AS AND A2 BUSINESS STUDIES TEXTBOOK

NICHOLAS GRIER
MA, LLB, WS
AND
MORRISON HANDLEY-SCHACHLER
MA, DPHIL, CPFA

OLD BAILEY PRESS

OLD BAILEY PRESS
200 Greyhound Road, London W14 9RY

1st edition 2001

ISBN 1 85836 438 8

British Library Cataloguing-in-Publication.

A CIP Catalogue record for this book is available from the British Library.

Acknowledgement
All material reproduced from official publications is used by kind permission of the Controller of Her Majesty's Stationery Office or the Office for Official Publications of the European Communities.

Printed and bound in Great Britain

Contents

Contents

Contents

Preface

Recently, there have been changes to the way in which A levels are examined. In particular, traditional A Levels have been divided into two connected examinations, these being AS (Advanced Subsidiary) Levels and A2 Levels, the level of the latter being broadly equivalent to the traditional A Levels.

The implementation of AS Levels and A2 Levels has not been without its difficulties, and at the time of writing (summer 2001) the Government is reviewing these two examinations. This book has therefore been revised on the assumption that whatever the outcome of the Government's review, a qualification broadly equivalent to the traditional A Level, and equivalent to the new (post-2001) A Level, will remain or be put in place. This book remains primarily appropriate for those studying Business Studies at A Level but is also serviceable for those studying the subject at AS Level.

The first five chapters examine the nature of business and the business environment, define fundamental terms, and introduce concepts of structure and organisation.

The next 16 chapters explore the various functions associated with raising capital, identifying and serving the needs of customers, producing goods, and managing human resources. Three chapters are then devoted to financial management, as a way of building on and developing previous material.

Finally the important theme of communication is addressed, before the whole subject is revised by a review of the interactive nature of business in the community and the global environment.

However, while the structure remains unchanged, the detailed material has been extensively revised. Since this textbook was first published there have been dramatic changes in the political, economic, legal and technological environments of business. These changes have been incorporated throughout the book, reflecting their impact on all the functional areas of marketing, production, human resource management and accounting.

June 2001

Chapter One

Introduction

- Introduction to the syllabus

- Aims of the syllabus

- Examination structure

- The textbook

- Study methods

Introduction to the syllabus

The syllabus for this subject, a copy of which you must obtain, is made up of many different topics. However, the subject areas do have a common link as they are all concerned with business and the environments in which businesses operate. By studying this subject you will acquire factual knowledge and understanding of the principles and problems involved in business from the point of view of managers, employees, owners and society at large. You will be equipping yourself for a future role in business and will be laying an essential foundation from which you will be able to branch into the specialised 'professional' areas such as legal, accounting, marketing, personnel, production, distribution and data processing, or pursue your studies at a more advanced academic level such as a degree or diploma in Business Studies.

Aims of the syllabus

a) To enable students to examine critically the aims, objectives and practices of business organisations from their economic, environmental and social aspects. Candidates will be expected to consider these problems from the point of view of the nation, the local community, industry, the proprietors, management and employees of industry, consumers.
b) To enable students to become familiar with the width and depth of business by a study of the integrated nature of business problems, allowing them to develop their skills of analysis, evaluation and synthesis in a business setting.

The syllabus is designed to convey some of the basic factual information surrounding businesses and their operations and to enable evaluation of them and their place in today's society. The underlying theme of the syllabus is the objectives of business organisations and how these objectives are attained.

Examination structure

For Business Studies A Level, there are five compulsory examination papers plus one additional assessment unit which may be completed either by an examination paper by or a 3,000 word coursework project. The first three papers form the Business Studies AS Level. The examination papers are as follows:

Unit 1

Marketing and Accounting and Finance
Chapters 7–19
1¼ hour examination.

Unit 2

People and Operations Management
Chapters 15–21
1¼ hour examination.
   Each of these two examinations consists of two compulsory questions designed to test your knowledge and comprehension of the subject matter and your ability to apply it to pieces of information presented to you in the form of text, graphs, charts and numerical tables.

Unit 3

External Influences and Objectives and Strategy
Chapters 3–6 and 26
1½ hour examination.
   This examination consists of a case study with questions requiring analytical and evaluative answers.

Unit 4

Marketing and Accounting and Finance
People and Operations Management
Chapters 7–25
1½ hour examination.
   This examination consists of a decision-making case study. You will be required to reach and justify a business decision on the basis of numerical data and other information.

Unit 5

Business Report and Essay or Project

Either a 1½ hour examination or a coursework project.

The examination is divided into two sections. Section A requires you to write a report to a business owner or manager on the basis of information provided. Section B requires you to answer one out of four essay questions.

The coursework project consists of a written piece of work approximately 3,000 words in length plus tables, figures and appendices. You may choose any topic relevant to the Business Studies syllabus but should ensure that you demonstrate a knowledge and understanding of the real business world.

Unit 6

External Influences and Objectives and Strategy

Chapters 8–15 and 26
1½ hour examination.

This examination consists of a case study with questions requiring analytical answers demonstrating an understanding of the relationships between different business issues.

The textbook

Read the syllabus very carefully; by the end of a Business Studies course you should understand and be able to discuss each of the topics mentioned. Even at this early stage in your studies it would be worth your while to look up any terms which you do not understand and make a note of them for future reference.

One of the difficulties which you will have to learn how to overcome is that the syllabus appears to consist of a number of apparently unrelated topics whereas, in reality, all business decisions are interdependent; you will be expected to show, in your examination answers, your understanding of this interdependence.

One answer to the problem is to organise your learning in as logical an order as possible, so that one topic leads naturally on to the next and each topic reinforces what has gone before until the last topic dealt with draws together and co-ordinates every topic you have studied. This textbook arranges the material according to a logic which is explained below; other textbooks to which you may refer may adopt a different logic (in fact there are probably as many 'logics' as there are textbooks!) but you should find the logic of this textbook sensible and easy to follow.

The material is divided into 26 chapters, each corresponding roughly to one week's work, thus leaving ample time for revision at the end of the year.

Chapters 2–5 present an overview of 'business' and define some basic types of business organisation.

Chapter 6 identifies the main sources of business finance.

Chapters 7–19 take a more detailed look at the operational functions of business, such as marketing, production, personnel, purchasing and research and development, with chapters 7–12 concentrating on marketing.

Chapters 13 and 14 look at some of the interrelationships between marketing, research and development, production, purchasing, personnel and accounting, and their effect on location and siting decisions.

Chapters 15–19 examine the personnel function.

Chapters 20–21 study human behaviour within organisations and questions of leadership and motivation.

Chapters 22–24 study the important topic of finance and the work of the accountant. Also examined are sources of finance and methods for interpreting financial data.

Chapter 25 looks at an issue which is implicit throughout the whole course, namely the importance of communication, both within the business organisation and between it and its suppliers, customers and government. Communication may be written, oral, numerical or graphical.

Chapter 26 examines the relationship between government and business, and draws the whole programme together by looking at various 'themes', such as the size of the organisation, ethical considerations, conflict and co-operation, change, interdependence and the management of scarce resources.

The logic of this approach is emphasised in greater detail below:

Chapter 2: Business and the environment

Before embarking on a wide-ranging study it is necessary to map out the territory to be explored in broad terms, so that the detail to be studied later can be seen in context.

Chapters 3, 4 and 5: Basic business organisations and their objectives

Businesses take many forms, from sole trader to multinational. These need to be defined at the outset, so that differences in their objectives, organisational structures and finances can be explored in greater detail as the course develops.

Chapter 6: Sources of finance

The relationship between business enterprise and owners and financiers is basic to a study of capitalist business.

Chapters 7–19: Operational functions

Business is essentially about making operational decisions in order to achieve agreed objectives. These operational decisions fall into certain functional areas such as marketing, research and development, production, purchasing and personnel.

Chapters 7–12: Marketing

Chapter 7: The marketing concept, functions and markets

There is a very good reason for looking at the marketing function first of all because businesses these days claim to be 'market (or customer) orientated'; that is because they recognise that their success or failure ultimately depends on the extent to which they can identify and satisfy their customers' needs. An understanding of the nature of demand is therefore an appropriate starting place for understanding business functions.

Chapter 8: Product policy and planning

Market demand determines the quality and quantity of products produced, but management must determine if the cost of investing in the necessary production facilities is justified over the long term, by analysing the anticipated cash flows likely to occur over the lifetime of the product.

Chapter 9: Marketing, planning, research and forecasting

The techniques for understanding consumer behaviour and analysing demand are the province of marketing research. These and other techniques are used to develop sales forecasts, which are the basis for all business planning, in production, purchasing and personnel, and in setting financial budgets.

Chapter 10: Pricing

Product policy and pricing cannot be separated, because decisions regarding the quality and quantity of the product determine its cost and price determines the quantity demanded; the difference between price and cost determines the contribution and, ultimately, the profit.

Chapter 11: The distribution function

Chapters 8, 9, 10 and 11 need to be considered together because it is the product form, the price and the convenient availability of the product which most directly influence customer demand. Chapter 11 (physical distribution) links directly with Chapters 13 and 14 below in considering the issues involved in location decisions.

Chapter 12: The promotion function

Having designed and produced the product, priced it and made it conveniently available, businesses may still need to inform and persuade customers to buy and to negotiate the details of a sales contract. This is the role of sales promotion.

Chapters 13 and 14: Production and purchasing, location and siting of businesses

These two chapters are designed as a convenient revision of some of the issues dealt with so far, particularly the important theme of interdependence of all the functions. Location embraces marketing, production, purchasing and personnel issues, together with government policy. The problems of co-ordinating the different functions and resolving potential conflicts are important managerial responsibilities.

Chapters 15–19: Personnel management

Chapters 15 and 16: Personnel management and manpower planning. Personnel recruitment, selection and training

Manpower planning is based directly on analysis of the business's manpower needs, which in turn are based on operational plans based on the sales forecast.

Chapters 17 and 18: Performance appraisal and labour turnover. Job evaluation and remuneration

Work must be assessed and workers motivated. Payment must be negotiated between employers and workers or trade unions.

Chapter 19: Welfare, discipline and termination of employment

The health, safety and welfare of work-people, their discipline and the termination of their contracts are the responsibility of personnel management.

Chapters 20 and 21: Individual, group and organisational behaviour. Leadership and motivation

These aspects of human relationships are the responsibility of all managers.

Chapters 22–24: Financial planning and reporting. Interpretation of accounts

Having considered the sources of capital in Chapter 6 it is appropriate to consider the use to which financial resources are put within the business and how operational decisions and their outcome in the market place are reflected in the business's profit and loss accounts and balance sheets. Ratio analysis and the interpretation of balance sheets are considered as ways of measuring the performance of a business.

Chapter 25: *Management information and communication*

The importance of communication is implicit throughout the course but it is appropriate to consider it specifically at this stage, partly to reinforce its importance and partly as revision of earlier material.

Chapter 26: *Government, the community and business*

Explores the role of government as manager of the economy and as legislator. Opposing policies and the role of pressure groups are considered. The last part of this chapter is entirely devoted to section 6 of the syllabus and is designed to draw the programme together and reinforce earlier material by considering themes such as 'size of the enterprise', 'business ethics', 'conflict and co-operation', 'interdependence', 'the management of scarce resources' etc.

Study methods

The point has already been made that one of the difficulties of Business Studies is that the syllabus consists of many diverse topics which are interrelated but where the interrelationships may not become apparent until the course is completed. Another difficulty is that the study of business is the study of something which is alive and dynamic and constantly changing even as you study it. To overcome both of these problems it is essential that you make yourself receptive to *any* information about the world of business from the start of your studies and try to keep yourself up-to-date by extensive background reading. Make a point of reading at least one 'good' newspaper such as the *Financial Times* or *The Times*. Do not restrict your reading to the business pages only but read the editorials, correspondence and political news and try to 'think through' how these and other items may be of relevance to 'business'. Try to read specialist journals such as *Management Today*, the *Journal of Marketing* and *Accountancy*. Watch or listen to current affairs or business related programmes such as *Panorama* or *The Money Programme* on TV or *Money Box* on BBC Radio 4 – take notes on these to remind you of particularly interesting items.

The internet is a further source of information on the business world. Most large companies now have their own websites which are intended to convey information about their business to customers, investors and the general public. These and other business-related sites can usually be easily found using a search engine such as Google or Altavista. Spend time exploring the information available on the web from companies and other organisations.

Inevitably all these items of information will come to you piecemeal and in no particular order – some items you will not understand at the time but may find useful later on. The best idea is probably to open a file under each of the 26 headings of the 26 chapters in this textbook and save newspaper clippings, copies of journal articles, examples of advertisements, company balance sheets etc in the relevant file, where it will be ready to use when you come to that chapter.

Obviously there is too much information for you to collect everything, so it may be a good plan for you to choose one industry which interests you and try to gather everything which you find relevant to that industry. This will give you useful examples with which to illustrate your essays.

This textbook is designed to give a formal structure to your studies, but you are strongly advised to supplement it by collecting material as suggested above, by taking careful notes of lectures and seminars and from other textbooks which may be recommended and by attempting all the assignments and exercises. Other textbooks will reinforce this one and may cast light by looking at the same material from a different angle; attempting all the assignments will give you practice in recalling information and in essay writing – and practice makes perfect!

A final word about writing essays:

a) Read the question very carefully and be sure you understand exactly what the examiner wants; you will not get any marks for writing a good answer to the wrong question. If it is for homework, read as widely as possible before starting to write; whether it is for homework or in the examination, spend several minutes carefully planning your answer, making sure that your plan contains all that you need to say and nothing that you do not need to say, and that it is structured to include an introduction, a development and a conclusion.

b) Try to answer the question in the first sentence! This is probably impossible, but do make clear to the examiner the direction your argument is going to take, so that he can follow it and see how you develop it.

c) Write in short, clear sentences.

d) Make sure that each paragraph contains no more than one part of your argument and its development – do not try to get too much into each paragraph.

e) Where appropriate, quote source material, such as the names of authors or theorists or a journal article.

f) As far as possible support your argument with examples, preferably drawn from your reading of current business affairs.

g) Finally, plan your conclusion carefully. Either use it to draw your whole argument together (but be careful to avoid mere repetition) or use it to hint at further developments, related to but outside the immediate scope of the question.

h) Write in proper standard English, avoiding slang, abbreviations, spelling mistakes and grammatical errors. Marks are given for presentation, and it would be foolish to lose any through carelessness.

i) Always check your work very thoroughly before you hand it in. Check the structure of every sentence, the spelling of every word and the accuracy of every computation.

Chapter Two

Business and the environment

- What is 'business'?

- Form, place and time utilities

- Exchange for mutual benefit

- The business environment

- Business functions

- Business model

What is 'business'?

Business can be defined as:

> 'The human activities performed by individuals or organisations of extracting, manufacturing or buying and selling goods or providing services in exchange for other goods, services or money, to the mutual benefit of the individuals or organisations concerned.'

This definition can be further expanded:

'Activities ... performed by individuals or organisations'

If an individual extracts (for example by growing vegetables), manufactures (for example by knitting a jumper) or buys goods or services for his own use or consumption he is not a businessman; he is merely a consumer. Even if he sells his own property (for example, his secondhand car) he is not doing so as 'a business'. Only if he extracts, manufactures or buys more than he needs for his own consumption and exchanges or sells the excess could he be said to be acting as a business. When two or more individuals act together for a common purpose they are 'an organisation' and if the common purpose is to extract, manufacture, buy or sell in exchange for other goods, services or money they are 'a business organisation'.

'Extracting'

Any activity which extracts goods in their raw (ie unprocessed) form (known as raw materials) from the earth or sea is known as 'primary production', because it is usually the first stage of a long chain of processes before the goods are ready for final consumption by individuals. Farming, fishing, forestry, mining and oil-drilling are examples of primary production, also known as extractive industries.

'Manufacturing'

Most raw materials undergo some form of processing before their final consumption. These processes may include a change of form (eg a chemical reaction, oil-refining, seasoning timber, cleaning wool, iron-smelting), machining (eg sawing timber, spinning wool, making engine parts) or assembly (eg furniture manufacture, knitting woollen garments, building cars). Manufacturing is known as 'secondary industry' because it is the second stage between extraction and distribution.

'Buying and selling'

Some businesses only buy the finished products of other businesses and sell them, either to final customers or to other businesses. These include wholesalers, retailers, franchises and other distributors and factors, brokers and other agents (which will be defined in greater detail in Chapter 11). These are known as 'tertiary industries' because they are the third stage, after extraction and manufacture, before final consumption. They are also known as distributive industries and are included among service industries.

'Goods or ... services'

Goods are physical, tangible items while services are intangible, invisible. Services may include banking, insurance, computer software, transport and tourism, which together make up most of the UK's 'invisible earnings'. Services include catering and entertainment. They may also be provided in conjunction with the sale of goods, eg delivery, installation, after-sales service or maintenance (of industrial machinery or domestic appliances such as washing machines). Other services may facilitate purchase, eg advertising gives the buyer information, or credit facilities make it easier to pay for the goods.

'Exchange'

This is the heart of our definition. All business activity involves exchange; the manufacturer makes and sells to the shop-keeper in exchange for a price, the shop-keeper sells to the customer for a price, the worker exchanges his labour for a wage, the shareholder invests his capital in exchange for a dividend, the banker lends money in exchange for interest. All of these relationships will be explored in greater detail in the following chapters.

'Other goods, services or money'

In our economy the most common form of exchange is goods or services in exchange for money. When goods or services are exchanged for other goods or services this is known as barter. Some workers may be paid in kind, ie in goods rather than cash. Other workers may enjoy special discounts as part of their conditions of employment, for example bank employees may get low-interest mortgages.

'Mutual benefit'

This, together with the concept of exchange, is also at the heart of our definition. In a free economy nobody is forced to buy or sell anything; buyers have a wide range of goods and services to choose from and sellers are free to decide where and when they wish to sell. Sellers compete with each other for the buyers' custom and buyers are free to buy from whoever they think is offering the best deal. In other words there is a constant process of bargaining between buyers and sellers, and competition between sellers.

This does not mean that you can take your supermarket trolley full of goods to the check-out and haggle with the cashier until you have agreed a price because most of our consumer goods are already priced; but, provided that you are able to exercise a choice, you are free to buy other goods or to buy the same goods from some other shop and, in time, this would force the first shop to offer lower prices or better service in order to retain your custom.

There are large sections of the economy, for example in the capital goods markets and in secondhand markets, where buyers and sellers do spend time negotiating (bargaining, haggling) before the final details of price, delivery etc are agreed.

The point is that only when both buyer and seller are satisfied is the bargain struck; that is when there is mutual benefit.

Form, place and time utilities

It is often assumed that this process of bargaining only refers to price. Indeed, much of classical economics theory is concerned with the laws of supply and demand and the workings of the price mechanism. But buyers want benefits other than just the lowest price; they want the product to be in the most suitable form for them, they want it to be available at a place convenient to them and they want it at a time which is convenient to them. In economist's terms they seek 'form, place and time utilities'. Sellers have to compete with each other to 'provide goods or services in the right form, at the right place and at the right time for the right customer'.

Equally, the seller wants benefits other than just the highest price; he wants to stay in business and therefore wants loyal customers, or he may wish to expand his business by attracting new customers. The seller will also often be willing to sell at a discount in return for quicker payment.

Exchange for mutual benefit

So far we have only considered the idea of 'mutual benefit' from the point of view of the exchange of goods and services for a price, but exactly the same concept applies to everything else in business. The employee exchanges his work for a wage and conditions of employment; if he is not satisfied with the wage or conditions of employment he may take another job, subject to there being another suitable one available. For his part, the employer is free to hire or fire workers, subject to the availability of labour and to the law. (See Chapters 15–19.)

The shareholder invests his capital in return for a dividend and the banker in return for interest; if they are not satisfied with the security offered or with the return on their investments they are free to invest their money elsewhere, subject to available opportunities and to the law. (See Chapters 6 and 22–24.)

The idea of exchange, of two parties negotiating an agreement which is to their mutual benefit, is fundamental to our understanding of business. It underlies every other concept; when problems arise in business it is usually because one party or the other has become dissatisfied with the exchange and believes that he is no longer enjoying a benefit.

Thus, declining sales are probably because customers are not satisfied with the product, the price, or the service; labour disputes because the workers are not satisfied with their wages or conditions of employment; bankruptcies because the financiers are not satisfied with the security offered in exchange for their investment.

The business environment

But the two negotiating parties (seller/buyer, employer/employee, lender/ borrower) do not negotiate in isolation; they are both working in an environment which dictates their relative bargaining positions.

The *economic environment* dictates whether customers have a lot of money to spend or very little and this influences the type of goods they want to buy and how much they are prepared to spend. Equally, the economic environment dictates the amount of work available and therefore whether labour is in abundance or in short supply; this affects the level of wages which the worker can negotiate. Also, the economic environment dictates the availability of money and therefore the returns paid on investments or loans; this influences the extent to which a business can afford to borrow in order to finance its activities.

The economic environment is itself affected by the *political environment*; to some extent the way the economy is managed will be the result of the political aims and objectives of the government in power.

The business and the parties with which it negotiates also work within a *legal environment*. For instance, the business may be subject to the provisions of the Companies Acts; the sale of goods and services subject to the Sale of Goods Act, the Trade Descriptions Act or the Consumer Safety Act; the employment of workers subject to the Employment Act or the Health and Safety at Work Acts (see Chapter 26), the provision and use of finance subject to the Companies Acts (see Chapters 6 and 22–24).

The types of laws which Parliament enacts may be the outcome of the political environment and pressure from lobbies or pressure groups; these, in turn, may reflect movements within the social and cultural environment. For instance, concern for the environment has led to the formation of 'Green' parties and pressure groups and to legislation for the control of industrial pollution.

The *social/cultural environment* determines the types of goods which people want to buy, particularly tastes and fashion. The ethnic and religious environments, which are particular sub-sets of the socio-cultural environment, may have a direct influence on a customer's style of living and therefore on his demand for certain goods. The socio-cultural environment may also affect a person's attitude to work and this may influence his attitude to the wages or conditions of employment offered by the business.

The *technological environment* describes the level of scientific and technical development which is available to the business, particularly in the areas of production, automation, data processing and information technology.

Inevitably, the more business activities are automated the less the demand for human workers, and this has a direct effect on levels of employment and wage negotiation.

The *physical or geographical environment* describes the physical world in which the business is located. This includes the availability of raw materials, power, climatic/seasonal conditions and the existence of road, rail, sea or air transport systems; these things have a direct influence on where the business is located and, therefore, on the costs of materials and distribution and on the availability of labour.

Finally, we may identify the *institutional environment*. This describes the types, number and availability of institutions with which a business may need to form working relationships and/or negotiate contracts. These include:

- banks (to provide financial services);
- wholesalers and retailers (to provide distribution services);
- professional firms (to provide professional services, such as legal advice, accounting);
- educational institutions (to provide training for employees);
- market research agencies (to provide market information);
- advertising agencies (to conduct advertising);
- employment agencies (to help find appropriate labour);
- carriers (to provide carriage of goods by road, rail, sea or air);
- insurance companies (to provide property and employment insurance);
- public utilities (to provide services such as water, electricity, gas, refuse disposal etc);
- suppliers (to provide necessary raw materials, parts, finished goods, machinery, office stationery etc);
- communications media (to communicate advertisements or public relations material).

To summarise, we have defined business in general and specific categories of business; established the importance of exchange; recognised the importance of mutual benefit; identified the process of negotiation and the existence of different types of business environment and their effect on negotiation.

Finally, the concept of 'functions' must be introduced.

Business functions

A function is a 'major business activity which has to be performed, usually concerning the negotiatory and exchange relationship between the business and some part of the environment'. Thus, all businesses must perform the following five functions:

Financial and accounting function. Raising capital from investors and/or lenders. Raising revenue from sales. Managing the use of capital and revenue inside and by the business.

Personnel function. Recruiting and employing labour appropriate to the business's needs. Managing all issues relevant to the employment of labour.

Purchasing function. Acquiring raw materials, machinery, parts, equipment and other supplies necessary to the business.

Production or processing function. The conversion of the materials or other supplies into a form suitable for sale to the business's customers.

Marketing function. The identification of customers' needs and the conduct of the exchange process between the business and its customers.

To these may be added three 'secondary' functions:

Entrepreneurial function. The provision of enterprise, initiative and leadership which is 'the function of management'.

Research and development function. The activity of investigating, developing and implementing new processes or new products, to improve the business's performance, cost effectiveness or products for sale.

Public relations function. Managing relationships between the business and the public or the communications media.

Business model

The concepts discussed in this chapter may be summarised in a simple model, as shown opposite. This model shows the business with its five main functions, four of which (finance, marketing, personnel and purchasing) have negotiation and exchange relationships with external 'markets'. These institutions make up the business's immediate surroundings or 'micro-environment'.

The various 'markets' work within the macro-environment, made up of the economic, political, legal, socio-cultural, technological and physical or geographical environments.

Within the business each function has to communicate with every other function. These, and other relationships, will be discussed in later chapters.

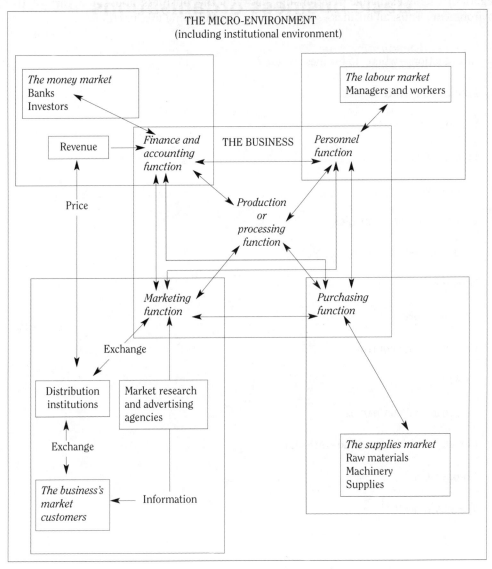

THE MACRO-ENVIRONMENT
(Economic, political, legal, socio-cultural,
technological and physical (or geographical))

THE MICRO-ENVIRONMENT
(including institutional environment)

The money market
Banks
Investors

The labour market
Managers and workers

Revenue

Finance and
accounting
function

THE BUSINESS

Personnel
function

Price

Production
or
processing
function

Marketing
function

Purchasing
function

Exchange

Distribution
institutions

Market research
and advertising
agencies

The supplies market
Raw materials
Machinery
Supplies

Exchange

The business's
market
customers

Information

Chapter Three

Basic business organisations

- Introduction – where do businesses start?

- Public and private sectors

- Sole traders

- Partnerships

- Companies

- Classification of companies

- Legal requirements of companies

- Directors

- Annual reports

- Ownership and control

- Growth

- Multinational companies

- Cartels, joint ventures and consortia

- Co-operatives

- The public sector

Introduction – where do businesses start?

Looking at today's giant businesses, such as British Petroleum (BP), Imperial Chemical Industries (ICI), BSkyB, Sainsbury's and Barclays Bank, it is difficult to realise that most businesses start off in a very small way. Indeed, many businesses start off as somebody with an idea – and ambition!

This chapter will define different businesses, ranging from 'sole traders' to 'multinationals', and will compare the objectives of different types of business in both the *private sector* and the *public sector*. The next chapter will consider the problem of managing and organising different types and sizes of business.

Public and private sectors

Mixed economy

The economy of the United Kingdom is what is known as a 'mixed economy'. By this we mean that some part or sector of the economy is owned and operated by private citizens, either as individuals or collectively, while the remaining sector is owned and operated by bodies created by either national or local government. The former is known as the *private sector* and the latter as the *public sector*.

Objectives

Broadly speaking, the private sector has the objective of profit, whereas the public sector has the objective of 'public welfare'. This is explored in greater depth below.

The public sector

The public sector comprises departments of state, including social services, health, education and the armed services, and public corporations, which include local authorities and nationalised industries.

The private sector

The private sector may be sub-divided into:

Unincorporated businesses:

1. Sole traders.
2. Partnerships.

Incorporated businesses or companies (which have to be registered with the Registrar of Companies):

1. Limited liability partnerships
2. Private companies.
3. Public companies.

These terms will now be explored in greater detail.

Sole traders

A sole trader is a person who enters into business on his own account, manages that business, and is solely responsible for providing the capital and making the decisions. His reward is the profit which the business may make and the satisfaction of 'being his own boss' but, in return, he must accept the risks of loss if the business fails.

Examples are:

1. small farmers, market gardeners;
2. local retailers (tobacconists, confectioners, grocers, butchers, greengrocers, hardware shops, 'corner shops' etc);
3. local services (hairdressers, window-cleaners, restaurants, car-repair workshops etc);
4. local manufacturing (self-employed craftsmen, small engineering workshops etc).

(*Note:* a sole trader does *not* mean only one person – all the above may employ other people, but if the business is *owned* by one person only, then it is classified as a sole trader.)

The sole trader is the most commonly occurring form of business enterprise in the UK.

Legal requirements

1. None, if trading under his own name.
2. Compliance with the Business Names Act 1985, if trading under a name other than his own.
3. (Possibly) a licence to trade from the local magistrates' court or other licensing authority.
4. Declaration of accounts to Inland Revenue, for taxation purposes.
5. Declaration of accounts to HM Customs & Excise for Value Added Tax (if turnover exceeds the VAT threshold, which is announced annually in the budget).
6. Compliance with employment laws, if any other person is employed by the business.
7. Compliance with other laws or by-laws relevant to his particular trade (for example a restaurant would have to comply with the Food and Drugs Act).

Liabilities

The sole trader is *personally liable for any debts incurred by his business.* This means that his house, car or other possessions might have to be sold in order to pay his business debts.

Objectives

The objectives of the sole trader are:

Profit. Of course the sole trader will seek to make profits, and the larger the profit the greater will be his personal financial gain. However, the sole trader may not wish to work as hard and as long as he would need to do in order to maximise his profits (the economist's objective of 'profit-maximisation') and may settle for a level of profit which gives him a personally satisfactory standard of living ('profit-satisfying') at an acceptable level of work.

Self-satisfaction. This comes through being his own boss and making decisions about his own life.

Survival. The sole trader will want his business to survive for at least as long as his own working life.

Status. He will want to enjoy the respect of the community he works in.

Immortality. Many sole traders wish to build up a business to leave to their heirs, thus providing the heirs with a living and preserving their own name.

Advantages of being a sole trader

- *Customers* are often *personally known* to the sole trader – he can therefore *react immediately* to their changing needs and tastes.
- *Flexibility, quick decision-making* – he does not have to spend time consulting others before making his decisions.
- *Motivation* – he will be motivated to work hard, because he is working for himself.
- *Privacy* – he is not required to disclose his accounts to anyone apart from the Inland Revenue and Customs and Excise.

Disadvantages of being a sole trader

Financial constraints
Because capital resources are limited to the sole trader's own resources plus whatever he can borrow:

- *Expansion is constrained* through lack of capital.
- *Economies of scale* may not be obtainable.
- *Bulk purchasing facilities* (and therefore lower prices) may not be available.
- All of the above may lead to a *weak competitive position*.

Human constraints
No matter how enterprising the sole trader may be he may lack some essential skill, for example he may be good at selling but not at financial management. These deficiencies may necessitate professional advice and consultancy, which can be expensive.

- He has to cope with *legal requirements*; for example, completing VAT records places a strain on one man and detracts from running his business.
- He is very vulnerable to *environmental changes,* eg population movement away from his locality, increased car-ownership encouraging his customers to shop elsewhere, etc.
- He cannot easily take a *holiday,* nor can he afford to be *sick,* without running the risk of neglecting his business.

Contribution to the economy

Sole traders are declining in importance as business, particularly retailing, becomes increasingly dominated by large companies.

Nevertheless:

- they provide *service*;
- they may make or sell *specialised products* which large companies are not prepared to make or sell;
- they provide *employment,* often in areas otherwise remote from major centres of employment, and serve *remote communities*;
- small retailers provide manufacturers with an *outlet* not necessarily provided by larger, multiple retailers. (Some manufacturers produce products specifically designed for the small retailer to sell, enabling them to compete with large multiple retailers.)

Performance of business functions

Even though the business may consist of one man only, the five main functions of business (financial control, marketing, purchasing, production and – as soon as somebody else is employed – personnel) still have to be performed. Obviously this may be too much for one person, because of excessive work-load and lack of knowledge of some functions. The problem may be overcome by sub-contracting, co-operation and hiring functional specialists as below:

Sub-contracting
Typically, sole trader manufacturers or retailers will appoint accountants to handle their financial affairs. Small manufacturers may sub-contract marketing to a marketing agency or task force.

Co-operation
A manufacturer with limited resources may arrange for a larger manufacturer to produce and/or market the product on a larger scale, with a share in the profit. This is quite common in exporting, where it is known as 'piggy-back exporting'.

Hiring functional specialists
The sole trader manufacturer may hire a book-keeper/accountant or a sales manager, so that he can concentrate on his speciality of production.

In all these cases the aim is to enjoy the benefits of specialisation while still retaining sole control of the business.

However, in the case of a partnership, the benefits of specialisation may be retained, but control will now be shared.

Partnerships

A partnership exists when two or more people 'carry on a business in common with a view of profit' (Partnership Act 1890). The rewards, in the form of profit, are shared between the partners, management decisions are made jointly and losses are the personal responsibility of each partner (subject to the provisions set out below).

Partnerships are most common among professional people such as solicitors, accountants and doctors, but any two or more people *jointly* running a business for profit are a partnership within the meaning of the Partnership Act.

Legal requirements

1. Partnerships are formed by contract between the partners. The agreed details are usually written in a document commonly known as a partnership agreement. If the partnership agreement is silent or ambiguous on a particular matter, the partners may consult the terms of the Partnership Act instead.
2. New members may only be admitted by agreement of all the members. Members may not be expelled (unless the partnership agreement permits it); however, partners may apply to the court for the partnership to be dissolved, after which a new partnership may be formed.
3. All partners participate in management but the right of junior partners may be restricted by the partnership agreement.
4. Unless the partnership agreement states otherwise, day-to-day decisions may be made on a majority basis, but major decisions, such as a change of business, must be unanimously agreed.
5. Sharing in both profits and losses is equal under the Partnership Act, but the partnership agreement may vary this; typically the senior partners may contribute more capital and take a larger share in the profits.
6. A partnership does not possess corporate status. Each partner is an agent of the firm and of his fellow partners for anything done in the course of the partnership's business. Each partner has unlimited personal liability for any debts incurred by the firm.
7. The Limited Partnership Act 1907 permits some (but not all) of the partners to enjoy limited liability; they take no part in the management. (This is rare, as a limited company is usually preferable.) Note that a limited partnership is different from a limited liability partnership.
8. The members of certain professions, such as accountants, doctors and solicitors, used not to be permitted by statute to form limited liability companies. This was to ensure that the members of those bodies were personally liable for their mistakes. This in turn encouraged the maintenance of high professional standards. Indirectly, however, it accounted for the high fees charged by professionals because of:

    a) the risk of expensive litigation;
    b) the fact that in practice partners' personal assets might not be very substantial;
    c) the need to carry extensive insurance cover against the consequences of their mistakes.

However, since 2000, many of these professions have been allowed to form limited liability partnerships and, in some instances, limited liability companies. This was because the imposition of personal liability on all partners in a partnership was seen as unfair and uncompetitive compared to the position in the USA and elsewhere in Europe.

9. The partnership must, of course, comply with other legal requirements as set out under 'Sole traders' above.

Objectives

These will be similar to those of the sole trader, ie profit (at a 'satisfactory' level), self-satisfaction (through exercising considerable, albeit shared, control over decisions), survival, status and immortality (through occasionally being able to persuade one's partners to elect one's heirs to the partnership).

Advantages of partnership

*   Each partner contributes *additional capital*, enabling growth or greater economies of scale to be achieved.
*   *New blood,* new ideas (balanced by the experience of older partners).
*   *Specialisation* by different partners in different aspects of the partnership business.
*   *Shared responsibilities* and decision-making.
*   *Less personal stress* than the sole trader may experience.
*   *Privacy*, there being no requirement to publish accounts (except, of course, to Inland Revenue or HM Customs & Excise).
*   *Continuity*, as the death of a partner does not mean the end of the business; his share may be 'purchased' by the surviving partners.
*   *Withdrawal of capital*: partners leaving the partnership may generally readily take out whatever capital they have contributed. In a company a shareholder may normally only get his capital back by selling his shares, provided that he can find someone willing to buy them and the company articles permit him to sell them. Many small companies restrict the transferability of shares.

Disadvantages of partnership

*   *Personal unlimited liability* for debts (as with sole traders).
*   *Slow decision-making* because all the partners must be involved (unless the partnership agreement permits some delegation of authority).
*   *Limited borrowing ability*, as the types of asset a partnership could offer as security for a loan are generally restricted to any land and buildings that the partnership and the partners own.
*   *Young or new partners* sometimes find it difficult to make their initial capital contributions.
*   Each partner is deemed to be *responsible* for the actions of his fellow partners, even if he neither approved of nor authorised those actions.

Limited liability partnerships

A limited liability partnership is a new trading or business organisation which came into being in April 2001. Limited liability partnerships are regulated by the Limited Liability Partnership Act 2000 and to some extent by the Companies Act 1985 and the Insolvency Act 2001. Limited liability partnerships exhibit characteristics of both partnerships and companies. At the time of writing they are so new that not many businesses have been incorporated as limited liability partnerships.

Similarities with partnerships are as follows:

- The relation between the partners is governed by a partnership agreement, which, as with partnerships, is not disclosed to the wider world; and where there is no partnership agreement, or it is silent or ambiguous on any matter, the law looks to the Partnership Act 1890 for guidance. Unlike companies there is no memorandum or articles of association.
- It is relatively easy to withdraw capital from a limited liability partnership (subject to the terms of any agreement to the contrary).
- Each partner is an agent for the limited liability partnership, as is a partner for any partnership.
- The tax treatment of profits is closely related to the tax on partnerships.
- A limited partnership has no shares, so they cannot be offered to the public or traded on the London Stock Exchange. This means that, as with a partnership, the limited liability partnership has to look to capital from the partners, or loan capital, if it wishes to broaden its capital base.

Similarities with limited companies (see pages 25–32) are as follows:

- The partners' liability to the partnership in the event of the limited liability partnership's insolvency is limited to the amount of capital each partner has put into the limited liability partnership, and no more.
- Assuming a partner is acting in the course of his business, he will not personally be liable for his acts: the limited liability partnership (of which he is a partner) will instead be responsible for his acts. If a partner does something very foolish which causes the limited liability partnership to become insolvent, the limited liability partnership's creditors may only claim against the insolvent limited liability partnership and not against the individual partners.
- Limited liability partnerships must publish their accounts annually with the Registrar of Companies.
- Limited liability partnerships may grant a mortgage over assets other than land and buildings and so may borrow to the same extent as a company.
- Many of the requirements of the Companies Act 1985 and the Insolvency Act 1986 apply to limited liability partnerships, particularly in relation to disclosure of information, accounting and winding up.
- Limited liability partnerships have a separate legal personality (explained at page 26).

Legal requirements
1. Limited liability partnerships are founded by incorporation with the Registrar of

Companies. This requires the completion of certain specified forms in a manner similar to the incorporation of a company.
2. There will normally be no restriction on the number of partners a limited liability partnership may have, subject to the terms of any partnership agreement.
3. The management of the limited liability partnership will normally be detailed in the partnership agreement, as will the decision-making processes within the limited liability partnership.
4. Profits and losses will be divided up as stated in the partnership agreement.
5. There is no prohibition against professionals such as doctors, accountants and solicitors becoming limited liability partnerships; indeed it is anticipated that many will do so. It is unlikely that this will cause a reduction in their fees, but it does mean that certain activities, such as the provision of accounting and legal advice, may stay in the UK instead of being provided elsewhere to minimise the risk of litigation.
6. As with partnerships, limited liability partnerships will still need to comply with the legal requirements set out under 'sole traders' above.

Objectives
These are similar to sole traders and partnerships, but with the added benefit that a limited liability partnership, like a limited liability company, might be prepared to undertake ventures that partners, with unlimited liability, might not. The limited liability partnership ought to encourage entrepreneurs, as a limited company does, while retaining most of the benefits of partnership.

Advantages of limited liability partnerships
As stated above, these are broadly the same as partnerships and limited liability companies, with the added benefits or differences that:

* although the limited liability partnership is responsible for the acts of the partners acting in the course of the their partnership duties, each individual partner is only personally liable to the limited liability partnership to the extent of his contributed capital (subject to any agreement to the contrary amongst the partners);
* limited liability partnerships will undertake ventures that partnerships might be unwilling to try because of the financial risks involved;
* limited liability partnerships will undertake necessary work on which the economy survives, such as auditing company accounts, which otherwise few partnerships would do because of the risks, or would only do for a very large fee;
* the borrowing ability of a limited liability partnership is greater than that of an ordinary partnership;
* takeover bids of limited liability partnerships could not take place because the partnership interests are not freely traded.

Disadvantages of limited liability partnerships
These are the same as partnerships and limited companies, except that:

- it is not possible to offer limited liability partnership interests to the general public, nor may a limited liability partnership be listed on the London Stock Exchange;
- as there are no shares, there is no payment of dividends nor capital growth in quite the same manner as a share;
- as with directors of companies, under certain circumstances incompetent or fraudulent limited liability partnership partners could find themselves personally liable for their limited liability partnership's debts;
- as with limited companies, creditors dealing with limited liability partnerships may well insist on personal guarantees from the individual partners if the creditors are not confident that the limited liability partnership would pay its debts.

Companies

How do they work?

The following section explains in very simple terms how companies are formed and financed. Later sections and Chapters 6 and 22–24 explore the system in greater detail. Companies are regulated by a number of statutes, in particular the Companies Act 1985 and the Insolvency Act 1986.

Let us assume:

Bill and Ben are partners. They decide they need £100,000 with which to expand their business. They decide to form a private limited company and register it with the Registrar of Companies.

They each pay £50,000 to the company. This is known as their 'investment' in the company. In exchange the company gives them each 50,000 shares with each share having a 'nominal value' of £1. A share is a unit of ownership in the company. As Bill and Ben have paid the full amount of the nominal value of each share, they cannot be asked to pay any more to the company for their shares unless they agree to do so. They could, if they wished, pay only a part of the nominal value of each share. They would then still receive their shares, but they might at a later date have to pay the company the amount remaining unpaid on each share. The £100,000 that Bill and Ben paid to the company, and for which the company gave them shares, is known as the company's 'share capital'.

As Bill and Ben are the only shareholders in the company, they have entire control of the company. If they wish, they can invite some friends to buy shares in the company, but this may mean that they lose total control of the company.

As all companies need some form of management, Bill and Ben will appoint a board of directors to run the company. In a small company, the largest shareholders are often appointed, or appoint themselves, as the directors.

If the company prospers, the directors will give a share of the company's profits to Bill and Ben by means of a dividend.

If the company fails, Bill and Ben may find that their share capital is all used to pay the company's creditors and Bill and Ben lose their investment. However, Bill and Ben cannot lose more than the nominal value of the shares they acquired.

The Stock Exchange

If Bill and Ben's company can establish a good trading record, after some years, and following various legal requirements, it would be possible for Bill and Ben to have their company 'listed' on the London Stock Exchange. This means that members of the public could buy and sell the shares in the company. The London Stock Exchange is the principal market place for the purchase and sale of shares in the UK. If the company is successful, Bill and Ben could sell some of their own shares and possibly become very wealthy. The market value of the company's shares depends on the laws of supply and demand: the keener the public is to buy shares in the company, the higher the price for each share.

Limited liability

As a sole trader or a partner in a partnership, the sole trader or the partner has 'unlimited personal liability', which means that he risks his entire livelihood if his business fails. He is thus less likely to undertake any trading activity that may involve him in a risk which could potentially ruin him and his family.

While this is good in one way, in that he is likely to carry on his business activities with great care and thoroughness, it is disadvantageous in another in that he will be less prepared to take a commercial risk. If too many people are too cautious with their money in this way, the economy of their country will stagnate and nationally living standards will decline.

However, if a bold entrepreneur knew that the most he could lose was his investment in a limited company, he would be much more likely to invest in a new commercial venture. If the venture were successful, it could create economic growth and employment and would stimulate the development of new technology. If the venture were unsuccessful, he would lose his investment – and no more.

It is sometimes said that the invention of the limited company was one of the best ideas in commerce since the development of double entry book-keeping.

Separate legal personality

In law a company has its own legal existence which is separate from its members (members are the people who own the company; only if a company has shares, which not all companies do, does it have shareholders). The company can employ people, it can own property and it can sue and be sued. The company's assets belong to it alone and not to its members. Equally, the company's debts are owed by the company and not by its members. The company is responsible for any negligent acts performed by its employees or agents in the course of their employment with the company.

This principle of separate legal personality was clarified by the House of Lords in *Salomon v Salomon & Co* (1897). Salomon incorporated his business as a limited company in which he held 20,000 shares, his wife, four sons and daughter having one share each. He lent money to the company, and, to protect his loan, the company gave him what was effectively a mortgage over the company's assets. This meant that if the company went into liquidation (ie became bankrupt) he would have a prior right to the company's assets. This duly happened. The other creditors objected to this, saying that he effectively was the company and should not be entitled to benefit at their expense. But the court held that he and the company had separate legal personalities and that it was perfectly valid for the company to grant him personally a mortgage over its assets.

Advantages of limited companies

- The members' liability to the company is limited to the nominal value of their shares or to any guarantees they may have given.
- A company has a legal personality separate from its members.
- A company has no restriction on the maximum number of members it may have unless the articles provide otherwise.
- The shares in a company may not only provide dividends but also produce capital growth.
- The members may delegate the management of the company to directors.
- A successful company could eventually be floated on the London Stock Exchange, potentially enabling its founders to become very wealthy.

Disadvantages of limited companies

- Companies must regularly disclose their accounts to the general public, thus allowing competitors to see how well or badly the company is doing.
- A company has to bear the cost of incorporation.
- Compliance with the requirements of the Companies Acts can be burdensome.
- Under certain circumstances incompetent or fraudulent company directors may find themselves liable for their company's debts.
- It is difficult to withdraw capital from a company.
- Some companies can be subject to unwelcome takeover bids.
- Most companies need to have their accounts professionally audited.

Classification of companies

Registered companies may be classified by the extent to which their members' liability for debt is limited, and according to whether the company is public or private.

Types of limitation of members' liability

Companies limited by shares
The members' liability is limited to the nominal value of their shares. Therefore they have no further liability once their shares are fully paid up. This is the most common form.

Limitation by guarantee
Each member's liability is limited to the amount he has guaranteed to contribute if the company is wound up following its insolvency. This usually applies only to non-profit-making organisations such as charities or professional associations.

Public and private companies

A public company may potentially offer shares to the general public; a private company may not. Public companies have to disclose more information about their accounts than private companies do. They also generally have to comply with more complicated legislation.

Public company

The Companies Act 1985 defines a public company as a company:

1. limited by shares;
2. with an authorised share capital (minimum £50,000);
3. with a memorandum stating it to be a public company;
4. registered as a public company under the Companies Act;
5. with two or more members;
6. with authority to invite the general public to subscribe for its shares or debentures, though as a matter of practice only companies which have a Stock Exchange listing will do this.

Only public companies, commonly known as 'plcs', may be admitted to listing. Most plcs choose not to be listed.

Private company

A private company is defined as a company:

1. with one, two or more members;
2. with limited liability, limited to the nominal value of its shares or to the value of any specified guarantee. However, it is possible to have an unlimited company, in which case members or shareholders are personally liable for all the company's debts. An unlimited company cannot be a public company;
3. *not* permitted to offer shares to the general public (unlike a public company). Capital resources are therefore limited to the resources of its members;
4. that is not a public company.

Legal requirements of companies

Registration of companies

A company is incorporated by registration with the Registrar of Companies, a government official, who maintains a record of all the companies in the United Kingdom. If the incorporation documents are correct, he supplies a certificate of incorporation which specifies the company's name, its registered number and where it was registered. Although the company's name may subsequently change, its number and nationality never does. The certificate of registration is conclusive proof that the registration requirements have been satisfied.

Documents to be filed

On registration there must be filed with the Registrar:

1. the memorandum of association;
2. the articles of association;
3. a statement of first directors and secretary to include not only their personal details but also their written consent to act in that capacity. The address of the registered office is also to be given in the statement;
4. the statutory declaration of compliance with the provisions of the Companies Acts given by a solicitor, director or secretary;
5. a statement showing the nominal capital and details of shares to be issued on incorporation.

Memorandum of association

This regulates the company's external relationship with investors, customers and creditors. From the memorandum one can ascertain:

1. the name of the company;
2. its status as either a private or a public company;
3. its nationality;
4. the principal purpose for which the company has been set up;
5. the liability of its members;
6. the initial authorised share capital of the company; and
7. the name and addresses of the first subscribers or members of the company.

Name. The company's name must not be the same as any other company name, nor must it be a name prohibited by the Department of Trade and Industry under the terms of the Business Names Act 1985. The company's name will also have to be specified outside the company's place of business, its registered office and on its headed paper, cheques etc.

Nationality. A company, once incorporated in one country within the United Kingdom, may not move its registered office outside that country.

Objects clause. Formerly of great importance, but increasingly less so nowadays, the objects clause sets out what activities the company can pursue. It was originally designed to ensure that investors knew the purpose for which their money was being used, and to protect investors from enthusiastic directors who might be misusing the investors' funds. Nowadays objects clauses are generally drafted very broadly to allow a company to carry on almost any legitimate activity.

Limited liability. This states the extent to which members' liability to the company is limited; and if the company is a guarantee company, this will be narrated here too.

Authorised capital. This states the total number and the nominal value of the shares that the company could issue to shareholders.

First subscribers/members. This states who the initial shareholders of the company are or, in the case of a company without shares, the initial members. The first subscribers/members must sign the memorandum and have it witnessed and dated.

Articles of association

These regulate the internal administration of the company. The principal matters dealt with are:

1. alteration to share capital;
2. allotment of shares;
3. transfer and transmission of shares;
4. calls on shares;
5. borrowing powers;
6. meetings;
7. directors' powers and duties;
8. dividends and reserve fund;
9. accounts and audit;
10. notices;
11. winding up.

Special requirements for public companies

There are special rules that apply to public companies that do not apply to private companies. This is because a higher standard of accountability is expected of a company that could potentially offer its shares to members of the public, even if as a matter of practice not all public companies choose to do this. These rules include:

- the amounts that directors may borrow from their companies are restricted;
- the payment of dividends must not reduce the overall capital position of the company;
- at the time that a public company is created there must be a minimum nominal share capital of £50,000 and all shares must be paid up to at least 25 per cent of their nominal value;
- if the company acquires non-cash assets from a seller and in return gives the seller shares in the company, those assets must be independently valued to ensure that the company is not paying an inflated price for them;
- public companies must hold regular shareholders' meetings; private companies may dispense with this requirement.

Directors

Directors are responsible to the shareholders for the day-to-day management of the company's affairs, their powers being defined in the articles of association and under statute. Directors are not supposed to act beyond those powers, and if they do they may be personally liable to the company for any loss which they may cause the company to suffer. However, the members of the company may, if they wish, choose to ratify the directors' actions, provided that the actions are legitimate and done in the best interests of the company.

One director is usually appointed managing director, with power to take certain decisions without reference to the board of directors.

The board of directors appoints a company secretary to act as chief administrative officer of the company.

Annual reports

Annually the company must send a copy of the company's accounts (see Chapters 22–24) and directors' report to the Registrar of Companies. The company must also send an 'annual return' detailing the current membership of the company together with details of its directors and company secretary. Once these documents are lodged with the Registrar of Companies at Companies House, any member of the public may inspect them.

Ownership and control

Theoretically a limited company is managed democratically by the votes of its shareholders, each ordinary share counting as one vote. In practice, however, many shares, particularly in companies listed on the Stock Exchange, are owned by relatively few institutions (eg insurance companies and pension funds), and the 'small' shareholders choose not to exercise their rights. Provided that the dividends are satisfactory many shareholders take no further interest in the company; of course, takeover bids or other 'boardroom battles' for the control of a company stimulate interest, but essentially the shareholders' objectives are either profit or security.

Differing objectives

The growth of companies, where ownership is separated from control (unlike sole traders and partners, where ownership and control are synonymous), has created a potential clash of interest between shareholders, directors, managers and workers.

The shareholders' objectives are profit, either in the short or long term, and/or security (a safe long-term investment); and/or (in the case of large shareholders) a majority shareholding, giving them control over the company through the directors whom they can appoint to the board.

The objectives of the employees of the company are often more concerned with survival and job security; high salaries or wages; good working conditions, job satisfaction etc.

If the employees' objectives are compatible with the interests of the shareholders there is no clash of interests, but if they are not there is a potential clash. The directors, who are directly responsible to the shareholders, will tend to identify more closely with shareholder interests. The managers, who are employees of the company but who derive their authority from the directors, may experience a personal conflict of interest (see 'Objectives' in Chapter 4 and 'Role problems' in Chapter 20).

Growth

Businesses have a tendency to grow. This is because:

1. Retained profit re-invested leads to greater efficiency and therefore greater sales.
2. Businesses will seek the advantages which come from economies of scale.
3. Businesses will seek the security which comes from operating on a larger scale, in many different markets.
4. Businesses will seek to exercise greater control over their environments.
5. Businesses are run by human beings, and ambitious managers will achieve personal satisfaction by running larger enterprises – they may be motivated by responding to the challenge of the larger enterprise or by the pursuit of power.

Growth is limited by:

1. financial constraints, because growth usually requires further investment, from either retained profit, loans or additional capital;
2. market size limitations, because a business cannot grow unless there is a large enough market;
3. lack of personal ambition in the owners or managers.

How is growth achieved? By:

1. selling more of the existing products to existing markets;
2. selling new products to existing markets (while retaining existing products);
3. selling existing products to new markets (while retaining existing markets);
4. selling new products to new markets (while retaining existing products and markets).

These are marketing solutions, which will be discussed in greater detail in Chapters 7–12.
Growth may also be achieved by some or all of the following:

1. acquisition of subsidiaries;
2. amalgamation and mergers;
3. horizontal, vertical or lateral integration.

Acquisition of subsidiaries

Subsidiary companies may be acquired by obtaining the majority shareholding in an existing company or by the creation of a new company in which the parent has the majority shareholding.

Holding companies

A holding company is one which has control over another company (or companies) either by holding sufficient equity (shares carrying voting rights) in the company, or by acquiring the right to appoint the directors of it.

This type of business organisation allows for centralised control (over, say, policy-making) and yet de-centralised operation, and companies within the 'group' are still able to retain their own individuality. Sometimes holding companies are created for the sole purpose of holding the shares of several subsidiaries.

Amalgamations and mergers

Amalgamations between companies (often rival companies) occur when two or more companies will mutually benefit from it.

Generally an amalgamation can take place by either merger or absorption.

Merger. This is usually the merging of companies in which each company involved is dissolved and its business assets and liabilities transferred to a new company which has been specially incorporated for this purpose.

Absorption. Absorption involves one company taking control of another (ie to become a 'holding company') by the outright purchase of the other company's investors' shares (either by cash or by exchanging shares in the 'holding company'). Shares may also be purchased through the London Stock Exchange ('take-over'). The company once taken over may continue as a subsidiary company.

Advantages of amalgamation
- an increased capital base, through combining the capital resources of both companies;
- improved management (often one of the motives for an amalgamation is for one company to obtain another company's managerial talent);
- rationalised capital investment (ie the pooling of buildings/machinery etc);
- a wider market, because both companies' markets are combined into one;
- pooling of research and development costs (these costs can be very large, and certain areas of research are 'pooled' on an industrial basis anyway);
- rationalised selling and distribution;
- the eradication of wasteful competition, because both companies are now co-operating instead of competing;
- the acquisition and exchange of valuable industrial 'know how', patents and goodwill.

Disadvantages of amalgamation
- With an increase in size of the company group structure, the control function may become remote, particularly as far as personnel relationships are concerned.
- The problem of integration (eg in the disruption to personnel and procedures, etc) may be very great.
- There could be a loss of trade name (perhaps), goodwill and 'industrial secrets'.

Direction of growth

There are three 'directions' in which a company can achieve growth. These are horizontal integration, vertical integration and lateral integration.

Horizontal integration
This is the linking up of companies producing the same product or service, or operating at the same level of processing. The amalgamation of the Midland Bank with the Hong Kong and Shanghai Banking Corporation, resulting in HSBC becoming a household name, is an example of horizontal integration.

Vertical integration
This is effected by expanding into the different processes carried out in order to produce and sell a product or service. A company can expand vertically 'forwards' towards its markets (eg a large film company purchasing a chain of cinemas) or 'backwards' towards the raw material supply (eg a motor manufacturer acquiring blast furnaces, or a clothing retail 'chain' buying into the textile industry). Ultimately all the successive processes carried out come under one source of control.

Lateral integration
This is directed towards increasing the range of products sold by integration with other firms which produce entirely different products.

Conglomerates

This is a merger of companies that have no important common characteristics (such as making the same product or operating the same process). Often the connection between constituent companies is so loose within the conglomerate that capital investment and profit policy directed by the central policy makers may be the only related interest. Conglomerates have a habit, over time, of being broken up into smaller units as the difficulty of managing the whole becomes more apparent.

Multinational companies

The drive to growth, discussed above, leads to the internationalisation of business and ultimately to the formation of multinational companies (hereafter referred to as MNCs).

Typical stages of internationalisation are passive exporting, active exporting, limited fixed investment in exporting and major involvement in international or multinational companies.

Passive exporting
This is usually a small company which receives an unsolicited enquiry from abroad, which results in a sale.

Active exporting
These are usually small to medium-size companies which actively seek export sales, but without necessarily modifying their products to suit export markets or setting up specialist export divisions.

Limited fixed investment in exporting
These are companies which commit some of their resources to an active search for export sales, which produce products specifically for export and which set up export departments to handle export business.

International companies
These have major involvement in international business: companies which regard their international business as at least equal in importance to their domestic business, which have specialist international divisions, which may approach international business through exporting, licensing or capital investment, which have manufacturing or marketing subsidiaries in foreign countries.

Multinationals
Companies which are truly multinational are registered in more than one country, have shares quoted in all or most stock exchanges and have directors from several countries. Common characteristics of multinationals are:

- overseas subsidiaries which are complete industrial and/or commercial organisations covering research and development, manufacturing, and sales and after-sales functions;
- involvement in several countries, which may be at different stages of economic development;
- generation of a universally accepted and understood corporate policy for guidance and direction of the overseas subsidiaries in pursuit of declared aims and objectives.

Operational environments and strategies of multinational companies

The progressive globalisation of world trade has reduced the importance of the domestic economy for many businesses. Foreign production by MNCs is already in excess of 20 per cent of world output and growing at a rate which outstrips world output growth. Even if MNCs are indifferent to it, they are playing a leading role in expanding international interdependence.

The driving force behind the growth and expansion of MNCs has been the belief that vertically integrated companies linked by a global strategic plan should possess a distinct competitive advantage over under-capitalised and technologically backward local businesses in the exploitation of any profitable overseas markets. MNCs should be more effective in mobilising, directing and controlling the resources at their disposal; have better opportunities of achieving economies of scale because of their larger production base and market horizons; be able to draw on a wealth of corporate experience in strategic planning, forecasting, market research, finance, production and marketing; and keep in close and constant contact with their overseas subsidiaries because of developments in high capacity cable and satellite communications, computers and jet planes.

Another motive for overseas investment has been the attempt to secure and protect supplies of key raw material. Moves by MNCs have been counter-balanced in the last decade or so by host countries which have become increasingly reluctant to allow foreign countries to control (through MNCs) the extraction and processing of their prized indigenous raw materials.

The comparatively lower labour costs of many overseas countries have also been an incentive to MNCs to transfer the manufacture of their products to selected areas in the world.

Benefits attributed to the presence of MNCs are:

- encouragement of transportation, banking and insurance, because these services are required by the MNCs;
- provision of, and training in, management and professional skills;
- exploitation of local natural resources, particularly where this necessitates large capital investment beyond the resources of the host country;
- establishment of new industries, thereby creating demand for manpower;
- investment for capital projects beyond the resources of the host country;
- provision of new markets and developments of new products;
- positive contribution to the balance of payments of the local country.

Disadvantages attributed to the presence of MNCs are:

- policy-making generally resides at the MNC headquarters, which carries the danger that the interests of the host country will be disregarded;
- research and development facilities and programmes are almost invariably centred in the MNC's home country;
- concessions made to MNCs to make their original investments (such as import protection and special tax deals; financial support and subsidies; protection against expropriation and guarantee against legal discrimination; and provision of sensitive information) may exceed potential benefits;
- high payments to expatriate managers can create resentment among local employees.

Operational problems of multinational companies include:

- the complexities of activities conducted on an international scale, which are far greater than those in the domestic field. Communication with subsidiaries is more difficult;
- restrictions imposed by the host government, which will be concerned with such matters as the amount of local manpower employed; the prevailing wage rates paid; the contribution of the MNC to the local gross national product (GNP); the percentage of control exercised by foreign nationals; the imposition of taxes; transfer pricing designed to retain profit in the 'home' country rather than the 'host' country; environmental pollution; and the degree to which the MNC can assist in strengthening the local industrial base;
- controlling companies with a diverse range of cultures and languages, at different stages of industrial, commercial and social development;

- exchange rate fluctuations; transfer of capital into and out of subsidiaries; cross-border transfer pricing;
- centralised and decentralised control, ie the degree of independence to be given (or taken by) overseas subsidiaries;
- deployment of resources for investment, and the reconciliation of the differing needs and demands of overseas companies and countries;
- reconciliation of overseas markets which are subject to different cultures, political climates, languages, geography, time zones, buying behavioural patterns, buying power, distribution outlets, packaging design, and susceptibility to advertising and sales promotional campaigns;
- workers' attitudes to international investment plans.
- the growing complexity of the legal situations affecting MNCs. Basically, a government can only effectively legislate for the activities of those of its citizens and companies who are living or operating within its boundaries.

Cartels, joint ventures and consortia

These are special types of co-operation between businesses.

Cartels

A cartel is sometimes used to describe an agreement between businesses to limit output and not to compete with each other, thus ensuring higher profits for each member and higher prices and a lack of choice for the customer. A large number of national governments and international institutions, such as the European Commission, have taken steps to make cartels illegal.

Joint ventures

Sometimes two companies, or a company and a government department, will combine forces for a particular project. One company might provide the know-how, the other company or the government department the labour or the premises. The profits and losses, responsibilities and duties are split between the parties in a pre-agreed manner.

Consortia

A consortium is a group of separate companies which join together to accomplish a specified task. The project is not expected to last indefinitely but may involve specialist activities such as industrial/business requirements. The building of the Channel Tunnel was undertaken by an international consortium of companies. Most major civil engineering projects (dams, bridges, motorways) and major building projects (power stations, hospitals) are carried out by consortia.

Co-operatives

Co-operative societies originate from the first society founded in Rochdale in 1844. They are based on the idea of 'self-help'. Membership of a co-operative society is obtained by purchasing a share or shares. However, unlike the procedure in companies, the voting rights are one vote per member, rather than one vote per share. There is a maximum shareholding, and shares are not quoted on the Stock Exchange. The shares cannot be sold. If a member leaves the society, the society pays him back the money he originally paid for his shares; thus the society's capital may fluctuate daily.

Profits are distributed to members and to non-member customers through a 'dividend' on the value of goods purchased; nowadays this is usually in the form of reward card points, which can be exchanged for goods. It follows that the more a customer buys from the co-operative, the larger will be his dividend.

Examples of co-operatives are:

Co-operative Bank;
Co-operative Insurance Society;
Co-operative Retailing Society.

Collectively they are one of the largest retailing groups in Britain.

The co-operative movement is closely identified with socialism, and has links with the Labour Party. An interesting international example of the influence of the co-operative movement is Mondragon, Spain, which is based on the principles established by the 'Rochdale pioneers'.

Advantages of co-operative societies
- Stability of trade results from the loyalty of participant members.
- Profit is shared between participant members, and the management is democratically elected.

Disadvantages of co-operative societies
- Democratic management may suffer from a lack of business experience.
- It is claimed that, due to the apathy of the average member, management is not elected according to wishes of the entire membership. Control of a society may rest in the hands of a small nucleus of people. However, this is equally true of companies.

Management buy-outs and employee share schemes

Sometimes senior managers of an ailing company club together to buy the company's shares from its existing shareholders (commonly a holding company). This is known as a management buy-out. The managers often know more about the company than its former owners, and they are strongly motivated to make a success of their own business. Holding companies are often quite pleased to be able to sell their unwanted subsidiaries to people whom they already know and with whom they are likely to be able to continue to do business.

In many companies both senior managers and ordinary employees are encouraged to buy shares in their own company. Tax incentives enable them to do this relatively easily. Such employee share schemes, as they are known, are believed to motivate the employees and to diminish the problem of industrial action.

Building societies

A building society is, in a sense, co-operative in its concept. It is a kind of bank which is engaged in borrowing money from its membership in order to lend it to other members, on security, for the purchase of property, normally for the members' own private occupation.

The public sector

We have seen that the public sector includes the departments of state and public corporations.

Public corporations

These are created by Royal Charter or, more commonly, by Act of Parliament. Local authorities are public corporations, empowered to issue municipal stock and raise loans. They have many potentially profit-making trading ventures, such as rented council housing, transport services, leisure facilities, airports and harbours. The extent to which these enterprises make profits or are subsidised by public rate-payers is a matter of political debate.

The use of funds raised from charges for specific services, such as council house rents, may be restricted to certain types of expenditure or their use for other expenditure may require formal approval by the members of the council.

Formerly many industries, such as ship-building, telecommunications and the railways, were owned by the state. Since the 1980s many of these industries have been privatised, with varying degrees of success, with either all or a majority of the industries' shares being held by investors. It is increasingly recognised that while the state tends not to run such industries efficiently, privatised companies tend to be too profit-driven at the expense of wider social considerations such as safety, respect for the environment and consumers, or employees' interests.

A distinction must be made between the 'nationalised industries' (wholly owned by the state) and 'mixed enterprises', where the state only holds shares in a company.

Although there are scarcely any nationalised industries in the UK today, there are still many places in the world where governments own majority shareholdings in large industrial companies.

Nationalisation versus privatisation

This has been a subject of political debate, the argument broadly speaking centring on whether the industries should be run 'as businesses', ie profit-making, or 'as public services', ie catering for social welfare and, if necessary, subsidised by taxes.

Advantages which are *claimed* for nationalisation

Economies of scale. Some industries, eg railways, may be best organised on a large scale.

Capital expenditure. Some industries may require such large sums of capital investment that only the state is capable of providing the necessary capital.

Control of monopoly power. The nationalised industries, although they are monopolies, are answerable to the public through Parliament.

Control of the economy. Because of their potentially enormous size (about 20 per cent of gross domestic product, about 20 per cent of investment and about 1.5 million employees in 1980), control of the nationalised industries meant, in effect, control of the economy. Price policies and investment policies in the nationalised industries affected prices and spending power throughout the economy.

Price discrimination. Any business benefits from price discrimination (see Chapter 10). However, nationalised industry may choose to discriminate in favour of socially needy groups such as old-age pensioners, thus pursuing social objectives rather than profit.

Social benefits. Service not otherwise profitable (eg rail services to remote rural areas) may be subsidised from public (ie taxpayers') money, for political reasons rather than profit.

Strategic reasons. Defence industries may be brought under state control.

Rationalisation of assets. Rather than have several private companies wasting their assets by competing (eg several adjacent railway lines, or gas pipes) it is more economical to have one – state-owned.

Investment. Ailing industries can be modernised by state investment.

Socialism. The 1918 Labour Party Constitution Clause IV committed the Labour Party 'to secure for the workers … common ownership of the means of production, distribution and exchange …'. In 1995 the Labour Party recognised that any attempt to re-nationalise the industries privatised by the Conservative governments since 1980 would be neither economically feasible nor politically desirable, and voted to abandon Clause IV. However, the basic arguments between left-wing politicians, in favour of greater state control, and right-wing politicians, in favour of greater private ownership through free-market policies, remains.

Arguments against nationalisation and for privatisation

Privatisation. The Conservative governments of the 1980s and 1990s pursued policies committed to returning nationalised industries to private ownership in the belief that private investment, the pursuit of profit, and the greater efficiency resulting from competition will benefit the economy. The Office of Fair Trading and certain government-appointed regulators are empowered to protect the interests of consumers.

Bureaucracy. Large organisations become bureaucratic and, therefore, inefficient and insensitive to customers.

No profit incentive. Private enterprises are motivated by the pursuit of profit; nationalised industries are 'cushioned' by taxpayer subsidies, and therefore are not subject to the discipline of a competitive free market.

Political interference and the corporate state. There may be fears about increasing political intervention in commercial decision-making and about the growth of the power of the state.

Chapter Four

Business objectives and organisation

- Introduction

- SWOT analysis

- Matching the firm to the environment – a two-way process

- Setting objectives

- Objectives: the concept

- Strategic planning

Introduction

The management of any business involves:

1. knowing where the business is now (situation analysis);
2. deciding where you want the business to be (setting objectives);
3. planning how to get there (strategic planning);
4. organising the work necessary to carry out the plan (organising);
5. making sure that you know when you have arrived – and if not why not (controlling).

SWOT analysis

The manager of the firm must consider the external environment and the firm's existing (or potential) resources. A useful 'tool' for doing this is the so-called 'SWOT analysis', which stands for 'strengths, weaknesses, opportunities and threats'. The manager identifies the firm's:

1. strengths (relative to the environment and to the firm's competitors);
2. weaknesses (relative to the environment and to the firm's competitors);
3. opportunities (arising from the environment);
4. threats (arising from the environment).

He then sets objectives, and plans to build on the strengths and remedy the weaknesses in order to take advantage of the opportunities and counter the threats.

The relationship between the firm's immediate (micro-) environment usually involves short-term operational decisions, whereas the macro-environment involves more long-term strategic decisions.

The essential point to note is that the relationships are dynamic, never static. Thus the firm's resources change from day to day as it wins or loses contracts, employees join or leave it, new products are designed, investments succeed or fail. It is impossible to list all the variations in the external environment but a commonly used framework for assessing these is called 'PEST analysis', which considers the influences on the company of political, economic, social and technological factors in the outside world. Naturally these categories can overlap, but the following examples will illustrate how changes in each of these areas of the environment can influence the company.

Political

- Changes in government may affect the level of support for private business as opposed to the public sector.
- Political instability may make long-term investments appear too risky.
- Changes in company law may encourage or discourage different types of business.
- Changes in employment law may make it more or less difficult to make workers redundant.

Economic

- Inflation reduces customers' purchasing power and therefore demand.
- New taxes may change the distribution of income and therefore create changes in purchasing power.
- Physical geography and climatic conditions can seriously affect the viability of industries in different parts of the world. For example, mining of some minerals may become more and more difficult as the more accessible seams are depleted.
- Good or bad harvests worldwide will directly influence the prices of goods generally and therefore performance of agriculture and the goods industry, even in those areas not directly affected by fluctuations in production.
- Changes in interest rates may make it advantageous or disadvantageous to invest in new plant.

Social

- New fashions may create opportunities.
- New beliefs, for example 'social responsibility', may impose constraints.
- Population movements and/or fluctuations in birth or death rates will influence the size of the population and therefore the demand for all products.

Technological

- New processes may bring about a competitive advantage or (if it is a competitor who has the new process) a disadvantage.

Matching the firm to the environment – a two-way process

Management's task is to match the firm to its environment. The manager must recognise that this is a two-way process; just as he responds to changes in the environment so the environment will be influenced by his decisions. Thus a decision to close down a plant (because of a decline in demand, brought about by changes in the economic or cultural environment) may create high local unemployment (reducing the demand for other goods or services); a decision to advertise (to increase sales of a particular brand) may increase demand for all brands, including competitors' (eg tobacco advertising); a decision to delay payment of a debt (to solve a cash flow difficulty) may arouse suspicions of financial weakness (and thus make further credit more difficult to obtain).

Setting objectives

Once all the relevant information about the business's current situation, resources and environment has been collected and analysed, the next step for management is the setting of objectives. This is necessary so that all the people involved, both managers and workers, will know what the business is trying to achieve, what resources are required to achieve it, what policies and plans are to be followed – in other words the setting of objectives is one way of ensuring that everybody in the business is pulling in the same direction.

Definitions

A major difficulty for students considering the subject of 'objectives' is that the word is used to mean different things by different writers and is often used in conjunction with other words such as 'mission', 'aims', 'targets 'and 'goals': sometimes synonymously, sometimes as having different meanings. Before proceeding further we must therefore attempt a definition of these words, and at the same time we shall attempt to define some other words often used in the same context, namely 'policies', 'strategies' and 'tactics'.

Objective
'Objective' describes in broad terms what the business wants to achieve. Examples might include:

- to generate profit;
- to generate sufficient cash resources to enable the business to continue;
- to perform a needed public service;
- to contribute towards improving the ethical and moral standards of society;

- to provide opportunities for its workforce to achieve their personal ambitions;
- to achieve market or industry leadership;
- to optimise customer satisfaction.

The word 'aim' is often used synonymously with 'objective' and sometimes used in the sense of an ultimate goal, with 'objective' being used to describe the smaller steps which have to be achieved before the goal can be accomplished.

Mission
'Mission' defines what the business wants to be, particularly the way in which it wishes to be perceived by its customers and its public. It therefore defines the business's corporate personality and long-term ambitions.

Target
'Target' defines very precisely and in quantifiable or measurable terms what has to be achieved in order to achieve the objective. Thus examples would be:

- 'to achieve a 10 per cent return on investment in each of the next five years';
- 'to achieve a 20 per cent share of the market within 18 months';
- 'to reduce labour turnover to 10 per cent per annum within one year'.

It is necessary that targets should be precisely defined so that they can be used as criteria or standards against which actual performance can be measured; if the actual performance is not 'up to standard' management will need to investigate the cause or causes.

The major characteristics of targets are that they:

- have specific time limits for achievement;
- are couched in specific quantifiable terms, such as: percentage market share; return on sales; labour production ratios, maximum raw material losses through breakages and handling; cost reduction percentage; maximum hours lost through strikes;
- are subordinate to objectives;
- assign individual and departmental responsibilities.

Targets are often 'operational targets' for each department to aim at, so that the business as a whole may achieve its objectives. The word 'goal' is often used synonymously with 'target'.

Policy
'Policy' describes how the business operates, its style, and its behaviour. Thus a business may claim that its policy is:

- 'to pay higher wages than the average';
- 'to maintain high quality products';
- 'to recruit only first class honours graduates for management training';
- 'not to offer bribes' etc.

It will be seen that 'corporate policy' helps to give the company an identity and ensures that all employees are likely to make decisions and act in a consistent manner one with another. Policy is therefore closely identified with mission.

Strategy

'Strategy' refers to major plans designed to achieve the company's objectives over the long term, usually defined as at least five years. Examples of strategic planning would include:

- brewers buying public houses over many years in order to control the sale and distribution of their beers;
- tobacco companies diversifying as the sale of tobacco declines;
- traditional food retailers selling non-food items etc.

Strategic decisions are made at a high level of management and involve all the functions of the business (finance, marketing, production, personnel and purchasing).

Tactics

Tactics are highly specific and detailed plans for a particular situation, to be carried out in the short run, usually defined as less than one year. Examples would include:

- introductory offers;
- a three-month advertising campaign to launch a new product;
- offers and counter-offers made by management or unions negotiating the annual wages agreement.

It is obvious that 'tactics' must be consistent with 'strategy'.

Tactical decisions are usually made at a lower level of management and only involve the department to which responsibility for the decision has been delegated.

Objectives: the concept

Having defined some terms we must now explore the concept of objectives in greater depth.

The earliest writers in the field of economics were interested in the reasons why businesses were set up and what their objectives were. Our discussion should therefore start with the early theories, particularly those of the economists.

Economic theories of the firm

Economic theories are based on a concept which assumes that the purpose of business enterprise is to make a profit. This concept is that the firm's function is to convert inputs – made up of a mixture of 'factors of production', ie land, labour and capital – into outputs of goods or devices for which customers will pay.

Since the firm can manipulate the relationship between the costs of the input and the price of the output in order to make a surplus, or profit, then it can be assumed that the firm is in business to make a profit. It has been assumed that the maximisation of profit is the true objective of business enterprise.

For the entrepreneur and the business, this has obvious advantages. For society, the advantages are twofold:

- If maximum profits are made, maximum revenue is obtained for society in general. This is Adam Smith's notion of the 'invisible hand': that the individual entrepreneur benefits society even if he did not intend to do so. By making profits the entrepreneur creates 'wealth', which can be shared among society at large.

- If profits are not being made, then this is a signal to society via the entrepreneur that resources need to be moved from one activity to another.

More modern economists, and others, criticise the theory on several grounds, arguing that:

- Increasing government intervention in and interference with business shows that the 'invisible hand' needs holding. Government intervention may be either to control 'anti-social' business behaviour or to provide investment which the private sector will not or cannot provide.
- The individual owner is no longer a dominant figure since today's large businesses are owned by many shareholders. Control of the business is in the hands of the professional manager, working mainly for a salary, whose objectives are not personal profit.
- The domination of large sectors of the economy by one or two firms means that competition is reduced and prices are not set solely by a 'pure' competitive market. Profit maximisation might mean that a monopoly is restricting output or charging abnormally high prices, rather than that industrial entrepreneurs are producing efficiently.

It is also pointed out that the taking of profit-maximising decisions needs perfect information and foresight, which managers do not have.

The argument between these two schools of thought has lain at the heart of the political debate since the early 1980s. The Conservative governments led by Margaret Thatcher and John Major pursued policies based on a belief in the social benefits of the market economy, similar to the theories of Adam Smith, whereas the Labour government which came into power in 1997 under Tony Blair has favoured more state intervention in business affairs.

The role of profit

While research has shown that profit is not the sole objective, it is still rightfully an important objective for the following reasons:

- It ensures the survival of the firm.
- It provides a source of finance by which the firm can renew or increase its assets.
- It provides distributable resources for stakeholders, especially shareholders.
- It provides a psychological spur for management to succeed.
- It provides a 'standard' measure by which one manager or one company can be compared with another.
- It is one of the most important factors in a potential investor's assessment of the company.
- It is an effective measure of how efficiently resources are being put to use.

Let us explore some of these concepts more thoroughly.

A basic question is: 'What is the reason for generating profit?' Is it to distribute it to shareholders in the form of dividends?

Unless the shareholder actually receives high dividends consequent upon higher profits, or is able to sell his shares at a higher price in anticipation of future dividends, he does not benefit from higher profits. Consequently, shareholders are more interested in the size of dividends than the size of the profits.

As the salary and status of an executive are directly related to the particular job he holds, and the greatest proportion of his income is likely to come to him via his pay cheque, it is reasonable to imagine that he will be ambitious to expand his departmental and personal responsibilities in anticipation of a larger pay cheque. Thus, he will be inclined towards those projects and activities which advance his cause and will oppose those which may retard his chances of promotion. It is difficult to imagine that the size of the dividend will be uppermost in his mind – although his legal responsibility must be to the shareholder.

Even when profit maximisation is the avowed aim of a company, the implementation of such a policy provides many problems of definition and application. Is the company interested in profit maximisation over the short or the long term? It can increase its profits in the short term by discontinuing expenditure on research and development activities intended to generate new products, but its profits will be lower in the long term because the new products will fail to materialise.

Profit – conclusions

Today it is not likely, if indeed it ever was, that firms exist only to make profits. The objectives of managers are very mixed. Within the limits set by serving a customer and creating sufficient resources for the company to continue, managers may be more or less entrepreneurial, some wishing to grow, others to remain independent; others again are mainly concerned with their own authority and rewards.

On the other hand, the pursuit of profit remains for the manager a proper objective. Those managers who maintain that it is the prime objective are intuitively recognising that the pursuit of one single all important objective keeps the mind focused on one thing at a time since it is difficult to concentrate on multiple objectives. It also helps to avoid conflicts of interest between one objective and another. Profit is, and will remain, an important standard by which managers are judged, and is therefore still the main objective of managerial performance.

Some economists support Behavioural Science theories in suggesting that managements' motives are much more complex than aiming for maximum profits might suggest. They suggest that managers aim for a satisfactory level of profit to keep shareholders contented and avoid the threat of being taken over.

In addition, many economists support the idea that all who are connected with a firm are 'stakeholders' who deserve benefit, so that profit for the shareholders is but one objective, and no longer the sole objective. The 'stakeholders' include shareholders, directors, managers, workers, customers, financiers, suppliers and the local community, all of whom have interests, sometimes conflicting, in the success or long-term survival of the business.

Behavioural science theories of the firm

These theories are put forward by sociologists and psychologists who look at how people behave in organisations. According to behavioural scientists, management decision-taking is not solely concerned with maximising the profits of a business but is a compromise between the conflicting 'business' objectives of each functional department and the private objects and personalities of the various decision-makers. In fact 'profit satisfying' is suggested as an alternative to 'profit maximising'.

1. Since each individual has his own objectives, business objectives, including profits, are set as a result of bargaining between the various parties or their representatives.
2. While objectives depend upon people they also change:
   a) over time (people and circumstances change);
   b) through changes in the environment (eg if new technology or legislation changes the business's position);
   c) with changes in the product or markets with which the business deals (since objectives will depend upon the industry in which the firm operates);
   d) with change in the size of the business.
3. Objectives are set to 'satisfy' various interested groups such as shareholders, managers, creditors, local community etc. This is the 'stakeholder theory'.

Clearly, objectives are set for all kinds of areas besides profit and profit-related factors. Personal and social objectives may play as important a part.

These theories, based upon research into organisations, seem to reinforce commonsense. They serve to remind us that man is more than an economic animal, whether he is owner, manager or worker. His motivations are complex. (See Chapters 20 and 21.)

Survival

Survival is obviously an overriding objective in every organisation. The first few months of the life of a business are usually the most crucial: its products will be unknown and unestablished, its advertising campaigns have had little chance to make any impact, repeat orders will not have begun to appear, its organisational structure will still be in a formative stage and it is likely to be subject to severe financial pressure due to low sales, heavy capital expenditure and difficulty in securing credit. However, survival through infancy is no guarantee of a subsequent happy life, as economic depressions and the activities of competitors may cause a business to re-examine its capacity for long-term survival.

The need to survive in the long run will lead the business to pursue some or all of the following strategies:

1. risk-spreading – by operating in more than one market or by having a wide range of products;
2. adaptation – by investing in market research and product research and development in order to remain sensitive to changes in the environment;
3. passive marketing – not attacking a competitor, and thereby not risking a response;
4. profit retention – ensuring that sufficient profit from successful trading is retained to guard against the bad times.

Customer satisfaction

Customer satisfaction is listed as a basic objective, because unless businesses achieve a satisfactory level of customer satisfaction they will soon go out of existence. The aim of the 'marketing concept' (where customer satisfaction measures its achievements) is to generate enough satisfied customers to ensure a profitable existence for a business.

Investment in market research is almost essential if the business is to identify the needs of its customers. This is discussed more fully in Chapters 7–12.

Growth

Growth is usually an implicit rather than an explicit corporate objective and is more likely to spring from internal pressure than from shareholders.

Growth may be measured against several yardsticks and is most commonly expressed in the following terms:

1. long-term profitable growth (ie a growth in the profit earned over several years);
2. increased sales turnover (ie a growth in the revenue earned over several years);
3. larger market share (ie a growth in the number of units sold relative to the competition);
4. industry or market leadership (ie gaining and retaining the largest market share);
5. expansion in number of new market or distribution outlets;
6. increased number of employees;
7. additional resources (ie higher level of capital employed).

A larger market share or leading position in its industry will not necessarily yield a business higher profits in the short term. If the expansion in sales has been gained through lower prices, it may have been achieved at a cost greater than the additional revenue – although higher profits may be earned in the long term.

The main obstacles to growth are seen to be:

1. resistance to change by key executives, who perhaps prefer an easy life to the rigours of attempting to exploit new products and new markets;
2. inflexibility of the organisational structure: the decision-making processes and the communication system, for instance, may not be easily adapted to larger scale;
3. lack of skilled manpower and other resources such as capital and land;
4. activities of competitors who may be applying effective counters to every move the business makes to extend its sales volume.

Cash flow

This will be discussed more fully in Chapters 22–24, but at this stage you should understand that unless a business has sufficient cash to pay its immediate 'creditors', ie its workers, suppliers, or short-term lenders, it will be insolvent and may have to cease trading. 'Cash flow' refers to the flow of cash in and out of the business and the amount of cash available at any time.

A business's cash flow position can exercise a decisive influence. If the business is unable to purchase and hold adequate stocks of raw materials and finished goods, or extend its credit base to attract new customers, or invest in long-term research and development programmes because of financial pressure, profits will be meaningless if survival cannot be secured and the business becomes insolvent. A strong cash flow provides an excellent launching pad for expansion.

All the objectives mentioned so far have an obvious commercial relevance: profit, survival, growth, cash flow, customer satisfaction.

Less obvious, although now widely recognised, is the responsibility to stakeholders.

The 'stakeholder' approach

The 'stakeholder' approach suggests that corporate objectives are, or ought to be, shaped and influenced by the collective pressures of those external organisations or (organised) groups of individuals which have significant contact with the company's operational activities, such as customers, suppliers, central and local government, consumer associations, trade unions, debenture holders and shareholders and members of the public whose lives are affected, directly or indirectly, by the activities of the company.

If the company intends its objectives to reflect, or take account of, the interests of these groups, it needs to know:

1. the composition, significance and relative strength of each group;
2. the legitimate claims that each group might have on the company, such as reliable standards of quality and after-sales service, reasonable stability in ordering patterns and avoidance of environmental pollution;
3. the degree to which the company is currently able to meet them; and
4. what evaluative standards to apply in attempting to reconcile conflicting claims.

A clear statement of corporate objectives is necessary to establish priorities.

Ethical and social responsibilities

Responsibility towards the community
The expectations and pressures of society have led businesses to a growing awareness of their social and ethical responsibilities. The most obvious are those concerned with ensuring that undesirable activities such as environmental spoilage and atmospheric pollution do not intrude on the enjoyment of public amenities.

Immediate action appears to be vital in a number of areas: conservation of energy sources, economies in the use of raw materials and the pursuit of recycling opportunities, and the conservation of land resources for future generations.

Responsibility towards the consumer
The fact that some consumers have been exploited (or believe that they have been exploited) by some companies has led to the growth of 'consumerism'. This manifests itself in the form

of pressure groups, the Consumers' Association and its magazine *Which?*, consumer programmes such as *Watchdog* and legislation such as the Trade Descriptions Act.

The central themes of consumerism are:

1. recognition of the need to protect the consumer from deceptive and misleading practices, monopoly pricing and dangerous products;
2. the growth of regulatory and quasi-governmental bodies which may take action against organisations which they believe have acted unfairly or illegally against the consumer;
3. educating and safeguarding the consumer about his rights to derive satisfaction from purchases – and hence from the vendor of the goods or services;
4. decisions by customers to buy only from suppliers whose policies are 'socially responsible', eg not stocking goods from countries with repressive governments.

The pressure of consumerists in Britain has been largely responsible for legislation which now requires the actual weight of products to be shown on their packaging; the true rate of interest on hire purchase agreements to be clearly stated on the transaction documents; motor car manufacturers to provide details of petrol consumption and emissions on common bases to facilitate direct comparisons; and cigarette packets to carry government health warnings.

Responsibility towards employees

If it is accepted that unhappy or discontented employees cannot work to their optimum level of efficiency, then it is in the interest of the employer to study the attitudes and motives of the employees with a view to improving performance. This is discussed more fully in Chapters 20 and 21.

Strategic planning

We have discussed 'objectives', both commercial and non-commercial, at some length, because unless a firm has a clear idea of its objectives, what it wants to achieve and what sort of firm it wants to be, it cannot sensibly set about planning its long-term strategies – the way in which it plans to achieve its objectives in the long run.

H Ansoff, a distinguished writer on corporate strategy, has identified four basic strategies for growth:

* market penetration – increasing the sale of the firm's existing products to its existing markets;
* product development – developing new products for sale to the firm's existing markets;
* market extension – selling existing products to new markets;
* diversification – developing new products for sale to new markets.

These four strategies may be visualised in the 'Ansoff matrix' shown opposite. How these four basic strategies are translated into operational plans will depend on:

* the firm's objectives;
* its resources;

- its environment; and
- how these are expected to change in the future.

Thus, for example, if the objective is 'growth', if the firm has a well-established and popular product, and if demand for the product is relatively elastic, the firm might select 'market penetration' as its strategy and 'price reduction' as its tactics.

The Ansoff Matrix

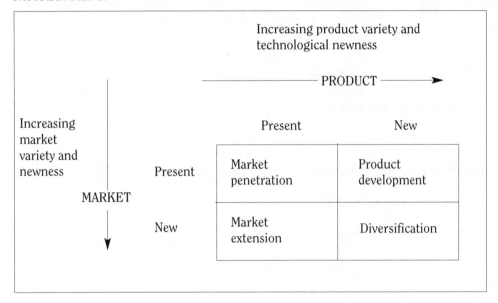

Alternatively, the objective of 'growth' might be pursued either by 'product development' (which would necessitate expenditure on technological research and development) or by 'market extension' (which would necessitate expenditure on market research). Where the objective is 'growth' and the environment is characterised by many relatively small businesses, each with differing market or technological strengths, the chosen strategy might be 'diversification' – through the acquisition of other businesses.

Once the broad strategic plans have been agreed at the corporate, or top management, level, they will have to be translated into operational plans for each part of the business. This is discussed in greater detail in the chapters on marketing, production and personnel.

Chapter Five

Organisational structures

- Organisation – introduction

- Management

- Organisation – some definitions

- Constructing an organisation

- The use of departments

- Definition of responsibilities and authority – organisation charts

- Types of organisation structure

- Organisational relationships

- The principles of sound organisation

- Span of control

- Delegation, centralisation and decentralisation

- Co-ordination

- Use of committees

- Board of directors

- Control

Organisation – introduction

If strategic plans are to be carried out by all the different parts of the business, acting in unison, it is evident that management must give careful thought to how the business is organised and how the work is to be co-ordinated. This is the theme of this chapter.

The subject of 'organisation' can be approached in two ways, structural and behavioural.

The structural approach looks at the formal organisation, ways of sub-dividing the work into areas of specialisation, the way in which authority and responsibility is allocated within the formal structure.

The behavioural approach recognises that, no matter how carefully the formal structure is designed and defined, it will only work if the human beings who make up the organisation are properly chosen, led and motivated.

There is, of course, a substantial degree of overlap between the two approaches. This chapter concentrates on the structural approach; Chapters 20 and 21 will concentrate on the behavioural approach, and Chapter 25 will concentrate on the theme of 'communication', which links both approaches.

Management

Before proceeding further we should consider what we mean by 'management'. The word is used in three senses: general management; departmental management; and the 'act' of management.

General management

The term 'general management' is used to cover all those managers, whether directors or not, who have responsibility for setting objectives, shaping the policy, planning, organising and controlling the company. 'Top management' or 'senior management' are terms often used, and titles might include chief executive, managing director or general manager. The term can also include senior functional managers, like the finance director, who are on the board of directors or report directly to it. The nature of general management changes with change in a company's size and complexity or in its environment. The fundamental role is similar in most companies and can be summarised as follows:

The organising role is to design the most appropriate organisation structure in order to suit the company's strategy. Further, it is to design the organisational roles so that people are best suited to the job.

The directing role is commanding and activating the organisation. This is the management task of implementing the plans and translating them into specific jobs for junior management, supervisors or workers to carry out. It also includes motivating the workers. Among the problems of direction are choosing the appropriate style of leadership. Styles of leadership are discussed more fully in Chapters 20 and 21.

Co-ordinating is the task of drawing together all the activities and efforts of the organisation. Budgets, meetings, committees and conferences are all examples of techniques or actions which are taken to ensure that everything is co-ordinated towards organisation objectives. Good co-ordination involves effective communications.

The controlling role is ensuring that work is properly performed by all members of the organisation. Control systems are instituted in order to measure performance. The major aspect of controlling is the feedback of information against present plans or standards so that deviations are highlighted for investigation and correction. As indicated above, the setting of quantifiable targets is an essential part of the control system.

Departmental management

Specific roles expected of departmental managers will be discussed in later chapters. At this stage you must recognise that departmental management consists of the following:

1. setting (departmental) objectives and targets, consistent with those set in broader terms at the 'corporate' or 'general management' level;
2. organising the work of the department – designing the structure, defining the roles, resolving conflict;
3. directing – commanding, activating and implementing plans, defining specific jobs, motivating workers in the department;
4. controlling – operating control systems, measuring performance within the department;
5. co-ordinating – the work of all the members of the department and ensuring effective communication with them and among them.

The 'act' of management

It will be seen that the only essential difference between the roles of general management and departmental management is a difference in size, limit of authority and responsibility, and degree of detail. It follows that the 'act of management' covers all the roles indicated above and may be carried out by any member of the organisation within the area for which he is responsible. Although we define 'management' as those people responsible for at least a department, the roles of management still have to be performed by supervisors, foremen, chargehands – people whom we do not normally classify as 'managers', but who, nevertheless, still have to 'manage' the part of the organisation for which they are responsible.

Organisation – some definitions

It is important to understand what organisation is and to be able to define it when answering examination questions posed in this area.

E F L Brech defined organisation as:

> 'That part of management which is concerned with the definition of the structure of:
> a) the responsibilities by means of which the activities of the enterprise are distributed among the managerial, supervising and specialist personnel employed in its service, and
> b) the formal inter-relations established among the personnel by virtue of such responsibilities.'

(This is a definition worth learning both for this topic and for others which follow.)

Other terms which must be clearly understood are 'to organise', 'organisational relationships' and 'the organisation structure', which are discussed below:

To organise

'Planning work and determining the activity necessary to accomplish that work, and the arranging of such activity into groups, divisions, departments and sections'.

Organisational relationships

'The position of management and the formal relationships which exist among positions in the organisation'.

Organisations consist of people who:

- have a common purpose;
- work in groups in order to achieve that purpose;
- use specialist knowledge and techniques;
- work together, because that is more effective than working separately.

Management works:

- towards the common and agreed objectives;
- through people;
- by using specialist management techniques;
- in an organisation, as defined above.

The organisation structure

'The superstructure (or framework) designed so that people can work together towards a common objective'.

'Organisation' is also sometimes used to mean the whole firm as a unit.

Constructing an organisation

There are three basic steps in the construction (or modification) of any organisation: determining the work which is necessary; dividing the work and allocating it to positions; classifying the positions into logical groupings.

Determining the work which is necessary

In order to do this correctly the following points are important:

1. establish the objectives of the work;
2. consider the workload required in order to achieve those objectives;
3. eliminate all unnecessary work (and duplication);
4. formulate procedures for carrying out the work;
5. ensure that essential work has not been omitted.

Professor Drucker, an eminent writer in business subjects, identifies three types of analysis which have to be performed at this stage:

1. activities analysis – determining what work needs to be performed and how the activities should be co-ordinated;
2. decision analysis – what type of decisions are to be made, and how each manager should be involved;
3. relations analysis – knowing what contribution each manager is to make, with whom he is to work, and what contribution other managers make to him.

Dividing the work and allocating it to positions

This step will entail the following:

1. the establishment of standards (for instance, it may be necessary to find out what constitutes a standard workload for one person at a given level of management);
2. it may be necessary to use management science techniques for this, including work study, organisation and methods study, job analysis etc;
3. obtaining the full co-operation of all people involved within the organisation.

Classifying the positions into logical groupings

It is very important that the positions are grouped according to the *type of work* rather than according to the personalities employed in positions at the time (this is known as the 'Principle of Orientation'). (See below, p79, 'The principles of sound organisation'.)

Almost inevitably the process of 'dividing the work' and forming logical groupings' will lead to the creation of 'departments' ie work groups whose members perform some similar work, usually under the leadership of a departmental manager.

The use of departments

The use of departments by grouping similar activities and employees means that a large number of subordinates can be directly managed, and gives the flexibility necessary to enable organisations to expand to cover business growth.

Methods of dividing work into departments include:

- Division into equal-sized groups. This method is used when skills are homogeneous and a specific number of employees is required to undertake various activities. This method is declining because of increased specialisation.
- By function. This is the most common type and involves the setting up of departments for production, marketing, personnel, finance etc. The exact departments required will be determined by the needs of the organisation.
- Territorial basis. This is more common where the enterprise covers many different locations. All the activities in one location may be assigned to the area manager.

- Product basis. This is increasingly used in large-scale enterprises concerned with diverse products where otherwise the organisation would be too complex.
- Customer basis. Where the customers are the key factor, they will influence how the organisation is grouped. This is particularly noticeable in service industries.

In larger organisations some or all of these groupings may be used.

Early forms of organisation as people are first recruited are likely to take a functional structure thus:

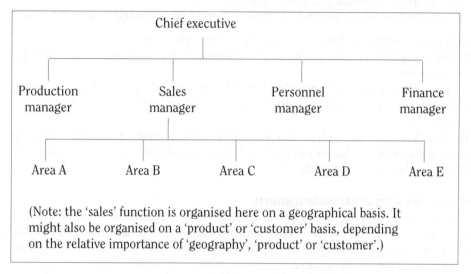

(Note: the 'sales' function is organised here on a geographical basis. It might also be organised on a 'product' or 'customer' basis, depending on the relative importance of 'geography', 'product' or 'customer'.)

When designing the organisation's management, take into account the following issues:

1. stratification – how many layers of management and levels of work there need to be;
2. formalisation – how formal communications and procedures have to be. The more bureaucratic the organisational style the more formal and systematised internal arrangements must be;
3. centralisation – management must decide the extent to which decisions can be delegated to others. Should all major decisions be taken by central head office management?
4. complexity – how complex can the organisation be? A simple hierarchy with clearly defined responsibilities and authorities is readily understood. By contrast a matrix type structure (discussed below) can be extremely confusing.

Definition of responsibilities and authority – organisation charts

For the organisation to work effectively it is essential for all responsibilities and authority to be clearly defined and communicated.

There are three methods of defining responsibility and authority and communicating them throughout an organisation so that everybody is perfectly clear as to what is required of them, what the parameters of their responsibilities are and what relationships they have with other people within the organisation. These are: organisation charts; organisational manuals; schedules of responsibilities.

Organisation charts

Examination questions often require diagrams of organisational structures incorporating one or more of the organisational relationships discussed in this chapter. Students should be able to draw charts to represent given relationships.

When constructing an organisation chart the following points should be borne in mind:

1. The chart acts merely as an *outline* of the organisation structure.
2. It should be presented clearly and be easy to understand. The minimum amount of detail should be shown.
3. There is no standard organisation and each firm has its own organisational characteristics. The chart should portray the organisation to which it relates and not attempt to depict the 'theoretical' norm.
4. If the chart is difficult to construct it may indicate that the organisation itself is defective and over a period of time has grown inefficient and unwieldy with lines of responsibilities and authority becoming distorted.

Advantages of using organisation charts

1. The preparation of an organisation chart requires the organisation to be analysed in detail. Such a study does, in itself, have benefits. Major weaknesses existing within the organisation (such as an overlap of authority or even certain areas of work not being covered adequately) will be revealed.
2. Relationships are highlighted.
3. The chart can be used for providing information to employees (particularly newcomers) about the nature of the business and the management structure. It also supplements the more detailed information available in the organisation manual. Furthermore it can be used for planning purposes, that is to be applied as a basis for any re-organisation or modification of the structure of the organisation.
4. An organisation chart can be used as a reference. When used as a medium of communication it can inform staff of changes within the organisation. Organisation charts used for this purpose will be displayed on departmental and corridor notice boards.

Disadvantages of using organisation charts

1. They give a static picture. Organisation charts become outdated very quickly. A chart shows the organisation at a particular time and in this sense is static. However, the business is dynamic and although the major structural framework of the organisation remains unaltered for a long period there are many changes within that framework (eg personalities) which necessitate the continual updating of charts.
2. 'Informal' relationships are not charted. The informal relationships are not portrayed and the absence of such information reduces the practical value of charts.

3. Charts may lead to 'bureaucracy'. A chart is inflexible and portrays definitive channels of communication and does not illustrate the 'short cuts' which are often taken.
4. Levels of importance are difficult to portray. Erroneous impressions are sometimes given by charts showing several managers on the same horizontal line, with the implicit suggestion that they are of equal importance and status. The actual relationships and weighted importance of different positions are very difficult to chart accurately.

Organisational manuals

These manuals are often called 'departmental' or 'procedure' manuals and will include details about each position (often in the form of a 'job description'), relationships, duties with related responsibilities and authority and standard principles and practices.

Schedules of responsibility

Schedules of responsibilities actually define the scope of responsibility and authority within each position shown on the chart and give descriptions of the work involved. Schedules of responsibilities will be drawn up specifying in detail the duties of personnel employed in particular posts and will include the following:

1. title of the job;
2. department in which the post occurs;
3. grade or level of the position, reflecting the relative position in the organisational hierarchy;
4. description of the duties involved;
5. the responsibilities carried and the corresponding authority;
6. relationships within the organisation in respect of superiors, colleagues and subordinates;
7. number and nature of subordinates;
8. position of the immediate superior to whom the person is responsible;
9. special responsibilities;
10. special limitations (eg in respect of levels of permitted expenditure on own authority, without having to refer to higher authority for approval).

Types of organisation structure

So far we have only considered the 'functional', 'departmental' organisation. However, analysis of the relationships between different positions reveals that there are many types of organisation structure, of which the simple departmental structure is but one.

This approach to the topic of organisation is concerned with the type of authority used and how and where it is allocated within the organisation.

Organisation has been classified into the following main types: line (or direct); line and staff; matrix; committee.

Line (or direct)

In a 'line organisation' all posts are concerned with the achievement of operational objectives. All authority is direct, passing from superior to subordinates.

Advantages of 'line' organisation
1. Responsibility is established and there is a clear-cut division of responsibility and the corresponding allocation of authority.
2. The decision-making process is quick.
3. It is very simple to understand and operate, and discipline is easier to maintain.

This type of management structure usually leads to a stable form of organisation.

Disadvantages of 'line' organisation
1. It is inflexible and rigid, and inappropriate for organisational growth.
2. The loss of an executive (by resignation, death etc) may have more serious effects than it would have in a more flexible organisation plan.
3. It can be autocratic and dictatorial, thus stifling the initiative and potential of junior management.
4. Executives may be overloaded with duties and responsibilities, leading to stress and illness (and bad judgment!). (This is discussed more fully in Chapters 20 and 21.)

Line and staff organisation (the most widely used approach)

In a 'line and staff' organisation, 'line' management is supported by specialist ancillary services (see opposite).

Disadvantages related to line and staff organisation
1. There may be friction between line and staff officers. Line officers often resist the activities of functional experts.
2. This may result in the misinterpretation of expert information which reaches workers through line officers.

Note: many textbooks refer to line and staff organisation as 'functional organisation'. This is because functional organisation in its 'pure' form is rarely used. The terminology used in examination questions should be studied carefully in the context of the subject matter of the question in order to establish what is required by the examiner.

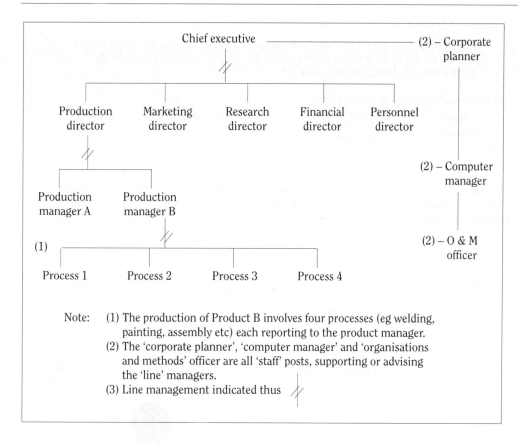

Note: (1) The production of Product B involves four processes (eg welding, painting, assembly etc) each reporting to the product manager.
(2) The 'corporate planner', 'computer manager' and 'organisations and methods' officer are all 'staff' posts, supporting or advising the 'line' managers.
(3) Line management indicated thus

Matrix organisation

This is a lattice of vertical and horizontal lines of authority bringing together a team of company specialists to work on a particular project (see overleaf). (A basic knowledge of the terminology is all that is required for the examination subject.)

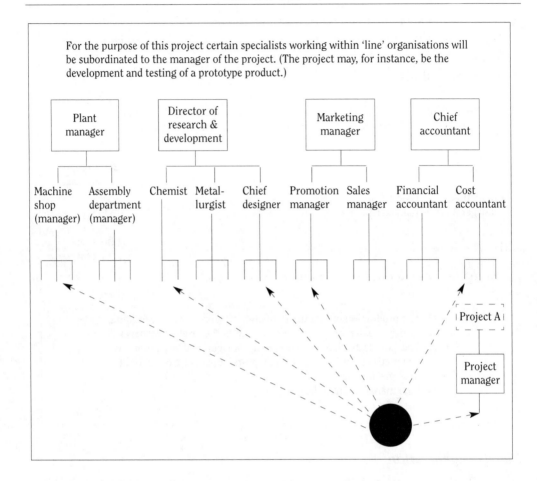

For the purpose of this project certain specialists working within 'line' organisations will be subordinated to the manager of the project. (The project may, for instance, be the development and testing of a prototype product.)

Committee organisation

The management is assisted by advisory committees such as are found today in the hospital service. Often there is a line organisation below the committee through which it manages. The work of committees is discussed in greater detail below.

Organisational relationships

The existence of any of these organisation types inevitably creates different relationships between the various positions. The various types of *relationship* existing within an organisation are akin to the types of organisational structure discussed above. The types of relationship are: line; functional; staff; lateral.

(Care should be taken over this part of the study. Staff 'relationship' has a different meaning from a staff 'organisation'. It is important that the meaning of *relationship* (ie as between people) should be differentiated from *organisation* (ie a structure into which positions can be slotted.)

Line relationships

A line relationship is the relationship which exists between a superior and his subordinates. An accountant and his clerks, the works manager and his foreman are examples of line relationships.

Functional relationships

This is the relationship exercised by a specialist appointed to carry out functional work throughout the organisation. This work is normally in an advisory capacity. The personnel manager will, for instance, have a functional relationship with the works manager in respect of the recruitment, training and general welfare of employees working within the latter's department. The accountant may have a functional relationship with the sales director on matters relating to the financing of sales, advertising and promotions etc. (It should be remembered that the functional head, eg the personnel manager, will have his own line organisation and therefore has a line relationship with his own staff.)

Staff relationships

This type exists where authority is representative and responsibility advisory. A managing director's personal assistant (PA) will communicate to line managers without any *personal* authority but will be accepted as being the 'voicepiece' of the managing director. In this respect the personal assistant exercises the managing director's authority. Having no personal authority he cannot take decisions himself, although he does have a duty to advise his chief on all aspects of the business and to offer his own recommendations.

The advantages of this are:

1. a good method of educating and training future leaders;
2. a saving of the time of top management who are relieved of mundane administration work.

The disadvantages are:

1. personal assistants often attain great 'unofficial' power and influence;
2. ambitious staff managers may try to assume authority over line managers.

Lateral relationships

This is the relationship which exists between people at the same level of organisation. It is not concerned with responsibilities or authority but rather with providing an avenue for communication and co-ordination between widely different aspects of work. Lateral relationships may be categorised into:

Colleague relations. The relationship that exists between people working in the same department and who are subordinate to the same superior.

Collateral relations. The relationships which are necessary for the interchange of ideas and opinions between people at the same level but in different departments within the organisation.

The principles of sound organisation

The principles formulated by H Fayol (a French writer on management) are listed below:

1. A unity of direction. No matter how the organisation is structured and to what extent decentralisation and delegation is applied only *one* person should ultimately be responsible for controlling all operations.
2. The scalar process. The ultimate authority (see (1) above) has control but also has the right to delegate authority to others through lines of command.
3. A unity of command. Each person should only answer to *one* superior.
4. The principle of correspondence. Authority handed down must correspond to the level of responsibility. If a person is delegated duties he must be given the authority necessary to accomplish them.
5. Span of control. The number of subordinates who can be *effectively* managed is limited and this number depends upon circumstances such as the nature and complexity of work. This number must not be exceeded.
6. Good communications. Both formal and informal lines of communication should be established and constantly reviewed.
7. The principle of orientation. All organisations should be planned according to the nature of the work and not according to the personalities occupying positions at the time.
8. The principle of exception. Only matters which are not going according to plan need be reported to management. Variances which are reported will be either favourable or adverse. In this way organisations will not be overburdened with masses of unnecessary detail.
9. Distinction in work. Different types of work have different characteristics and this should be allowed for in the planning of an organisation. For instance, tasks requiring individual craft skills should be separated from semi-skilled repetitive type work.
10. Simplification, specialisation and standardisation. These concepts should be introduced and encouraged wherever possible in the organisation, because they help to keep costs as low as possible.
11. Control over procedures. The procedures adopted by the organisation should be planned and controlled by some clearly established authority. Often a certain level of management will be responsible for the control of day-to-day procedures. Creative thought (perhaps expressed in the form of 'staff suggestion schemes') should be encouraged, however.
12. Planning. Planning should always precede work.
13. Flexibility. Organisations should be structured to allow for adaptation in the face of

changing methods, objectives, scale of operations, technological development and resources. Major changes in organisation will require comprehensive study.

14. Facility for access. All members of an organisation should have the right and be given the ability to submit complaints and suggestions to an appropriate superior.

Span of control

Fayol's principles of sound organisation include reference to the 'span of control', which is a very important concept in organisation design.

Both Fayol and L F Urwick, a British management consultant, have advocated a strict upper limit to the number of subordinates placed directly under the control of one manager. Urwick has postulated that the 'ideal number of subordinates for all superior authorities is four'; however, there are many factors, such as the complexity and nature of work, which may make a number greater than four acceptable.

There is no specific number of individuals which a manager can effectively supervise, but in any given case there will be a limit. It is this limit which makes proper organisation necessary and introduces the concepts of delegation and decentralisation. The ideal number of subordinates has been found to be anywhere between three and thirty, depending on the circumstances. The more recent theories developed emphasise that it is not possible to determine the exact number without examining the underlying factors.

Determining the span

Several factors are important when determining the span of control. Other than the nature and complexity of the work involved the personality of the manager must be considered and his ability to deal with people. A manager can reduce the amount of time actually spent supervising by:

- delegating authority in the performance of a well-defined task;
- drawing up clear and concise plans and policies;
- communicating these plans to subordinates;
- using objective performance standards (targets) to determine whether subordinates are following plans.

The importance of setting the span correctly

It is very important that the span of control is set correctly. Too wide a span means that the manager has to divide his time between too many subordinates, leading to:

1. a loss of personal contact between manager and subordinates;
2. possible loss of control over the group;
3. the possibility of sub-groups (with unofficial leadership roles);
4. an inability to inspect the output of the group;

5. the possibility of the general training and supervision of workers suffering, and as a result employee morale and output declining.

Too narrow a span of control leads to:

1. too many levels of management and high administration costs (such as management salaries);
2. delays in the decision-making process because of the length of the management chain;
3. too much supervision; as a result initiative may be stifled and morale adversely affected.

Delegation, centralisation and decentralisation

The degree to which authority should be concentrated or dispersed depends on *how much* authority there is. Delegation is part of decentralisation because authority must be delegated in order for decentralisation to occur. If there is no delegation, the organisation is centralised. The degree of centralisation decreases as more decisions are pushed down towards the work level, as they become more immediate in execution and as they become increasingly more specialist in nature. Centralisation involves a limitation of authority and a lack of delegation, and results in a slowing down of the decision making process. It also frustrates the initiative of junior managers.

Delegation

The main purpose of delegation is to make decentralisation of authority possible. This becomes necessary when a manager's span of control is too great and involves giving a subordinate authority for specific operations. It is only the authority which is delegated. The overall responsibility remains that of the superior.

Method of delegation
This can be oral or written (eg by schedules of responsibilities), specific or general. It is important that the delegation should not be too inflexible, and also not too wide in scope.

Principles of delegation
The following aspects are important:

*   the principle of delegating according to the results expected (and agreed) so that the subordinate has sufficient authority to achieve the results required;
*   the scalar principle, which is the chain of direct authority relationships throughout the organisation. This is essential: each subordinate must know who has delegated authority to him and to whom he is responsible;
*   the authority-level principle, which requires that each manager makes whatever decisions he can and only passes upwards those decisions outside the scope of his authority;
*   the principle of absolute responsibility, which states that it is only authority that can be delegated; the superior remains responsible for the activities and results of the subordinate.

Art of delegation

This essentially depends on personal attitudes and involves the extent to which the manager is:

- receptive to new ideas;
- willing to allow minor decisions to be made by a subordinate;
- willing to trust subordinates;
- willing to use only broad controls (rather than hour-to-hour or day-to-day control).

Centralisation

Advantages of centralised management

1. It gives better control over activity.
2. It enables procedures to be standardised throughout the organisation.
3. It eliminates a certain duplication of effort.
4. Staff, equipment and space can be utilised more efficiently. (Centralisation may, for instance, justify the purchase of a computer or other sophisticated machinery.)

Disadvantages of centralised management

1. Bureaucracy and 'red tape' increase, with the resultant increase in paper-work and record keeping.
2. Delays occur in the decision-making process, particularly at the work level.
3. Orders may be given by managers who are not familiar with the actual work situation.

Decentralisation

Factors determining the amount of decentralisation of authority

1. The cost. This can be in monetary, prestige or personnel terms.
2. The degree of uniformity required. If greater consistency is needed, this will be easier to achieve with a higher degree of centralisation.
3. Economic size. In a large firm, more decisions are made by different people and it is difficult to co-ordinate them. Where authority is decentralised decisions can be made more quickly.
4. The philosophy of management. Executives may prefer an authoritarian structure, where all the decisions are made at the top level of management, or a decentralised system where all managers feel that they have a greater influence in the organisation by being able to use their own discretion in decision making.
5. Availability of suitable management. If managers of the correct calibre are not available it may be more appropriate to concentrate authority in the top management area.
6. Use of control techniques. If control techniques are highly developed, a higher degree of decentralisation will be possible.
7. Nature of work. If the work is located over a wide geographical area, a greater degree of decentralisation will be necessary.
8. Environmental influences. These can be things such as government determination of prices and profits or restrictions on the use of labour. These factors may limit the amount

of decentralisation possible, but clearly defined policies and boundaries of authority may overcome the problem.

Co-ordination

It is not enough to design the organisation's structure; the work must be co-ordinated.

Definition

Co-ordination means the synchronisation of effort and then relating and integrating the tasks to achieve unity of effort. In other words, it is the process of timing activities and combining activities so as best to attain the overall objectives.

Division of responsibilities

In a small organisation, where everybody knows everybody else, teamwork and co-ordination are likely to develop naturally, but in a large organisation with a high degree of specialisation and division of responsibilities, co-ordination will require the full attention of top management. Co-ordination is ultimately based on the authority of top management. Some of the problems that arise in connection with departmental co-ordination are:

- Conflicting departmental objectives: a typical example concerns stock levels. The overall objective of stock control is to optimize level of stocks. The production controller will require high material stock levels in order to have long and uninterrupted production runs. The sales manager will prefer a high level of finished goods stocks so that customers' requirements are met promptly. The purchasing manager will wish to take advantage of discounts for ordering large quantities of raw materials. Finally, the accountant will want to ensure that working capital is not unnecessarily tied up in stocks.
- Sacrificing long-term corporate goals in the interest of short term departmental profits.
- the difficulty of co-ordination arising from having too many purchasing and sales departments (eg one for each division).
- Transfer price problems where one division makes internal 'sales' to another and an internal price has to be set on the transfer to allow proper evaluation of the performance of each division.
- The danger of separating certain aspects of work which need to be very closely co-ordinated. For example, physical distribution management is sometimes separated from other functions and yet needs to be closely co-ordinated with marketing management.

Individual jobs and the goals of the enterprise

Co-ordination will best take place when individuals are able to see how their jobs harmonise with the objectives of the enterprise. Communication of the overall policies and objectives is therefore an important adjunct to co-ordination. (This issue is discussed more fully in Chapter 25.)

Co-ordination and communication

The problems of co-ordination are related to those of communication since without efficient communication co-ordinated effort is difficult. (Communication will be discussed in greater detail in Chapter 25.)

It is important that when a manager communicates information or instructions to subordinates he must be sure that the latter understand, accept and, if appropriate, act on them.

It is equally important that subordinates report the completion (or not) of tasks, or other information useful to management.

There is often failure to transmit information upwards because subordinates may not realise what information higher management needs. This is a major problem as much of the information, relevant to high-level decisions, originates at low levels in the organisation.

Co-ordination through committees

Committees are often the only means of co-ordinating the various functions of a business and bringing together people in charge of different departments. Management brought together in committees hear the views of their colleagues and begin to understand their problems. Often, co-ordination involves a decision on matters which affect several departments. Each ought to have a voice in the decision yet none has the authority to decide in isolation.

Use of committees

Committees undertake a wide variety of work with varying degrees of responsibility. They may be either line or staff, formal or informal. Basically, a committee is a group of people charged with dealing with a specific problem.

Reasons for using committees

1. As a means for dissemination of ideas and opinions in a wide field of experience, and for making group recommendations.
2. For the representation of interested groups in policy matters. This enables a more balanced viewpoint to be put forward by drawing on a wide field of knowledge. It also enables these groups to feel more responsible for the final decision.
3. As a forum for transmitting information. All parties involved learn of the information simultaneously; this also results in a saving of management time. Co-ordination is improved.
4. For consolidation of authority. In this case the committee is used for crossing functional departments without referring the matter directly up the chain of authority.
5. To act as a good forum for management training and education and for using 'understudy' management development techniques.

Disadvantages of committees

1. The decision-making process is slowed down.
2. Aggressive, outspoken members may dominate meetings, and the authority of the committee may rest in the hands of one member or a small group within it.
3. As a result of disagreement, compromise action may be adopted.
4. Committees reduce the authority of 'line' managers.

Board of directors

Introduction

A committee with a very important role to play is the board of directors. Its role and the specific roles of the managing director and company secretary are discussed below.

The board of directors formulates broad policy and represents the highest level of management in a company. The directors of a company are required by law to undertake certain specific responsibilities which include safeguarding its assets and guarding against inefficiency and fraud. The duties of the board of directors are similar to those of 'trustees' as they have a fiduciary relationship towards the company which means that they must act in good faith for the benefit of the company *as a whole*. Their responsibilities are:

1. to act as custodians of invested capital. This includes a duty to safeguard investors' capital and ensure a reasonable rate of return;
2. to set main objectives (business strategy);
3. to formulate sectional policies (eg production, marketing, personnel, finance etc);
4. to ensure that all policy is within the limits set by the company's Memorandum and Articles of Association;
5. to design the organisation of the company in accordance with the objectives and policy;
6. to appoint executives and lay down their authority and responsibilities;
7. to review policy and organisation continuously and update them as and when it becomes necessary;
8. to control the overall activities of the organisation;
9. to sanction extraordinary expenditure (eg capital expenditure above a certain amount) and to authorise significant deviations from planned activity (eg a larger order received from an overseas source);
10. to authorise the disposition of distributable profits.

Executive and non-executive directors

Directors are often divided into executive and non-executive directors. Although all directors share the responsibility for the management of the company, non-executive directors are less involved with the details of running the company and are more concerned with strategy and policy. Non-executives are likely to be recruited from the ranks of existing directors of other companies and may be chosen for their track record at boardroom level. As a result, non-executives are usually older than executives but may at the same time have less experience in the industry in which the company works. Common differences between executives and non-executives are as follows.

Executive	Non-executive
A full-time director who has functional responsibilities within the company as well as being a director	Directors who act in a part-time capacity attending board meetings but taking no part in the day-to-day management of the company
	Very independent and voting is not influenced by 'career' implications
Has a working knowledge of the company and its activities	Broadens the outlook of the board by bringing in new ideas and opinion
Aids internal co-ordination	Providing communication channels to other companies (eg merchant banks, overseas market, suppliers etc)
Usually a specialist member of the management team	Expected to have general business knowledge
Has a responsibility for evaluating the 'practicality' of any recommendation put to the board	May be out of touch with the 'practicality' of certain decisions and may not be particularly interested in the practical side of the company

Corporate governance

Corporate governance is concerned with how companies behave and how they conduct themselves. It is concerned with the ethical behaviour of companies and with the quality of communication between companies and their stakeholders.

A number of reports were produced by committees sponsored by the London Stock Exchange and other bodies in the 1990s which made recommendations for the improvement of corporate governance in the UK. These reports included the Cadbury Report (1992), the Greenbury Report (1995) and the Hampel Report (1998). Among the recommendations made were the establishment of audit committees consisting of non-executive directors to facilitate communication between external auditors and directors and to improve the scrutiny of information contained in the company's annual accounts and the creation of remuneration committees to decide on directors' salaries and other benefits.

The managing director

The managing director is the 'chief executive' and takes a major role in the management of the day-to-day operations of the undertaking. Because of this he has certain individual responsibilities:

1. if also chairman, taking the chair at board meetings;
2. supervising, controlling and co-ordinating day-to-day operations of the business;
3. taking personal decisions on urgent or unexpected matters;
4. engaging in detailed financial planning and making related recommendations to the board;
5. personally dealing with major customers and suppliers and often negotiating in person with high level trade union representatives;
6. interpreting policy formulated by the board and seeing that it is carried out;
7. appointing senior staff and recommending executive appointments to the board;
8. maintaining a high level of morale within the company and promoting prestige, esteem and goodwill for the company outside it.

The company secretary

The company secretary has certain responsibilities in law, and usually other responsibilities too. He is not a director but acts as secretary to the board, and is therefore an executive officer of the directors of the board. His main duties are:

1. ensuring that the company fulfils its legal requirements. This includes the keeping of statutory books (such as the Register of Members) and making periodic returns (such as the Annual Return) and special returns (such as reporting changes in company directors);
2. ensuring that the Memorandum and Articles of Association are complied with;
3. the administration of meetings, of both directors and shareholders. This responsibility includes arranging the meetings, preparing agenda, recording minutes and ensuring that, if required, relevant action is taken in accordance with such minutes;

In addition, he is often responsible for the general administration of the company.

Control

The final role of management identified in this chapter is that of 'control'. Clearly all the other roles of situation analysis, setting objectives, strategic planning and organising have the common purpose of 'controlling' the business. However, in this context, control has a very specific meaning, which is defined by the following steps:

1. setting targets (performance standards, and criteria by which performance may be measured);
2. measuring actual performance against targets;
3. identifying variations of performance against target;
4. identifying the causes of such variations;
5. taking necessary action, particularly to prevent future under-performance or to build on past over-performance.

Chapter Six

Sources of finance

- Introduction

- Provision of finance

- Sources of finance

- The new issue market

Introduction

It is sometimes useful to visualise businesses, particularly manufacturing, as a system having inputs, processes and outputs. The inputs are managed by the three main functions of finance, personnel and purchasing, the processing is the function of production and the outputs (finished goods) are exchanged by the marketing function for revenue, thus:

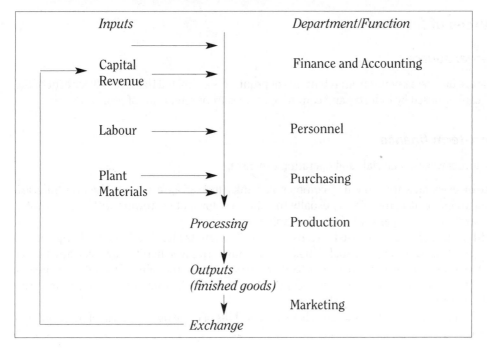

In this chapter we shall focus on the 'input' of capital:

Financial management provides the capital necessary to finance all the other functions, analyses capital projects and manages the company's working capital.

Cost and management accounting analyses costs and provides other data enabling management to plan and control other activities.

Financial accounting records the assets and liabilities and day to day transactions enabling the directors to account to shareholders as is required by statute.

Provision of finance

There are basically two kinds of finance required by a company: long-term finance and short-term finance for each production period before the revenue from sales is received.

There are four main factors to consider when cash is required:

1. What is the money required for and is it a short-term or a long-term requirement?
2. How much money is required and when?
3. Are resources available within the company, or is it necessary to go outside?
4. What will it cost to service any debts?

Having decided on the requirements choose the source which is the cheapest and most convenient for the requirement – a short-term source for a short-term requirement and a long-term source for long-term requirement.

Sources of finance

Internal sources

These are business savings from retentions of profit. It is estimated that over 70 per cent of the total capital raised by industry and commerce comes from retentions of profit.

Short-term finance

This covers wages, materials and operating expenses.

1. Bank overdrafts are allowed by commercial banks up to an agreed limit. The overdrafts are repayable on demand. This is usually the cheapest form of borrowing with interest rates charged at 1 or 2 per cent above the bank base rate.
2. Bills of exchange are used extensively in foreign trade. A bill of exchange is an unconditional promise, usually made by the buyer to the seller, to pay a certain sum of money on a specified future date. A bank will lend a sum to the value of the bill to its holder for the unexpired term. Interest charged on the loan is known as the discount. The discount rate fluctuates from day to day.
3. Acceptance credits: this is where a bank accepts bills of exchange on behalf of its customers

(debt factoring), paying the value of the bill (less discount) to the creditor and collecting from the debtor when the bill matures.

4. Trade credit: this is the purchase of goods or service on credit – of 30 days, 60 days, and longer in some cases.

5. Debt factoring is where a business obtains an advance from a third party (the factor), usually a bank, on the strength of some of the debts owed to the company. The company need not assign the debts to the factor; indeed the factor will not always want to accept the risk of non-payment. The company may arrange for the factor to collect the debts on the company's behalf. The factor advances the money to the business, after deducting an amount to cover interest, the expense of collecting the debt and the risk of non-payment. Invoice discounting is similar to factoring but the finance house advancing the money will have no involvement in collecting the debts.

Medium-term finance

This is for two to five years – to cover equipment, research and development.

1. Hire purchase of plant, equipment, machinery, vehicles etc is effectively a means of obtaining medium-term credit on fixed terms. A finance company purchases the goods and leases the goods to the user in exchange for regular payments. When the final payment is paid, the finance company transfers the ownership of the goods to the user.

2. Equipment leasing is similar to hire purchase in that regular instalments are paid but with this method the equipment does not usually become the property of the user. However, some leases may be arranged for the whole life of the equipment leased, in order to spread the cost as effectively as possible.

Long-term finance

This is over more than five years – to cover land, premises, long-term investments and the minimum levels of stock that the company needs to maintain to continue its operations. There may also be a need for permanent financing to enable the company to maintain a constant level of trade debtors, especially if customers are given generous credit terms.

1. Long-term borrowing can be done by means of a mortgage on land and buildings from a bank, an insurance company or a pension fund. Loans are usually repayable over up to 25 years.

2. Issue of shares to investors: the method of issue depends on whether the company is private or public. Private companies cannot advertise their shares, and only public companies listed on the Stock Market may invite the general public to subscribe for shares. There are several different types of share, of which the most common are 'ordinary' shares and 'preference' shares.

3. Debentures are bonds given in exchange for a loan for a specified period of time on which a specified rate of interest is paid. Most debentures are redeemable on a specified date and are usually issued in values which are multiples of £50 or £100.

Shares

Ordinary shares. These shares make the holder a member of the company, with voting and dividend rights. Normally members have one vote per share and the ordinary shareholders collectively own the 'equity' of the company. This means that they are entitled to all rights and benefits after the claims of debenture-holders and preference shareholders have been satisfied. The articles frequently reflect this principle by giving the ordinary shareholders the sole right to receive any surplus assets on a winding up.

Preference shares. These shares have the right to a fixed maximum rate of dividend which must be paid in full before any dividend is paid to the ordinary shareholders. If they are cumulative preference shares any unpaid dividends will be carried forward to be paid in a future year before the ordinary shareholders receive anything. Preference shares may also be participating, ie they have a right to a part of the surplus profits. The details of these rights will be specified in the articles of the company.

Debentures

These are not a part of the company's share capital. A debenture is a written acknowledgement of a debt by the company, and the debenture-holder is a creditor, and not a member of the company. He therefore has no voting rights unless the company grants him any. The income of the debenture-holders is a fixed amount of interest which is payable before any dividends; and in the event of liquidation of the company, the secured debenture-holder is entitled to repayment before any shareholders. It is common for the debenture to be secured on the assets of the company by means of a 'fixed' charge, such as a mortgage over land and buildings, or a 'floating' charge, which is a form of mortgage over moveable assets of the company such as its stock, any patents or licences, vehicles, etc. Both these charges must be properly registered with the Registrar of Companies or they will not give the charge-holder priority over the ordinary creditors in the event of a liquidation. Without this priority, debenture-holders would not lend their money to the company, or, if they did, they would demand a very high rate of interest.

A fixed charge is useful because the charge-holder can if necessary sell the mortgaged asset without any difficulty. With a floating charge, the debenture holder will find that certain debts need to be paid out of the secured assets before the charge-holder can take or sell them. These debts are known as 'preferential' debts and include overdue tax payments, outstanding VAT and arrears of wages.

Debentures may be a cheap way of raising capital; the debenture-holder has greater security and so does not require such a high income. He will not be able to interfere in the management of the company unless it is doing badly and the debenture deed allows him to appoint a receiver and manager. The main disadvantage to the company of this type of capital is that the interest must be paid regardless of the profits.

Securing debentures by a fixed charge may be inconvenient to industrial companies because of the need to change location with growth, with a resulting need to influence the change. The floating charge overcomes this problem as it permits the inter-change of assets. Certain companies, however, do make use of fixed charges, such as hotel and cinema companies, where the basic asset is a building with little likelihood of fundamental change.

Convertible debentures carry a right for the holder to convert the debenture to ordinary shares at a given date and price. This adversely affects the position of the ordinary shareholders but protects the debenture-holder against inflation if share prices rise.

Gearing

The ratio of fixed interest and preference capital to equity capital is referred to as the 'capital gearing'. In industries where there is little likelihood of sharp profit variation, high gearing is acceptable. It becomes dangerous, however, when applied to industries with erratic levels of profitability, because fixed interest repayments must be paid even if profit falls, leaving little or no profit available for dividends.

Bonus issues

There is no actual inflow of capital into the company on a bonus issue (or capitalisation issue): it is simply a correction of the divergence between issued capital and the retained profits. As the earnings and dividend are related to the issued capital and not to the total capital employed, a large divergence between the two values will possibly give an exaggeration of the earnings and dividend percentages. A capitalisation of the reserves overcomes this problem. Effectively, retained profits are turned into extra shares for the shareholders. Shares are allotted, fully paid up, to the existing shareholders on a pro rata basis.

Government assistance

The Department of Trade and Industry (DTI) and other bodies are authorised to provide assistance in the form of grants and loans to manufacturers and commercial concerns which are setting up business or expanding business in designated development areas.

The new issue market

The institutions engaged in raising long-term capital are collectively referred to as the new issue market. These institutions are:

1. Issuing houses: these are merchant banks and finance companies which specialise in providing means of raising capital.
2. Underwriters: these are insurance companies and investment trusts which are willing to 'underwrite' issues (see below).
3. Investing institutions: these are investment trusts, insurance companies, unit trusts and other corporate bodies, such as pension funds, which have large funds to invest.
4. Certain specialist capital-providing organisations.

Methods of launching a new issue

There are various methods of launching a new issue, depending on the size of the capital required, the risk to potential investors and the urgency of the required investment. Among the commonest methods are the following:

Direct offer by company

The company must comply with the *prospectus requirements* of the Financial Services Act 1986. It is usual to employ underwriters who, for a commission, guarantee to take up any shares for which the public do not subscribe. The other costs involved include brokerage, advertising, printing and other administrative costs. This method is rarely used except occasionally by banks which have the in-house expertise to carry out such an offer.

Offer for sale

In this case the offer is made by an issuing house or other body that has bought the shares from the company. The offer is subject to the prospectus requirements of the Financial Services Act 1986. Its advantage is that it guarantees the success of the issue for the company. The issuing house makes its profit on the margin between the price it pays and the price at which it offers to sell which must be stated in the offer. If the issue is very big and there is any risk of under-subscription, it will be underwritten.

The offer can be made on a fixed price basis or on a tender price basis. In the case of an *offer for sale by tender,* the minimum price is fixed and the public are invited to subscribe at any price above this minimum. An 'average' price is then chosen at which the shares will be fully subscribed for by those people who have offered over the 'average' price: all successful subscribers pay the same 'average' price.

The attraction of a tender offer to the issuing house is that it obtains a higher price for the capital. A straight offer for sale at a fixed price usually results in fixing a low price to attract subscribers and a resulting over-subscription. Investors on the other hand prefer fixed price issues because they are certain of their commitment. Where an over-subscription does occur, it is usually met with a ballot or rationing solution.

Rights issue

This is a method by which a company raises money from its existing shareholders. The members are offered the right to purchase new shares in the company proportional to their existing holdings at a price which is usually below the market price. The advantage to the company is that this is a cheap way of raising capital.

Placing

This is usually effected through the company's stockbroker who approaches various institutions or wealthy investors and 'places' the shares with them. Stock Exchange rules require that details of the securities must be advertised in the press before the placing. Permission to deal will be granted in the usual way. This method has been criticised as favouring certain investors, and the Stock Exchange usually requires that a fair proportion of these securities should be made available to the public before dealings are allowed to start.

It may be possible to place a block for shares with an institution privately without going through the market at all. A high-yield security will be necessary in this case to persuade the institution to forego easy marketability.

Chapter Seven

The marketing concept, functions and markets

- Introduction

- Marketing – some definitions

- The marketing concept

- The marketing function

- Markets defined

- Market classification

- Consumer and organisational markets

- Convenience goods, shopping goods and speciality goods. Low/high involvement

- Perishable goods (physical characteristics of product)

- Luxury goods

- Demographic and geographic classification

- Commodity markets

- Industries

- Market forms and structures

- Demand

- Segmentation

Introduction

Chapters 7–19 examine the operational functions of business, ie marketing, production, purchasing and personnel. Chapters 7–12 concentrate on marketing.

Many businesses these days claim to be 'market' or 'consumer oriented': to base their decisions on analysis of customers' needs. All business decisions are ultimately based on analysis of demand and the sales forecast, that is on how many of its products the company expects to sell in the future. Sales and sales forecasting are the preserve of marketing and therefore marketing has a key role in all business planning.

Sales forecasting is discussed in Chapter 9.

Marketing – some definitions

The first two define the 'marketing concept':

'The marketing concept is the view that all businesses exist in order to satisfy customer demand.'

'Marketing is making what we can sell, not selling what we can make. In other words, marketing is making what we know we can sell (because we know what our customers want), not just selling them what we can make (whether they want it or not).'

The next defines the 'function of marketing':

'Marketing is the process of determining consumer demand for a product or service, motivating its sale and distributing it for ultimate consumption at a profit.' (E F L Brech, *Principles of Management*: Longman, 1953)

The last three define 'marketing management':

'Marketing is the creative management function which promotes trade and employment by assessing consumer needs and initiating research and development to meet them; it co-ordinates the resources of production and distribution of goods and service; determines and directs the nature and scale of total effort required to sell profitably the maximum production to the ultimate user.' (Institute of Marketing)

'Marketing is the management process responsible for identifying, anticipating and satisfying customer requirements, profitably' (Institute of Marketing)

'Marketing management is the analysis, planning, implementation, and control of programmes designed to bring about desired exchange with target audiences for the purpose of personal or mutual gain. It relies heavily on the adaptation and co-ordination of product, price, promotion and place for achieving effective response.' (P Kotler)

It is not necessary for students to memorise each of these definitions, but they should all be understood. Try to distinguish between:

- the marketing concept – the idea that all businesses exist in order to satisfy their customers;

- the marketing function – the exchange process that all businesses must perform, exchanging their products for the prices paid by their customers;
- marketing management – management of a specific set of roles and tasks in order to perform the exchange function. These roles and tasks are identified as 'activities' in the table on page 87, below, and discusssed in Chapters 8–12.

The marketing concept

Evolution

In very simple economies producers and consumers live close together and know each other personally. Therefore the producer only produces what he needs to produce for his customers' known demands – there is therefore relatively little waste. However, production is on a very limited scale, with little opportunity for economic growth.

The industrial revolution changed this situation. Because of an increase in population there were more mouths to feed and people to clothe – there was therefore an increase in demand for food and textiles, creating an economic problem: 'how to increase supply?' The answer was found in capitalisation, ie making production more capital intensive through the use of machinery – and the resultant growth of an engineering industry to produce the machines.

But, to make machines efficient they had to be close to sources of power and concentrated in factories. This meant that producers were no longer necessarily close to their customers – and known personally by them. This meant that producers had to start producing against 'anticipated' (rather than 'known') 'demand' – with the attendant risk of waste if the customers did not buy. This was not a problem so long as demand exceeded supply, but throughout the nineteenth century production became so efficient that eventually supply exceeded demand.

This created a different economic problem – 'how to dispose of the excess production?'. The answer was found in classic economic theory – if supply exceeds demand, reduce price to stimulate demand. However, this solution has long-term dangers – if price is reduced, profits which business needs to survive may be eroded. In the 1930s weaker companies were forced into bankruptcy, leading to massive unemployment, and a further reduction in spending power.

The marketing concept attempts to reconcile the two problems – by identifying the customers' need (through market research) *before* producing the goods the risk of wasteful over-production should be minimised. While market research is necessary to identify the customers' needs, sophisticated distribution and advertising have also evolved in order to make the goods available and to tell customers about them.

Thus the adoption of the *marketing concept* by a business re-establishes communication links between seller and buyer by market research, distribution, sales promotion and advertising. Businesses which adopt the marketing concept base *production* on *identified and quantified consumer needs* and purchasing power; design advertising and other forms of promotion which will promote the desired reaction from identified consumer characteristics; and co-ordinate all activities with 'consumer satisfaction' as the prime objective. They are efficient because their goods are produced against 'known' demand.

Consequences for business

The implications for business of the adoption of the marketing concept are:

1. It does *not* mean that the marketing function is more important than other functions or that marketing should run the business.
2. However, it does mean that the business must define its objectives and its policies in terms of its customers' needs rather than in terms of its own existing resources or skills.
3. The business must also define its objectives in terms of the generic demand for its products, rather than the specific demand. Thus, for example:

   - The film industry is *not* just in the film business – it is also in the entertainment business.
   - A motor car manufacturer is not in the business of making and selling motor cars propelled by internal combustion engines, fuelled by hydrocarbon products – it is in the transport business.

4. The business must redefine its competitors to include not only those businesses which are making a specific product similar to its own but also other businesses competing for a share of the generic demand. Thus, for example:

   - The film industry is in competition with the television industry.
   - The motor industry is in competition with the railways and, in the near future, may face increasing competition from cars propelled by electricity, gas and other fuels.

The marketing function

Obviously, the marketing concept contains many controversial ideas, some of which we shall return to. However, whether one accepts the marketing concept or not, all businesses must perform the 'marketing function'.

The marketing function is the business function which is concerned with the process of exchange, ie exchanging the company's output of goods and services for the customers' expenditure of price. It is therefore distinguishable from the finance and accounting, personnel, purchasing and production functions.

The marketing function, within the context of the business system, lies in the area bounded by the dotted line in the diagram opposite:

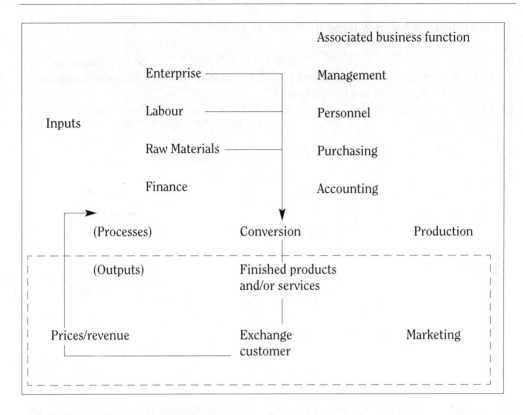

The marketing function is that function of the business which is directly responsible for the exchange process. It follows that marketing is the function of the business directly responsible for the total relationship between the business and the customer.

Tasks of marketing	Sub-function
a Identifying customers' needs	Marketing research
b Translating needs into products	Product planning
c Determining the product's price	Pricing value to the customer
d Making the product available	Distribution
e Informing and motivating the customer	Promotion (selling and advertising)

The marketing function may therefore be seen as a cycle:

```
                        Market research ─────────────► Pre-planning
                    ↗                                   information

         Needs                    Post-purchase information
           ↑                               │
           │                      Purchase behaviour:
                                  sacrifices
                          Price
  Customer – response ──► }      │ ──────────────────────► Producer
           │              Time effort                        │
  Communication                                              │
           ↑                                                 │
                            Product                        Offering
                              │                          ↗
     Promotion ◄──────      Price       } ◄──
                              │
                          Distribution
```

The **customer** has **needs**, identified and analysed by **marketing research** to provide **pre-planning information**. The **producer** responds with an **offering** represented by the **product**, **price** and **distribution**. **Promotion** is used to **communicate** the facts about the **offering** to the **customer** who makes a **response** by his **purchase behaviour** which involves a **sacrifice** of **price, time and effort**. This **behaviour** is analysed by **marketing research** to provide **post-purchase information**, which may lead to a refinement of the offering – and thus the cycle continues.

Notice that **marketing research, distribution** and **sales promotion** are widely recognised as the proper preserves of marketing management. But control over the **product planning** and **pricing** functions is often shared with production management and accountants respectively – and shared control leads at best to organisational problems and at worst to actual conflict between marketing management and the other functions.

The solution to this problem lies in a recognition by all the business functions of the **marketing concept** as the guiding philosophy of the business.

Sub-functions

The marketing function has been defined above as the business function concerned with the process of exchange. It therefore includes all the sub-functions which facilitate the process of exchange:

Sub-function	Activities involved
Marketing information and research	Economic, business, trade, industry, consumer, user, product, sales, distribution, packaging and advertising research and analysis
	Information handling and data processing
	Marketing operations research
	Competitive intelligence
	Sales forecasting
Product policy planning	Formulating product policies
	Determining and developing the company's product mix. Matching the product's specifications, packaging, pricing, performance and servicing to customer needs through product and service improvements. New product development
Pricing	Formulating pricing policies. Setting prices for each product in the product mix, at different stages in the product life-cycle, and for various markets and market segments. Initiating, or responding to, competitive price changes. Preparing competitive bids
Distribution	Formulating distribution policies. Selection, motivation and control of distribution channels. Planning and control of physical distribution. Warehousing, packing and transport
Promotion	Formulating promotional policies and objectives. Selection, planning and control of appropriate promotional tools ie personal selling, advertising, public relations, packaging and merchandising. Personal selling, sales reporting, sales analysis, sales budgets quotas and targets. Management of the field sales force
	Advertising, defining advertising objectives. Media selection, planning and control. Liaison with advertising agencies and media owners. Design of point-of-sale and display material
	Public relations. Communication between the business and its public
	Packaging. Package design
	Merchandising. Planning and implementation of point-of-sale promotions such as coupons, premium offers self-liquidating offers etc. planning and implementing trade promotions such as incentive schemes, sales contests, display competitions etc

Markets defined

In Chapter 2 we recognised that each function of a business operates within the business's 'main' or 'operational environment' – which consists of a number of 'markets'. This section explores the concept of markets in greater detail.

Definition

A market exists whenever people come together, either directly or indirectly, to buy and sell goods and services.

The interaction of the buying and selling functions in a free market decides what will be produced, by whom, how and who will buy it.

More specifically we can say that a market is made up of, on the one hand, people (either as individuals, groups or organisations) with needs, purchasing power (usually monetary), and the opportunity and willingness to purchase; and, on the other hand, sellers willing and able to sell.

Various points emerge from this definition:

- It is important to understand needs, as drives towards the act of purchase.
- Markets may expand or contract with changes in purchasing power.
- Markets may be created, or existing markets enlarged, by increasing the opportunity to purchase, through more widespread distribution.
- Markets may be enlarged by stimulating the willingness to purchase by sales promotion and advertising.

Markets may also be sub-divided into 'segments' consisting of groups of people or organisations having some characteristic which is not held by other segments eg different age groups, people living in different geographical regions etc. Clearly these segments may each be treated as separate markets. Therefore, although the concept of segmentation will be discussed in greater detail below, the principal market segments are included in the classification of markets which follows.

Market classification

Markets and products may be classified according to:

Criterion	Market classification
The usage of the product	Consumer/organisational/industrial
Customer's purchasing behaviour	Convenience/shopping/speciality Low involvement/high involvement
Physical characteristics of products	Perishable/durable
Social attitudes	Luxury/necessity
Demographic	Age/sex/family size/income/occupation/ education/family cycle/religion/ nationality/ social class
Geographic	Regions/nations/trading blocs/developed/ underdeveloped countries
Raw materials, undifferentiated primary products	Commodity markets

Kotler proposes a simple framework for analysing all markets, based on six questions:

1. What does the market buy? – objects of purchase;
2. Why does it buy? – objectives of purchase;
3. Who buys? – organisation for purchasing;
4. How does it buy? – operations of purchasing organisations;
5. Where does it buy? – outlets for purchasing;
6. When does it buy? – opportunities for purchasing.

To these may be added:

7. How much does it buy? – amount of product

Consumer and organisational markets

The consumer market

This is the market for products and services that are purchased or hired by individuals or households for personal (non-business) use. Consumer markets may be classified by customer category or by product types. Possible customer category classifications include:

- total population;
- national population distribution;
- regional population distribution;

- urban, rural, inter urban distribution;
- number of families;
- size of families;
- age groups;
- sex;
- education;
- occupation;
- race;
- national origin;
- class;
- religion;
- socio-economic groups.

Examples of product-type classifications are:

- foodstuffs;
- textiles and clothing;
- household articles;
- furniture;
- consumer durable and many others.

The organisational market

This may be sub-divided into:

The industrial market

This consists of individuals or organisations who acquire goods or services to be used *either* in the production of further goods or services which are for sale or rental to others, *or* as an integral part of such further goods or services. Industrial *markets* may be classified by type of industry, by number of employees, by turnover, etc.

Industrial *products* may also be classified in many ways:

According to the type of product. These are:

1. Products entering directly into manufacture:

   - raw materials from agriculture and extractive industries;
   - semi-manufactured goods which are incorporated into a product but in this process they are changed, eg basic chemicals, sheet steel, fabrics;
   - parts which are manufactured articles which can be installed as a component of a further product without change in form eg electric motors, thermostats and batteries;
   - contract manufacturing services which when part of the manufacturing process are contracted out to another company, eg dyeing, casting and shaping of material supplied by the customer.

2. Supplies of goods and services:

   - maintenance and repair items, eg spare parts, lubricants, cleaning material and paint;

- operating supplies which are used directly in everyday operation, eg stationery;
- business services provided by other companies, eg printing, cleaning and equipment maintenance, finance and insurance.

3. Capital investment items:

- installations which are part of fixed plant, eg large machine tools;
- equipment which is not regarded as fixed plant, eg hand tools.

According to government classifications. These include:
- agriculture, forestry, fishing, mining, quarrying;
- construction;
- manufacturing;
- transportation;
- wholesale;
- retail;
- finance, insurance;
- services.

The reseller market

This consists of individuals or organisations (middlemen, dealers, distributors) who acquire goods for the purpose of reselling them or renting them to others at a profit. Reseller markets may be classified by type of product (as listed for industrial markets) or by type of reseller (discussed in greater detail in Chapter 11): wholesaler, retailer, multiple, independent retailer, factor, franchise holder.

Note: in both industrial and reseller markets there may be several links in the chain from original producer to ultimate customer. Each link or intermediary may regard the next link as his market.

The government market

This consists of government units of all types – supranational, national, local – which purchase or rent goods or services for the purpose of carrying out the functions of government, ie the public, as opposed to the private sector, of a mixed economy. Government markets can be classified by area of responsibility (supranational, national, regional, local) or by relevant department.

Note: the purpose of grouping industrial, reseller and government markets under one category of 'organisational' markets is that they have certain characteristics in common which distinguish them from consumer markets.

Difference between consumer markets and organisational markets

Consumer markets	Organisational markets
'Original' demand	Demand is derived
Considerable variations in elasticity	Demand is relatively inelastic
Levels of product knowledge vary widely	Market is relatively knowledgeable
Many purchasing units (persons/households)	Few purchasing units
Some regional concentration of segments (but not very pronounced)	Regional concentration of industry

These differences may need an explanation.

Original/derived demand

All demand originates from consumers. Therefore the demand for organisational (particularly industrial) products is only derived from the consumer demand for the product of which the industrial product is a part. For example, consumers demand motor cars; the construction of motor cars requires steel; therefore the demand for steel used by the motor industry is derived from the consumer demand for motor cars.

Elasticity

This is discussed in greater detail in Chapter 10 below and is a measure of the extent to which demand fluctuates in response to fluctuations in price. Because of the considerable variety of goods purchased by consumers there are considerable variations in elasticity. However, industry's purchases of materials are largely essential (without material the business would cease to work), and therefore fluctuations in price have relatively little effect. Furthermore, once a business has installed capital equipment it cannot easily respond to a cheaper offer from another supplier.

Buyers in organisational markets are 'relatively knowledgeable' because they are professional buyers with access to the most up-to-date and sophisticated information.

Convenience goods, shopping goods and speciality goods. Low/high involvement

In determining the appropriate category for a given product or market three determining factors must be considered:

1. the customer's level of knowledge about the product before the purchase;
2. the customer's preference for one product or brand;

3. the customer's loyalty to one product or brand.

The benefit obtained by searching for and comparing different products is balanced against the price, time and effort involved (ie the 'sacrifice' element in the exchange process). These three factors vary considerably according to the market category concerned.

Customer purchasing behaviour in consumer and organisational markets can be compared as follows:

Consumer markets	*Organisational markets*
Convenience goods *(low involvement)*	There is no direct parallel in organisational markets, but the following classification is similar:
Customer has:	
complete knowledge of the product brand high preference for a particular brand low loyalty to the brand (he will switch to an alternative if his preferred brand is not available)made minimal effort to obtain product	*Straight rebuy* A routine purchasing procedure exists and there is an approved list of suppliers
Convenience products are usually:	
low priced small frequently purchased readily accessible	
Examples: confectionery, bread	

Marketing implications:

extensive (widespread) distribution is essential if customer's loyalty is to be retained
minimum sales service, because the customer already knows about his preferred brand
reminder advertising, because the customer does not need information about the brand

Consumer markets	Organisational markets
Shopping goods *(high involvement)*	*New buy*
Customer has:	
incomplete knowledge of the product or brand	The need for the product has not arisen previously so there is no experience in the company and a great deal of information is required
low preference for any brand low loyalty to any brand made maximum effort to obtain information before buying	
	Modified rebuy
Products are usually:	
high priced (relative to normal household expenditure)	A regular requirement for the type of product exists and the buying of alternatives is known, but sufficient
infrequently purchased	change has occurred to require some alteration to the normal supply
accessible only in main shopping centres	procedure
Examples: furniture, cameras	

Marketing implications:

selective distribution, particularly to main shopping areas, because the customer will
make an effort to 'search' for the product
high sales service, because the customer needs information
informative advertising

Consumer markets	Organisational markets
Speciality goods; 'prestige' products	*Deluxe services*
Customer has complete knowledge of product or (particularly) brand:	Businesses offering luxury goods and services, such as high-class hotel chains and some car-rental companies, will need to purchase the expensive goods and supplies which their customers expect
high preference for a particular brand high loyalty to his preferred brand makes maximum effort to obtain his preferred brand	
Products are usually:	
high priced luxury goods regularly (not necessarily frequently) purchased selectively distributed	
Examples: expensive perfumes, high quality pipe tobaccos, high quality motor cars	

Marketing implications:

product quality control is essential to maintain high quality
exclusive distribution, both to enhance the image and because the customer is willing to search for his preferred brand
high quality sales service
exclusive, reminder advertising, because the customer already knows about the brand but loyalty needs to be reinforced

Perishable goods (physical characteristics of product)

The physical nature of the product determines its 'life', from production to consumption. Perishable products, such as fresh meat and vegetables, or vaccines, need fast physical distribution, to deliver the goods before they deteriorate, and high environmental control (packing and storage) costs, to prevent the goods from deteriorating and becoming unsaleable. Durable goods do not need such expensive packing and distribution.

Luxury goods

This mode of classification is of relevance to consumer markets but has little relevance to industrial markets (except for 'prestige' products). Marketing implications for luxury goods are exclusive distribution and advertising, to create and reinforce the luxury image, and high price, to reinforce the image of high quality. Examples include Rolls-Royce cars and Chanel No 5 perfume. But the manufacturer may have to be ready to move into the mass market, eg with mobile phones and laptop computers.

Note: social attitudes change – today's luxury may be tomorrow's necessity.

Demographic and geographic classification

The demographic characteristics of the market obviously affect product policy, price, distribution and promotion – to be discussed later.

Both consumer and industrial markets may be divided regionally, particularly for the purpose of sales and distribution management – again, this will be considered later.

Commodity markets

Raw materials, such as wheat, coffee, sugar, tin, rubber etc, are traded in the various 'commodity markets', of which London is a major world centre. There are two major characteristics of these markets which distinguish them from the other markets discussed above.

Because the goods are relatively 'undifferentiated' (ie they do not have brand names, trade marks etc) the price is largely determined by the classical laws of supply and demand. Thus, if a bad harvest reduces the supply of a commodity such as tea, buyers will tend to offer high prices in order to secure the supplies which are needed by the industry. In time these prices are likely to be passed on to the consumer. Similarly, threats of war will tend to push up the price of rubber, oil, chromium and other necessary raw materials. On the other hand a switch from tin to aluminium by the canning industry will reduce the demand for tin and therefore the price of tin will fall – with disastrous effects for the tin-mining industry.

The commodity market is characterised by the necessity to secure long term supplies of essential raw materials. When the commodity is already available for sale it is traded at an agreed price, known as the 'spot' price, but when the commodity is not yet available it may be traded at a 'future' price.

'Futures markets' deal in a range of commodities such as wheat, sugar, cocoa, coffee, copper and wool which are purchased at agreed prices for delivery at some future specified time. Both purchasers and sellers hope to gain, but their motivations are different. The purchaser gambles that when delivery is taken the agreed price will be lower than the prevailing 'spot price', while the farmer may prefer a guaranteed price to the risk of the market price falling.

If the purchaser believes that the price is likely to rise he will tend to take a long position, in other words, he will buy futures with a view to selling the futures or the commodity itself when the price rises. If the seller believes that the price is likely to fall, he will tend to go short, in other words, he will sell futures in the hope of buying the commodity more cheaply at a later date and thereby making a profit. Going short carries a substantial financial risk, as it imposes an obligation to expend an unknown amount of money in covering the seller's position at a later date. It is evident that purchasing for a specialist manufacturer such as Nestlé is a very skilled job, requiring close monitoring of the macro-environment, especially the economic and political factors affecting the prices of coffee and cocoa.

Industries

There is obviously a close relationship between 'markets' and 'industries', in the sense that an industry exists in order to satisfy the demands of a particular market. This section explores the factors affecting the size and structure of industries.

Definition

An industry is a grouping of firms with common interests and associations.

Structure of an industry

The structure of an industry is dependent on many factors, which are explored in greater depth in the sections which follow. The most important are:

* number of firms in the industry;
* market share which each commands and the combined market power which the top four or five firms command;
* degree of differentiation existing between the products offered by the industry;
* price elasticity of demand and the responsiveness of the market to price changes;
* speed with which individual suppliers can react to changes in the industry demand;
* size and nature of the entry barriers preventing potential competitors from entering the industry (for example, the minimum level of capital needed by potential entrants to be able to compete effectively);
* distribution channels used by individual suppliers;
* nature of the competition between the suppliers in the industry (for example, whether it has a price or non-price emphasis);
* investment in research and development and technology, and the speed of product change in recent years;
* profit/cost/volume ratio and the relationship of fixed costs to variable costs and total costs;
* susceptibility of the industry to external pressures and influences, (for example, government, economic, technological and social);
* existing and potential challenge from other industries;
* history and prospects of industry mergers and acquisitions.

Entry barriers

Entry barriers protect and strengthen the market position of monopolies and oligopolies by making it difficult for potential entrants to compete.

Some products generate a greater customer loyalty than others: potential entrants will have to persuade their target audiences to test purchase their products, perhaps by offering them special inducements in the first place, such as free samples or gifts. The cost of the initial advertising campaign is likely to be very high and, if the company also has to offer lower prices, its return per unit might be much less than established companies', perhaps making the whole idea unattractive to the potential entrant.

Market forms and structures

Perfect competition

Its main characteristics are:

1. There is a large number of buyers and sellers, none of whom is large enough to affect the total supply or demand, nor powerful enough to dictate or influence the market price.
2. The market price is determined by the combined pressures of the aggregate demands and supplies of all buyers and sellers in the market and will change when the forces of demand and supply change.
3. Barriers to entry are low and potential entrants find no difficulty in competing. Ease of entry into and exit out of the market in response to movements of market prices ensures that over the long term companies produce up to the point where marginal cost (ie the cost of producing one more unit) is equal to the marginal revenue (ie the revenue earned by selling one extra unit). Although in the short term, the market price may be pushed up above the marginal cost, this cannot persist over the long term, as potential entrants would be attracted by the higher profits and their additional capacity would soon bring prices and profits down. By contrast, if market prices fell below marginal costs, the less efficient firms would be forced to leave the industry until prices rose.
4. The product is standardised, so buyers are indifferent to their point of purchase. Promotional activity such as advertising is pointless, because price is the sole purchasing determinant.
5. Buyers and sellers are fully informed of the market conditions, so that no one can buy or sell at an advantageous price.
6. As the market price is 'given' there is no advantage to any producer to charge a different price; his theoretically best strategy is to produce at the volume where any further increase in production will tend to cost more than the additional revenue earned. In the theoretical language of economics he will produce at that volume where his 'marginal cost is equal to his marginal revenue'.

Monopoly

A monopolist is a 'sole supplier' or, indeed, sole purchaser of a product. In practice there are no pure monopolists but any supplier having too large a share of a market may be able to charge a high price, to the disadvantage of the consumer. Alternatively, a purchaser having too large a share of the market may be able to force a very low price to the disadvantage of the supplier.

The Fair Trading Act 1973 and subsequent legislation minimises the opportunity for monopolies and control. The Director General of Fair Trading has the power to investigate accusations of restrictive practices with the help of the Competition Commission. The European Commission also has powers to investigate and if necessary prohibit abuses of a commercially dominant position by potential monopolists.

Even where a product has no apparent competitors in its own industry, it cannot ignore products in other industries. A monopoly supplier of electricity, for example, may be in competition with suppliers of gas to domestic customers and this will limit the price that the electricity company can charge.

Furthermore, if the monopolist is not protected by patents, he needs to be careful that he does not give too much encouragement to potential entrants. Procter and Gamble and Unilever are always acutely conscious of the German company Henkel and have not so far charged a price for their detergents on the UK market at the point where Henkel have thought it worthwhile to compete. This industry is also well protected by brand advertising.

The strength of a company's monopoly power is related to the degree of difficulties posed to other companies to enter into direct competition. If the monopoly power is based on a product differentiation which is primarily cosmetic (ie packaging and branding), competitors could probably invade the monopolist's territory effectively. The monopolist will, in these circumstances, not charge the full monopoly price, thus reducing the incentive to competitors to enter the market.

Oligopoly

This is a situation where the market consists of a few large firms and, possibly, a number of small ones. The products of each firm tend to be similar, so individual suppliers attempt to raise the appeal of their products by investing them with distinctive characteristics. This is known as 'differentiation'. Thus, detergents may be provided with special additives supposed to give them greater cleaning power, extra brightness, extra whiteness, more suds, or less suds. Nevertheless, customers probably view the market range as substitutes, although they will have their preferences.

Oligopoly results in a rough status quo which is unlikely to change dramatically. No supplier is likely to drop his prices as his competitors would merely follow suit, with no one except the customer better off. Nor is a supplier likely to raise his prices as he would lose business to his lower-priced rivals. Competition has to be exerted in non-price forms, the most common being advertising and sales promotion campaigns, improved after-sales service, speedier deliveries, improved quality and performances, guarantees and favourable credit terms.

An oligopolist market tends towards a common price in much the same way as a perfectly competitive market is supposed to do. The oligopolist demand curve, however, is not completely elastic: sales will not completely disappear if an oligopolist raises his prices, nor will his sales expand much if he reduces his prices, because his competitors will take retaliatory action.

The largest firms automatically assume price leadership, with the smaller firms following suit because they have no option. If a company initiates a price war in the belief that it can improve its market share, it may win but at the expense of short-term profitability.

The success of the marketing strategy of the oligopolist appears to depend on his ability to:

1. assess competitive reaction to his proposed moves;
2. anticipate future trends better than his rivals;
3. establish the profit/cost/volume relationship which will yield him the best returns;
4. establish which activities might give him an advantage, such as improved sales techniques, selective advertising campaigns or new products;
5. recognise the threat of potential competitors;
6. develop a sensitive marketing intelligence system to keep him fully informed on the current position and future prospects of the market;
7. (for the smaller company) establish a unique market 'niche'.

Demand

Throughout this chapter we have referred often to 'demand'. Obviously the idea of demand is fundamental to our understanding of the marketing concept and of marketing.

General definition

'*Market demand* for a *product* is the *total volume* that would be *bought* by a defined *customer group* in a defined *geographical area* in a defined *time period* in a defined *marketing environment* under a defined *marketing programme*.' (Kotler)

Note: each term must be precisely defined before the concept of market demand can be put to practical use. Possible interpretations of each are given below:

- Product: product items, product line, company sales or industry sales?
- Total volume: units or money value?
- Bought: ordered, despatched, received, paid for?
- Customer group:

  - (consumer markets) age, class, sex, income, ethnicity, religion, attitude, usage rate?
  - (industrial markets) size (output, labour etc), industry classification, usage rate?

- Geographical area: town, area, region, country, world?
- Time period: short term (typically up to one year) medium term (one to five years), long term (over five years)?
- Marketing environment: economic, political, technological, competitive, social, cultural?
- Marketing programme: alternative marketing mixes, levels of marketing activity.

Kotler's definition makes the important point that demand by a specified number of people at a particular place and point in time (over which the company has virtually no control) is a *function* of industry and environmental conditions and company marketing effort.

This suggests the concept of 'potential demand', ie the quantity which would be demanded under ideal environmental and marketing conditions.

We must also distinguish between:

1. generic demand – the demand for the benefit which the individual product provides, for example the demand for films (the product) is part of the generic demand for entertainment;
2. industrial demand – the demand for the products of a particular industry;
3. company/brand demand – the demand for a particular company's product or brand.

We must also distinguish between:

1. potential demand – the maximum that would be demanded under ideal environmental or marketing conditions;
2. realised/actual demand – the quantity actually demanded.

Demand may also be expressed by the simple formula

$$D = (N_{Pt} R)$$

Demand (D) = number of customers (N) at a particular place (P) at a particular time (t) x their average rate of purchase (R).

This is a very simple idea, saying that if 1,000 people have an average consumption of three units per year, then their annual demand will be 3,000 units. However, the important point to remember is that the company cannot influence the value of N (the number of people in its market) but it can influence the value of R (the average rate of purchase), through its price, advertising, sales effort etc. Therefore marketing management need to monitor changes in N, resulting from changes in the size of the population, from birth and death rates, emigration and immigration, as well as adjusting its own marketing effort.

Finally, we must consider the concept of *'elasticity'*. Let us assume that the 'demand schedule' for a particular product (ie the quantity which would be demanded at different prices) is as follows:

Price (per unit)	Quantity demanded (per week)
20p	6 units
15p	10 units
10p	15 units
5p	23 units

This can be plotted graphically:

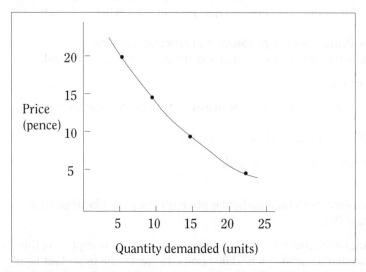

The potential demand is unaltered but the actual demand will normally increase as price falls or decrease as price rises. Luxury items are an exception to this general rule.

Clearly a critical problem for the marketer is to know what quantity will be demanded if he changes his price. If the market shows a substantial increase (or decrease) in demand with a relatively small change in price we say that demand is 'elastic'. Conversely if demand remains fairly constant, even after a relatively large change in price we say that demand is 'inelastic'.

Elasticity at a particular point on the demand curve can be measured by the following formula:

$$Ed = \frac{\% \text{ change in the quantity demanded}}{\% \text{ change in price}}$$

where Ed = demand elasticity.

Where the 'coefficient of elasticity' is greater than 1.00, demand is elastic. Where the coefficient is 1.00, demand is unitarily elastic. Where the coefficient is less than 1.00, demand is inelastic.

For practical purposes, elasticity over a wider range of the demand curve, known as 'arc elasticity', can be measured by the following formula, which calculates the change in quantity as a proportion of average quantity divided by the change in price as a proportion of average price:

$$Ed = \frac{Q2 - Q1}{Q2 + Q1} \times \frac{P2 + P1}{P2 - P1}$$

Where Q2 = new quantity demanded, Q1 = old quantity demanded, P2 = new price, P1 = old price.

$$\text{Demand elasticity} = \frac{\text{The difference in quantity demanded at different prices}}{\text{The difference in price}}$$

$$x \quad \frac{\text{The sum of the prices}}{\text{The sum of the quantities demanded}}$$

Using our demand schedule above, we have:

1 Price	2 Quantity demanded	3 $\frac{Q2-Q1}{Q2+Q1}$		4 $\frac{P2+P1}{P2-P1}$		5 Elasticity
20p	6					
		4/16	x	35/5	=	1.75 (elastic)
15p	10					
		5/25	x	25/5	=	1.00 (unitary elasticity)
10p	15					
		10/40	x	15/5	=	0.75 (inelastic)
5p	25					

Revenue is the result of multiplying the price per unit by the quantity demanded. Thus, in our example:

1 Price x	2 Quantity =	3 Revenue ((1) x (2))	4 Elasticity
20p	6	£1.20	
			Elastic
15p	10	£1.50	
			Unitary elasticity
10p	15	£1.50	
			Inelastic
5p	25	£1.25	

Where demand is elastic an increase in price reduces revenue, and a reduction in price increases revenue. Where demand is inelastic an increase in price increases revenue, and a reduction in price reduces revenue. Where demand is unitarily elastic revenue is not affected by a change in price.

The concept of elasticity is fundamental to marketing and to business in general and should be clearly understood.

Segmentation

So far we have only considered complete markets and total demands. However, it is essential to note that markets may be divided into segments, each of which can be treated as separate 'markets' with its own unique demand schedule.

Market segmentation is the sub-dividing of a market into homogeneous subsets of customers, where any subset may conceivably be selected as a market target to be reached with a distinct marketing mix.

Conditions necessary for market segmentation to be effective

For market segmentation to be effective three conditions must be satisfied.

1. Measurability. Are the particular characteristics which distinguish one segment from another measurable? Is the necessary data available or obtainable? (perhaps through marketing research). This may pose difficulties if the distinguishing characteristic is a psychological characteristic (eg the target segment's willingness to take risks, which may be important when introducing a new product) rather than some clearly definable demographic characteristic such as age or sex.
2. Accessibility. Is it possible for the marketer to reach the target segment through some specific advertising medium or distribution channel (eg specialist magazines, specialist stores, specialist features in national newspapers)?
3. Profitability. Is the segment large enough and has it sufficient purchasing power to justify and support separate marketing programmes? Has it sufficient growth in profits in the future? (For example, the teenage population 'bulge' was a target segment for the Ford Mustang. Saga holidays specialises in holidays for older people, targeting the growing population of pensioners.)

The benefits of segmentation

The marketer who segments his market will be better able to:

- identify market gaps, by comparing current market offerings against levels of customer satisfaction (an example is Surf – based on the discovery that there was a segment of the market seeking value for money and hostile to promotional 'gimmicks', Square Deal Surf was created);
- use his knowledge of different response rates from different segments to guide his total marketing budget. Different segments may respond differently to different marketing tools and the marketing effort should be allocated accordingly (eg advertising aimed at poorer segments may stress a competitive price, whereas advertising aimed at a wealthy segment may stress good quality);

- understand the workings of his market.

Bases for segmentation

Geographic segmentation. Markets may be segmented by region, climate, population density, cities, urban areas, rural areas and internationally by country, trading bloc, language groupings etc.

Demographic segmentation. Markets may be segmented by age, sex, family size, income, occupation, education, family life-cycle, religion, nationality, ethnic group, social class.

Benefit segmentation. Markets may be segmented according to which benefits are sought by the buyers. For example, some people buy toothpaste for health reasons, whereas others buy it for cosmetic reasons.

Volume segmentation. Markets may be segmented into heavy, medium, light and non-users; non-users into potential users and non-potential users.

Marketing factor segmentation. Markets may be segmented into those most responsive to price, those most responsive to advertising, etc.

Lifestyle segmentation. Markets may be segmented by differing values, attitudes, interests and opinions held by different groups of customers. Segments with the same lifestyle are likely to buy the same products, read the same newspapers, live in similar neighbourhoods, etc.

Socio-economic segmentation. Markets may be segmented into social class groups, which tend to share similar levels of income, and therefore purchasing power, together with similar values, attitudes, interests and opinions. In the United Kingdom the socio-economic groups most used in marketing are:

A – Senior professional and managerial;
B – Professional and managerial;
C1 – Junior professional, clerical, 'white collar';
C2 – Skilled manual working class, 'blue collar';
D – Unskilled manual working class;
E – Unskilled casual labour, pensioners on fixed incomes, etc.

Family life-cycle segmentation. As people move through life they often pass through different stages, for example from being single, through living with a spouse, having an infant, having teenage children, living with a spouse after children have left home, living on a pension, to living alone after the spouse's death. Each of these states represents a different market segment, with different needs and levels of income.

Chapter Eight

Product policy and planning

- Introduction

- Definitions

- Product policy decisions

- Alternative product strategies

- Stages in product planning

- New product development

- Product life-cycle

- Product portfolio management

Introduction

It is a matter of debate whether 'product policy' is a corporate rather than a marketing issue. More than anything else, a firm's products define what sort of business it is and therefore product policy might be considered as a corporate issue; on the other hand, products ought to be developed in response to customer needs and this takes product policy into marketing's area of responsibility.

Definitions

Kotler defines the product as:

> 'A bundle of physical, service and symbolic particulars expected to yield satisfaction or benefits to the buyer.'

This definition stresses the point that the product should be viewed from the customer's point of view; the customer does not just buy the physical product, he buys the services associated with or provided with the product.

Even more fundamentally he buys satisfaction of some need eg a camera is not just a bundle of plastic, steel and glass (as production and purchasing functions might see it); it delivers memories and satisfies the need for nostalgia.

Products and services

Products are physical ⎫ both are intended to satisfy consumer needs,
                       ⎬ and both are subject to the same marketing
Services are abstract ⎭ considerations.

Services are defined as:

> 'Activities, benefits or satisfactions which are offered for sale as such, or are provided in connection with the sale of goods.'

Note: services 'as such' are medical care, travel, banking, insurance etc.

Thus, products comprise the actual product or service as such; use services (installation, maintenance etc); acquisition services (location, information, delivery, credit etc assist in acquiring the product); associated services (sales promotion devices – providing a further inducement to buy – perceived as 'free' or 'extra' services).

Note: the service element (advertising, distribution etc) is more readily varied than the product element because of the high cost and relative inflexibility of production processes, tooling up etc. This is of significance in the strategy known as 'product differentiation' (see below).

Product item. This is a specific version of a product.

Product line. This is a group of products closely related by associated usage, and/or common customer group, and/or common distribution channel, and/or given price range.

Product mix. This is a composite of products offered for sale. Width, depth and consistency of product mix need to be considered: width – how many different product lines are there?; depth – how many items are there in each line?; consistency – how closely related are the various product lines?

Product policy decisions

Product policy may be seen as the result of the interaction of three variables: corporate objectives, corporate resources and market opportunities.

Corporate objectives

What is the company's business? This must be defined in terms of market needs (see discussion of the 'marketing concept' above). What are the company's objectives? They could include:

- return on investment;
- profit goals;
- market share;
- stability;
- risk spreading;
- growth etc.

Identification of the objectives will determine product policy: either offensive strategy (development of new products), or defensive strategy (defending established products). Examples of the relationship between objectives and product policy include:

Objective			Product policy
Risk spreading	– leads to	–	wide product mix
Growth	– leads to	–	new product lines through research and development
Market segmentation	– leads to	–	product diversification, wide and deep product lines

Corporate resources

What are the company's resources (as part of SWOT analysis)?:

1. Finance: how relatively strong is the company's cash position or borrowing power?
2. Raw materials: how relatively strong is the company's access to suppliers of essential parts or raw materials?
3. Plant: how efficient is the company's machinery and equipment?
4. Trained personnel: how well trained are the personnel to produce and sell the proposed new product?
5. Specialised experience: does the company have the necessary expertise?
6. Market location: how close is the company to either supplies or markets?
7. Time: how long before a competitor introduces a new product?
8. Other advantages: monopoly, patents, reputation, control over distribution channels etc.

Market opportunities

Opportunities may arise from changes in the political, economic, socio-cultural, technological, legal, demographic or competitive environment of the business (see chapter 2).

The relationship between market opportunities, corporate objectives and corporate resources

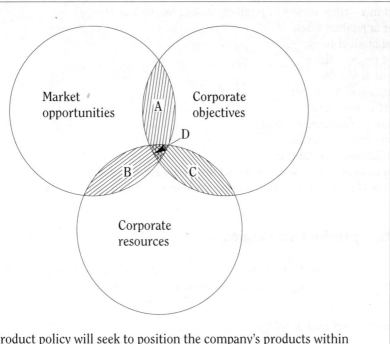

Product policy will seek to position the company's products within area D or to take up a position in area A, B or C and then try to modify corporate resources, corporate objectives or market opportunitities to enable the product to thrive.

A   When corporate objectives and market opportunities are coincident, but not resources, management will tend to concentrate on acquiring or developing appropriate resources, eg the pharmaceutical industry's heavy investment in scientific research.

B   When market opportunities and resources are coincident, but not objectives, management may have to reconsider their objectives, eg the Ford Motor Company's decision to enter the small car market.

C   When objectives and resources are coincident, but not market opportunities, management (and particularly marketing) may concentrate on market creation through advertising and sales promotion, eg 'new' cosmetics.

D   Where all factors coincide, immediate short-term study and exploitation will be undertaken.

Factors in product policy decisions

Product policy decisions will include:

- product mix – what variety of products should be produced?
- number of product lines;
- width of product lines;
- range of product sizes;
- quality of products;
- modification of products;
- branding of products;
- elimination of existing products;
- addition of new products;
- standardisation of products;
- planned obsolescence – so as to attract demand for 'new' products;
- how many of each type of product to be made in a specified time period?

Alternative product strategies

Four alternative product strategies can be recognised: undifferentiated marketing, concentrated marketing, segmentation, and product differentiation.

Undifferentiated marketing

There is a convergent, standardised, homogeneous product mix. The company concentrates on one (or a very few) standardised product(s), marketed in the same way to all markets (eg British Gas before the liberalisation of the energy markets).

Advantages
The unit costs of production and marketing are minimised through scale economies, because the average cost of production and marketing is lower as a result of the large volume.

Disadvantages
It makes no allowance for the heterogeneous nature of the market and may therefore miss profitable market opportunities.

Concentrated marketing

There is a convergent, standardised, homogeneous product mix, and the company concentrates on one segment of the market.

Advantages
There are scale economies of production and advertising, but not as great as with undifferentiated marketing.

Disadvantages
As with undifferentiated marketing there is no spread of risk, nor does the strategy make allowances for changing tastes, needs, etc in the target segment.

Segmentation

There is a divergent, various, heterogeneous product mix – the company produces many different products, each designed to satisfy the needs of different market segments, and each differently marketed (see 'Segmentation', above, chapter 7) eg executive cars, family saloons, estates.

Advantages
With wide market coverage there is high spread of risk, because if one segment fails others may still survive.

Disadvantages
There are high unit costs of production and marketing, because there will be no economies of scale.

Product differentiation

There is a convergent, standardised, homogeneous product mix with 'pseudo-differentiation':

1. The company produces essentially the same product for all markets, but differentiates in some minor way (eg packaging, branding, colouring) and differentiates the marketing for each segment. This is common with detergents.
2. The company produces the same product, but differentiates through marketing. For example, Guinness uses different packaging (draught, bottles and cans) and different advertising to target both the 'traditional' and the 'trendy' segments simultaneously.

Advantages
It keeps production unit costs low because of scale economies (but not marketing costs) and achieves wide market coverage.

Disadvantages
Because claimed product advantages may not be 'real', customers may switch brands to obtain sought-after benefits. The success of this strategy is therefore dependent on the extent to which customers believe claimed advantages to be real.

Stages in product planning

We have seen that the first stage must be the SWOT analysis of corporate resources and market opportunities, together with consideration of corporate objectives. From this analysis three questions may need to be asked:

1. Is our present mix making the best use of resources, responding to market opportunities and achieving corporate objectives?
2. If not, which products should be eliminated or modified? Apparently these should be the products making the smallest contribution to profit (or perhaps even making a loss) but ask the following subsidiary questions:

    a) is the product complementary to others, which may be profitable? ie sales of the profitable products may depend on the unprofitable and eliminating the unprofitable one may lose sales of the profitable one;
    b) does the unprofitable product give entry to an important customer/industry?
    c) is it certain that eliminating the unprofitable product (which may nevertheless be making a small contribution) will increase overall profitability?

3. If the present product mix is not right, are there 'gaps' in the market (opportunities, 'niches') which could be filled by a new product or products?

New product development

Once it has been decided to develop new products, experience shows that the following stages are most likely to lead to success: idea generation; preliminary appraisal; concept testing; commercial planning and appraisal; product R & D, marketing research; prototype testing; test marketing; regional launch, post- launch monitoring and evaluation, and national launch.

Idea generation

The purpose is to generate as many ideas as possible – ideas cost nothing! The more there are, the more likely it is that some will succeed. Techniques for idea generation include:

*   brainstorming;
*   analysis of competitors' products and advertising;
*   marketing research – particularly group discussion;
*   'new product development departments', specifically to generate and develop new ideas, have been set up by some large consumer goods companies.

Preliminary appraisal or screening

From now on, each stage *reduces* the number of ideas, eliminating the unprofitable or technically impossible and – hopefully – leaving only the successful ideas to be marketed. Questions asked would include:

*   does the idea 'fit' our corporate objectives?
*   is it technically feasible?
*   are the resources available?

The aim is to avoid either of two types of error:

1. Type I errors occur when the firm decides to go ahead with a new product, which then fails to achieve its targets.
2. Type II errors occur when the firm decides *not* to go ahead with a new product, which a competitor then launches successfully.

Concept testing

At this stage the firm starts to spend money on researching the more likely product ideas. Concept testing is a particular form of marketing research where the public's reaction to the 'concept' of the new product is measured and analysed.

Commercial planning and appraisal

If the customer reaction to the concept appears to be favourable the firm will have to conduct a detailed analysis of the projected costs and revenues, and therefore projected profits/losses and cash flows associated with the new product (see sales forecasting). This will have to be conducted over the projected life of the product or the strategic planning period, whichever is the shorter. More sophisticated techniques for this analysis are discussed in chapters 22–24, but at this stage consider the following simple example:

Assume that the product's sales life is expected to be five years. Sales in year one are forecast to be 2,000 units, year two 5,000 units, year three 10,000 units, year four 8,000 units and year five 3,000 units.

The price in year one will be £10 per unit, but this will fall to £9 in year two and to £8 in years three, four and five (as competition gets keener).

The product will take one year to develop, technical research costing £20,000 and marketing research costing £10,000.

Advertising and selling costs in year one will be £20,000, but these will remain £10,000 for the remaining four years.

Production costs are expected to be £4 per unit.

These assumptions can be analysed as follows (see overleaf):

	Development year	Year one	Year two	Year three	Year four	Year five	Totals
Sales ('000 units)	0	2	5	10	8	3	
Price (per unit)	–	10	9	8	8	8	
Revenue (£'000)	0	20	45	80	64	24	233
Production costs @ £4 per unit (£'000)	–	8	20	40	32	12	112
Gross profit (£'000)	0	12	25	40	32	12	121
Technical research (£'000)	20	–	–	–	–	–	20
Market research (£'000)	10	–	–	–	–	–	10
Advertising/selling (£'000)	–	20	10	10	10	10	60
Non-production expenditure (£'000)	30	20	10	10	10	10	90
Profit/loss (£'000)	(30)	(8)	15	30	22	2	31
Cash flow							
Balance b/f (£'000)	–	(30)	(38)	(23)	7	29	31
Income (£'000)	–	20	45	80	64	24	
Outflow (£'000)	(30)	(28)	(30)	(50)	(42)	(22)	
Balance c/f	(30)	(38)	(23)	7	29	31	

Whether a total profit of £31,000 on a total investment of £202,000 is worthwhile is for management to decide. Perhaps more important is the question 'can they afford a negative cash flow for three years?'.

R & D, market research

If it is decided that the product will yield the profits and cash flows required, the product will be given the 'go ahead'. At this stage the company commits itself to major expenditure on the new product – technical R & D and new product market research are both expensive and speculative. Because of the long 'lead times', between the idea and the eventual launch, associated with many products, it is probable that there will be no return on the initial investment for several years.

Prototype testing

The R & D will include the production of prototypes, for technical research and for market research (product testing). The market research will include:

- product testing, to test the acceptability of the product to customers;
- package testing, to find the most acceptable package design;
- brand name development (see below);
- distribution research, to obtain distributors' reactions to the product;
- advertising research, to discover which media the customers patronise and which messages are most effective.

Brands and branding

The concept of the brand name is so important in modern marketing that it is necessary to discuss it in detail.

A brand is a name, symbol, term, mark or design which enables customers to identify and distinguish the products of one supplier from those offered by competitors.

When a brand has been on the market for some time it takes on a 'personality' by which people describe, remember and relate to it. A brand name conjures up an association of ideas according to its public image, past customers' experience of using the product, and the degree to which it has become a household word (for example, all vacuum cleaners are Hoovers and all gas water heaters Ascots). A brand image is, therefore, a composite of beliefs, prejudices and associations which facilitate the identifications of qualities and characteristics with specific products (for example, a washing up liquid is 'kind to hands', Volvo cars are 'safe and dependable'). These need to be thoroughly researched at this stage, so that the name and image of the new product will ensure that it is appropriately 'positioned' in the minds of potential customers and in relation to competitive brands.

The company should consider, before launching the product, what market position it is targeted to occupy, the special qualities it possesses, the uses to which the product will be put, the nature of the satisfaction the customer is expected to extract from its use, the channels through which it will be distributed, its relationship to competitive products and the media which will be used to publicise it.

Brand names fall into five broad categories:

1. contrived names with no associated corporate ties (for example, Daz, Jif and Lux);
2. contrived names possessing phonetically symbolic associations (for example, Swish curtain rails);
3. descriptive names (for example, Head and Shoulders shampoo and Whiskas cat food);
4. generic brand symbols combining a common name for all the company's products (for example, Polyfilla, Polycleanse and Polycell);
5. combination of company name and a brand name (for example, Gillette Rightguard, Gillette GII, Gillette Contour, Gillette Shaving Cream).

115

Brand names promise quality and performance, suggesting what the customer can expect. They are of especial importance when there is little difference between the performance and value of competitive products as customers are buying the product image and not the physical product. The brand name stamps the brand's personality on the product, assists the customer to identify it and is an implicit guarantee of quality and performance.

Although the aim of a brand manager is to ensure widespread recognition for his brands, there is a danger of it being over-successful. When a product type becomes known by the name of one of the brands, the courts may rule that the brand name has been elevated into a descriptive generic name and the owner of the brand name loses the exclusive right to its usage. Nylon, escalator, aspirin and zipper were once brand names, so nowadays market leaders are very aware of the need to avoid their brand name becoming a generic term.

New brands: barrier to entry. Few new brands and products achieve lasting success, either having failed to surmount the barriers to entry or, perhaps, never even being launched. The principal barrier is probably financial. A new brand unavoidably involves a heavy cash outlay, research and development, manufacture and testing of prototypes, market research exercises, including pilot runs, the construction of new plant or the modification of existing plant, the training of manpower and salesmen and the initial promotional campaign, before there is any resultant cash inflow.

Another major entry barrier to be surmounted is to offer a brand which is better and different. If the new brand offers only a similar or marginally superior performance, why should potential customers buy it? A new brand has to break down existing brand loyalties, whereas an existing one has to fight to retain these loyalties. The strengths and weaknesses of competitive brands and the effectiveness of the marketing strategies of competitors, will influence the 'height' of entry barriers: if the barrier can be raised high enough then prospective entrants will be deterred. Brand loyalty is often a most effective barrier.

Test marketing

To return to our 'stages of new product development', the penultimate stage is test marketing. By this stage the product is in its most acceptable form (as a result of product testing); the price has been agreed; the packaging and brand name have been decided; advertising campaigns have been planned and the advertisements produced; the salesforce has been briefed.

In a test market the product is marketed normally in a region which has been selected to be representative of the population as a whole. The results are carefully analysed to decide if it is worth 'going national'. Evidence shows that of product prototypes which are *not* test marketed about 50 per cent are likely to fail when they 'go national'. (Only about 5 per cent of all new product ideas are successfully marketed!)

Remember that, in test marketing it is the *marketing* which is being tested – the complete marketing mix, not just the product.

Regional launch, post-launch monitoring and evaluation, national launch

If the test marketing is successful (or perhaps as part of it), the product is then launched in a region, where the market's purchases, attitude to the product and its price, and recognition of advertising messages can all be monitored and evaluated. If the regional launch is successful the product may then be launched nationally.

Product life-cycle

Some marketing theorists hold that products are like living organisms, in that they are conceived, are born, mature, decline and die. The stages in a typical product life-cycle are development, introduction, growth, maturity, saturation, and decline. These stages, together with sales and profit curves, characteristics of each stage, marketing objectives, typical consumer types, relative demand elasticity to different marketing variables and financial objectives, are set out below and on the following pages:

The product life-cycle

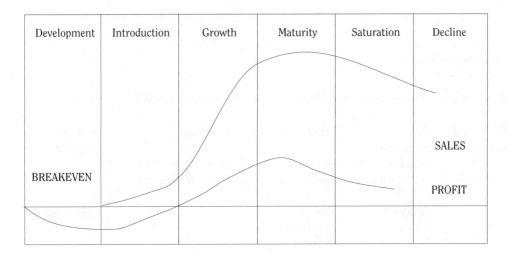

Characteristics of each stage

Product evaluation	Launch	Competitive reaction	Stabilising	Total market declines – one brand may enjoy temporary increase in share
R & D	New brand has short-term (monopolistic) advantage	Total market grows	Sales increasing, but a slower rate – eventually level off, or decline	
Market research		Brand grows or retains share	Most customers own/use a brand – therefore brand preference is significant factor	Over-capacity – mergers
Test marketing		Increase in per capita consumption		
		Volatile, unstable	Per capita consumption declining	Substitutes appear

Marketing objectives

Development	Introduction	Growth	Maturity/saturation	Decline
Marketing Research	Create maximum awareness	Penetration	Retain share	Test for abandonment.
Testing	acceptance	Reinforce loyalty	Capture share from weaker competitors	Search for 'new' uses/images
	Establish brand loyalty	Maximise gain from introductory promotion.		
	Maximise 'monopolistic' advantage	Distribution		
		Word-of-mouth		

Consumer type

Development	Introduction	Growth	Maturity	Saturation	Decline
Being defined through marketing research	Innovators Young, rich educated trend-setters, risk-takers	Early adopters. Young/ middle-aged rich/middle income 'The Joneses' (trendy but not 'eccentric')	Early majority	Late majority. The majority + laggards – middle/old-aged, middle/ lower income, cautious, conservative	Majority being eroded by brand-switching (by innovators) to substitutes

Relative elasticity of marketing variables

Development	Introduction	Growth	Maturity	Saturation	Decline
	1. Quality	1. Advertising	1. Price	1. Quasi-quality (packaging etc)	1. Advertising (new uses)
	2. Advertising	2. Quality	2. Advertising	2. Advertising	2. Service/ quality
	3. Price	3. Price	3. Quality	3. Service/ quality	3. Price
	4. Service	4. Service	4. Service	4. Price – already forced down, little remaining flexibility	

Financial objectives

Development	Introduction	Growth	Maturity	Saturation	Decline
	Break-even	Profit/ through growth in sales	Profitability reaches its peak	Profit/ through reducing costs	Cutting losses

Comments on the product life-cycle concept

The concept has validity as a descriptive model but not as a predictive model. Thus, while some products and/or brands may be seen to have behaved according to the product life-cycle theory, imaginative marketing has given other products/brands a new and very profitable lease of life, when the strict adherence to the theory 'predicted' decline.

The theory may become a self-fulfilling prophecy. If management are too dependent on the theory they may withdraw marketing support from a mature product in order to devote funds to the development of a replacement product; inevitably the existing product, deprived of its marketing budget, will decline and management may be forced to introduce the replacement without adequate testing, thus having two failures instead of one success.

Product portfolio management

An interesting combination of product life-cycle theory and market structure concepts appears in the approach to product portfolio management advocated by the Boston Consulting Group. They argue that most companies have a range (or portfolio) of products, which will have differing market shares and which will be in markets growing at different rates. Furthermore, market leaders (having the largest share) will generate most cash because of economies of scale. Finally, products which are in fast growing markets will consume more cash (in order to compete) than products in slow-growing, mature markets.

From these basic ideas the Boston Consulting Group constructed the 'BCG Matrix':

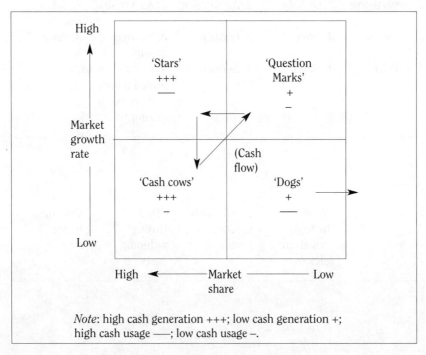

Note: high cash generation +++; low cash generation +; high cash usage ——; low cash usage –.

The model suggests that a company may have some 'star' products which generate a lot of cash, because of their high market share, but will use a lot because of the high growth rate of the market. As the market settles down the need for cash declines, but the high market share ensures high cash generation – such products are 'cash cows', whose excess cash can be used to finance the development of the most likely 'question marks' (new products in high growth markets), which may become the future 'stars'. 'Dogs' (low market share products which will consume excessive cash if they are to grow) should probably be dropped from the portfolio.

Chapter Nine

Marketing planning, research and forecasting

- Introduction

- The marketing mix

- Marketing research

- Secondary data

- Primary data

- Data analysis

- Marketing objectives and targets

- Sales forecasting

Introduction

We have seen that the marketing function is concerned with the management of exchange and the company's response to demand. We have also seen that demand is not just a function of price, but also of other factors such as advertising and sales promotion. Marketing management is therefore the management of all the variables such as product quality, price, distribution channels, sales force, and advertising which collectively respond to and influence market demand. These variables are known collectively as *'the marketing mix'*.

We have also seen that all management involves situation analysis, setting objectives and targets, strategic and tactical planning, organising and controlling. Situation analysis requires reliable management information, which in the marketing area is provided by 'marketing research'.

All planning involves making choices between several alternative plans. Strategic planning necessitates analysis of probable long-term environmental changes; tactical planning requires analysis of how the market is likely to respond. Both therefore require long-term and short-term 'sales forecasting'.

This chapter therefore deals with the following topics:

1. the marketing mix;
2. marketing research;
3. marketing objectives and targets;
4. sales forecasting.

The marketing mix

Obviously demand for the firm's products will be maximised when customer satisfaction from the consumption of the product is maximised, which will occur when the product is exactly what the customer wants and customer sacrifices in order to obtain the product are minimised. Demand for a firm's products can be influenced (either increased or reduced) by varying those factors over which the firm has direct control in order to vary the level of customer satisfaction and customer sacrifice. These factors fall into four categories (as defined by E Jerome McCarthy).

The factors in the marketing mix

These factors, sometimes described as 'marketing tools', are:

1. product (quality);
2. price;
3. place (distribution, availability);
4. promotion (selling/advertising, informing or persuading).

Varying the factors in the marketing mix
The process of determining the optimal mix of the factors is exactly what the science or art of marketing consists of. The number of possible combinations of the factors is obviously very large. All four factors can be varied:

1. The product's actual quality can be varied. Its 'image' (quasi-quality) can be varied by variations in the advertising and sales promotion, and its presentation may be varied by changing the packaging.
2. Price can be varied in order to stimulate or reduce demand, as demonstrated by the price mechanism.
3. Place: the availability of the product (and therefore the amount of effort the customer must sacrifice in order to obtain the product) can be varied by distributing the product more or less widely or by varying the distribution 'channels' employed.
4. Promotion: the number and deployment of the field sales force may be varied. Advertising expenditure may be increased or reduced. Advertising themes may be changed. The advertising media employed may be varied.

Professor Neil Borden of the Harvard Business School conceived the idea of a 'mix', and wrote that:

'The marketing mix refers to the apportionment of effort, the combination, the designing, and the integration of the elements of marketing into a program or "mix" which on the basis of an appraisal of the market forces, will best achieve the objectives of an enterprise at a given time.'

Principles in determining marketing mix

While the number of possible 'mixes' is virtually infinite, certain principles should be followed:

1. Consistency: it is essential that each variable should be consistent with each other. For example, a high quality product should be supported by high quality distribution and advertising.
2. Balance: different markets show different levels of sensitivity to different marketing variables. Management must identify the most important variable(s) and ensure that due emphasis is given to these, with support from the other variables. For example, if the market is very price-sensitive it may be necessary for the advertising to stress the price advantages of the product.
3. Diminishing returns, budgets and opportunity cost: despite the fact that one variable may be a 'key' variable it is seldom advisable to place *all* the emphasis on this. This is because sales response to each variable normally shows an increasing and then a diminishing return, for example:

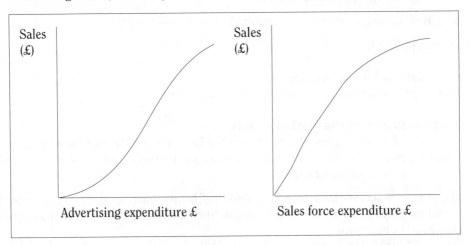

4. All marketing decisions have to be made under a budget constraint. The opportunity cost of each increase in sales achieved by an increase in expenditure on one variable, is the increase in sales achieved by an increase in expenditure on another variable which is foregone (£1 spent on improving the product cannot be spent on advertising – the question being which £1 will give the best return).

Therefore, the theoretical task of marketing management is to set its marketing mix at a point so that the marginal product of each of the variables is equal.

Marketing research

Introduction

Marketing research is essentially applied research, whereas market research suggests answers to the question 'Is there a market?' Marketing research answers the more practical question 'Is there a market and how should it be penetrated and developed?' Marketing research obtains information about the dynamics of marketing: market research is more static.

Definitions

BIM (British Institute of Management):

> 'The objective gathering, recording and analysing of all facts about problems relating to the transfer and sale of goods and services from producer to consumer.'

Kotler:

> 'Systematic problem analysis, model building and fact finding for the purposes of improved decision-making and control in the marketing of goods and services.'

The scope of marketing research

Marketing information is an aid to management decision-making. It has many uses, for example:

* identification of consumer needs;
* more precise characteristics of customers may be defined, eg age groups, stage in family life-cycle, income levels, educational backgrounds, geographic distribution, urban/rural distribution, ownership of consumer durables, where and how they shop, what media they see etc;
* product research, including acceptability of the product; brand name; suitability of package: shape, size, protection, labels;
* price research, including customer's sensitivity to price changes; competitive prices; elasticity;
* distribution research, including structures of distribution channels; distributors' attitudes to the product; levels of service provided by distributors;
* advertising research, including amount of advertising expenditure by brand and media; customers' recall of advertising messages; pre-testing;
* market measures, including sales volume and trends; opportunities for expansion of market; market share of major competitors; identification of major economic and/or social forces affecting the market.

Steps in research planning

For all kinds of research, the following are essential:

1. defining the problem, deciding what information is needed;
2. estimating 'value' and 'cost' of research;
3. deciding the likely sources of the information:

   a) secondary – will this be enough?
   b) primary.

If primary research is to be undertaken, additional steps are needed:

4. defining the population of interest, and the population from which the information will be gathered;
5. deciding whether to undertake an exploratory or pilot study;
6. deciding between a one-shot survey, a panel or an experiment from the main survey;
7. planning the data collection method;
8. deciding the sample;
9. planning the fieldwork;
10. timing the research, especially the fieldwork;
11. planning resources – people, stationery, computer-time;
12. planning the editing and analysis of data and writing of the research report.

Value of market research

Before money is spent on research – on gathering and analysing marketing information – its value should be weighed against its costs. The value of information is the value of the improvement in decision-making that can be achieved with the information, ie the marginal gain from having better information must be greater than the marginal cost of obtaining the information.

This means that it is necessary to form a hypothesis of the probable research findings before committing expenditure, so that the cost-benefit of the proposed research can be evaluated.

Problem definition

The first step in any market research project is the formulation and definition of a problem. The researcher should be made fully aware of the nature of the problem facing the executive and what the objectives of the project are. He needs to know the operational and environmental pressures and constraints affecting the executive and the resources currently and potentially available to him. What criteria will be applied to decide the success or failure of the project? How many alternative courses of action are available to the executive? What is the time span within which a decision has to be made? What is his attitude to risk?

The definition of the problem usually conditions what can be achieved, so it is up to the researcher (in consultation with the executive) to prepare a plan which will ultimately meet the requirements of the executive.

Problem diagnosis involves tracking down the relevant change factors which have caused the problem. If it is a complex problem there may be many contributory factors. As it is often impossible to specify the problem parameters at the outset, a preliminary survey is necessary to clarify the issues involved. For example, falling sales may be due to a variety of causes such as product obsolescence, inadequate advertising, confusing price structure, inconsistent quality, strong competitive pressures or a lower level of economic activity. Problems cannot be specified satisfactorily until their key issues have been identified. It is not enough to know their symptoms, their causes must be known. Symptoms are only signposts, not the heart of the problem.

Preliminary survey

The aims of a preliminary market research survey are to define:

1. the problem situation;
2. the key factors on which full information is required;
3. the data sources to be tapped;
4. the resources and time needed to complete the survey;
5. the control measures needed to check its progress.

When the preliminary survey has been concluded, the company will have three options open to it:

1. not to proceed further because the survey has not provided evidence strong enough to justify any further expenditure and effort;
2. to proceed on a limited scale: selected areas may be chosen for detailed study;
3. to proceed to a full scale survey because the potential benefits outweigh the associated costs.

Types of data

Data for research purposes may be classified into secondary and primary data.

Secondary data is data already compiled by some agency other than the user. The use of it is known as 'desk research', and the principal sources are:

1. internal company records;
2. external government statistics; trade association reports; published academic research etc.

Primary data is data which is not already in published material and which must, therefore, be obtained by the researcher.

Secondary data

Secondary data or primary data?

Research into secondary data should always be undertaken *before* primary research. Apart from the fact that secondary data is relatively cheap to obtain, the information sought can often be obtained entirely from secondary data, and if primary data has to be obtained the secondary data will be useful to assist in compiling it.

Uses for secondary data are:

1. as background information for identifying and defining the problem;
2. to establish hypotheses about possible solutions to problems, or subsequent testing by primary research;
3. as guidance on research method (when similar primary research has been done before);
4. in sample planning, for defining the population and the sample frame;
5. as an independent check on primary data.

Sources of secondary data

Internal records
Advance arrangements are necessary to ensure that internal data will be available in the form required. This involves liaison with, for instance, company accountants.

The most commonly used internal data are: Sales records broken down by: customer, area, region, product, salesmen, industry, size of order, time, handling cost. Area managers' and salesmen's reports, sales turnover, sales expenses, stock control records, production statistics, transport statistics, advertising expenditure statistics.

External data
There is a wide variety available of which the most commonly used are:

Government publications
- Ten year Census of Population
- Census of Distribution and Census of Production
- Annual Abstract of Statistics
- National Income and Expenditure
- Business Monitors (every month and every quarter) giving output of industries, export etc
- Overseas Trade Accounts of the UK (exports and imports)
- Family Expenditure Survey (annual) broken down geographically and by class of household

In recent years, government has increasingly recognised a responsibility to provide statistical information as well as to seek it. Since the Statistics of Trade Act 1974 specifically referred to the provision of a statistical service for industry, the volume of published statistics has increased steadily and a Business Statistics Office was formed in 1968 to create data banks for storage and access. The Department of Trade and Industry as well as other government departments, have developed information services which are unparalleled for range and depth by an individual organisation. Information is received from around the world, although chiefly from Britain, on business performances and trends in most industries which, after processing, are published in routine monthly, quarterly and annual reports and digests giving relevant statistics in trend and forecast formats. Examples of routine publications are *Monthly Digest of Statistics, Annual Abstract of Statistics, Annual Report of National Income & Expenditure* and *Department of Employment Gazette*. However, many government statistics are based on census returns which take a long time to collect and process, so are not issued frequently as a consequence. These include the Family Expenditure Survey and the Censuses of Production, Distribution and Population.

Non-government sources

- Industrial MR Association
- AC Neilson
- Attwood Consumer Panel (about 9,000 households return diaries recording purchases. Panels are sensitive to change or trends)
- Media – TV audience measurement
- National Readership Survey
- BRAD (British Rate and Data)
- Statistical Review of Press and TV advertising
- MEAL (Media Expenses Analysis)
- *Retail Business*
- The *Economist* (special reports)
- *The Times* reviews
- Trade associations
- Technical trade press
- Chambers of commerce
- Company financial statements – balance sheets and profit and loss accounts.

Trade and technical journals and newspapers

These can be valuable sources of data on:

- the availability of new materials and the uses to which they might be put;
- the projected activities of competitors;
- home and overseas markets and industry trends;
- annual accounts and company chairmen's statements; and
- the national and international economic situation.

Semi-official sources

Marketing data can be extracted from many semi-official sources. Most public libraries contain reference books such as *The Stock Exchange Year Books,* Dunn & Bradstreet's *Guides,* Kelly's Directories and Kompass Directories. Trade associations (ie companies in specific industries and trades pursuing common interests) generate or collect marketing data which is then made available to their members in the form of interfirm comparisons and special reports, while other semi-official sources which might provide similar data are the British Productivity Council, the Confederation of British Industries, Chambers of Commerce and Professional Institutes.

Scrutinising secondary data

Information collected from secondary sources should not be accepted unquestioned. The following aspects should be examined:

1. the character of the collecting or sponsoring organisation. In some cases data is collected to 'prove' something, and may be biased, eg information from political pressure groups;
2. the objectives of the original study. If these are not reconcilable with the objectives in hand, the data may not be suitably classified;
3. the methods employed. Inaccurate data will have been produced if sample selection or data collection were badly done. Reputable organisations either append a full description of their methods, or willingly explain them on request;
4. the definitions used: eg family, department store, employed, income. Are these the same definitions as the ones used in the research?
5. timeliness: the data may have become out of date.

Primary data

Primary data may be obtained by observation (looking): audit, recording devices and direct observation of people; experimentation (testing): controlled experiments and test marketing (data collection may involved both interview and observation technique); interview (asking): personal interview, telephone interview, and mail interview.

Observation

1. It may be possible to collect information at lower cost and more accurately through observation. It may be more accurate because brand usage reports show a 'halo' effect (the upward bias reflecting the prestige which respondents associate with a well-known brand; for example Johnson's Wax showed a 50 per cent variance between respondents' reports and observation of the actual brand at hand).
2. Observation can cover both current and past behaviour; for example, instead of asking 'what brand of TV do you own?' or 'what brand of detergent have you just bought?', it may be simpler to ask 'may I see it?'
3. Sometimes observation is the *only* source of information, eg department stores 'shopping' to ascertain competitive prices.
4. The observational approach can only measure current events and what can be seen; it cannot provide answers on customer motivations, opinion and attitudes.
5. Observation by non-personal means can be achieved by mechanical and associated devices:

    *   galvanometers (commonly called 'lie detectors') measure emotional response to brand stimuli by change of pulse rate and increase in perspiration;
    *   ophthalmographs measure reactions to advertisements;
    *   tachistoscopes test recall of brand names;
    *   audimeters record TV channel and time.

6. Many market research organisations use panels to provide basic data. A panel is a permanent sample which may be housewives, shopkeepers or specified segments of the population. The members of the panel are measured on the same items, such as their weekly food basket. The composition of the panel will change only when its members are

unable to continue, in which case a replacement is sought with similar characteristics. Over a period, a behavioural pattern emerges from which trends can be extracted. Thus, if a company alters its advertising campaign, or changes the design of its container, or makes special offers, then over the period in question the effect of the introduction of this one change can be measured, provided nothing else alters during the same period. Of course, there are bound to be many external factors impinging on the panel choice as well, but a strongly constructed panel does offer valuable data for comparison purposes.

7. Omnibus panels operate on the same basis, but the data collected changes according to the needs of the researchers. On such occasions, panel members may be asked to comment on the appeal of a new sales promotion campaign, whereas on another occasion they might be asked to comment on some new product features.

Experiments

Experiments are designed to find out what would happen if a change were introduced into the marketing situation, eg if a new product were launched. Researching this area by asking 'what would you do if ...?' questions does not produce satisfactory results; better is to introduce respondents into the changed situation and record what they do or their verbalised reaction. Test marketing can be a form of experiment.

Administering experiments

In an experiment, a selected variable is put into effect, and its results measured. For instance, respondents are shown an advertising film and the resulting change in their level of brand name recognition is measured; or salesmen receive a period of sales re-training and the change in sales achieved is measured.

Measuring change

There are three possible methods to use to measure change (the effect of a variable):

1. take a measurement before as well as after the variable is introduced (time series design);
2. expose a number of individuals or groups to different levels of 'treatment' (eg one-week, two-week and three-week re-training periods) and compare them (cross-sectional design);
3. a combination of (1) and (2).

Reasons for distorted results

It is possible for the amount of change measured in an experiment to give a distorted impression of the effect of the variable because:

1. other factors have changed in the intervals between the two measurements in a time-series design; or differ between individuals or groups in a cross-sectional design;
2. the individuals or groups have matured between the two measurements (time-series);
3. the fact of having been measured (asked questions) on a previous occasion changes the individual's reaction on the second occasion (in time-series experiments).

Experiment design to avoid distortion

Careful design of experiments is needed to avoid these 'errors'. Useful techniques are:

1. random selection of respondents;
2. random assignment of individuals to groups;
3. use of a control group, which is not subjected to the treatment. Changes in the behaviour of the treatment group compared with that of the control group can then be more reliably attributed to the effect of the treatment.

A laboratory experiment

This is conducted under carefully controlled simulated conditions. However, there is the risk that respondents may not act in the same way under real conditions.

A field experiment

This is conducted in a natural environment (eg under normal shopping conditions), but in one where the investigator is able to control or manipulate at least one decision variable.

Test marketing

This is a practical example of the experimental approach. A company chooses representative market areas to test the response of customers to a selected product. As the object of experimentation is to reduce the risk element, the company has to ensure that its sample is large and representative enough to enable accurate conclusions to be drawn. Test marketing, of course, means publicly exposing one's products and proposals, so if the company intends to gauge customer reactions to its new product (or characteristics) it will generally use a short period for test and evaluative purposes in order to avoid the danger of competitive products beating it to the full market. Sometimes test marketing persuades a company to proceed no further.

Theme and media experiments

These use permutations of advertisements in roughly comparable markets, one of which will be the 'control' area and the other the 'test' area. The control area will be subjected to a normal campaign and the test area to an experimental one. More than one theme or media experiment can be conducted simultaneously by using as many test areas as are required for comparison with the results from the control area. Thus, customer response against alternative advertising strategies can be measured in terms of actual sales before the advertiser is committed to large scale expenditure. Each test period is broken down into three distinctive time spans. The first is used as a trial run to check sales under normal conditions in the control and test areas, while the second uses the intended experimental conditions and the third resumes normal advertising again in the test area to check the effects of carry over from the experiment. Sales, stock and purchases are checked at the beginning and end of each period and a close check made to ascertain that no undue influences have affected either the control or test areas. Problems may crop up in its operation as the maintenance of strictly comparable conditions in the control and test areas may be difficult, while tests may take several months to complete and evaluate.

Interviews

There are three main types of interview:

Personal interviews

Interviewers ask questions of one or more respondents in a face-to-face situation. The interviewers' role is to get in touch with respondents (often at home or in the street), ask the desired questions and record the answers.

Personal interviewing is time-absorbing and expensive, especially when random sampling is used, but interviews can be longer and more probing; research into motivations, for instance, is always conducted by personal interviewing.

Telephone interviews

These are used when only a limited amount of information is required, eg 'coincidental' determination of television programme audience sizes and reactions. Calls are placed to a sample of telephone subscribers while the programme is showing.

Telephone interviewing can obtain a limited amount of information swiftly and economically, but there is an in-built bias in a sample of telephone subscribers because not everyone has an instrument.

Mail interviews

Questionnaires are prepared and mailed out to selected respondents who are asked to complete and return them; usually a stamped self-addressed envelope is provided.

Mailed interviews can be conducted with respondents anywhere in the UK for the same low cost. If required the respondent can remain anonymous, and may, therefore, be willing to reveal 'private' information. On the other hand the response rate is typically low, and those who do not reply often feel differently about the question from those who do. Follow-ups to eliminate bias increase the cost per complete interview.

Interviews may be structured or unstructured, direct or indirect. Structured means that a formal questionnaire has been designed; questions are asked in a pre-arranged order and with pre-arranged wording. Direct means that the purpose of the question(s) has not been disguised.

The advantages of the structured and direct interview are:

1. Questions can be asked in an orderly way, to prevent one question or its answer from influencing the response to another.
2. Exact wording is worked out, first, to avoid misunderstanding, and, secondly, to avoid influencing the answer by the phrasing used and to ensure that the required information is obtained.
3. Questionnaires can be pre-tested.
4. All respondents are asked the same questions in the same order, thus maximising control of interviewing and reducing variability in answers caused by differences in interviewer characteristics.
5. It is less demanding of interviewer skill, resulting in lower pre-interview training cost.
6. It facilitates editing, computer coding, and tabulating and analysing data.

133

The problems of the structured and direct interview are:

1. It is difficult to get complete answers to questions on personal and motivational factors.
2. The approach does not encourage the respondent who knows more to reveal additional information.
3. No 'new' aspects of the subject can be introduced.

In an attempt to solve these problems, unstructured direct interviews are usually used for exploratory studies. The interviewer is given only general guidance on the type of information required, and is left free to ask the necessary direct questions to get the information, using the wording and order most appropriate in the context of the individual interview.

The unstructured (direct or indirect) interview is also used in research into motivation, where a structured questionnaire is difficult to compose as it tends to suggest answers. When used to determine motives, an unstructured interview is known as a depth interview.

Focus groups

An effective method of eliciting opinions and motives is through an unstructured group discussion led by a skilled interviewer, who encourages the group to discuss the topic under investigation freely.

The advantages of unstructured interviews are that they are flexible and can elicit information that cannot be obtained through structured interviews. Their problems are that there are higher pre-interview costs through the need to use higher calibre interviewers, and that editing and tabulating are most complicated.

Uses of primary data

The time and cost involved in the collection of primary data means that it is only used when secondary data is unavailable or inadequate. It is usually concerned with the generation of characteristics and descriptive profiles of target audiences:

1. Demographic and socio-economic characteristics: these class actual and potential customers by age, occupation, geographical location, education, income, family size and composition, sex, social class, religion, leisure pursuits and membership of clubs and societies. Marketers are usually interested in attempting to establish whether there is any relationship between specified combinations of individual characteristics (or groups of individuals who collectively can constitute a market segment) and product features.
2. Knowledge of product characteristics: there must be some correlation between the knowledge which a target audience possesses of a company's products and the volume of sales.
3. Attitude: this may be described as the conviction of a person about any object or idea. The attitude of potential customers to a specific product determines whether or not they are favourably disposed towards it and, if not, what has to be done to change it.
4. Motives: these may be described as the drives, wants, needs or impulses to act in a certain way; they are those elements in a person's make-up which cause him to act in the way he

does. Marketers are more likely to be able to develop effective advertising campaigns if they are able to identify with and appeal to, the basic motivations of their customers.

5. Behaviour is physical activity which takes place at a certain time under certain circumstances and conditions. Marketers are usually concerned to establish just what their current and potential customers are doing, or have done, on such points as: their purchases, purchase volumes, prices paid, for whom, when, terms of payment and whether the purchase is for a new or replacement item.

Data analysis

The final stage of the market research process is the analysis of the data which has been collected by any of the means discussed earlier in this chapter.

Market research data only have significance when they provide the basic raw material for information. Data analysis is concerned with editing, coding, tabulating and presenting collected raw material into a form suitable for problem solving and decision making.

The market research report

The report must provide its readers with the information they require and in the format they are able to understand and appreciate. If the readers are not technical experts, there is no point in including technical data which would only serve to confuse and annoy them. The normal requirements of clarity and conciseness apply, but each report must be tailored to individual demands and the circumstances in which the exercise is carried out.

Obviously, the market research report must be as accurate as possible. The possible causes of inaccuracy are as follows:

1. biased source lists (electoral registers become outdated, or may be distorted for political reasons);
2. incorrect sample drawing;
3. non-random field selection in random surveys;
4. bad or incorrect quota basis data;
5. poor question formulation (leading questions, ambiguous questions);
6. poor fieldwork control and checking;
7. interviewer bias;
8. poor interviewer briefing;
9. 'family' interviewing in individual contact surveys (children often 'prompt' mothers to give a different answer from their first response);
10. untruthful respondents (not necessarily deliberately lying – they may give the answer they think the interviewer wants!);
11. non-contactable respondents: not all respondents chosen randomly will be available for interview;
12. careless recording of answers;
13. inaccurate coding;

14. list order biases (respondents tend to choose the first item when they are asked to indicate a preference on a list of items) – this can be minimised by order rotation;
15. 'hunch proving' (can extend to the whole research programme being biased to 'prove' a client's or researcher's hunch);
16. poor editing.

Marketing objectives and targets

Corporate plans provide the framework within which marketing plans should be developed and operated. The four basic strategies (penetration, product development, market extension, diversification) provide the framework within which more detailed marketing strategies can be devised. The two strategies discussed below are market share and positioning.

Market share

Everything seems to be in favour of the large company. Operational economies in manufacturing, distribution and marketing ought to be gained as sales expand, thereby further strengthening the competitive power of the larger company. It can afford more expensive and sophisticated equipment, more costly and penetrating research, more skilled and highly trained personnel, quantity discounts on its purchases and advantageous advertising terms and it can offer its customers lower prices as a consequence of its lower operational costs. The publication during the early 1970s of the results of studies conducted by the Boston Consulting Group and the American Marketing Science Institute (the originator of the PIMS (Profit Impact of Market Strategies) approach) suggested a strong linkage between profits and market share – the larger the market share possessed by a company, the better the return on its capital employed.

In addition to the apparent economic advantages of large scale operations, executives also seem to enjoy the status of working for a large company – if it is the market leader, so much the better. Yet in spite of the encouragement from so may quarters to become larger, there is no automatic guarantee that a large market share will generate larger profits. What the decision makers are searching for is the optimal market share. Figures 1 and 2 show the factors which might be taken into account in locating the optimal market share and market share strategies.

Figure 1: Locating optimal market share

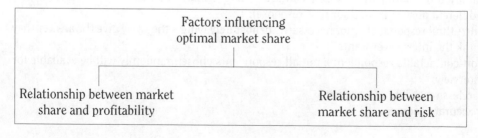

Figure 2: Market share strategies

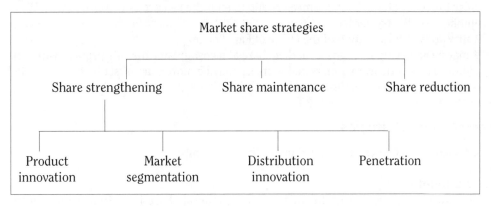

Relationship between market share and profitability

An analysis of past corporate performances may provide a rough guide to the manner in which profits have corresponded to changes in the size of market share. There comes a point, no matter how efficient the company, when it finds that any additional sales or increases in its market share, can only be achieved at a cost higher than the associated benefits. Potential customers, loyal to competitors, may be too costly to entice away, or competitors may have a grip on some market segments too costly to break. Statistics produced by the Centre for Interfirm Comparisons or analyses of the annual accounts of competitors can be sources of information, in attempting to identify that market share which will give the company its highest return on capital employed.

Relationship between market share and risk

The nature of the risk to company survival and/or advancement tends to vary according to the size of its market share. The risk element will be high for a low market share company because:

1. It does not possess a large enough number of loyal customers on which it can rely for continued support.
2. It will find it difficult to withstand any concerted and prolonged attack on its position due to its limited financial resources.
3. It cannot afford the detailed and expensive market research necessary to identify the most profitable market segments.
4. It will be unable to achieve the economies of scale available to larger companies.
5. It may not have the resources to respond to rapid switches in consumer tastes. (On the other hand, small companies are often more flexible than large companies.)

The risk factor will be at its most dangerous to a high market share company if its market share rises above the optimal level. The company is potentially vulnerable on three counts:

1. It is a sitting target for smaller companies who can use it for comparative advertising in order to attract attention to themselves and to shift the balance of power (eg Avis: 'We're number two. We try harder.').
2. It may attract the attention of the Office of Fair Trading.
3. It may be achieving its highest market share at a cost greater than its profits justify: the additional revenue from a marginal increase may be more than offset by the associated costs. (See 'perfect competition' and 'oligopoly' above.)

Market share strategies

Market share strategies can be studied under three headings:

Share strengthening
A company which is operating below its optimal market share is neither achieving the economies of scale nor the profitability levels potentially open to it, so it is logical to pursue a policy of increasing its market. Four main avenues are open to it:

Product innovation. A new and improved product may offer the best prospects for achieving a larger market share. Where a completely new product is to be put on the market, no factual information or potential consumer demand will be available and even market research may be able to offer little better than a broad indication of the likely prospects.

Where the innovation is based on an existing product, the company will usually have access to information which will allow reasonably accurate forecasts to be created, but even in this case there is no guarantee of success. The company will have to decide whether its chances of success in attaining higher sales and market share are worth the risk of losing some or all of its investment in the selected project.

Market segmentation. An increased market share may be sought by pursuing an intensive policy of market segmentation and increased product variety to appeal to a large number of segments.

Distribution innovation. Market shares may be increased by the use of different distribution routes and outlets. Mail and telephone ordering have been used as distribution channels by a number of retailers. Avon Cosmetics have reverted to the supposedly old-fashioned idea of door-to-door selling and have carved out a sizeable share of the cosmetic market. Timex Watches have encouraged the sale of their watches through such outlets as chemists and supermarkets in addition to the conventional jewellery outlets. The development of computer databases has led to a growth in direct marketing, aimed at residential neighbourhoods or individual households.

Throughout the 1990s there was a substantial increase in the use of the internet as a forum for buying and selling, with the sellers including both established offline businesses such as Tesco and specialised online businesses such as the online auction house eBay. Although many online retailers experienced severe losses and there were high profile company failures, such as the collapse of the web-based clothing store Boo.com in 2000, there were also a number of success stories, especially among established companies looking for a new method of advertising and distributing goods and, more commonly, services with relatively low distribution costs, including banking, insurance, theatre tickets, airline and rail tickets and package holidays. The distribution of recorded music over the internet can be expected to increase in the next few years, although this may be dependent on distributors' ability to prevent illegal copying of music files.

Penetration. Market share may be increased by more aggressive selling and advertising.

Share stability
A company which is satisfied with its present market share will adopt a policy of share stability. It will attempt neither to increase nor reduce its market share. This presupposes:

1. that the company will attempt to ensure that it has a worthwhile replacement for those of its products nearing the end of their life-cycle by anticipating the obsolescence of its own products (see 'product life-cycle' above;)
2. that the company will pursue a multi-brand strategy similar to that developed by Unilever and Procter and Gamble in the detergent market to prevent its competitors establishing a foothold – such a strategy is known as 'market fortification'; and
3. that the company in a saturated market will adopt a 'confrontation' strategy, which may involve intensive advertising and promotional campaigns, in an effort to guard its market share.

Share reduction
A company which feels it has over-extended its resources may decide to reduce its market share in an endeavour to strengthen its overall position. It will then reverse the normal marketing practice by raising its prices and cutback on its advertising in order to reduce the level of consumer demand.

Market positioning

The process
Market positioning is the process of:

1. identifying the individual needs of each market segment and the extent to which these are met by competing products;
2. selecting those segments on which the major marketing effort will be concentrated;
3. deciding on the message and media to be used to generate a unique character for the product it is intended to promote in order to distinguish it from competition products.

Role of positioning
The role of positioning is to strengthen the purchasing power of the messages directed at selected target audiences. Their effectiveness is likely to be improved if satisfactory answers can be extracted from the following sets of questions:

1. What market positions do our products occupy in the minds of our target audience relative to competitive products?
2. What criteria do our target audience apply in their purchase decisions?
3. In order to maintain or reposition our product do we need to change the product, the marketing or both?

Although each supplier needs to have market position which he attempts to achieve or reinforce by advertising to his target audience, his actual market position is set by his customers. When a competitive product is the overwhelming market leader or occupies a distinctive role in the market, all other products tend to take their position from it and often relate their own advertising to it.

Identifying the market

Market positioning requires a supplier to identify a specific market segment to which he intends to appeal and create an image for his product which will give it a special niche in the market. The more pronounced and distinctive the product image he can create – provided that his potential customers find it acceptable – the better his chances of success. Consequently, market positioning is the process by which a supplier brings together his product and his target audience; it is the deliberate creation of a community of interests.

Sales forecasting

Introduction

Most decisions that human beings make are based on some estimate of what will happen in the future. Business and marketing decisions are also based on forecasts of the future, in particular sales forecasts. Typically, sales forecasts involve managerial judgment (subjective) and mathematical techniques (objective). The forecasting process may be modelled as follows:

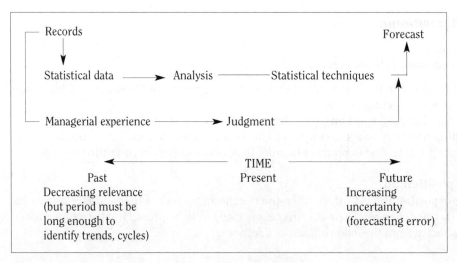

140

Why forecast?

In marketing the reason for forecasting falls into two main categories: long-term forecasting and short-term forecasting. Long-term forecasting is mainly concerned with *strategic* decisions such as new product development, entering new markets, investment decisions, projected cash flow etc. For example, when developing a new product, the business must forecast the likely profit or loss in order to decide whether or not to proceed, as illustrated below:

New product appraisal

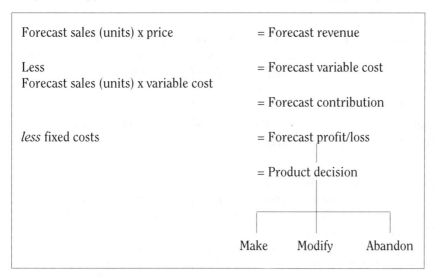

Forecast sales (units) x price   = Forecast revenue

Less   = Forecast variable cost
Forecast sales (units) x variable cost

                                        = Forecast contribution

less fixed costs   = Forecast profit/loss

                                        = Product decision

Make   Modify   Abandon

Short-term forecasting is mainly concerned with budgeting (providing finance, purchasing materials, hiring labour), production scheduling, and marketing planning (tactics, rather than strategy).

Difference between long-term and short-term forecasting

Apart from the obvious difference of time (long term is normally in excess of three to five years, short term any period up to one year, with medium term covering the interval) there is an important distinction to be made regarding the role of marketing planning in forecasting.

In the long term it may be assumed that demand will be determined primarily by external forces such as changes in the economic, social, technological environment rather than by one firm's marketing mix. In any case it is almost impossible to forecast with any accuracy far into the future what a firm's marketing mix and resultant sales response will be.

In the long term, therefore, the forecast may precede the plan:

Forecast ———————————————————➤ Plan

But in the short term the firm's marketing mix may be assumed to have an immediate effect on sales.

In the short term, therefore, the plan must precede the forecast:

Plan ⟶ Forecast

Example: assume a firm is considering three different marketing strategies (mixes), M1, M2, M3. M1 is high advertising, low price, M2 is low advertising, low price and M3 is high advertising, high price. The resultant sales response for each mix is forecast, and the data arranged in tabular form as follows:

	Marketing mix		Sales forecast (units)	Contri- bution per unit	Gross contri- bution	Net contribution (after deducting) advertising)
	Advertising	Price				
M1	£10,000	£1.50	110,000	£0.50	£55,000	£45,000
M2	£5,000	£1.50	100,000	£0.50	£50,000	£45,000
M3	£10,000	£2.00	60,000	£1.00	£60,000	£50,000

Obviously M3 would be chosen and the forecast would therefore be 60,000 units. (The fact that M3 is forecast to achieve sales of only 60,000 units might persuade management to choose a different strategy so as to make better use of their productive capacity, labour etc, but this might be at the cost of making smaller profits.)

Clearly, long-term forecasts provide the framework for short-term forecasting. Whether forecasting in the long term or short term, the first stage must be to consider the firm's macro-environment and to identify any changes taking place which may influence the firm's future sales.

Types of long-term forecasting

Demographic forecasting
Changes in the birth rates and death rates, immigration and emigration will influence the total number of customers in a potential market ('N' in the formula $D = N_{Pt} R$, in Chapter 7).

Economic forecasting
Reports can be obtained from various government departments, banks and other organisations. Economic forecasts are based on estimates of the population, inflation, productivity, unemployment etc. The company should be able to relate the economic forecasts to its own industry, and to its own position within that industry, by taking into account:

- changes in gross national product and contributory components, number of people unemployed and output levels by standard industrial classifications;
- changes in exchange rates, influencing exports and imports;
- quantitative and/or qualitative restrictions on imports and exports;

- introduction or withdrawal by government of selective taxes and subsidies;
- energy conservation and anti-pollution programmes;
- changes in level, composition and movement of population;
- changes in direction and magnitude of national and international trade-cycles;
- changes in inflation and interest rates;
- legislative measures affecting the market, such as credit trading regulations;
- changes in number of new houses built, new cars manufactured etc, which will affect dependent industries;
- changes in industrial structure (ie firms entering, or leaving, the industry).

Technological forecasting

With the rapid development of technology, forecasting for new products and processes has become a major element of planning. Some of the techniques used for such technological forecasting are:

- the Delphi techniques which involve systematically obtaining the opinions of a number of experts as to what type of technological developments are likely to take place and when these are likely to occur;
- the trend technique by which relationships or trends are established between two industries so that developments in one industry can be forecast from developments in the other, eg forecasting of developments in commercial aviation from developments in military aircraft;
- morphological analysis, which is the systematic examination of all possible techniques in a given field.

However, technological forecasting is extremely difficult because many important discoveries arise from chance occurrences, eg the discovery of penicillin, and many inventions which are technically sound may not find public acceptance in the market place, and thus do not become commercial propositions.

Forecasting methods

The method chosen will depend on the time period to be forecast, the relevance and availability of appropriate data, and the required degree of accuracy. Obviously, the more sophisticated the technique the greater the accuracy to be expected. However, the more sophisticated the technique the higher the cost. The best method (or combination of methods) is the one for which the sum of these two costs is minimised. Forecasting methods fall into two categories: surveys (subjective – 'what people say'); and quantitative techniques (objective – 'what people do, or have done').

Surveys

Surveys of buyers' intentions to buy. Superficially, the obvious technique is to ask potential customers 'how many units will you buy in the forecast period?'. However, consumers are seldom able to answer such a question with any accuracy, particularly if the product is a new, previously unsold item (see 'concept testing').

Test marketing may be included under surveys or used to refine a previous survey as this tests the buyers' intentions to buy under 'real' marketing conditions. Surveys of intentions to buy are rather more reliable in industrial markets, where the buyers are relatively 'expert', but there is a danger of bias as buyers may inflate their estimates in order to ensure supply.

Salesforce opinion. Salesmen may be consulted to obtain sales forecasts. The advantages of this are:

1. Salesmen are closest to customers, and are therefore better able to judge developing trends.
2. Salesmen gain confidence in sales quotas derived from such forecasts, thereby increasing their motivation.
3. Estimates from different salesmen enable forecasts to be broken down by product, territory, customer and salesman. Individual errors are likely to be compensated. (Individual forecasts may be aggregated to form a 'synthetic' forecast.)

The disadvantages are:

1. Salesmen may be biased (optimistic or pessimistic).
2. They may over-react to changes in the market.
3. They may not be aware of other forces (eg economic) or company plans.
4. Salesmen are employed to sell – time spent away from selling is misuse of their time.

Expert opinion may be consulted. The advantages of this are that different points of view are considered and balanced, and the technique is relatively quick and cheap. The disadvantages are that the technique is dependent on subjective opinions, the responsibility is dispersed (because the expert is only an adviser, not responsible for the final decision), and that it is better for aggregate forecasts than for detailed breakdowns.

Quantitative techniques
Associative techniques. Analysis of past sales may establish a correlation between sales and some other factor or combination of factors, in other words between sales as the dependent variable and other factor(s) as the independent variable(s), for example changes in the weather and sales of ice-cream or umbrellas; changes in interest rates and sales of houses.

Sales may then be forecast on the basis of a forecast of the independent variable, using correlation analysis.

Extrapolative techniques. These are based on historical time series. Techniques include moving averages, exponential smoothing, and least-squares. Past observations may be fitted to a time pattern or decomposed into trend, cyclical, seasonal or random elements for extrapolation into the future.

The advantages of this are that the forecast is objective, and that computer programs can handle very complex data. The disadvantage is that a forecast is only as good as the data used – there may be a need for human judgment to refine the forecast in the light of additional data.

Causal methods. Market dynamics are analysed with a view to building a (mathematical) model of the process. Market testing may be included to test and refine hypothetical models.

Approaches to forecasting

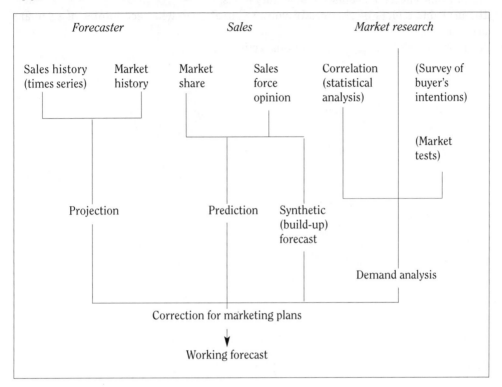

Models

Very close analysis of a market over a long period of time may enable the analyst to construct a model of how the market 'behaves'. Such models can be used either for forecasting or for testing alternative plans and their probable outcomes.

A model is a representation of something else: in order to be meaningful, it should express the central qualities and relationships of the latter and assist in the prediction of future events. Explanatory (ie descriptive) marketing models are intended to show events and situations as they are, while decision models are designed to improve the quality of decisions.

Marketing models can assist analysts and observers to understand the probable impact of changes in the values of selected variables.

A change in the value of any marketing variable affects most marketing activities. Its probable impact on the other marketing variables can be isolated and explored by applying a range of values to one selected variable in a relevant marketing model. Thus, marketing models can be used to examine:

- the probable effect of changes in price levels;
- the significance of applying alternative advertising media or different levels of promotional expenditure to nominated product lines or individual products;
- the probable effect of changes in the level of customer credit;
- the probable effects of changes in inventory levels;
- the probable effects of changes in volume of sales (ie what economies of scale are achievable?);
- the probable rate of decay in promotional activities.

Chapter Ten

Pricing

- The nature and importance of pricing

- Pricing objectives and policies

- Price calculation in theory

- Price calculation in practice

The nature and importance of pricing

Pricing has been the subject of extensive study by economists and accountants.

The role of price in the marketing mix

The role of price in the marketing mix can be demonstrated by the following diagram:

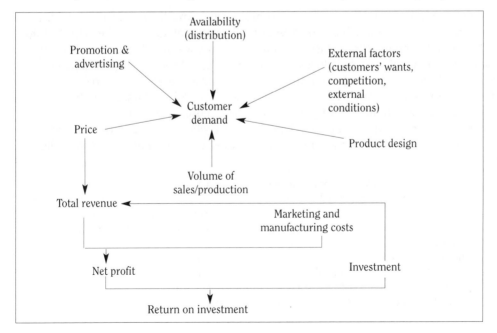

The diagram shows that price, together with product design, promotion, distribution and other external factors, has a direct influence on demand. In this sense price can be said to have a 'promotional' effect, as recognised in the workings of the 'price mechanism'.

Price is a unique part of the marketing-mix in one other very important way. It is the only part which contributes (via the formula PQ = R, Price x Quantity demanded = Revenue) directly to the firm's pool of resources; all other marketing activities (advertising, selling, market research etc) are costs incurred in anticipation of a return on the sums invested.

Customer attitudes to price

Research shows that:

1. While consumers have a generally high awareness of price, they do not have the perfect knowledge which classical economic theory demands.
2. Awareness of price increases in proportion to the frequency of the purchase.
3. The effect of non-price variables on the purchasing decision is often at least as important as the effect of price.
4. Consumers' perceptions of price are more important in determining the purchasing decision than the actual price.
5. The role of price in the purchasing decision increases in importance in inverse proportion to the available purchasing power.

Differences between the economist's and the marketer's attitude to price

Economists tend to attach importance to price, while marketers tend to attach more importance to non-price variables. The reasons for the apparent dichotomy lie in the historical roots of both disciplines. When classical economic theory was first being formulated, traded goods such as raw materials, bulk foodstuffs and even finished consumer goods were relatively standardised, with no differentiation through advertising and branding. Therefore the major differential was price. Secondly, average income was low and discretionary purchasing power severely limited, which meant that price was the major purchase-constraint.

Marketing, on the other hand, developed at a time when the assumptions of the classic theory were becoming increasingly invalid. As J G Udell says (*Journal of Marketing*, January 1964):

'i) In today's competitive economy, supply – or production capacity – generally exceeds demand; and therefore, nearly all sellers are forced to be either completely competitive or almost collusive in their pricing. Because there may be little or no freedom for a company to deviate from the market price, heavy reliance must be placed on product differentiation and sales effort.

ii) The relatively well-to-do consumers of today are interested in more than just price. They are interested in product quality, distinctiveness, style, and many other factors which lead to both physical and psychological satisfaction. Consumers not only can afford but want product differentiation and sales promotion. From them the consumer receives a great deal of

psychological satisfaction and utility. It is only logical that consumer-oriented managements would choose to emphasize products and sales efforts in an attempt to satisfy consumer desire.
iii) It is through successful product differentiation that a manufacturer may obtain some pricing freedom. Products known to be identical must be priced identically in the market place. A departure from identical prices would result in all patronage going to the seller or sellers with the lowest price.'

Situations in which price is of great importance

Despite criticism of the classical economic theory there are certain situations where price is of critical importance. These are:

1. when the price must be set for the first time for:

    a) a new product;
    b) an existing product being introduced to a new distribution channel, or market;
    c) sealed-bid pricing (jobbing contracts etc);

2. when the firm is considering a price change which is either:

    a) correcting an initial pricing error; or
    b) a change in policy, eg from 'skimming' to 'penetration';

3. when the firm is considering the appropriate reaction to a competitor's price change;
4. when the firm is considering how to price several related items in the product line – product line pricing.

Pricing objectives and policies

Pricing decisions for individual products must be made within the context of an overall pricing policy.

Environmental factors

Type of industry. In general, it is probable that industrial markets will be more aware of price, whereas consumer markets may be more influenced by non-price variables such as branding and advertising.

Structure of industry. Economic theory regarding price under monopoly, oligopoly or perfect competition is relevant to the price setter.

Product category. Primary products are relatively undifferentiated except by price. Secondary products may be differentiated by branding. The demand for tertiary products (services) tends to increase with economic development.

Product offering. The greater the degree of product differentiation the greater the degree of price freedom which the product enjoys. A 'new' product poses unique pricing problems and opportunities, whereas the price of modified and existing products must be related to the price previously charged.

Product line considerations. The relationship between different items in the product line will be reflected in pricing policies. Management must consider how the price of one item may influence sales of another.

Market development. Price elasticity will vary according to the stage in the product life-cycle.

Demand factors. Management must consider the extent to which demand is 'economically' or 'psychologically' influenced by price or non-price factors.

Cost factors. Are economies of scale obtainable? What are competitors' costs? Have competitors more or less pricing freedom than we have?

External factors. These are political – prices/incomes policies etc; legal – laws relating to price-fixing; economic – obviously the most significant external influence on prices; and technological – substitute products, processes and relative prices.

Competitive factors. Price may be used as a barrier to entry, but a high price may attract competition or substitution.

Distribution factors. Attitudes of channel members to firm's pricing policy may be a potential area of channel conflict. Total distribution costs (TDC) are directly affected by volume, and volume may be determined by price.

Resource inputs. These include suppliers – high prices may lead to pressure for higher suppliers' prices; unions – high profits lead to greater wage pressure; and finance – investors influenced by price policies (inverse of unions).

Other executives. Salesmen will tend to favour low prices, easier sales. Finance may tend to favour high prices. Advertising will be concerned with consistency of relationship between price and 'image'. Production will tend to favour price policies which lead to steady production flow.

Time span of decision. For how long must price be maintained? What is the competitive response likely to be in the short run and the long run?

Corporate and marketing objectives

These must be clearly identified before pricing decisions are made, because marketing objectives are derived from corporate objectives and pricing objectives are derived from marketing objectives.

Maximise return on investment. For the profit maximisation objective, management must consider the time-span of the decision; is profit to be maximised in the short term or the long term?

Consolidate sales/market share. The emphasis is likely to be on service, distribution and building customer loyalty rather than on price.

Expand sales/market share. The following points must be considered:
1. Price elasticity – is demand for the product elastic or inelastic?
2. Price awareness of customers – do they know the present price?
3. Communication needs – can customers be effectively informed?
4. Competitive response – how will customers respond?

These will determine whether or not a change in price is likely to expand sales.

Achieve price/margin stability. Non-aggressive policies and pricing at industry norm will be essential.

Early cash recovery. The emphasis will be on quick return on investment, because of liquidity problems or uncertain (eg political) future. Dependent on elasticity of demand and firm's competitive position, the price is likely to be high.

Enhance prestige, quality image. The price is likely to be set high, to enhance consumers' price/quality perceptions.

Meet or discourage competition. Competition-oriented pricing policies, aimed at creating barriers to entry (usually low prices), will be needed.

Active price policies

Having identified corporate and marketing objectives, the firm can determine whether price is to play an active or passive role in pursuing these objectives: in other words, whether price is to be the key element in the marketing mix.

Skimming. Pre-conditions for this are:
1. a sufficiently large segment whose demand is relatively inelastic, not sensitive to a high price;
2. unit costs relatively unaffected by small volume, because there is a high ratio of variable to fixed costs;

3. high price is unlikely to attract competition.

The policy aims at 'skimming the cream' by taking advantage of the target segment's willingness to pay a high price, and is therefore essentially discriminatory. Its advantages are that it enhances the quality image and leaves room for adjustment if the initial price is too high.

'Sliding down the demand curve', experience or learning curve pricing. This is an initial high price, lowered as the market develops and productive capacity expands. It is similar in effect to skimming, but not deliberately discriminatory.

Premium pricing. This is a high price policy designed to enhance a quality image.

Fraction below competition. This is a low price policy aimed at maintaining constant competitive pressure, but without attracting too strong a competitive reaction.

Penetration. Pre-conditions are a highly price-sensitive market, with high price elasticity; economies of scale in production or distribution being available, because of low ratios of variable to fixed costs; and a low price which is likely to discourage competition. The policy is to charge a low price, and communicate this fact widely, so as to stimulate market growth and capture a large share.

Discrimination. Price discrimination occurs when two or more prices are charged which do not reflect a proportional difference in marginal costs. Examples are discrimination by product version, when two versions of the same product (eg 'standard' and 'luxury' versions) are disproportionately priced, relying on the psychological effect of price differentiation to obscure the true difference in quality and marginal cost. Discrimination also occurs by place (eg theatre seats are differently priced although cost is evidently the same), by time (eg out of season fruit) or by customer (eg tourist).

For a price discrimination policy to succeed there must be a segmented market with varying demand intensities, no opportunity for low price group to resell to high price group, little chance of underselling and the cost of segmenting and controlling the market must not exceed the marginal increase in revenue gained by price discrimination. Short-term gains must be balanced against possibility of long-term loss of customer goodwill.

Stay-out policy. Jobbing firms with full order books may not want extra work, but may be afraid not to bid for contracts in case they are not invited to bid in the future. Under these circumstances they may enter a very high bid with the deliberate intention of losing the contract, but, if they win, with sufficient profit margin to sub-contract.

Put-out pricing. This is very competitive pricing aimed at eliminating a weak competitor.

Deviations from pricing policy

The following should be seen as variations from the basic pricing policy, or as short-term deviations to achieve some short-term objective.

Planned deviations: discounts. A price discount may be given to some customers for carrying out some agreed function (eg reciprocal advertising) or for performance of an agreed contract (eg payment within a specified time). There are also trade discounts, being the difference between the retail price and the lower price charged to wholesalers or stockists. Quantity discounts may also be offered which pass on economies of scale to the firm's customers.

Planned deviations: promotional pricing. In conditions of oligopoly most promotion is defensive rather than aggressive. Price-off deals are short-term deviations from the normal price aimed at maintaining brand share.

Unplanned deviations: price-cutting. A 'price war' may be described as an unplanned deviation from the normal pricing policy.

Passive price policies

Price leadership. The market leader is not free to pursue active price policies if the custom of the industry is to 'follow the leader', thus negating the effect of price differentials. Thus any pricing policy which leads to informal collusion (charging the industry norm) or formal collusion (price agreements) is passive within the industry. This is typical of oligopolies. Clearly, such policies may not be passive so far as substitute products are concerned.

Price calculation in theory

Example (from Kotler, *Marketing Management, Analysis, Planning and Control*).

Assume the following demand schedule:

Price (P)	Quantity demanded (Q)	Revenue (R)
£0	1,000	£0
£50	800	£40,000
£100	600	£60,000
£125	500	£62,500
£150	400	£60,000
£200	200	£40,000
£250	0	£0

Now, assume the following costs:

Fixed costs   £6,000
Variable costs   £50 (per unit)

All the information in our example can be displayed as in the following table:

P	Q	R (P x Q)	Fixed cost = £6,000	Variable cost = £50 x Q	Total cost	Profit/ loss
£0	1,000	£0	£6,000	£50,000	£56,000	– £56,000
£50	800	£40,000	£6,000	£40,000	£46,000	– £6,000
£100	600	£60,000	£6,000	£30,000	£36,000	£24,000
£125	500	£62,500	£6,000	£25,000	£31,000	£31,500
£149*	404	£60,196	£6,000	£20,200	£26,200	£33,996
£150	400	£60,000	£6,000	£20,000	£26,000	£34,000
£151*	396	£59,796	£6,000	£19,800	£25,800	£33,996
£200	200	£40,000	£6,000	£10,000	£16,000	£24,000
£250	0	£0	£6,000	£0	£6,000	– £6,000

It can therefore be seen by inspection that profit is at a maximum when price = £150. (* In the above table prices either side of £150 are shown to illustrate the point.)

Theoretically, therefore, if the demand schedule and costs are known it is possible to calculate the profit-maximising price.

However, the model is open to criticism on various grounds. It assumes a short-run profit maximisation objective; one product only; that fixed and variable costs are known; and that the firm has perfect knowledge of its demand schedule. It ignores the effect of any non-price variables such as distribution channel members, advertising, competitive activity etc.

Nevertheless, provided that it is recognised that the model simulates reality but does not portray it exactly, it is an essential starting point in understanding the relationship between price, demand, costs, revenue and profit.

Price calculation in practice

In practice, pricing techniques may be divided into three groups: cost-oriented, demand-oriented and competition-oriented

Cost-oriented techniques

'Cost-plus' and 'mark-up'

The technique is:

1. Calculate full unit cost (ie labour and material plus overhead contribution).
2. Add agreed percentage.
3. Total equals price.

'Mark-up' is the term usually used in the retail trade, whereas 'cost-plus' is the term usually used in manufacturing, particularly non-routine contract work such as jobbing. In general:

1. Mark-ups vary inversely with unit cost: the higher the cost, the lower the mark-up.
2. Mark-ups vary inversely with turnover: the higher the turnover, the lower the mark-up.
3. Mark-ups are higher on private brands, rather than manufacturer's brands.
4. Mark-ups vary directly with brand loyalty: the higher the loyalty, the higher the mark-up.

But these 'rules of thumb' are frequently varied, eg 'seasonal' mark-ups (which are discriminatory and demand-oriented, reflecting some customers' willingness to pay a higher price for out-of-season goods).

The advantage of mark-up or cost-plus pricing is that costs are more readily known than demand. The technique is simple and convenient. If it is the custom of the industry, prices will tend to be similar, thus minimising price competition.

However, there are serious disadvantages; first, the calculation of full costs necessarily involves more or less arbitrary decisions about overhead allocation, and the base of the pricing calculation is therefore suspect; and, secondly, the technique takes no account of demand factors and therefore there is a risk that potential profits may be forgone.

Target pricing

The technique aims to provide a target rate of return on total costs at a specified volume. The procedure is:

1. Estimate the percentage of capacity at which the factory is expected to operate in the period under consideration.
2. Calculate the costs of producing this output. Specify the target rate of return.
3. Mark-up total costs by the target rate of return. The result equals the target revenue.
4. Divide the target revenue by the number of units planned to be produced.

The result equals price $\left(\dfrac{R}{Q} = P \right)$

The technique is open to criticism because it uses an estimate of sales volume to derive price, ignoring the fact that price may be a major determinant of sales volume. The technique is therefore more suitable when demand is inelastic.

Break-even pricing

Given the objective of breaking-even within the time under consideration, management may calculate the prices. The pricing decision then becomes a matter of judgment 'Can we achieve break-even sales quantity at this price?'

The break-even formula is:

(Revenue) PQ = (Total costs) Cf + CvQ

in which P = price, Q = quantity, Cf = fixed costs, and Cv = variable costs per unit.

Demand-oriented pricing

While it is theoretically desirable to base price decisions on demand factors rather than merely cost factors the problem is that demand is much more difficult to quantify that cost. At best the firm may have an idea of the general shape of its demand curve, but this is liable to constant fluctuation under the influence of competitive activity, advertising effort, the appeal of substitute products, environmental factors etc.

However, some idea of 'yesterday's' demand curve is better than nothing and when this is coupled with more or less precise knowledge of the firm's costs and informed judgment of the effect of environmental factors upon demand it is possible to calculate a 'very good' if not an 'optimum' price.

Obviously, the difficulties of estimating demand are greatest when the product is new, because there is no historical data upon which judgment may be based. The best that the firm can do is to study the demand for the most similar alternative product.

The techniques of demand estimation are by direct interview, by experiment, and by statistical inference (see Chapter 9).

Direct interview

Respondents are asked to say what price they would be prepared to pay for the test products, or to indicate the price-range within which they would expect the product to be located. Care must be taken to avoid biased answers, by masking the true object of the enquiry and by inviting price comparison between the test product and established, known products.

Nevertheless, the technique is open to the criticism that it is unrealistic, because it forces respondents to make a judgment in the test situation rather than the 'natural' shopping situation. (See marketing research.)

Experiment

Price is varied in different stores or test-markets or at different times and the resultant demand is analysed to discover the 'best' price. The major difficulty is that none of the other independent variables (competition, advertising, promotional activity, the economic environment, the weather etc) are likely to remain constant throughout the experiment and it is therefore very difficult to isolate the effect of price alone. The use of a control group is desirable. The technique is also potentially dangerous in that the goodwill of the customers who pay the highest prices may be lost, if they learn that the product is sold elsewhere at a lower price (compare with 'price discrimination'). This danger may be overcome by a laboratory, rather than a field, experiment. (See marketing research.)

Statistical inference

Historical data regarding price and sales volume, together with other relevant information, is analysed in order to determine the relationship between price and demand. Once again, the difficulty is to isolate the price/demand relationship from the effect of other variables.

Demand-oriented pricing techniques are:

1. Discrimination. Different prices are charged to different markets or segments in order to maximise the gain from different demand schedules.
2. Product line pricing. Setting prices which will achieve objectives (profit or sales) for the whole line.

    The relationship which exists between products in the product line is interrelated demand, where demand for one affects demand for another. This may take the form of:

    a) Substitution. One product is a real or perceived substitute for the other; for example, if A is perceived as far superior to B, but its price is perceived as only slightly higher, demand will drift towards A. If A is perceived as only slightly superior to B, but its price is perceived as far higher, then demand will drift toward B.
    b) Complementary. One product complements another, so the sale of one may assist sales of the other. It may be more profitable to sell one product at a very low margin in order to earn high profits on the other. This is similar to 'loss-leaders' in retailing.
    c) Interrelated costs. Where each product is expected to absorb a share of the overhead costs (absorption costing), a change in the demand for one will affect the company's cost structure and may give a false impression of relative profitability. Absorption costing is an accounting practice which has no relevance to demand; in marketing marginal costing is always preferable because this gives a truer measure of the relationship between demand, supply, costs and profit.

Sealed bids

In most government markets and some other organisational markets suppliers are commonly invited to 'tender' for the supply of specified goods. Their tenders, representing the lowest price at which they would be willing to supply the goods, or perform the contract, are normally required to be submitted by a specified date in sealed envelopes (to avoid corrupt practices). The envelopes are opened, usually in public, and the contract is awarded, all else being equal, to the lowest bidder.

As it is a 'winner takes all' situation, with no opportunity for subsequent price adjustment, the pricing decision is based on own costs (partly) and analysis of competitors' likely bids (primarily). The latter may involve analysis of competitors' past bids, and analysis of the present state of competitors' business – whether order books are relatively full or empty. It may be assumed that the competitor with a full order book will bid high and the competitor with an empty order book will bid low. The problem with sealed bid contracts is that a low bid may win the contract, but forgo potential profits; a high bid may lose the contract and incur losses arising from the costs (product research, preparing drawings, analysing costs, etc) which may be necessary to prepare the bid.

Chapter Eleven

The distribution function

- The functions of distribution

- Division of distribution functions

- Structure of distribution – channel dimensions and structure

- Channel stability

- Choice of channels

- Channel selection

- Alternative strategies for controlling channels

- Distribution institutions in the UK

- Physical distribution

- The total distribution cost concept

The functions of distribution

The distribution functions are:

1. concentration and dispersal of goods;
2. accumulation, assortment and allocation of goods;
3. transfer of possession of goods from buyers to sellers;
4. the physical care and protection of goods, while in storage or transfer;
5. contact, negotiation and transaction between buyers and sellers;
6. transfer of ownership of goods from buyers to sellers.

These functions are necessary because of the imbalance of place, time and form which exist between where, when and what the producer produces and where, when and what the buyer wishes to purchase. Types of imbalance and the associated distribution functions are summarised in the table opposite.

Type of imbalance	Associated distribution function
Geographical, spatial (goods are produced in one place but consumed in another)	Physical storage and transportation
Time lags (goods are produced at one time but consumed at another):	
1. Seasonal production, regular consumption (eg frozen foodstuffs)	
2. Regular production, seasonal consumption (eg Easter eggs, fuel)	
3. Continuous production, periodic consumption (eg washing powders)	
Large scale production, small scale consumption (goods are produced in large quantities but the unit of consumption is the individual, family, company etc)	Breaking bulk and storage Concentration, sorting, dispersion
Specialised production, various consumption (the industrial producer achieves economies of scale through specialisation, but the consumer wants variety, eg shopping basket contains products from several specialist industries)	Accumulation, assortment, allocation
Exchange processes:	
1. production for consumption	Contact, negotiation, transaction
2. income for expenditure	Ordering, invoicing, payments, receipts
(Marketing manages the exchange function, the distribution system provides a mechanism for exchange between producers and ultimate consumers)	
Communication, information	Provision for information
(Sellers need information about the market and the market needs information about products. The distribution system helps to	(Information about products must flow downwards from the producer, information about markets must flow upwards from provide such information) the distributor.) Note that the communication system is often inadequate because producers and distributors have different objectives. Marketing research and advertising take place to bridge this gap

Division of distribution functions

The functions and associated management are normally divided into commercial, channel distribution – those functions which facilitate buying and selling, and enable the transfer of ownership and possession to take place – and physical distribution – the function of storing, protecting and transporting goods.

Structure of distribution – channel dimensions and structure

Economic factors

Each 'sort' represents a different stage in the distribution channel; therefore additional stages will be introduced so long as economies can be gained (and by-passed if they incur diseconomies). Economies may be achieved by spreading the fixed cost of making a sale or delivery over more product units, or by reducing the number of transactions.

Channel dimensions and structure

Channel structure (the number of vertical intermediaries) and dimensions (the number of sales outlets), and stability, are dependent on these economic factors.

Channel dimensions and structure are concerned with:

1. intensity/selectivity (ie number of sales outlets):

   a) Intensive distribution refers to a large number of sales outlets, achieving the most intensive coverage of the market.
   b) Selective distribution refers to a small number of sales outlets, catering for the exclusive needs of a particular market segment.

2. directness (ie number of institutions in the vertical channel):

   a) Direct distribution describes the producer selling and delivering the goods directly to the customers.
   b) Indirect distribution describes the situation when the goods pass through various intermediaries ('middlemen', such as wholesalers and retailers) from the producer to the customer.

Determinants of the intensity or selectivity of distribution

Intensity and directness tend to vary inversely. The characteristics of selective distribution are:

1. significant selective market (see 'speciality goods');
2. high retail margins;
3. effective barriers to competition (eg through branding);
4. consumers willing to spend time searching for their preferred brands expect service;

5. no or limited economies of scale in distribution;
6. low (infrequent) replacement rate by consumers.

The characteristics of intensive distribution are:

1. low income mass market;
2. low margins;
3. anticipated early competition (no barriers);
4. consumers spend little time, expect little service;
5. considerable economies of scale in distribution;
6. adequate capacity (for expansion);
7. high (frequent) replacement rate by consumers.

Thus, for example, convenience goods such as biscuits, which are consumed frequently, have relatively low margins available for distribution, require no sales service and, where the customer is not prepared to spend much time on searching for his preferred brand, will demand intensive distribution and the channels will tend to be indirect (producer, wholesaler, retailer, customer).

Conversely, shopping goods such as furniture, which are bought infrequently, have relatively high margins available for distribution, require considerable sales service and where the customer is willing to spend time and effort in shopping around, will demand more selective distribution, and more direct channels (producer, retailer, customer).

Industrial goods may have either a high or a low replacement rate (office stationery or manufacturing plant) but because the number of potential buyers is limited, distribution is likely to be direct (producer, user, or producer, stockist, user).

Reducing the number of transactions

The following grossly simplified examples illustrate how economies may be achieved by a reduction in the number of transactions.

Example 1 (selective distribution)

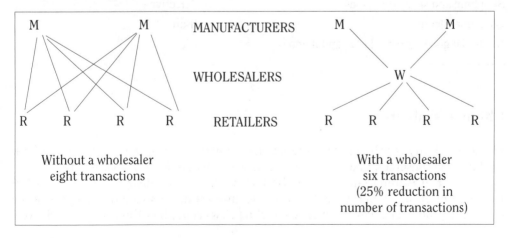

Example 2 (intensive distribution)

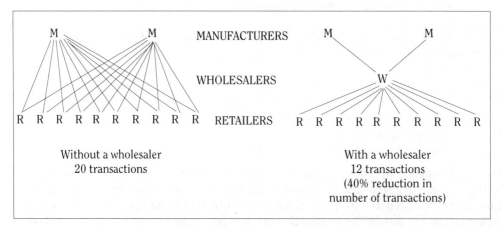

Without a wholesaler
20 transactions

With a wholesaler
12 transactions
(40% reduction in
number of transactions)

Notes:

1. In Example 2 (intensive distribution) the existence of a wholesaler is more likely to be economically justified than in Example 1 (selective distribution).
2. Intensity and directness tend to vary inversely because the greater the number of outlets, the greater the economies which can be achieved by reducing the total number of transactions by using the services of a wholesaler. This is a very important point to remember, because 'middlemen' are often accused of leading to higher consumer prices. In fact, in intensive distribution systems, they help to keep total costs down.

    In general, the pattern to be expected is:

Type of goods	Distribution structure
Convenience goods	Intensive
Shopping and speciality goods	Selective
Consumer goods	Indirect
Industrial goods, particularly capital goods	Direct

Channel stability

Channel stability is achieved when functions are performed to the satisfaction of both producer and consumer. Under these circumstances functions become routinised.

However, it is important to recognise that producers and distributors are (usually) independent of each other; they have a mutual interest in satisfying the demands of the ultimate customer but they may have conflicting views about how this should be achieved.

Furthermore, as both producers and distributors are seeking profits it is evident that the total profit which can be earned by a distribution system must be shared between them and this can lead to conflict.

In general it can be said that, while 'competition' exists in distribution systems on the horizontal level, 'conflict' exists in the vertical channel.

Examples of competition

Mail order catalogues compete with traditional retail outlets, as does 'mixed merchandising'. This is diversification by retailers to spread high fixed costs, and to create competition with traditional outlets. Examples are:

- specialist magazines through associated outlets, competing with traditional newsagents (eg *Amateur Photographer* in camera shops, *Practical Householder* in DIY shops);
- car care products through driving schools, competing with garages etc;
- mortgages through banks, competing with building societies.

Conflict and power in distribution channels

The existence of conflict in vertical distribution channels is the result of the struggle for the balance of economic power between producers and the various intermediaries. Changes in distribution structure, and therefore in channel stability, are largely caused by changes in the relative power of producers, intermediaries and consumers.

The sources of power are financial, purchasing power; market position power ('brands' versus 'own label'); and information power.

Financial, purchasing power

The relative bargaining power of manufacturers and, for example, multiple retailers depends on relative size and extent of dependence on each other. Thus, the growth of the multiple has tended to shift bargaining power away from the manufacturer. Because the multiples can buy in bulk at favourable terms they are able to compete strongly with the independent retailer; because of their size and because there are relatively few of them manufacturers also tend to supply them directly (similar to industrial markets).

This has threatened both the small, independent retailer and the wholesaler, who have therefore come together to form 'voluntary groups' (see below) for mutual protection. This development has been welcomed by manufacturers as it creates outlets in competition with the multiples, and therefore shifts power back towards the manufacturer.

Market position power

Market position power is dependent on user/customer loyalty to the brand or to the distributor. Thus:

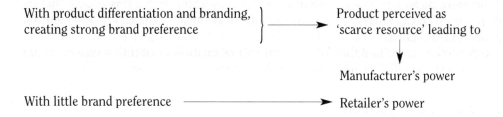

Branding and distribution

The development of retailers' own brands is an attempt (often very successful) to shift customers away from dependence on manufacturers' brands, and thus increase the retailers' power.

A manufacturer has three broad options open to him: to sell his entire output under his own label, to sell his entire output to a retailer(s) under the latter's label or to sell to both markets in an effort to obtain the best of both worlds.

Own label brands may be defined as consumer products manufactured by, or on behalf of, distributors and sold under the latter's name or brand exclusively through his own outlets. *Manufacturers' brands* can be defined in similar fashion as products bearing a manufacturer's name or brand which are not sold or supplied exclusively to any single retail organisation.

A manufacturer with little market power may elect to sell his output direct to retailers if it appears that the cost of establishing an independent brand will be beyond his financial capacity or the attendant benefits are not justified. The own-label producer is faced with conditions comparable to those of the producer in the perfectly competitive market. He is given (or agrees to) a predetermined specification at a fixed price to manufacture a product, so the lower the cost at which he can supply it, the greater his profit. He will have no advertising to do and research costs will be at a minimum because innovatory products will be developed by those companies offering manufacturers' brands. He will also face tough competition from other manufacturers who have the expertise and excess capacity and, as entry into the industry is usually easy (the products being simple to manufacture), the producer is in a weak negotiating position relative to the distributor and may find there is little alternative to becoming dependent on the distributor.

Manufacturers' brands stand the best chance of success when:

1. Sizeable economies of scale are available to them in their production process.
2. The cost of entry into their market is high.
3. Their prices are not high enough to attract competitors.
4. There are significant differences between competing brands, encouraging the promotion of product differentiation through the generation of a competitive image.

From the distributors' angle, own label brands have several advantages:

1. They are usually 10 to 30 per cent cheaper than manufacturers' brands.
2. They promote store loyalty and company identification.
3. They offer a higher profit margin than manufacturers' brands.
4. They enable the distributors to control quality, prices and inventories.

Information power

Retailers are close to customers and therefore may have better information about customers' preferences, attitudes etc. The manufacturer's use of marketing research is one way to restore 'the balance of power'. The advent of credit card shopping means that the retailer can match purchases with the actual identity of the customer, which is very powerful information.

Choice of channels

The choice of channels is of great importance. The main considerations are:

Consumers' characteristics

1. preferences for: supermarkets, self-service, mail-order, door-to-door salesmen or status shops;
2. preferred method of payment: cash, credit or hire purchase;
3. geographical location;
4. usage: heavy, light, frequent, occasional;
5. brand loyalty: how much effort will they exert to locate a specific brand.

Product characteristics

Perishable products such as meat, fruit and vegetables need short channels, perhaps direct from producer to consumer like 'pick your own' strawberries, but the need for breaking bulk and assortment necessitate wholesale markets such as the new Smithfield and Covent Garden sites.

Channel selection

The stages in channel selection (by the manufacturers) are:

1. Determine the role which distribution is to play within the marketing mix. The role will usually be that of supporting a key strategy (for example, the strategic objective of selling typewriters for home, rather than office, use might be supported by distribution through furniture stores etc.

   Occasionally distribution is the 'key' strategy (as when brewers enter the wine trade to gain greater economies from their distribution channels, the pubs).
2. Consider product characteristics and consumer preferences as in 'Choice of channels', above.
3. Select appropriate channel(s). The following factors should be taken into account in selecting distribution channels:

   a) territory covered by the distributor;
   b) financial status – stocks held and ability to extend credit;

c) product knowledge;
d) market knowledge;
e) size and quality of distribution sales force;
f) training which may be necessary;
g) display facilities;
h) warehousing facilities;
i) maintenance and after-sales service, which the distributor can provide;
j) contracts with or access to key customers (particularly in the case of industrial stockists);
k) complementary products sold by the distributor;
l) relative importance of manufacturer's product to distributor's other lines – the manufacturer is aiming at 'manufacturer dependence'.

4. Persuade intermediaries (selected channel members) to co-operate.
5. Help the distributor to sell the product by:

a) advertising, promotional support;
b) offering reasonable margins;
c) contributing to or organising joint advertising and promotion;
d) providing training;
e) giving prompt, reliable service;
f) giving replacement guarantees.

6. Manage and control channels by:

a) mutual visits;
b) training of distributors' staff;
c) supplying information about products;
d) encouraging involvement in decision-making;
e) obtaining regular reports.

As indicated above, distributors are independent of manufacturers and therefore the methods of control have to be by persuasion and motivation and mutual self-interest. Contracts such as agency agreements may be drawn up between manufacturers and distributors but these are only as strong as it is in the interest of both parties for them to be.

Alternative strategies for controlling channels

The wish to have greater control of the channel leads to alternative vertical strategies:

1. Integration forwards: the manufacturer acquires ownership and control of distributors, eg breweries and pubs.
2. Integration backwards: the distributor takes over control of the supplier.
3. 'Extending' forwards (positive co-operation with retailers, rather than control, eg consignment stocks, promotional support).

Distribution structure in UK

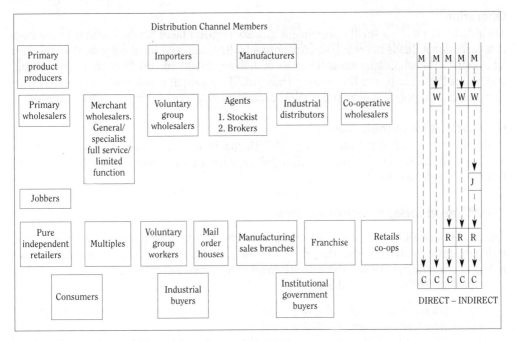

Distribution institutions in the UK

Independent merchant wholesalers

The functions of these are locating source of supply, collecting, storing, breaking bulk, assembling and dispersing (to retailers or industrial users). Their advantages are economies of scale obtained from spreading the fixed costs of the above functions over several units.

There is a tendency towards specialisation, limited line and limited function because of diseconomies from slow-moving lines. Independent merchant wholesalers are declining because multiples do their own wholesaling, there is a tendency towards direct distribution and voluntary retail groups are being formed.

Rack jobbers

These provide and service 'racks' or shelf-space in supermarkets with non-food lines. In return for a commission on sales, rack jobbers accept full responsibility for selecting, displaying, promoting, supplying and delivering and stock-controlling. Thus the retailer avoids risk involved in purchasing. The manufacturer gains a sales outlet more attractive to retailers than the manufacturer's own salesmen. The hiring of shelf or floor space by manufacturers is particularly identified with department stores, which are diversified retailers of luxury and durable consumer goods.

Cash and carry wholesalers

Operation

The retailer (typically a small independent grocery retailer) takes his own vehicle to the cash and carry depot, loads his requirements onto a trolley, and pays for the goods at warehouse 'check-out'. The wholesaler saves the costs of delivery, credit and credit control, and selling, and passes these savings to the retailer, thus providing a small retailer with a relatively low-cost source of supply and enabling small independent retailers to compete with multiples.

Implications for manufacturer

Cash and carry is a distinct retail segment with special needs. It enables manufacturers to pursue a 'direct to retailer' distribution policy, with a convenient and economic way of reaching a large number of small retailers.

Unaffiliated independent retailers

The majority of all UK shops are owned by independent retailers, many of whom are 'pure' independents; in other words, they do not belong to any group or chain. Therefore small independent retailers are still the main channel of distribution for consumer goods but they are declining. The reasons for the decline are:

1. Large retailers (especially multiples) enjoy the benefits of low-cost bulk purchase, passed on to consumers in lower prices.
2. Declining numbers of consumers are willing to pay for personal service because of increasing social acceptance of the low-cost self-service concept;
3. The small retailers' lack of capital inhibits modernisation and therefore inhibits greater efficiency and lower operating costs.

Therefore this system has evolved:

1. 'defensive alliances' – voluntary groups and chains (see below);
2. growth of cash and carry (see above);
3. continued need for local expert sales assistance or after sales service. (See 'Sole traders' above.)

Voluntary groups and chains

('Group' means one wholesaler with several retailers; 'chain' means several wholesalers, several retailers.)

Operation

An independent wholesaler(s) and retailers agree to co-operate to combat the greater buying power of multiples. The wholesaler(s) organises central purchasing, advertising, promotion and capital finance.

The retailers undertake to purchase most of their merchandise from the group wholesaler (usually about 60–80 per cent). The retailers gain economies from the bulk buying power of the group; freedom to concentrate on selling-out, rather than buying-in; and lower physical distribution costs through group rationalisation.

The wholesaler gains a guaranteed market.

Implications of voluntary groups for manufacturer
1. economies of distribution (bulk deliveries, few outlets);
2. low sales representation and management costs;
3. easier credit control, fewer bad debts;
4. groups' more aggressive pricing and promotional policies benefit the manufacturer;
5. groups tend to favour brand leaders, therefore it is harder for the little-known brands to gain acceptance;
6. groups discourage sales direct to retailers in the group; thus the manufacturer tends to lose contact, influence and control at the retail level.

Mail order houses

Operation
The mail order distributor solicits orders by press advertising, direct mail or agent/catalogue. The distributor receives the orders and despatches the goods by post.

Reasons for growth
1. the difficulty of retail shopping in congested areas with car parking problems (mail order was originally designed to serve the needs of low-density rural areas of the American mid-west and expatriate British families in India – it is still successful in Scandinavia for similar reasons);
2. working housewives, with little time to 'shop around';
3. the customer's willingness to accept the validity of printed advertising as adequate product information – supported by an unconditional money-back guarantee.

Distributor's gains and losses
The distributor gains because display and personal selling costs are eliminated; he has direct contact with the market; he has lower fixed costs of warehousing etc (no need for expensive 'prestige' sites) and a lower wages bill, because of more capital-intensive storage and handling; and there are no intermediary margins.

He loses because of relatively higher return rates (goods not accepted by customers) and bad debts.

Costs of mail order incurred relative to other distribution methods

Printing	high
Advertising	high
Agents' commission	high
Warehouse	low
Administrative costs	low
Distribution	high

Doorstep selling

The goods concerned are either:

1. high-value products (eg vacuum cleaners, double-glazing, encyclopaedias). Team of trained 'high pressure' salesmen saturate an area before moving on to another area. There is no 'repeat-purchase' element involved; or
2. low-value, regular purchase 'convenience' products (eg Avon Cosmetics, Kleen-e-ze). Regular, low-pressure coverage is used to build up a regular clientèle.

In-home selling

This is similar to low-value regular purchase doorstep selling (see above) but supported by a party (usually a coffee or tea-party) organised by a private hostess. The agent demonstrates the product, and the hostess usually receives a free gift or other small incentive. It is suitable for products requiring demonstration and some personal selling. Savings in intermediary margins are offset by relatively high representation and promotional costs. Typical products include Tupperware, cosmetics and lingerie.

Manufacturer's own branch

This is suitable where trade is characterised by frequent product changes or by a very wide range of product styles, and where the limited stock-holding facilities of retailers would weaken the advantages to be gained by such policies (eg shoe manufacturing and retailing). Pre-conditions are available capital to invest in retailing, and the ability to maintain the goodwill and business of traditional retailers while establishing own branches.

Franchising

From the customer's point of view franchising appears the same as a manufacturer's own branch (see above), but in fact the franchiser does not own the retail outlet; he merely grants the retailer a licence to use his name and processes under the terms of the franchise agreement.

The franchiser provides product and marketing know-how, site selection, equipment, training, publicity, and use of the brand name.

The franchisee (retailer) pays a fee, royalty or share of the profit; agrees to accept the franchiser's policies regarding price, product range, advertising, inventory and sales quotas; only stocks and sells the franchiser's product (eg Kentucky Fried Chicken, ice cream vans).

The franchiser gains exclusivity, control at retail level, rapid expansion with minimum capital (compare with 'Manufacturer's own branch', above), and aggressive dealers with local expertise.

Agents

This is a frequently misused term, taken to include both representatives who take title to goods and those who do not (eg especially export agents). Strictly, an agent (in law) does not take title to the goods, but merely negotiates business between two principals, the buyer and the seller.

'Agents' who do take title may be either industrial stockists carrying competing lines or industrial distributors. In the latter case, manufacturer and distributor negotiate an exclusive 'agency' agreement, defining territory covered by the distributor, lines carried, and an agreement not to carry competitive lines. The manufacturer agrees not to supply competing distributors.

Both types of agent relieve the manufacturer of the cost of servicing small accounts.

Brokers

Brokers do not carry stock. They negotiate the terms of sale between manufacturer and stockist, and receive a commission on the deal.

Jobbers, factors

These carry stock, maintain warehouses and despatch goods. They are of advantage to the manufacturer:

1. where the narrowness of the product line cannot support its own sales force;
2. where there exists a specialised market for some item in the product range;
3. to extend the operation into markets too remote for its own sales force;
4. particularly for new product launches (through contract salesforce hired ad hoc).

Industrial agent

The manufacturer's agent acts on behalf of one principal (or a few related but uncompetitive principals) and is paid by commission on sales. He carries out the functions of personal selling, negotiating delivery, service and (occasionally) price. He submits market reports, handles enquiries and complaints and agrees (through the agency agreement) not to handle competitive lines, in return for which the manufacturer agrees not to supply competitive dealers, unless a prior agreement exists.

The selling agent

He is usually employed by small firms unable to finance their own marketing and salesforce: a complete sales and marketing department 'for hire'. His functions may include marketing research, promotion, selling, invoicing, and credit control.

Physical distribution

The major functions of physical distribution are storage and warehousing, and transport.

Storage and warehousing

Warehouses or depots are needed to store finished goods, or parts. They can hold 'buffer' stocks when goods are not made to specific orders, or they can be strategically located close to major conurbations to provide quick service to customers. They can also be used to break down bulk into smaller units, by shipping the goods from the factory to the depots in bulk to reduce transport costs.

Transport

Goods can be transported by road, rail, canal, sea and air, or a combination of several of these methods. Goods which deteriorate rapidly, or which are required quickly will need fast transport such as road or air. Many of these goods, such as frozen meat and other frozen foods, need refrigerated transport. Other goods such as oil, petroleum, chemicals, gases, flour, sugar, use bulk container type transport (road tankers, and tanker type vessels at sea and on canals).

Decisions required

The major decisions therefore relate to the number and size of warehouse facilities, and the mode of transport.

The total distribution cost concept

The relevance of the decisions to marketing is that the level of customer service, and therefore the level of sales profitability, is affected by the distribution service given to customers. Therefore it is a mistake to make physical distribution decisions in isolation, eg a decision to reduce costs by reducing the number of warehouses may be a mistake because the resultant loss of sales may cost more than the potential saving.

The traditional approach to physical distribution required the distribution manager to decide on the best way of transporting manufactured products to their destinations. The modern approach starts from the other end of the process with management studying its target markets, their purchase behavioural patterns, their geographic locations, their individual and collective requirements for speed and frequency of delivery and the services offered by competitors. Only then will the company arrive at an integrated and comprehensive set of decisions on the distribution channels to be used, the location of its warehouses, inventory levels and the nature of the transportation to be used to move the products to its customers, in order to achieve the highest level of customer service commensurate with lowest costs.

From the point of view of customers, the level of service they receive from suppliers is likely to be a dominant factor in their purchase deliberations, including:

1. the speed with which a normal order is implemented;
2. the speed with which an urgent request can be met;
3. the condition in which the goods are received;
4. the replacement of defective goods; and
5. installation and after-sales service: whether these are free or charged.

The concept of analysing the effect of distribution costs on total profitability is known as the 'total distribution cost' concept. The costs involved are as follows: number, capacity and location of warehouses; inventory carrying costs; customer service; obsolescence; alternative facilities use; transport costs; and costs of capital in stock or in transit.

Number, capacity and location of warehouses

These should be related to the levels of customer service. Increasing the number of warehouses in order to improve customer service will obviously increase warehouse costs, but the cost of 'lost' sales will decline. The optimum level of customer service (ie number of warehouses) is when the total of these costs is at a minimum.

Inventory carrying costs

These costs are reduced by more frequent turnround (smaller inventories, smaller warehouses, lower rents, lower capital costs etc). Equally, a distributor's cost will also be reduced by more frequent turnround. Thus, it may pay the total system to use a more frequent, more expensive mode of transport (air rather than sea, road rather than rail) in order to reduce inventory cost, and therefore total costs.

Customer service

Sales are affected by stock outs and unreliable delivery. Therefore it may be necessary to hold buffer stock to avoid disappointing customers.

Obsolescence

Obsolescence arises when goods have been produced but the market no longer wants them. Obsolescence costs arise from over-stocking to ensure customer service. In the case of perishable or fashion items obsolescence can arise from extended delivery times; more rapid delivery, although itself more expensive, may eliminate such costs.

Alternative facilities

The opportunity-cost of warehousing is the investment in production, promotion etc which must be forgone. ('Opportunity-cost' is a term used by economists to demonstrate that the cost of any purchase is an alternative purchase which has to be forgone.)

Transport costs

Different modes of transport have different fixed and variable costs associated with them. Often the more 'modern' modes such as air and road have lower fixed costs (fewer goods 'tied up' in stock, easier documentation etc) but higher variable costs (freight per tonne-mile) than older modes such as sea and rail. The transport cost decision can therefore be treated as a breakeven problem.

If the volume is expected to be small it will pay to use air (low fixed costs, high variable cost), but if it is large it will pay to use sea (high fixed cost, low variable cost).

Costs of capital in transit

Different modes of transport have different associated cash flows. The faster the mode the sooner the customer can be invoiced and payment received; on the other hand, the faster the mode the higher the freight cost. Therefore the cash flow of alternative systems should be calculated. (Clearly these should be discounted to present-day values.)

All of the above costs should be analysed together and for their effect on each other and total business profitability before making physical distribution decisions.

Chapter Twelve

The promotion function

- Introduction
- Personal selling
- Size of sales force
- Organisation of the sales force
- Sales staff
- Management of the sales force
- Advertising
- Structure of the advertising industry
- Planning an advertising campaign
- Public relations (PR)
- Sponsorship
- Branding
- 'Ethics' of advertising

Introduction

The promotion function of marketing has six major sub-functions:

1. personal selling;
2. media advertising;
3. sales promotion;
4. merchandising;
5. public relations;
6. sponsorship.

The balance and composition of these sub-functions together make up the promotion mix.

Note: where this chapter refers to a 'salesman' or 'salesmen' it includes both salesmen and saleswomen.

Personal selling

Except where a company sells by mail order, personal selling is an essential component of the promotion mix, because it is the only component which can actually negotiate and agree the contract of sale. The personal salesman:

1. locates and contacts new potential customers;
2. informs the customer about the product: its price, special features, availability etc;
3. persuades the customer to prefer the product;
4. answers questions about the product;
5. demonstrates the product;
6. negotiates the contract of sale;
7. builds the relationship between the customer and salesman's company;
8. deals with complaints;
9. provides his company with information and advice about his area and his customers.

Size of sales force

The number of salesmen required depends on the number of existing potential customers that have to be covered, the frequency of calling, the average time spent with each customer, and the time spent in travelling from one customer to another. In the consumer goods field, selling to retail shops, the salesman is making repeat calls to collect orders and generally maintain good relations with the buyers. Regular repeat calls on fixed routes in a clearly defined territory is the mode of operation. Salesmen selling consumer goods in densely populated areas where there are many retail shops can make up to 20 calls per day.

A salesman in a rural territory may be able to average only ten calls per day because of the distance he has to travel between each customer. At the other extreme a company selling goods to organisational buyers has fewer customers and their salesmen may well spend several hours with each customer on each visit, averaging two or three calls per day, or less. The salesman's role in organisational or industrial markets is frequently that of a technical consultant; his work is more varied and more flexibly planned than the work of the consumer goods salesman.

Organisation of the sales force

Sales forces are usually organised on one of the following bases:

• by geographical area;

- by type of product;
- by type of customer;
- by size of customer;
- by type of industry;
- some combination of the above.

The basis most commonly used is geographical area. Each salesman is assigned a specific territory, the boundaries of which are clearly defined after considering:

- the number of existing and potential customers;
- the frequency of calls on these existing and potential customers;
- the physical geography of the territory;
- the concentration of customers and the distances to be travelled;
- the mode of transport to be used, eg on foot, by car, by public transport;
- the capacity and calibre of the individual salesman, eg the type of workload appropriate to the salesman's age and experience.

Sales management should try to achieve an equitable workload for each individual salesman, and each should receive the reward for his effort accordingly. If commission schemes are to be used, the rate of commission should be related to the sales target and potential of each separate territory. Areas of equal geographical size are not necessarily of equal sales potential.

Sales staff

Selection

The sales manager, perhaps in collaboration with the personnel department, must draw up a detailed job description for their business's own particular type of salesman and a specification of what attributes, characteristics and qualifications their 'ideal' salesman should have.

A good salesman needs:

- good health;
- energy;
- determination;
- faith – in himself, his company and its products;
- empathy, to identify with the customer and his needs and think as the customer does;
- intelligence, to manage his territory efficiently, to absorb the product and market his knowledge, etc;
- an acceptable personality;
- a good appearance;
- equanimity.

Training

The types of training should include;

- induction training – an introduction to the company;
- product training – anything from one week to two years depending on the technicalities and complexity of the product, eg a single product like food, packed in a can, sold to retailers: one week; a range of machine tools: up to two years, possibly in addition to a five-year apprenticeship in the machine tool industry;
- training in sales techniques – covering the techniques of pre-approach, approach, presentation and/or demonstration, negotiation, and closing the sale;
- training in administration – covering form filling (expenses, order, requests, complaints etc), report writing etc;
- field training – up to three months accompanied by a sales trainer (could be a specialist trainer from headquarters, sales manager, area manager, sales supervisor, senior salesman) who should be competent to train;
- continuous training – consists of meetings with superiors to discuss progress and problems, lectures by specialists, refresher courses, sales meetings, sales conferences, films sales bulletins etc to develop salesmen to their full potential.

Remuneration

There are three main types of remuneration for salesmen:

1. Salary only: this offers security but offers no incentive for extra effort. This type of remuneration is paid where a large part of the salesman's job is of a servicing and advisory nature, typically in industrial markets, or senior sales staff.
2. Salary plus commissions on sales: the payment of a basic salary gives the salesman a sense of security but he needs to put in effort to get additional pay by way of commission.
3. Commission only: usually very high commission is paid; the goods may be speciality goods where there are no repeat sales and the salesman has to push hard to make a sale. This type of remuneration does not create loyalty to the company. It is more common in consumer markets.

Management of the sales force

The sales manager needs to be able to forecast, plan, organise, motivate, communicate and control. He requires the ability to lead, motivate and inspire a predominantly extrovert group of salesmen, needs skill in handling human problems and may carry out all or some of the following tasks:

The planning function

The sales manager:

- provides short-term, intermediate and possibly long-term forecasts on which company targets can be based.
- plans sales campaigns in accordance with marketing objectives;

- plans to achieve a profit of X per cent on sales;
- estimates costs for budget purposes;
- analyses markets to identify new uses for existing products, and new product prospects – in collaboration with market research;
- plans the overall activities of area managers, sales supervisors and salesmen in the areas, or regions;
- plans and organises the sales office according to the expected workload;
- plans and assigns territories for effective coverage;
- sets standards of performance and conduct for all sales staff, both internal and external;
- plans his own time;
- plans regular sales meetings;
- plans for the general development and promotability of sales staff and salesmen;
- plans to use available support services where applicable.

The action function

The sales manager:

- recruits quality salesmen with future potential;
- continually trains new and experienced salesmen in basic skills, attitudes and interpretation of company policy;
- strives to motivate and develop each salesman to his full potential;
- considers dismissals, recommends promotions, demotions and transfers;
- keeps salesmen informed of new products, advertising campaigns etc;
- directs the activities of area managers, regional managers, sales supervisors, salesmen and sales office staff;
- supports and directs the application of sales, advertising and promotion programmes;
- consults with salesmen and customers on problems of service, delivery etc;
- maintains discipline;
- continually encourages salesmen, especially after failure (to get a big order or contract), provides incentives, and gives recognition for a job well done;
- liaises with heads of other departments such as production, finance, accounts, design, personnel;
- works in close conjunction with the marketing manager and the heads of other working functions – advertising and sales promotion, marketing research and distribution.

The control function

The sales manager:

- maintains standards of performance and conduct;
- establishes the frequency of calls on each class or type of customer, and adjusts the frequency when necessary;
- maintains an efficient record system to provide a quick analysis of performance for each product, area and salesman;

- periodically and systematically evaluates the performance of each individual salesman, and the overall performance of the sales staff;
- constantly reviews performance;
- determines in what areas performance is progressing according to plan;
- investigates the causes of lack of progress against plans and takes remedial action;
- controls costs as per budgets.

Advertising

Definition

'Advertising is a non-personal communication directed at target audiences through various media to present and promote products, services and ideas, the costs of which are borne by an identifiable sponsor.'

Structure of the advertising industry

A diagrammatic representation of the structure of the advertising industry appears below and on the opposite page.

Advertisers

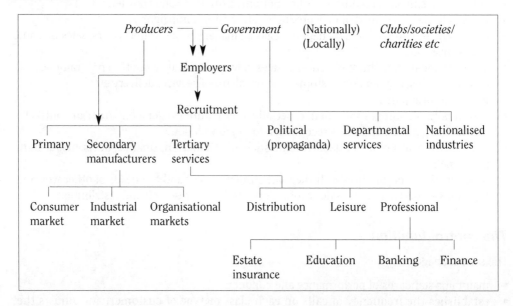

Agencies

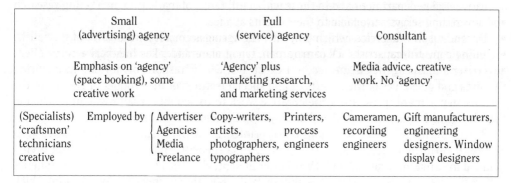

Media Owners

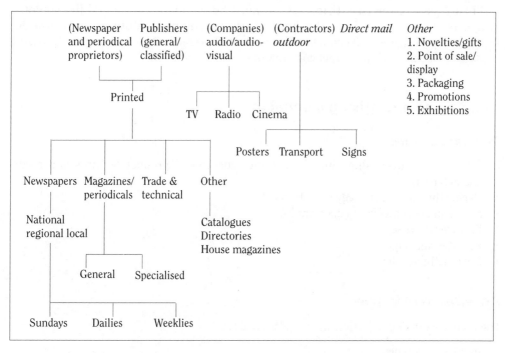

As shown above, advertisers include manufacturers and suppliers of goods and services, government departments, clubs and societies and private individuals – in other words anybody with something to communicate, who is willing to pay media owners to carry the communication, is an advertiser. Marketing is concerned with advertising which has the objective of selling a good or service, but the principles are equally applicable to a government department wishing to publicise a public service or to a charity wishing to raise funds.

While advertisers may deal directly with the media owners it is customary to work through an advertising agency. The table shows that there are various types of agency ranging from those who merely take a commission for booking space or time with the media, to those with a creative design department and to those with a full range of marketing, marketing research and advertising services available to their clients at a fee.

Depending on the services which they offer the agencies employ a wide range of specialists, including copywriters, artists, TV cameramen, typographers etc. The link between the client advertiser and the agency is the account executive, who is responsible for communicating the aims and objectives of the advertiser and special features of the product or service to the creative department, presenting the creative work to the client for approval and ensuring that the advertisement is booked and displayed in the appropriate media.

The media break down into various types, printed, audio-visual, outdoor. Each varies in its ability to perform a specific advertising task; eg, a specialist magazine is better at giving detailed information than TV, but TV is better at capturing the attention of a wide audience with a simple, dramatic message. The skill of media selection is choosing the medium which will best achieve the advertising objective at the lowest cost.

Finally, part of the advertising system must be the market itself and the potential customers who make it up. Understanding the customer, his needs, attitudes, and knowledge of what media he is most likely to see, is an essential prerequisite for planning advertising messages that will reach the target customer most cost effectively.

Planning an advertising campaign

The broad stages are:

1. Identify the advertising objectives, target customers, product features and media characteristics.
2. Decide the creative strategy (how to say it).
3. Select and cost media (media planning).
4. Prepare advertisements.
5. Run the campaign.
6. Analyse the results.

Advertising objectives

The main advertising objectives may be classified as:

1. to create awareness;
2. to provide information;
3. to persuade;
4. to remind;
5. to reinforce the purchase decision.

These objectives are closely linked to a model of buying behaviour developed by Lavidge and Steiner (see next page).

This model suggests that customers move through various stages from 'awareness' (of a need), 'knowledge' (of products that will satisfy the need), 'liking' and 'preference' (for particular brands) to 'conviction' (that it is the best buy) and 'purchase'. Subsequently they experience 'satisfaction' which the advertiser will wish to 'reinforce', or 'dissatisfaction' which the advertisers will wish to overcome.

Therefore the advertiser must identify which state his target customers have reached (through marketing research – the product life-cycle concept is also relevant to this analysis) and set his advertising objectives accordingly. Thus, a new product will seek to maximise 'awareness' and 'knowledge' of what it can do, whereas a more established product will seek to reinforce brand 'preference' and the market leader, with a major market share to defend, will 'remind' regular customers.

The more precise advertising objectives are made, the easier it is to plan a campaign and the easier it is to measure the effectiveness against set objectives. From the objectives detailed targets must be derived.

Thus targets should be set in quantifiable terms, eg, if an advertiser discovered, through marketing research, that 30 per cent of the market were aware of his product and 10 per cent had tried it he might set his advertising targets as follows:

'After a three month campaign 50 per cent of the market should be aware of the product and 15 per cent should have tried it' – the success of the campaign, measured through marketing research, will therefore be determined by the extent to which these targets are actually achieved.

Consumer behaviour (adapted from Lavidge and Steiner)

Consonance	REINFORCEMENT	Reminder ↑	Posters TV etc
Advertisements minimise cognitive dissonance		SATISFACTION	
Motives Advertisements stimulate desires, persuade, stimulate purchase	PURCHASE	↓ CONVICTION	POS (point of sale) Retail store ads Display Price-off deals 'Last chance' offers etc
Emotions Advertisements change attitudes, persuade	PREFERENCE	↑ LIKING	Argumentative copy 'Image' Status advertisements etc
Thoughts Advertisements create awareness and provide information	KNOWLEDGE	↑ AWARENESS	Announcements Slogans, jingles Descriptive copy

Identifying target customers

When advertising objectives have been established, the next stage is to identify target customers, with particular reference to their reception of alternative advertising media. A 'consumer profile' should be identified, covering the typical customer's age, sex, social class, income, geographical location and size of family; also needed are his attitudes to product, company, advertising etc; readership of newspapers and magazines; TV-watching characteristics, etc.

Industrial buyers should be broken down into three groups:

1. Who influences the purchase?
2. Who decides the purchase?
3. Who makes the purchase?

Thus, for example, while technical information about a new machine would be communicated to engineers through the specialist magazine, financial information about it might be communicated to financial and managing directors through the business press – in both cases being followed up by the personal salesman calling with detailed technical and financial information and a demonstration.

Identifying product features

The third stage is to specify, in detail, the unique features of the product which are to be communicated. These features may be physical and technical or, as is the case with many consumer products, impressions or images. The unique features, (known as USP – Unique Selling Points) are the basis (or copy-platform) on which the copywriter bases his work, the designer his illustration, etc.

Selecting the media

When the objectives of the campaign, the customers which the campaign must reach and the message which the campaign must get across have been identified, the final stage is to select the media most suitable for achieving the given objectives.

Different media have different characteristics, as follows:

*   geographical coverage (eg national or local newspapers);
*   social class (eg readers of the *Daily Telegraph* or *Sun*);
*   age group (eg viewers of TV at different times of the day);
*   power to reach special groups (eg hobby magazines);
*   ability to inform (eg posters on railway stations);
*   ability to demonstrate (eg cinema film);
*   high impact (eg whole page advertisements in newspapers or dramatic music on TV);
*   repetition (eg slogans on radio or TV);
*   timing (eg seasonal campaigns at Christmas, peak viewing hours on TV or Saturday newspapers advertising gardening and leisure products).

Merchandising

Included in the 'promotion mix' is the manner in which the product is presented for sale, including packaging, point of sale material, display stands etc.

Promotions

Also included is a specific sub-function known as 'promotions'. This is also known as 'below the line' advertising, with media advertising being 'above the line'.

Sales promotion aims to persuade non-users to try the product and regular users to increase their purchases, by offering some inducement to buy, over and above the benefits implicit in the product itself. Such inducements may be financial (eg a money-off offer), tangible (eg a 'free' gift) or intangible (eg an opportunity to enter a competition).

Every promotion aims to achieve either a long-term growth in brand share, or a short-term gain in brand share, or both. Obviously, the new or recently introduced brand (in the launch or growth phase of the product life-cycle) aims to achieve long-term growth. This can only be achieved by inducing non-buyers to 'try' the product in the hope that they will buy again. The emphasis will therefore be on promoting small pack sizes (to induce trial), or 'free' sample (buy one, get one free), or competitions etc where the prize is so attractive that regular users of competitive brands will be induced to switch brands.

By definition the established brand in a mature or saturated market cannot hope to achieve long-term growth. Its aim must be to achieve short-term gains at the expense of the competition, recognising that many of the buyers so induced to buy will revert to their original brands after the promotion.

The difference in the two objectives (long-term growth and short-term gain) is reflected in their relative cash flows: the long-term growth promotion is expected to yield profits in the future, through the increase in loyal customers, whereas the short-term gain promotion must yield profits immediately.

All promotions (except for new products) have some element of subsidy to the regular user (the regular user benefits from the money-off offer, the free gift etc). It is therefore important to segment the market into users and non-users, identify significant characteristics of non-users and try to aim promotion specifically at them.

Public relations (PR)

Definition

The Institute of Public Relations defines public relations thus:

> 'Public relations practice is the deliberate, planned and sustained effort to establish and maintain mutual understanding between an organisation and its public.'

It is therefore broader in scope than marketing alone, embracing such areas as:

1. Corporate and financial PR: this projects the image of an organisation and helps to maintain its position in the stock market. Product sales may be affected by favourable or adverse publicity about the company and its financial management.
2. Community relations: environmental issues such as pollution, land development, establishment of new factories etc will affect the public's attitude to the company and, by association, its products.
3. Industrial relations: publicity about industrial relations may affect attitudes toward product quality and deliveries.
4. Relation with opinion leaders: the attitudes of the general public towards a company and its products may be influenced by opinion leaders such as politicians, journalists, broadcasters, teachers, leaders of specialised institutions, societies or other 'pressure groups', who, in turn, may be influenced by their relationship with the company.

Public relations is sometimes erroneously called 'free advertising'. While it is true that it is not paid for in the sense that an advertisement must be paid for, it does represent a considerable investment of man-hours in identifying opportunities for good publicity, identifying risks of bad publicity, devising publicity material, press statements etc, maintaining good public relations with influential persons and institutions etc.

Public relations must be planned and co-ordinated in conjunction with marketing.

Sponsorship

A comparatively recent addition to the range of promotional tools is sponsorship, when a company contributes to the cost of public entertainment such as a concert or sporting event. Often the sponsor awards a substantial cash prize to the winner of a sporting event, and sometimes he pays the costs of a team or an individual player.

The objectives of sponsorship are:

1. favourable publicity for the product or service (eg Cornhill Insurance sponsorship for cricket Test matches);
2. association of the image of the sport with the product (for example, the Milk Marketing Board sponsored women's netball, thus overcoming poor publicity for milk, particularly among potential young mothers);
3. obtaining publicity otherwise not allowed (eg Embassy sponsorship of snooker obtains extensive TV coverage, despite the ban on TV advertising of cigarettes).

Branding

The subject of branding has already been introduced in Chapter 8, where the importance of researching and selecting an appropriate brand image was seen to be an important stage in new product development. This section examines branding from the advertising and sales promotion point of view.

There are three fairly distinct sequential levels of brand acceptance by consumers. The aim of each brand manager is to reach the final stage.

Brand familiarisation. The first task is to create an awareness of a new product by the target audience and, in the early stages of its life-cycle, this is usually attempted through intensive advertising in selected media, distribution of free samples or a low-priced introductory offer. The short-term target is to persuade customers to test-purchase, in the hope that they will then become regular purchasers.

Brand preference. Brand preference is the second stage of brand acceptance and occurs when consumers deliberately choose a specific product in preference to competitive products. Unless the brand reaches this second stage, there is no chance of it ever becoming successful.

Brand loyalty. This is the last stage in brand acceptance and occurs when a customer wants this product and no other. If it is not immediately available he will either search for it or defer his purchase until it is available.

It will be apparent that these three stages are closely linked to the advertising objectives of creating awareness, persuading and reminding. It will also be apparent that the three stages relate to the different types of market, convenience goods and speciality goods.

'Ethics' of advertising

There are two main arguments against advertising: that it is wasteful of scarce resources, and that it is immoral. Because this is a controversial topic, students are advised to be familiar with the arguments on both sides.

Wasteful

The 'wasteful' argument falls into two main streams:

1. that advertising persuades people to consume things which are unnecessary and therefore wastes natural resources;
2. that advertising adds to costs.

It is true that mankind is consuming the resources of this planet at an ever-increasing rate, threatening our future existence. But is this the fault of advertising? It is rather the fault of human greed – by consumers who want a 'better' life and by financiers in pursuit of short-term profits.

Ironically, it is the technique of mass persuasion advertising which may become necessary to reverse the trend of over-consumption.

In other words, it is not advertising which is to blame, but the use to which advertising is put.

The 'adding to costs' argument is more complex. If cost accountants insist on treating advertising as a variable cost then it is apparent that some arbitrary percentage will be included in the direct cost of each unit – and passed on to the customer in the selling price.

However, if advertising is treated as an investment, as it should be, then increased sales will lead to lower average unit costs, which can be passed on to consumers in lower prices.

It follows that where the market has potential for growth, advertising benefits the consumer, but where the market is saturated, advertising is merely defensive and therefore does not increase sales and reduce costs. It is noticeable that critics of advertising tend to concentrate their argument in oligopolies such as the detergent market.

Immoral

The 'immoral' argument also takes two main streams:

1. that advertising persuades people to consume 'immoral' products such as tobacco or alcohol;
2. that advertising uses 'immoral' appeals, such as sex.

So far as the first is concerned, advertising does not claim any moral standpoint – it is up to society to decide what may be morally and legally sold. Equally the use of sex in advertising merely reflects current social values.

This section has only hinted at the main issues. There are many others, such as:

- the role of advertising as a barrier to entry, which protects the jobs in the defended industry;
- the extent to which informative advertising is legitimate but persuasive advertising may not be;
- the corruption of aesthetic values;
- the use of advertising in 'good' causes such as charities;
- the role of advertising in under-developed economies, which may persuade people to waste their limited wealth on unnecessary or harmful products.

Students are advised to prepare their own arguments for and against advertising.

Chapter Thirteen

Production and purchasing

- Introduction

- Design, research and development

- Types of production system

- Problems facing the production manager

- Quality control

- Stock control (or inventory control)

- Purchasing department

Introduction

We have seen that all business decisions are ultimately based on demand. We have seen that marketing research attempts to identify the form (quality) of product which customers need and are most likely to buy and sales forecasting attempts to measure the quantity which they will be most likely to buy within a given planning period. The production function is the business function which is responsible for translating this information into saleable products or services.

(Services. It is important to note in passing, that, although this chapter is primarily concerned with manufacturing tangible goods, the same principles apply to service industries; they must also identify customer needs and decide what quality and quantity of service they should 'produce'.)

How does this work in the production function? In the long term the company must analyse:

- long term macro-environmental factors, particularly the economic and technological environments;
- corporate objectives;
- corporate resources, already available or which will be needed.

From this analysis two fundamental strategic decisions must be made:

1. capital investment in factory and plant, which will depend on long-term forecasts of demand and therefore, the capacity which should be available to satisfy that demand;
2. location. Closely linked to the capital investment decision is the decision where to locate the business – this is discussed more fully in the next chapter.

Capital investment decisions lay down the nature and shape of production processes, in some cases, for many years. For instance, the steel and chemical industries involve complex capital-intensive manufacturing processes, so significant increases to their basic production capacities can only be introduced by completely rebuilding or re-equipping their existing plant or building a new one as it is rarely practical and economic to add piecemeal extensions on to existing plants. Obviously, investment decisions of this magnitude are not made very often and even when they are, it can take several years from the date of the original decision for the plant to become fully operational. The investment decisions are virtually irreversible except over the very long term because land and buildings and plant and machinery are geared to a certain product, production processes and level of output. By contrast, the light engineering and clothing industries are usually labour-intensive, their capital investment relatively low and even fundamental changes in their operational processes can often be introduced without too much upheaval. They also tend to be more responsive to changing demand patterns and their equipment is more readily adaptable to the new demands.

In the short term (up to one year, dependent on the nature of the industry), production management must:

1. plan and carry out a programme of machine replacement and maintenance;
2. maintain sufficient stocks of raw materials, parts and finished goods to satisfy the anticipated demands of marketing;
3. hire, and manage, workers with appropriate skills and in sufficient numbers to produce the planned number of goods.

Daily, production management must respond to the actual orders as they are received from the sales department and schedule or reschedule production so as to meet promised delivery dates or other priorities.

Organising the production function involves:

1. deciding the type of production method;
2. planning the factory layout and organising the work into departments or sections, depending on the amount of specialisation involved in the production of the finished goods;
3. controlling, which involves the setting of measurable targets, particularly quality standards and levels of output per man or per shift, and monitoring performance on a regular basis. This is discussed under 'quality control' below.

Design, research and development

Having considered this overview of the production function we must now examine the work of two departments – design, and research and development – which are closely related to production but should be considered independently.

The design department is where new product concepts or product modifications are designed.

The research and development department is where technical research takes place. This research may take three forms:

1. Pure research: this is relatively unusual in business, where most research has a clear commercial application in mind. However, some major companies, particularly in the pharmaceutical industries, do finance pure research – from which they often gain commercially valuable 'spin-offs'.
2. Product research and development: if the company is 'market-oriented', a substantial part of the research and development department's work will be concerned with researching and developing new products, the idea for which may have originated from marketing research findings.
3. Process research and development: the technical problems of making goods as cheaply as possible may be investigated by research and development, sometimes to the extent of designing their own machinery.

Types of production system

Although all production systems differ somewhat, there are two basic types of production systems. One is based on intermittent production and the other is based on continuous production.

The type of production system adopted depends on the type of market being served, the marketing strategy and the type of product.

The most extreme example of intermittent production is 'jobbing', where the company produces specialised products to each customer's individual specification. At the other extreme is continuous production, or 'flow' where the company produces a homogeneous product for mass sales and distribution. In between is 'batch', where the company varies the flow-line to produce different versions of the same basic product. Evidently 'jobbing' and 'batch' production are related to 'segmentation marketing', whereas 'flow' is related to 'undifferentiated marketing'.

In terms of the *unit cost* of the product or service being produced, the continuous system usually yields lower unit costs than does the intermittent system. This is because of economies of scale in which quantity discounts can be taken, specialization of labour can be utilized, and special-purpose machines can be used.

The *storage costs* per unit are usually lower in continuous-production systems, because the raw materials are in storage a short time and the goods-in-process inventories move through the plant very rapidly.

The *time required* for production is usually shorter in continuous-production systems than in intermittent-production systems. In an automobile plant, a home-appliance plant, or a paper plant, products move rapidly through the production process. In assembly-line operations, found in mass-production industries, it is not unusual to find automobiles, appliances, or other products coming off the assembly line every few minutes. On the other hand, products in intermittent-production systems are usually in a state of partial completion for several days or several weeks.

In most continuous-production systems *fixed-path materials-handling* equipment is used. Fixed-path equipment includes conveyors, chutes, rails and robots. Since a continuous-production system is based on one or a few standard products which are manufactured with a predetermined sequence of operations, relatively inflexible materials-handling devices can be used effectively. The most dramatic recent development in continuous production systems is the use of robots controlled by computer, to replace many traditional human labour tasks.

In intermittent-production systems, variable-path materials-handling equipment is prevalent. Since various products are produced and a great deal of flexibility must exist in the system, portable materials-handling equipment is essential. Examples of this type of equipment are carts, lift trucks, skids and cranes.

There is usually a significant difference in the amount of money invested in intermittent- and continuous-production systems. Because of special-purpose machines, fixed-path materials-handling equipment, and costly control mechanisms, as well as the larger scope of operations, the continuous-production system usually requires a larger capital investment than does the intermittent-production system.

In general, continuous-production systems utilize special-purpose equipment, whereas intermittent-production systems use general-purpose equipment. The general-purpose machines in intermittent production provide greater flexibility in terms of products which can be produced than is the case of continuous-production systems.

Finally, the marketing characteristics of companies which use continuous-production systems often differ from those of intermittent-production systems. With intermittent production, the marketing effort is directed toward getting and filling individual orders for varied products. In continuous production, the marketing effort is expended in developing distribution channels for the large volume of output and persuading the customers to accept standardized products. For example, refineries and paper plants produce certain grades of gasoline and paper, and it is difficult for the consumer to obtain another grade unless he can purchase a sufficiently large volume to justify the expense of changing the continuous-production process.

Problems facing the production manager

External pressures

These include:

- shorter product life-cycles which have created the need for speedier introduction of new products;
- industrial over-capacity;
- expansion of inter-industry competition or substitution (eg plastics replacing wood and aluminium and man-made fibres replacing natural fibres);
- broader product ranges;

- delivery ex-stock for spare parts and replacements;
- higher quality and reliability specifications, combined with lower costs and selling prices.

Internal pressures

Internal pressures on the production function can influence product design, material handling, plant layout, production scheduling and control, inventory levels, cost control, job evaluation and wage systems as well as unit and total production costs.

The most common internal pressure points on production are:

- increased mechanisation;
- a higher proportion of service personnel (ie maintenance men, production controllers, progress chasers, material handlers) and a correspondingly low proportion of direct workers, out of the total labour force;
- the requirement for senior personnel to be qualified, hence the need for training instead of reliance on 'experience only';
- determination of wage and salary levels, when the individual contributions of different jobs cannot be isolated;
- a growing dependence on computing staff and facilities;
- attempting to meet the needs of the workforce for more challenging and satisfying work.

Quality control

No matter how carefully marketing has priced and advertised the product the final determinant of whether customers buy – and keep on buying – the product is product quality, including design. This means that the production function has a responsibility to the market – the responsibility to maintain control of quality.

Responsibility for quality control takes two forms:

1. The commercial responsibility is the simple one of maintaining quality at the level which will satisfy customer expectations, and minimise customer complaints.
2. The legal responsibility is the 'duty of care' which all businesses have towards their customers.

Quality control must be maintained at all stages of production:

1. incoming raw materials and parts must be inspected;
2. processes must be regularly examined;
3. machinery must be maintained;
4. workers must be trained;
5. work in process must be examined periodically;
6. finished products must be inspected before they leave the factory.

Clearly, it is not possible to inspect every single unit, particularly where goods are produced by flow production. Therefore work must be sampled according to statistical standards. Goods involving the safety of customers, such as car brakes or dangerous drugs, must be sampled more rigorously than other less critical items.

Stock control (or inventory control)

Inventories

Inventories fall into two broad categories.

Raw material and work in progress inventories

The primary purpose of inventories is to insure the manufacturer against shortages of raw material and work in progress which could delay production. As it is expensive to hold stocks, most companies attempt to minimise their stockholding, but it may be even more expensive if the company runs out of stocks and costly plant and workers are left idle.

Finished and semi-finished goods

Stocks of finished and semi-finished goods are held to cater for fluctuations in customer demand. These inventories act as buffers, as it is easier to even out production levels over the long term. Stocks will be built up in periods of low demand and run down during high demand. Where customers are offered a range of options on a basic product, the company may stock partly finished goods which can then be built to individual customer requirements.

Stocks

Stocks in all forms, raw materials, work-in-progress and finished goods often represent a disproportionate amount of the working capital of a business.
 Stocks will be held for some or all of the following reasons:

- to take advantage of bulk discounts;
- to run the factory more efficiently by keeping production at a steady rate;
- to provide reliable customer service;
- to decouple individual processes from each other;
- to produce economic production runs on equipment.

Stocks in any form tie up company capital, so the fundamental question has to be asked: is the cost incurred by holding stock justified by the benefits derived from that stock?
 Computer technology has led to the development of 'JIT' (Just In Time) inventory control systems which try to minimise the cost of holding inventory by making materials, parts and finished goods available at the time when they are required for the next stage in the production and distribution system – no earlier, because that means unnecessary stock, and no later, because that causes unnecessary delay.

Fundamental considerations

Stock control must attempt to balance two opposing costs:

1. When to order?
2. How much to order?

For the first, ordering frequently will reduce the amount of money tied up in stocks (by maintaining lower stock levels), but increasing the fixed costs associated with placing orders. For the second, large orders will reduce the order costs and take advantage of discounts but will increase the capital tied up in stocks.

Variety reduction or standardisation

Before discussing stock control systems it is important to point out that no stock system, however complex, can be justified for controlling the level of items which should not be stocked in the first instance.

The best starting point for any stock system is a *variety reduction; standardisation* exercise. Elementary checks of the stock items will often reveal considerable duplication of similar items. Only when the range of stocked items is at a minimum, consistent with production requirements can stock control be considered to be effective.

When to order

Refer to the accompanying Figure 1, which demonstrates stock movement over time.

The point on the graph marked ROL (reorder level) is the level to which we should theoretically allow the stocks to fall before placing an order for replacement.

The 'lead time' represents the period of time required by our supplier before delivering the order. The rate of consumption during the lead time determines the ROL. For example, if an item is used at the *average* rate of 100 per week and it takes two weeks to deliver a new order then the ROL becomes 200. In general:

ROL = Lead time x Usage rate during lead time

Stock charts
Figure 1

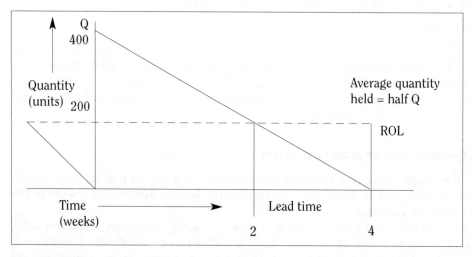

Figure 2

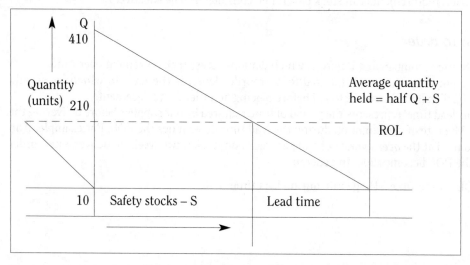

To compensate for fluctuations we must carry a safety stock (Figure 2 above).

Now the ROL was determined by the *average* usage rate, but on *some* occasions that rate was 105 per week. Then we could set the ROL at 210 units. We are now carrying a safety stock of ten units as an insurance against the possibility of a high rate of usage occurring during the lead time. Since the safety stock ties up capital it can be considered as the insurance premium against the possibility of a stock out.

If the usage rate of the item could on a few occasions rise to 140 per week, should the ROL be set at 280 units? For a safety stock of 80 units, is the insurance premium too high? Four points must be considered:

1. on how many occasions usage rate reached a very high level;
2. the service level required – the risk of stock out we are prepared to accept for certain items;
3. the length of the lead time;
4. the price of the item involved.

These factors taken together can be resolved by statistical methods which are outside the scope of this manual. However, an intuitive analysis will indicate some of the main points for determining safety levels. For example:

1. If the item is low priced with fairly low usage we can afford fairly high safety stocks.
2. If the lead time is extended then it is unlikely that maximum usage will occur over the whole of this period. Therefore the safety stock can be reduced.
3. If the item is critical and stock out costs likely to be high, then a high safety stock can be justified.

Deciding how much to order

Deciding the order quantity requires the minimisation of two opposing costs: those of placing the order and holding the stock. The expenses associated with these costs are shown below.

Order costs	Holding costs
Finding a supplier	Loss of interest on capital tied-up
Telephone and postage	Storage space and services
Passing invoices	Deterioration and obsolescence
Checking incoming goods	
Updating stocks and documentation	
(The larger the order the lower these unit costs will be!)	(The more ordered in excess of current usage the higher these costs will be!)

ABC analysis

Any firm operating a stock control system must relate the cost of running the system to the value of the stock item being controlled. Obviously low value items do not justify the same rigorous control (and its cost) as the more expensive items.

A useful approach in attempting to relate the cost of control to the value of the items may be exploited by classifying stocks into categories along the following lines:

1. determine the annual usage value (AUV) of each category of stock item

    eg Price per item x Annual usage = AUV.

2. arrange items in descending order of AUV.

3. accumulate the per cent number and per cent AUV of the items.
4. plot them in a chart form …

The result will be like Figure 3 below. It is usually found that a relatively small proportion of the items account for a relatively high proportion of the total annual usage value. (Pareto's law holds that 20 per cent of all items account for 80 per cent of costs.)

This analysis now gives us a basis for applying the various degrees of control relative to the value of the items.

'A' category items justify strict control. Maintain stocks at minimum. Order in small quantities frequently. Examine stock movement frequently.

'B' category items order on ROL basis. Maintain accurate records. Review order quantities and order points fairly frequently, or when major change occurs.

'C' category items use simple controls.

Figure 3: ABC analysis

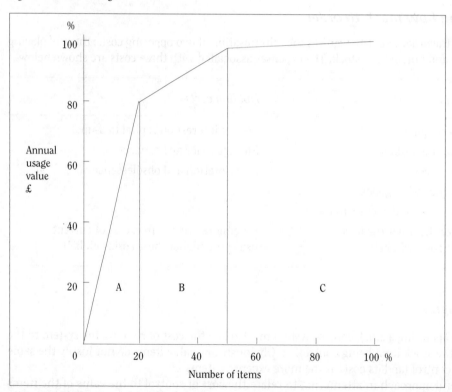

Purchasing department

Planning the re-order of materials, discussed under stock control above, involves careful liaison between the production and purchasing departments and sales forecasting.

We have already seen, in the reference to commodity markets above, that the purchasing department is responsible for:

1. maintaining stocks of materials at the appropriate level;
2. buying material at the lowest possible price, by:

    a) comparing prices offered by competing suppliers;
    b) entering into futures contracts, if appropriate;

3. ensuring the quality of material purchased;
4. (acting under instructions from the user departments) ordering, re-ordering, receiving and making payment for all goods, plant, equipment used by the company;
5. working within the agreed purchasing budget.

Chapter Fourteen

Location and siting of businesses

- Introduction

- Factory location

- Factory siting

- Wholesale and retail location

Introduction

We have seen, in Chapter 13, that the two most important strategic decisions, so far as the production function is concerned, are: capital investment; and location.

We have also seen, in Chapter 11, the importance of not treating physical distribution costs as merely additional costs but of integrating distribution with marketing and stock control decisions.

When considering location the principles explored in Chapter 11 can be extended to include the cost of delivering materials as well as the costs of distributing finished goods to customers. We should now view the business as a total *logistics system*, involving the flow of materials from suppliers into the business, through production processing and out as finished goods to be distributed to customers.

Suppliers ➤ (Materials) ➤ Production ➤ (Finished goods) ➤ Customers
process

Where the production process is located between suppliers and customers depends, to a large extent, on what happens during the production process.

If the production process adds weight or volume it is likely that it will be located close to the market, because the distribution costs outward will be relatively more expensive per tonne-kilometre than the delivery costs inward. Thus, for example, brewers and soft drink manufacturers, who add water to dry ingredients, will locate close to markets.

If the production process reduces weight or volume it is likely that it will be located close to the source of raw materials, because distribution costs outward will be relatively cheaper per tonne-kilometre than the delivery costs inward. Thus, for example, dehydrated food plants will be close to the source of supply.

However, location is not just concerned with the relative costs of transporting materials or

---

finished goods. It is useful to visualise the location problem as a network of conflicting forces and influences pulling in different directions:

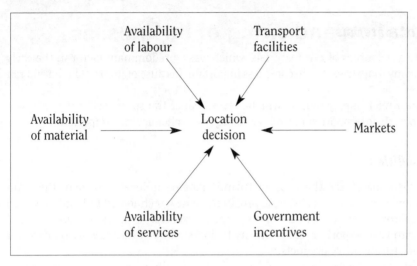

Factory location

The best location will be the one which provides the best compromise after balancing the advantages and disadvantages.

Any decision must be taken with an eye to the future – developing technology, communications and changing attitudes may change what is good location initially into a poor one later.

The principal factors influencing the choice of plant location are: availability of workforce; availability of materials; transport facilities; availability of services; government incentives; proximity to market.

Each of these is dealt with in greater detail in the paragraphs which follow:

Availability of workforce

1. The required number of *suitably skilled personnel* should be available at the right wage level.
2. The presence of a *local supply of unskilled labour* is normally necessary.
3. There should be scope for *development of personnel* potential through local training facilities. In an industrial area staff will move between jobs, and technical colleges and polytechnics will specialise in appropriate training courses.
4. Where a district has developed around an industry it will have acquired a pool of skilled and experienced workers and subsidiary industries and specialisation will exist.
5. If staff are to be relocated with the move of the plant sufficient *housing* must be available.

6. An area offering *good local amenities*, eg shops, entertainments and communications, is much more attractive to staff than a remote one.

Availability of materials

1. Proximity to the sources of raw materials, which was a predominant factor in the early location of many industries, has become less important, because of improved road and rail facilities.
2. A location near main supply sources will, however, reduce transport costs.
3. Proximity to ports for imported raw materials, eg petro-chemicals, is important.

Transport facilities

1. Transport costs may force the manufacturing plant to be located near to the main materials supply or markets. (The close proximity of new technology to London, which represents approximately 15 per cent of the home market size, is proof of this.)
2. For plants with large export orders promixity to docks may be necessary, particularly for those manufacturing heavy products.
3. In the case of export goods which are of low weight and bulk, proximity to a large airport may be equally desirable.
4. The main modes of transport used for supplying the home market are rail and road. Rail operators will provide private sidings, special collection and delivery services, and charge industrial rates related to usage, distances carried etc.
5. The low cost of road haulage, the development of large efficient motorways, and the door-to-door delivery service have made it a very important mode of industrial transport.
6. The development of container freight transport, a combination of road, rail and sea haulage (sometimes including air transport), has helped to reduce the problem of locating the factory. (This does not apply to all industrial processes – some materials/goods are not suitable for containerisation.)
7. In some cases water transport by river or canal may be used to advantage (for example, Ford Motor Company located near the Thames at Dagenham). Water transport is much more widely used on the Continent than in the UK.

Availability of services

The important services which normally need to be taken into account are gas and electricity, water, drainage and waste disposal.

Power supplies

The source of power is no longer a predominant factor in location of industry. The development of the North Sea oil fields and the national gas distribution grid and the national high-tension electricity grid mean that these major power sources are available almost everywhere. One factor which has contributed to the decentralisation of industry over the past 50 years has been the availability of these 'new' types of industrial power.

Water

Water may be required in production processes – steam, cooling, mixing and washing. Its supply and degrees of purity and softness are essential factors in determining location of certain industrial processing plants.

Effluent disposal

The disposal of effluents (eg in the chemical industry) is a major problem and is another factor which may influence factory location. Changing public attitude, environmental pollution regulations and central and local government policy are important further considerations.

By-products

A ready market for any by-products may be a useful incentive. One company's waste product may be another company's raw material.

Commercial services

The existence of banking, advertising and other commercial institutions may be of importance.

Government incentives

A very important factor will be the government aid which is aimed at directing new industry to certain underdeveloped areas. Obviously the policy of central government is dynamic and incentives will be changing constantly (changes which students should keep abreast of). However, some of the important allowances given by the government over the past few years are listed below:

- Government grants may be available for new buildings and works in certain development areas. Particularly large grants may be given in Northern Ireland in order to encourage business there.
- Loans are available, at favourable terms, to firms moving or expanding and are related in size to the number of new jobs created.
- Certain removal grants are available to cover expenses of moving plant and stocks to the new location.
- Allowances are paid for the training and transfer costs of certain classes of employee undergoing training courses.

Proximity to markets

As indicated in the introduction to this chapter this factor may be important if the product is heavy or bulky or if there is no other overriding factor operating. There is a tendency for sub-contractors to set up near large plants which may take all or most of their output, as in the case of the Midlands car industry.

Summary

In deciding the location of a factory there are a great many conflicting influences which come to bear:

1. What type of process is operated?
2. Does this have special requirements concerning power, water or communications?
3. Is there a need to be near to main suppliers because the raw materials are heavy or bulky?
4. Is there a need to be in close proximity to markets because products are heavy or bulky?
5. What are the labour needs?
6. Are there special labour requirements related to experience, training, housing etc?
7. What grants are obtainable from the government?
8. How do these grants affect location decision?

Factory siting

Once a location (or a general area) has been chosen, the actual siting of the factory also presents problems. There will be a variety of conflicting factors here, and the management must consider (assuming that planning permission has been obtained) town site, suburban site and rural site.

The advantages and disadvantages of each of these are detailed below:

Town site

Advantages:

1. Amenities are normally good.
2. Transport facilities are good.
3. Services, eg banks, hotels, are good.
4. Reliable supplies of power and water and adequate drainage services are available.

Disadvantages:

1. The cost of land is high.
2. Rent and rates tend to be high.
3. Skilled labour tends to be available but demand for labour may be high (in a competitive 'industrial' environment). As a result labour turnover may be high.
4. Planning permission may be difficult to obtain. (The Town and Country Planning Act 1962 requires that permission must be obtained for buildings, expansion and alterations to buildings, etc. Such permission may be refused or granted with certain conditions, for example by stipulating size and design of the buildings. Also local by-laws relating to noise, effluent and transport may be more stringent in urban areas.)

Suburban site

Advantages:

1. The cost of land is moderate.
2. Rent and rates are moderate.
3. Amenities are adequate.
4. Skilled labour from the town and unskilled rural labour will be available.
5. Expansion should be easier than in the town and planning permission less difficult to obtain.
6. Transport inwards of raw material and outwards of finished products will be less difficult than at a town site.
7. Services will be adequate.
8. There should be adequate supplies of power and water, and adequate drainage services.

The disadvantage is that the labour force may require transport, parking facilities, etc.

Rural site

Advantages:

1. The cost of land should be lower, and there are certain grants for factory construction available from central and local government.
2. Rent and rates tend to be lower.

Disadvantages:

1. Amenities are normally provided by the company.
2. There will be an adequate supply of unskilled labour (male and female), but skilled workers will normally have to be transported in or have housing provided for them.
3. Expansion at low cost may be possible, although environmental 'attitudes' may result in opposition to any expansion.
4. Transport services are limited. (Transport of materials in and finished goods out may be eased due to the provision of private rail sidings, large unloading bays etc).
5. Commercial services are normally inadequate.
6. Electricity may be available from the grid, but other services such as drainage may be inefficient.

When the area has been decided on and the site selected, the factory itself as a working unit must be considered. Of course, many more factors will be evaluated and deliberated over before construction work starts. (It is worth remembering at this stage that it is often not so much the case of building a *new* factory as of taking over and modifying second-hand premises. The main factors discussed here are applicable to either case.)

The object of the factory is to produce as efficiently as possible, which means that attention must be concentrated on the *factory building* and its *design*, its *layout*, *equipment* and the handling of materials as well as the overall task of production management which comes later when the factory is ready to start working. The design, layout and equipment are, of course, dependent on whether the factory is operating a jobbing, intermittent system or a continuous flow system, as discussed in Chapter 13.

Wholesale and retail location

Obviously, retailers locate their premises close to centres of population; the number of customers and their average purchasing power will determine the size of – and therefore the capital invested in – the shop. Wholesalers can take advantage of low cost rural or 'back street sites'.

The most interesting recent development in retail location is the emergence of the one-stop shopping hypermarket, often located in out-of-town sites. This type of development enjoys considerable economies of scale but its dependence on a car-driving population has serious social consequences for the elderly and the infirm.

Chapter Fifteen

Personnel management and manpower planning

- Introduction

- Personnel manager's responsibilities

- Functions of a personnel department

- Manpower planning

- The process of manpower planning

- Personnel policy

Introduction

The Institute of Personnel Management (IPM) has defined personnel management:

> 'Personnel management is that part of management concerned with people at work and with their relationships within an enterprise. It applies not only to industry and commerce but to all fields of employment. Personnel management aims to achieve both efficiency and justice, neither of which can be pursued successfully without the other.
>
> It seeks to bring together and develop into an effective organisation the men and women who make up an enterprise, enabling each to make their own best contribution to its success both as an individual and as a member of a working group. It seeks to provide fair terms and conditions of employment, and satisfying work for those employed.
>
> In particular, personnel management is concerned with the development and application of policies governing:

> a) manpower planning, recruitment, selection, placement and termination;
> b) education and training;
> c) career development;
> d) terms of employment, methods and standards of remuneration;
> e) working conditions and employee services;
> f) formal and informal communication and consultation both through the representatives of employers and employees and at all levels throughout the enterprise;
> g) negotiation and application of agreements on wages and working conditions: procedures for the avoidance and settlement of disputes.

Personnel management must also be concerned with the human and social implications of change in internal organisation and methods of working, and of economic and social changes in the community.'

Four important points emerge from this definition:

1. Personnel managers have both a line and a staff role.
2. Personnel management may be seen as a system, with inputs, processes and output.
3. Personnel management must follow the same stages which we have already identified:

    a) situation analysis;
    b) setting objectives, policies and targets;
    c) strategic and tactical planning;
    d) organising;
    e) controlling.

4. All managers have responsibility for 'personnel management' in so far as their own subordinates are concerned.

Line and staff role

A personnel manager fulfils a dual role in an organisation. He is a 'line' manager in respect of his own department but has a 'staff' relationship with other departments. 'Line management' is effectively action management, whereas 'staff management' is advisory. Thus a personnel manager cannot make changes in another department directly but must advise the appropriate line manager. This dual responsibility occasionally causes 'personality clashes', particularly as a number of line managers prefer to deal with their own personnel matters. Each personnel manager must resolve these problems by the most appropriate method. However, the specialised knowledge of the personnel manager is generally recognised (eg in industrial relations, law).

Before personnel management had evolved fully, line managers were apprehensive about the apparent interference of the personnel manager in their sphere of authority. Over a period of time a greater appreciation and acceptance of the personnel manager's role has grown up because of his objective assessment of problems, his skill in carrying out negotiation and consultation, and his knowledge of the 'human relations' aspects of the organisation.

Lupton, in trying to justify personnel management as a specialist function, makes the following two remarks:

'The reasonable satisfaction of human needs is an inescapable function of management, and a necessary prelude to efficiency.'

'Personnel management aims to achieve both efficiency and justice. These aims and functions are best carried out by people who are specially trained for the job.'

Personnel management seen as a system

Inputs

Recruitment
Selection
Negotiation
Contracts of employment

The personnel manager
'operates in the labour market'

Processes

Training
Development
Working conditions
Health and welfare
Avoidance and settlement of
disputes
Termination of employment

Managing and maintaining the workforce

Outputs

Performance of work

Productivity is the output from the system

Stages of management (manpower planning)

Situation analysis
This is the identification of the company's manpower needs, derived from corporate plans, sales forecasts and production plans, and an analysis of existing manpower's strengths and weaknesses. In addition there must be an analysis of the availability of labour, particularly as influenced by economic and demographic forces, and a recognition of opportunities or constraints imposed by law.

Setting objectives, policies and targets
Personnel objectives and policies must be consistent with corporate objectives and policies. Targets will include productivity measures and improved labour turnover.

Controlling
This is measuring performance against targets, and taking action to remedy any variances. Such action may include recruitment, training and termination of employment – and so the cycle continues.

Collective responsibility for personnel management

The human resource is perhaps the most important resource used within any business and its management is the responsibility of *all* managers. Personnel managers may use their particular skills and knowledge of personnel management to advise other line managers.

This chapter and the next four examine personnel management from the 'functional line management' point of view. The following two chapters examine the subject of the management of the human resource from a behavioural, non-functional viewpoint.

Personnel manager's responsibilities

The personnel manager is responsible for a number of broad areas including:

1. control and performance of the personnel department, personnel records etc;
2. advising top management on policy;
3. advising 'line management' on particular problems and personnel matters;
4. communicating personnel policy etc to all employees;
5. manpower planning;
6. negotiation and industrial relations;
7. acting as company representative on committees, both internal and external.

Functions of a personnel department

The functions given below are not necessarily all undertaken by personnel departments in all kinds of organisations. They represent, however, the range of responsibilities normally covered by the personnel function throughout industry and commerce and largely reflect practice in those companies where the personnel function has been established for some time.

Employment

This includes:

1. manpower planning;
2. liaison with both the Department of Education and Skills and the Department of Trade and Industry and with any other sources of labour supply;
3. application of company's terms and conditions of employment;
4. interview of applicants, engagements, transfers, releases, dismissals;
5. induction of new employees and checks on their progress;
6. maintenance of personnel records and statistics;
7. employee interviews and consultations;
8. grading of employees, for wage and salary levels;
9. agreeing hours of work and overtime;

10. legislation relating to employment;
11. attendance at appropriate committees relating to employment.

Training and education

This includes:

1. provision of instructors;
2. introduction of new supervision and management procedures;
3. encouragement of further education for employees through correspondence colleges, day release classes, attendance at technical and evening institutes, evening classes and lectures;
4. management development;
5. supervision and control of notice boards and information bulletins;
6. provision of suggestion schemes, works tours and a library; maintenance of a staff magazine.

Wages and salaries

This covers:

1. administration and review of company's wage and salary structure;
2. assessment and control of differential rates and special payments;
3. consultation when necessary with time study or organisation and method consultants in respect of incentives.

Industrial relations

This covers:

1. Negotiation with trade unions;
2. Provision of information on conciliation and arbitration procedure;
3. maintenance of machinery for joint consultation, eg joint production committee, works councils;
4. interpretation and dissemination of company personnel policy;
5. acting as company representative in outside negotiations affecting personnel;
6. advice on administering industrial relations legislation.

Welfare employee benefits (including health and safety)

This includes:

1. administration of canteen, sick club and benevolent and savings schemes;
2. pension and superannuation funds and long-service grants;
3. legal aid and other advice on individual problems;

4. transport, housing, billeting, shopping and other related problems of staff where applicable;
5. provision of social and recreational facilities;
6. application of the provisions of the Factories Act and the Office, Shops & Railway Premises Act;
7. fatigue studies and rest pauses;
8. accident prevention: participation in safety committees, safety education, investigation of accidents, accident statistics etc;
9. administration of workmen's compensation schemes.

Manpower planning

Introduction

Manpower planning is a relatively new activity for most firms. A great deal of attention has been devoted to the planning of other economic resources, such as capital or raw materials, but the importance of planning for manpower has been overlooked. This is now changing. One reason for this is that in recent years labour supply has become a critical factor in the operation of many companies.

Since labour costs make up a substantial part of the total running costs of many firms, it is important to ensure that labour resources are utilised as effectively as possible. The ability of the firm to compete successfully may well depend on how accurately labour costs are predicted and controlled.

Finally, it is clear that in a number of companies manpower planning has developed concurrently with overall business planning. If a company is examining and determining its strategic objectives for a period of five years or more ahead, it can scarcely ignore the manpower implications of these objectives.

Unique characteristics of manpower as a resource

Manpower is a resource, but it is completely different from all other resources, such as land and buildings and plant and machinery, because:

1. It may refuse to accept the manner and conditions in which management has decided to deploy it.
2. It may leave the company of its own volition irrespective of the problems so created.
3. It may go on strike.
4. It cannot be considered as a homogeneous resource (for example, although manpower as a totality may be in abundance, there may be a chronic shortage of skilled mechanics or computer programmers).
5. It can be retrained in various disciplines if the composition of the demand for manpower changes.
6. Its level for remuneration is subject to continuous negotiation and, in recent years, the increase in its rate of earnings has outstripped the general level of inflation.

7. Its ideas of what is socially acceptable are changing rapidly: it may decide that certain types of jobs (such as those associated with coal face working or refuse collection) are socially unacceptable or that monotonous and repetitive jobs must be modified to inject an element of interest in their completion.

The manpower planning process involves:

1. defining overall objectives for a given period ahead (eg in terms of forecast sales, output of goods or services);
2. converting these objectives to manpower (or man/hour, man/day) requirements, taking account of changes in production methods, product mix etc;
3. estimating how many of the existing labour force (of different occupations or grades) will leave the company, or their present job, during the forecast period and how many will have been trained to replace leavers;
4. considering what effect changes in working hours and holiday will have on the labour force;
5. assessing the possibilities of recruiting extra men and women to make good losses from wastage and/or to meet additional demands;
6. determining where and when critical manpower shortages are likely to arise;
7. forecasting changes in the demand for manpower generated by a miscellany of factors such as new technology, productivity improvements, product market variations, and changes in national and international business conditions;
8. deciding how these problems can best be overcome (or how the company should 'adjust' to them);
9. developing the capacity of manpower to exploit, or adapt to, the speed of technological, economic and social change;
10. the co-ordination and direction of all manpower policies covering recruitment, training, dismissals, redundancies, promotions, transfers, job evaluation and wage and salary negotiations, towards common organisational goals.

Manpower planning in the company organisation

If the manpower planning function is to make a real contribution to the efficiency of the company, top management must ensure that it is fully integrated with other parts of the firm's long-term planning and strategy.

Two basic elements are necessary. Every 'line' manager should be made aware of the importance of considering the manpower implications of the decisions he takes; and there must be somebody responsible for co-ordinating manpower planning over the whole organisation – normally the personnel manager or director.

The process of manpower planning

Corporate strengths and weaknesses

An essential factor which needs to be taken into account in compiling the corporate plan is a 'resource profile' which analyses (in manpower terms) the strengths and weaknesses of the human resource component.

In order to assist in the compilation of a human resource profile, a set of standard questions can be used:

1. Who are the key personnel in the business?
2. What knowledge and skills do they require?
3. Does each key person know what is expected of him? Are clear policy directives available to which easy reference can be made for clarification?
4. Are clear guidelines laid down covering recruitment, training, dismissals, redundancies, promotions and wage and salary rates?
5. How are policy changes transmitted throughout the organisation? What changes are made to ensure that the targeted personnel receive and understand important communications?
6. What formal and informal contacts are maintained with trade union officials? Are they adequate and beneficial?
7. Does each key person have adequate coverage?
8. Who is involved in decision – making processes? What arrangements are in force to see that decisions are implemented? How are actual performances monitored?
9. What principles are applied in developing organisational patterns such as departments and areas of delegation?
10. How does the business identify and adapt to change?

The manpower planner should carry out periodic and systematic analyses of the characteristics and features of the manpower resource to extract and interpret changes in its distribution and composition. Separate analyses should be made of distinctive categories such as executives and supervisors and of those engaged in specialist activities, because without a suitable categorisation, wastage and recruitment problems cannot be studied adequately. Recruitment policies will be directly influenced by the age distribution of manpower (eg if there is a disproportionate number of personnel in the higher age groups in key specialisms).

The rate of labour turnover (discussed in greater detail below) is a fairly good indicator of corporate morale, but it should be supported by detailed analyses of changes in the rate so that corrective action can be applied where necessary. Trends and patterns should be established for retirements, resignations and dismissals according to age groups, department, jobs and specialisms. The personnel department should ascertain, where possible, the reasons why each person has left and code each of the reasons to establish whether there is any cause for alarm.

Manpower requirements

The sales forecast is converted into a production schedule which is fragmented into a work programme by department, activity, product and component. Each task should be assigned standard operational times, based on work study techniques or on past experience, especially where the tasks are of a routine or repetitive nature and the output expected from each machine type is known.

The manpower required may also be calculated by means of predetermined ratios of manpower to the expected product mix. These ratios, however, should also take into account changes in absolute as well as relative volumes – 200,000 units should not require twice the number of man – hours as 100,000 units because of the benefits of economies of scale. Manpower requirements may also be influenced by changes in productivity rates generated by improved machinery, higher utilisation of manpower and better methods of production control.

Manpower deployment

Productivity and efficiency can be measured in many ways, the most common being production ratios and indices. Where these are used for productivity agreements and payment-by-results schemes, the workforce, or their representatives, must be fully conversant with, and agreeable to, the basis of measurement.

Productivity potential should initially be related to the data available from existing records, so that the range of actual performances of different groups and levels of personnel can be compared.

'Activity sampling', method and work study exercises can yield valuable data on work patterns. The collected data should identify where opportunities exist for improvements in productivity.

Personnel policy

Plans in this area are concerned with the essential management functions of motivation. Personnel plans will consider carefully recruitment, selection and training of staff, staff welfare needs, manpower planning, health and safety regulations, salaries and investigations into labour turnover and redundancy costs.

The policy overall will be aimed at recruiting and retaining an efficient labour force; increasing efficiency through better working conditions; improving labour and management relations.

There are certain recognised principles which must form the basis of any personnel policies. These are:

1. democracy in management, on which co-operation and collaboration depend;
2. recognition of individuals and their need for job satisfaction;
3. justice, equity and consistency.

Examples of major policy statements (bearing in mind that these must be specific and positive, rather than vague and general) are as follows:

1. employment policy: to procure efficient personnel, and to enable them to derive

satisfaction from their jobs by offering them attractive working conditions, security and opportunities for advancement.

2. training policy: to provide adequate training facilities in order that employees may improve performance of their present tasks and prepare themselves for promotion.
3. wages and salaries policy: to pay wages and salaries that compare favourably with those other local firms according to a structure which gives due reward to the ability, experience, responsibility and working environment of each employee.
4. industrial relations policy: to establish adequate procedures to deal with grievances and labour problems promptly, and to make every effort at all times to improve the relationship between the company and its employees through joint consultation.
5. welfare policy: to provide services and benefits that compare favourably with those offered by other employers, and such social amenities as are sincerely desired by employees and are mutually beneficial to them and the company.

Each of these major policies then requires detailed implementation by consequential policy statements covering such subjects as:

1. employment: job analysis, recruitment methods, selection techniques, employment of married women, placement of the aged and disabled, policy about retirement, promotions, transfers, dismissals, redundancy;
2. training: induction of new employees, apprentices, operatives' training, supervisory training, management development;
3. wages and salaries: sliding scales, cost of living differentials, incentive schemes;
4. industrial relations: steps for building better management, eg trade union relationships, grievance procedures;
5. welfare: pension scheme, sickness benefit, medical services, transport, housing facilities, canteens, sports and social activities, help with personal problems.

Written personnel policies

Although there is general agreement on the need for personnel policies, there is some dispute over whether these policies need to be in writing.

The major advantages of written policies are:

1. The kinds of action that must be taken to achieve the goals set up by the company are clearly indicated.
2. There is clarification of thinking by management on personnel problems.
3. Co-operation and teamwork are encouraged by co-ordinating the actions of different sections and departments.
4. Uniformity and consistency are given to decision making.
5. Managers and supervisors are guided in determining actions and attitudes in a variety of situations.
6. Help is given with the delegation and decentralisation of authority, thus contributing to improved organisational relations.
7. They aid in supervisory training and management development.

8. They assure workers of the interest of shareholders and management through a practical statement and demonstration of goodwill.
9. They tell employees of the rules under which they are expected to work, thus helping induction and training.
10. They foster high morale and improve union relations by encouraging consistency in dealing with grievances and other problems.

The major disadvantages of written policies are:

1. They mean entering into a form of contract which may be binding on the business and from which it is difficult to withdraw.
2. There are difficulties in setting out a policy which covers the whole range of future possible problems.
3. A written policy may prove impossible to uphold if circumstances change.
4. A written policy is rigid and may restrict management's freedom of action in individual cases.

The above disadvantages can often be overcome by suitable wording of the policy and if the written policy is prepared with proper care and attention. Generally most major companies have written policies which are worded so as to provide management with some degree of flexibility.

Chapter Sixteen

Personnel recruitment, selection and training

- Introduction

- Job analysis

- Job description

- Job specification

- Recruitment

- Training principles and methods

Introduction

The recruitment of suitable employees is often an expensive task and, if the employee recruited is unsuitable after a short period, the total cost is lost. Research has shown that most unsuitable employees were so when recruited and improved recruitment techniques would have established this at the outset.

There is a detailed procedure which helps to minimise the number of recruitment mistakes. The stages are job analysis, job description, and job specification.

Job analysis

The starting point is job analysis, which has been defined as:

> 'The process of examining the job to identify its component parts and the circumstances in which it is performed.'

The detail and approach may vary according to the purpose for which the job is being analysed. The first step in job analysis is to ask those who know what is involved in a job to express it. The sources for information about jobs are normally supervisors and the workers actually doing them.

It is probably better practice to interview the holder of the job first, and then check the information obtained with his superior. If any marked differences of opinion emerge, the job should be discussed with them together until a common understanding is reached. The analysis should cover:

1. initial requirements to perform the job;
2. duties and responsibilities that the job entails;
3. environment and conditions of employment;
4. the social background of the job.

In working through such a check-list, the analyst must beware of being unduly influenced by the personality and qualifications of whoever happens to be doing the job at that particular time. Job analysis is a tool of management aimed at eliciting the detailed information as objectively as possible.

Job description

The production of a job description will normally follow on from job analysis. Job description has been defined as:

'a broad statement of the purpose, scope, duties and responsibilities of a particular job'.

The aspects that may be included in a job description are as follows:

1. Title of the job: as well as the title of the job, the location and position within the organisation should be included.
2. General description of the job: this should include the constituent parts of the job and how this job differs from the others that appear similar. It should also include a description of the level of responsibility included in the job.
3. Physical aspects of the job: this covers the physical working conditions of the job at the time that it is described.
4. Training requirement: this will set out the initial and also the subsequent training needs to enable the job to be carried out efficiently.
5. Social interaction: this will indicate whether the job is one that is carried out in isolation, or requires the individual to be part of a work team.
6. Conditions of employment: this would include such aspects as promotion possibilities, employee services in operation, the normal working hours, and overtime schemes.

Job analysis and job descriptions are required to provide the basic data needed by planners on what now exists as the work to be done and what may be the requirement in the future.

Job specification

When the job has been looked at, the next stage is to consider what kind of person is required to carry out the job efficiently and to the satisfaction of the organisation. This would take the form of a job specification. Such a specification will then form the basis for selection of persons to fill jobs.

The aspects that would be included in a personnel specification are as follows:

1. Education and intelligence: this would include a description of the level of academic knowledge required; the type of intelligence required should also be stated.
2. Physical make up: this will include the age level of the individual required and in general terms the type of physical strength or appearance needed,which could vary according to the nature of the work.
3. Experience: this should indicate the type of experience that would be essential if the job was going to be carried out successfully.
4. Aptitudes: if there are any special aptitudes which are directly related to high performance in the job, they should be stated.
5. Personality: the personality requirements to enable the job to be carried out should also be indicated.
6. Interests: it can be an aid when carrying out the selection process if the nature of an interest or hobby can be directly related to certain characteristics of the job.
7. Initiative and drive: this should indicate the energy content of a job. In some jobs there may be a requirement for an individual to work on his own initiative, whereas in others this may not be necessary.

A job specification sets out what qualities and qualifications a person ought to have, if he is to do a particular job to the level required.

Recruitment

After a job specification has been completed, the personnel department can proceed with the job of recruiting candidates. Obviously whenever a vacancy arises, some thought should be given to finding a suitable individual from internal sources.

This may give a promotional opportunity to someone with ability within the organisation, and hence ensure that the individual will probably stay with that organisation. Internal promotion may motivate other employees but may, of course, also cause some jealousy.

If a vacancy offers a promotional opportunity, there may be a case for advertising internally. In this way, any employees who are interested will apply thus increasing the 'pool' of candidates, and the organisation does not place in an embarrassing position employees who do not wish to be considered and who, without the internal advertisement, might have been offered the job.

The *external source* of labour comprises those people who form the population of the country working or seeking work, modified by recruitment by competing organisations and by additions from the educational system, retraining programmes and redundancies elsewhere.

The size of the external labour supply will be affected by changes in the birth and death rates, by changes in school leaving or retirement ages, by changes in economic and social conditions and by immigration and emigration.

Reduction of the age of retirement and change in the opportunities for young people to engage in further and higher education will affect the size of the available labour force.

Externally, the personnel department will need to develop contacts with the various sources from which prospective employees are likely to be obtained.

This will include job centres, youth employment offices, schools, colleges and universities, private employment agencies, and some professional associations and trade unions who run their own advertising and sometimes recruitment services.

The personnel department may advertise 'at the factory gate' or in newspapers, journals and magazines, dependent on the type of vacancy.

Media advertising is an expensive but effective method of recruiting. Close control of expenditure will have to be set against the importance of recruiting the right person.

The personnel department will have to assess the success or otherwise of using different media, and ensure that the money being spent is 'cost-effective'.

In addition to advertising and letting various outside bodies know what vacancies are available, the personnel department can sometimes recruit individuals by keeping present and former employees aware of job opportunities.

Sometimes informal contacts with managers in similar organisations can help towards solving recruitment problems.

As well as the demographic, economic and social environment, recruitment takes place within a legal environment. The employer's freedom to recruit whom he will is constrained by Equal Opportunities and Race Relations legislation and by closed – shop agreements with trade unions.

Application forms

Application forms are used by personnel managers in the initial screening of candidates for employment. Sometimes they are sent out to candidates in answer to enquiries being received from an advertisement. At other times they are filled in by candidates when they call at a personnel department and before they are seen by the personnel manager or a member of his staff.

The advantage of getting candidates to complete a standard application form is that a good deal of basic information concerning work history, education qualifications and personal circumstances can be considered before deciding whether it is worthwhile to interview the candidate.

This is particularly beneficial to the candidate if he has to take time off from work to attend an interview and especially if he has to travel from one part of the country to another for the interview, only to discover that he would not be suited to the job and that this could have been foreseen from a study of his application form.

Common to most application forms are groups of questions covering:

1. personal information: name, address, date of birth;
2. education: schools, college or university, evening classes, professional qualifications;
3. employment: previous employers and occupations, present wage or salary;
4. medical history: major illnesses or disabilities;
5. spare time activities and interests;

6. space for the candidate to write about himself, why he wants the job, what he can offer etc;
7. names of referee(s).

Some firms use a different application form for a different (and recognisable) level of employment. For example, the form to be completed by a newly graduated person can have an expanded education section and a relatively small employment section, whereas forms to be used by people applying for jobs where no academic or professional qualifications are demanded can have a very small section devoted to this aspect.

When an application form is sent out by a firm in answer to a request following an advertisement, a copy of the job description and specification can usefully accompany it at this stage so that the candidate has a clear idea of what the job entails and what kind of person is being sought.

Interviewing

Interviews are carried out in many ways: by the departmental manager in small firms, by a personnel officer with technical assistance, by panels of senior executives sitting together, and by variations and combinations of all these. For very senior posts the 'interview' may extend over several days' residence. For overseas jobs the interview will usually include the candidate's spouse.

Whatever the form, the four purposes of interviewing remain the same:

1. to enable the employer to obtain further information about the candidate to decide his suitability for the job in question;
2. to give the candidate all relevant information about the job and the organisation;
3. to decide how well the candidate will fit in with existing employees, socially and professionally;
4. the public relations aspect of leaving the candidate with the feeling that he has had a fair chance.

The first purpose has been the constant study of specialists in selection for many years and much has been done to perfect methods of getting information from candidates.

But the second purpose has been comparatively neglected. Job descriptions may have been sent to candidates, and these may be expanded orally at the interview, but far too often candidates are not shown the actual place or office where they will be working, nor do they see anything of the people with whom they will work. Ideally, candidates should meet the latter to see how well they would get on with each other.

If the fourth purpose is kept continually in mind, it will greatly influence the manner in which any interview is conducted. For a candidate to feel that he has been fairly treated, he must be given the chance to ask any questions he wishes.

Seven-point plan

Interviewing demands skills in which few senior managers have been properly trained. These skills can be improved by adopting a systematic approach. Probably the best-known system is the seven-point plan, devised by the National Institute of Industrial Psychologists, which is an attempt to list the items that must be considered during an interview:

1. physical characteristics: health, appearance, manner;
2. attainments: experience, education;
3. intelligence: ability to grasp problems quickly;
4. aptitudes: manual, verbal, numerical;
5. interests: any relevant hobbies (which may illustrate the candidate's personality);
6. disposition: leadership, sense of responsibility, sociability;
7. personal circumstances: for example, commitments which might affect the candidate's ability to do the job.

Having previously evaluated the job's requirements, the selector should attempt to link these and the differences shown between the candidates in order to find the best 'match'. The relative importance of each of these items will obviously vary according to the nature of the job. Therefore the interviewer may 'weight' each item to reflect its relative importance, and then score each candidate against each item. The sum of the scores will give an objective measure of each candidate.

The interviewer
The interviewer should follow certain well-established rules during his time with the candidate:

1. He should be aware of his own prejudices and allow for them. Also he should not be swayed by 'halo effects' which result from favourable conclusions being reached about an individual stemming from just one particular trait which he possesses.
2. Notes of fact may be taken during the interview, with the candidate's agreement. But notes concerning the interviewer's assessment of the candidate should be written after the latter has left the room.
3. The interviewer must remain detached. There should be no question of obtruding his own personality into the conversation in order to create an impression.
4. He should appear interested throughout, and not appear to be bored.
5. He should encourage the candidate to speak freely and should do the minimum amount of talking himself.
6. The questions that he does ask should be phrased so that they are clearly understood.
7. The interviewer should be as thorough as possible and, with experience, an interviewer should learn to gauge how much time he needs for each type of applicant.

Selection tests

In considering a candidate for employment, use may be made of certain selection tests, some of which have been developed by national organisations.

Intelligence
There are many dimensions to intelligence, and, if it is felt desirable that a person's mental abilities should be measured, care should be taken to ensure that the tests do measure qualities that are important to the job. Many firms these days use differential test batteries which give a 'profile' of a number of mental factors or abilities.

Aptitudes

Apart from the test mentioned above, special tests have been developed which cover such aspects as sensory capacities, co-ordination, dexterity etc.

Personality

Personality tests are designed to identify the most significant personality traits which the individual displays or perhaps the degree to which he tends towards one extreme or the other of a trait-dimension (eg dominance, submissiveness). Some of these tests have been criticised on the ground that it is possible to falsify the answers through knowledge of what behaviour is acceptable or desirable, but evidence shows that they are useful in matching the personality to the job.

An alternative to the inventory personality test is to place the person in a situation which clearly resembles or simulates a critical real-life situation and to observe his behaviour from the personality aspect as well as perhaps his technical, administrative or intellectual ability.

Performance

It can often be useful to develop a test designed to measure the level of accomplishment of the candidate: his education, technical knowledge, operational ability at a particular trade etc. A test in shorthand and typing for secretarial candidates falls in this category.

Medical

Many offers of employment are made conditional upon the candidate satisfactorily passing a medical examination.

Tests of any kind should only be used after an assessment has been made of the part played by the factors being examined in the satisfactory performance of the job under review. This can be done by giving the tests concerned to people already doing similar work and relating to their score an evaluation of their performance.

Tests are not exclusive methods of selecting personnel. Tests should be used in combination with application forms and interviews and only where appropriate. A good selection test must be sufficiently reliable, its results not being influenced too much by chance factors.

The demands on reliability must be very high if a test is to have any value for the selection of individuals. It must also be relatively consistent. It should also be sufficiently valid, measuring the capacity or personality trait which it purports to measure and predicting with reasonable certainty the future performance of the tested individual.

Review of procedure

Following up the success (or failure) of candidates appointed under a recruitment procedure is essential if the effectiveness of that procedure is to be kept under review.

Training principles and methods

People in industry and commerce are constantly in learning situations. They change their jobs, new machinery or processes are introduced into departments, promotion takes place, reorganisations occur. Each new situation creates a 'learning' problem before the individual feels competent to deal with the new daily routines.

Training involves overcoming 'blocks' in the path of effective learning. It is concerned with direct job performance but it can also be effective in changing attitudes. This aspect becomes more important with the increase in plant productivity bargaining. Training officers have an increasing part to play in helping management and workers overcome their mutual suspicions.

Relationship between education, training and staff development

Education and training overlap but need to be distinguished. Education imparts knowledge, training imparts skills. Education is a process of acquiring background knowledge of a subject. Normally this takes place at schools, technical colleges and universities or by private study. Training is learning to use this knowledge in specific work-situations. It is thus concerned with job performance as well as with the application of knowledge to work.

Further education given in conjunction with training gives workers a job perspective and helps them to understand the need for change and hence for retraining; it may also help workers to accept the responsibilities that go with the job.

Both education and training are means of communication and agents of change. The distinction between 'training' and 'staff development' is usually that training applies to lower levels of work and manual skills, whereas staff development applies to the personal development of managers.

Reasons for the need to train and retrain

These include:

1. There is a shortage of suitably qualified manpower at national level.
2. Manpower as an industrial resource is increasing in cost.
3. Pressure from competitors to reduce costs and meet delivery dates requires more efficient use of manpower.
4. Technological changes necessitate training in new skills and retraining for those with obsolete skills.
5. Introduction of new operating procedures necessitates retraining.
6. Larger industrial complexes require new supervisory and management skills to overcome problems of co-ordination.
7. Staff must be developed to fill key posts, in case the present occupant leaves.
8. Employees hired for their potential must be developed.
9. There is a growth in plant bargaining.

In addition, the social responsibility felt by a firm for its employees often extends to providing education such as a pre-retirement or supervisory education scheme.

The training officer

The training officer's function within the firm is to provide for change. There is little point in training which merely reinforces what people are already doing. He tends to be regarded as an agent of change, and may well be involved as an organisational analyst identifying the need for structural changes in the organisation.

While the training officer organises the training programme and takes part in the formulation of training policy, the whole process remains the responsibility of management. The evaluation of training is an important step in revising policy and setting fresh goals.

Setting up a training function

This involves a two-phase process with the first phase at top management level and the second phase at line management level.

First phase at top management level

The relevant steps at this level are:

1. Analyse: ask questions about the way in which manpower is employed in the business, and the problems that exist.
2. Formulate: plan changes in the working environment and changes in manpower utilisation by training. This may include employment of a company training officer.
3. Implement: obtain the co-operation of all concerned. Analyse specific training needs and formulate detailed plans for departments. Put the programme into action in each section and evaluate each department's programme. Make any changes in other features of the firm suggested by the analysis.
4. Evaluate: evaluate the results of the training programme in terms of optimisation of the company's manpower resources with regard to plans for the future.

Second phase at line management level

This is the 'implementation' section of the first phase.

1. The training officer gains the co-operation of all involved: management, workers, unions.
2. Line managers analyse their sections' skills and training needs.
3. Line managers, advised by the training officer, formulate plans, including methods, cost and manpower allocation.
4. Plans are put into operation. Line managers may take part in on-the-job training and may receive training themselves.
5. Evaluation: did the line managers get what they wanted from the programme?

The entire training process is the responsibility of line management and an integral part of management strategy. It is important that open communication should prevail, and the whole exercise should be well documented. 'Evaluation' stage of any programme should be the basis for revision of the policy before setting up a new programme.

Types of training

Training may include:

- induction training for new staff;
- job training so that operators use correct working methods in the shortest time;
- supervisory training, to improve knowledge both of the technical and administrative aspects of the jobs and how to exercise leadership and authority;
- managerial training, to provide for planned succession of staff to greater responsibilities;
- executive development, to give training in management methods and techniques to increase the capabilities of existing members of management.

Industrial training techniques

These include:

1. Job instruction: this is carried out on the job, with little or no special provisions or concessions to the trainee.
2. Vestibule training: this is done in the training school, where training is on equipment identical to that used in production and many shop floor operations.
3. Simulation: this is an analogue or reproduction of a system, used where it is too difficult or dangerous for the particular skill to be learnt in real life, eg training of airline pilots.
4. Role playing: this is a type of simulation which requires trainee to know background to role in order to achieve realism in solving problems.
5. Sensitivity training: this is carried out in T Groups, which are formed to teach principles of interaction and attitude change.
6. Case studies: these attempt to improve the thinking process and widen attitudes by examining similar situations from which general principles may be learnt.
7. Films/TV.
8. Lectures.
9. Discussion: (with (7) and (8) above), this gives an opportunity to share experience and learn from each other.
10. Job rotation: this provides experience in responsible posts in several functions. It is important in management education and development because it encourages the transfer of knowledge and skills from one job to another.
11. Programmed learning: pre-set learning instructions are learnt at the learner's own speed, enabling him to assimilate knowledge without the high cost of personal instruction.
12. Action learning: management development programmes, pioneered by Professor Revans, involve staff working in industries other than their own.

Evaluation of training programmes

Evaluation in this context can be simply described as assessing the overall worth of training. Generally it is better to plan the evaluation programme before giving the training. This necessitates the following questions being asked at the policy formulation stage:

1. What are the objectives of the training programme?
2. At what level are the objectives set?
3. Against what criteria is training to be evaluated?
4. When should evaluation take place?
5. Who should do the evaluation?
6. To what extent are changes in the firm the result of training?
7. Is it possible to compare the costs of training with financial gains in performance (cost-benefit analysis)?

Theoretically, the purpose of evaluation is to compare the marginal cost of training with the marginal gains in performance which may be directly attributed to the training. In this way the business may decide if the training is cost-effective.

Chapter Seventeen

Performance appraisal and labour turnover

- Introduction

- Performance appraisal

- Management by objectives (MBO)

- Labour turnover

- Exit interviews

Introduction

In simplistic terms, the performance of an organisation is the cumulative effect of the performance of all employees. Obviously the relative seniority and responsibility of each job has a 'weighting' effect but the performance at all levels needs to be reviewed systematically and on a regular basis. Labour turnover is often used as one aspect of personnel management performance appraisal and is thus included in this section, although it is also relevant to termination of employment and manpower planning.

Performance appraisal

Definition, purpose and methods

Performance appraisal is the judgment of an employee's performance in his job. It is in effect, a formal and systematic assessment by a superior of his subordinates. Most managers have a subjective judgment, often changeable, of their subordinates, but this requires to be formalised and made in a prescribed, uniform way at agreed intervals (usually six-monthly or annually).

There are a number of purposes for performance appraisal, including:

- to improve performance;
- to provide information for decision-making and control;
- to help to provide standards and to communicate objectives;
- to act as the foundation of a differential payment and rewards system;
- to provide objective criteria and facts in order to minimise subjectivity of judgment;

- to give data by which future performance can be assessed, eg whether an individual is worth promoting;
- to indicate training needs, eg areas of performance which need improvement which might involve training;
- to motivate individuals or groups by making them aware of their performance against standards;
- to raise morale by enabling good performance to be recognised;
- to provide feedback whereby future standards and objectives can be modified in the light of current performance.

The major methods of performance appraisal are:

1. ranking, whereby a manager ranks his subordinates in order of merit;
2. grading, whereby employees are graded in, say, five grades, eg poor, below average, average, above average, very good;
3. a rating scale whereby subordinates are given points (on a scale usually up to five points) for a predetermined list of personal characteristics or work factors;
4. a strengths/weaknesses system whereby a manager writes a list of strong/weak points of a subordinate in relation to his job. It also requires the manager to assess promotion potential and training needs of each of his subordinates;
5. the appraisal interview whereby the subordinate is encouraged to talk about his successes and failures over the appraisal period. The manager and subordinate should use the interview to try to solve some of the problem areas. The interview may be used as a method in itself or in conjunction with other methods.

Problems

While the methods for measuring performance may easily be defined, there are a number of problems involved, including:

1. Determining the standards of measurement and deciding upon the criteria to be used, quantitative or qualitative, are not easy. How accurate are the standards anyway? (It has, for example, been suggested by sociologists that the accuracy of time study techniques for determining rate-fixed times may be as low as 40 per cent. Measuring workers' performance against standards which may be wrong 60 per cent of the time would seem to be of little value.) In any event we always have the problem of who is the standard or average worker against whose performance other people's results are to be measured.
2. Individual performances are almost always affected by the work of others (the machine operative needs a ready supply of parts to machine, for example). Where team-working is involved then the team has to be measured as a unit and workloads balanced. Managers and supervisors are dependent on others for their rewards, and their performance must be measured on their skills in leadership through the total performance of their division or department.
3. Any attempt to measure, whether in the physical sciences or the social sciences, is accompanied by errors of observation or bias.

4. Behaviour changes when performance is measured, as the Hawthorne studies demonstrated. This change is known as the 'Hawthorne effect' (see Chapter 20 below).
5. Some criteria may conflict with others, for example some accounting ratios used for judging short-term performance may not be suitable bases for making decisions about long-term requirements.
6. When more than one criterion of performance is used, it is essential to ensure that individuals understand which is the most important.
7. A particularly strong or weak characteristic may weigh heavily and cause other job factors to be ignored.
8. Devising an appraisal scheme suitable for varying jobs, eg research, marketing and production, which all have different criteria, is very difficult.
9. The standards are often set by the informal organisation (see Chapter 20 below).
10. Emphasis may be placed by subordinates upon short-term favourable results at the expense of medium to long-term objectives.
11. Appraisal is often time consuming and can *create* conflict rather than resolving it.

Nevertheless, despite these many problems, performance appraisal is generally regarded as an essential tool of modern management.

Management by objectives (MBO)

MBO is a systematic technique which attempts to improve the overall company performance by a comparison of actual objects achieved against pre-determined targets, either quantitative or qualitative. It involves participation and the provisions of management information to a greater degree than usual.

MBO is a system which covers all levels of an organisation. It contains the following major features:

1. Standards and times are set in agreement between subordinates and superior basically through a management appraisal interview.
2. Standards are integrated with organisational goals.
3. Objectives or standards which depend on results and outcomes are set for each individual.
4. Measures are both quantitative and qualitative.
5. Time is specified for the key activities involved in the person's jobs.
6. Standards are integrated with organisational control systems so that feedback is available.
7. Standards are set relative to the position in the organisation, but at a level which raises the efficiency and motivation of the person.
8. Standards are set to assume an improvement in an individual's weakness. The claimed benefits of MBO are that participation increases motivation and delegation, feedback increases control and efficiency, standards increase predictability and measurability and the system increases commitment, co-ordination and communication. There may, however, be problems as set out below:

   a) It is doubtful whether any one system can cover so many purposes which range from staff development to motivation.

b) It is costly in managerial time and paperwork.

c) It confuses performance with potential, control with procedures.

d) It may raise hopes of promotion which the organisation cannot fulfil.

9. MBO is complementary to corporate planning. It is a system designed to allow individuals to set objectives by which they can contribute to organisational goals and their own personal goals. By integrating individual goals with organisational goals, organisational weaknesses can be overcome. On the other hand, like corporate planning, it needs firm commitment on the part of senior management to make it work and an acceptance of participation. Monitoring performance against objectives set will be difficult, and may, in fact, seem threatening to the individual.

10. MBO is a mechanistic, systematic way of looking at a lot of organisational problems at the same time. For this reason it may not work as well as its enthusiastic supporters suggest. But like corporate planning it may be that the process is the important thing. By adopting MBO a firm is:

a) demonstrating interest in its staff as individuals;

b) deliberately adopting a procedure to set time aside for looking at their objectives;

c) systematically examining its own strengths and weaknesses internally;

d) inviting participation in the setting of objectives.

Labour turnover

Definition and measurement

'Labour turnover' is used to describe the movement of workers into and out of a firm's employment, and is calculated in the form of an *index of labour turnover*. The index is an expression of the total number of separations as a percentage of the average number of employees over a period of one year, as follows:

$$\text{Net labour turnover} = \frac{\text{Total separations in period}}{\text{Average working force}} \times 100$$

Since some separations are unavoidable (eg women leaving to have babies) or, in some cases, desirable, as when employees may be encouraged to leave to get advancement their present firm cannot offer, the formula may be adjusted to take these factors into account, in which case the calculation is:

$$\frac{\text{Total separations} - \text{Unavoidable separations in period}}{\text{Average working force}} \times 100$$

An annual calculation is considered the best since shorter periods may contain particular unusual influences; sometimes, however, quarterly indices may be produced when it is felt that they may indicate seasonal trends.

There is one great weakness about this method of calculation since it obscures the extent of the stable element of the labour force. For example, a labour turnover index of 33⅓ per cent could mean either of two things:

1. If a different third of employees left each year, none of the original employees would be left after three years.
2. If labour turnover affected only a particular third of jobs the holders of which constantly left after only one year's service, then two-thirds of the original labour force would still remain after three years.

These two situations differ markedly in the degree to which the labour force consists of experienced workers, ie it ignores the very important matter of labour stability. An index of labour stability thus needs to be calculated at the same time as that of turnover. Such an index is:

$$\frac{\text{Stability index or}}{\text{skill wastage index}} = \frac{\text{Number with over one year's service now employed}}{\text{Total employed one year ago}}$$

This assumes a worker to be experienced after one year, but the actual period may be adjusted as necessary.

The standard index has been criticised, then, in that it is heavily influenced by the previous employment history of the firm and lacks information about the length of service of those leaving. Although simple to calculate, it is of very limited value for comparing 'turnover rate' of different organisations.

A company's 'turnover rate' will be affected by a number of factors, but primarily by the nature of its business. There are annually published labour turnover statistics on an industry basis and any external comparison should be with a firm of a broadly similar size in the same industry, eg the hotel and catering industry has traditionally had a high turnover rate. Because women are more likely to leave work to bring up children, and married women may also be more likely to change jobs if their husbands are offered jobs in a different region, the female employees' labour turnover rate is generally higher than the turnover rate for male employees.

Costs

It is often widely assumed that the only cost of an employee leaving is the direct costs of obtaining a replacement, which can be high particularly if the job needs to be advertised or recruitment takes place through an agency. However, in addition to these replacement costs there may be others, including:

*   lost production in replacement period;
*   lower production in induction and job training period;
*   overtime payments at premium rates to other employees during the replacement period;
*   cost of training the new employee;
*   administrative costs of a leaver and a new employee (eg personnel records, payroll);
*   higher level of spoilt work while replacement is being trained;
*   possible use of a more highly skilled employee in replacement period;
*   need for other employees to learn how to work with the new recruit;
*   possible effect on morale and productivity.

So management action should be usually aimed at reducing the labour turnover rate. However, in organisation dependant on a continual supply of new people with new ideas, such as an advertising agency or a university a relatively high labour turnover may be acceptable.

Methods of reducing labour turnover

A high labour turnover rate may be a natural outcome of that particular business or it may reflect a failure of personnel policy. Separation or 'exit' interviews (described below) can often establish the real cause and specific remedial action taken. The following are some of the remedial actions available to management:

- ensure that selection procedures are adequate – this is essential if the leavers mainly comprise recent joiners;
- ensure that supervisors and managers are performing their tasks, including man-management, properly;
- ensure that employees' abilities are being used as widely and effectively as possible;
- review or introduce job evaluation;
- review pay and personnel policy;
- improve training;
- improve communication;
- ensure that working conditions are as good as possible;
- promote group and individual morale and group cohesiveness;
- increase job satisfaction.

Exit interviews

As shown above, the direct and indirect costs of labour turnover are high, and it is important for management to know why employment was terminated either voluntarily or involuntarily. The separation or 'exit' interview is an essential tool to gather data to determine the causes for labour turnover. Reasons for its use are:

1. to get information from dissatisfied staff;
2. to retain the employee's goodwill;
3. to improve the firm's employment situation;
4. to improve staff policies and practices;
5. to determine the true reason for leaving.

The main purpose of the interview is to obtain information, and, in general, the employee should not be persuaded to withdraw his resignation. The interview must be held in private and the person interviewed must be assured that information obtained will be treated as confidential. From information gained at such interviews definite trends may be established enabling administrative action to be taken to reverse them and reduce turnover. If it proves impossible to interview an employee who has resigned, a questionnaire may be sent to him after he has left.

Reasons for 'separations' fall into three main categories:

1. voluntary separations (avoidable);
2. separations due to management action (these may be avoidable or unavoidable);
3. involuntary separations (unavoidable).

Employees who leave voluntarily mainly leave because they dislike or are bored with the job; they dislike the pay and/or the conditions; they see little prospect of advancement. In all these instances they leave because they think they will be able to do better elsewhere.

Those who are dismissed by the management leave for reason of:

1. unsuitability (inefficiency, incompatibility);
2. discipline (lateness, persistent absence, insubordination etc);
3. redundancy (due to trade recession or end of contract).

All these reasons for leaving, in so far as they are due to shortcomings of the business, are capable of a certain amount of control; for example:

- Jobs can be made more attractive.
- Pay can, within limits, be increased.
- Conditions can be improved.
- Suitable workers can be given better prospects of promotion.
- Better selection methods will reduce the number of unsuitable employees.
- Means can be found to improve timekeeping, the health of employees and the quality of supervision.

The effects of redundancy can often be minimised by absorbing employees affected in jobs on other contracts. Trade recession alone is uncontrollable by the management itself and the effects of this can often be mitigated.

A high labour turnover for 'avoidable' reasons, apart from its monetary cost to the company, is a very serious matter. Every disgruntled leaver is potentially a source of ill will towards the company. When employees are in any case difficult to find and costly to engage and train, it is essential not to neglect the warning signs of high turnover.

Chapter Eighteen

Job evaluation and remuneration

- Introduction

- Job evaluation

- Introduction to remuneration

- Determination of overall wage and salary levels

- Additions to wages and salaries

- Collective bargaining for wages

- Hours of work

- Productivity agreements

- Company pay policy

- Financial incentives

- Profit sharing and co-partnership

- Pensions

Introduction

Job evaluation is the process of placing jobs in order of their relative worth in order that employees may be paid fairly. It is normally carried out in two stages:

1. establish an order of ranking for various jobs;
2. apply a set of money values when (1) above is established.

Job evaluation

Methods

Job ranking
This is the simplest form of job evaluation. Each job is assessed as a whole and its relative importance to the organisation is established. Duties, responsibilities and qualifications necessary are considered and jobs grouped together according to an approximate correspondence of difficulty or value. A number of grades are then determined to the requirements of the organisation, jobs fitted into these grades and a wage level set for each grade.

Job classification
This method is very similar to job ranking and differs only in the sequence of events in that the grades and salary levels are identified before the jobs are considered in detail; jobs are then related to the salary level.

Points system
Jobs are broken down into a number of factors such as training and supervision required, and each factor given a weighting. The 'value' of a job can then be assessed by totalling the points awarded to its component factors. This method is extremely complex to implement due to the wide range of factors likely to be involved and the varying degree of importance of each factor. Current feeling is that points systems introduce unnecessary complexity without a commensurate improvement in the quality of the ranking obtained.

Time span of discretion
This method is concerned with the length of time a worker can be left alone by his superior. This is particularly suitable for management and supervisory appointments.

Problem areas

The major problems of job evaluation are:

1. the establishment of the criteria to be used;
2. the weighting to be given to each factor;
3. limiting the number of categories or grades to manageable proportions;
4. the effect of training;
5. the possibility of becoming too rigid in grading and thus losing employees;
6. the prejudice of the evaluator – this is normally overcome by the use of a job evaluation committee;
7. the time and effort needed – job evaluation is still predominantly used by larger companies (over 5,000 employees);
8. the difficulty of having the evaluations accepted by employees – again a committee, with employee representation, can often overcome this.

The Institute of Office Management job classification scheme is widely used to grade jobs up to supervisory level. Gradings, on a scale of A to F, depend on the degree of training, supervision and experience required to carry out the job.

For many large companies, job evaluation is essential to avoid numerous claims regarding pay by employees. There are a number of problems, particularly when introducing job evaluation, and the participation of employees and their acceptance is vital.

Introduction to remuneration

The terms 'salaries' and 'wages' relate to the payment of individuals in gainful employment. The term 'pensions' relates to the remuneration of individuals after gainful employment has ceased.

Traditionally, the remuneration paid to manual workers was referred to as 'wages', while the rewards for 'white-collar' (ie management and clerical) workers were known as 'salaries'. These terms are still used although the distinction between the two categories of workers is becoming increasingly blurred due to social pressures and the introduction of legislation concerning terms and conditions of employment.

The payment of wages is usually linked with contracts of employment which are terminable at relatively short notice, ie one week, one day or, in exceptional cases, one hour, and whose wage levels are determined by negotiation between trade unions and employers or employers' associations. Wages are usually determined by hourly rates with allowances for overtime and are generally paid weekly or fortnightly.

Payment of salaries, however, is usually associated with a longer period of notice to terminate employment, for example one month, or even more, and the determination of salary levels is by individual negotiation. Salaries are usually paid monthly and many salaried employees are not permitted to claim overtime.

Consideration should be given at this stage to the term 'remuneration'. Wages and salaries are terms in common usage which describe that part of an individual's reward received in the form of cash, or equivalent, at regular intervals. The balance of the individual's reward may include such items as pensions, sickness benefit, paid holidays, provision of company cars and other 'fringe benefits', share of profits, and commission.

Determination of overall wage and salary levels

One of management's most difficult decisions is the determination of overall wage and salary policy. Obviously the most important factor will be the impact of wage settlements on costs, and therefore on prices and profitability.

High wages and salaries are likely to attract more job applications and thus give management a wider field of choice when recruiting. While high wages do not in themselves guarantee high productivity and a stable labour force, it is indisputable that they do play a large part in the maintenance of morale and the reduction of labour turnover.

The degree of unemployment in an area will have a significant effect on the wage and salary levels in that area. This is particularly true when union influences are weak.

Union pressure may result in high wage levels in unionised companies. Alternatively non-unionised businesses may also pay higher than average wage levels in an attempt to keep the unions out. However, if the wage levels in a business are too high, for either reason, other employers in the area may object on the grounds that the business is destabilising the labour market and call for a reduction in wage levels over time.

Limits on a business's wages policy are set by its level of profitability. A business which is losing money may not be able to afford to pay more than a minimum level of wages, while one which is known to be profitable will be expected by the workers, and perhaps the community, to pay generously.

A business which is anxious to promote its reputation as a good employer and a good corporate citizen may decide to pay high wages to ensure good public relations.

Other factors which may influence the level of wages and salaries paid might include the stability of employment, the magnitude of fringe benefits, changes in the cost of living and comparability with similar firms in the industry.

Factors affecting pay

A wage or salary is influenced by many different factors. Some of these affect the basic pay for a particular job while others affect the pay of individual employees. They include:

Environmental factors
1. Supply of and demand for labour: when there is a high level of unemployment supply of labour exceeds demand, which will tend to depress wages.
2. Cost of living: workers will seek wages which at least keep pace with rises in the cost of living.
3. Government intervention.

Job factors
1. Difficulty of the job.
2. Working conditions, particularly if they are unpleasant or dangerous.
3. Responsibility.
4. Qualifications or skills required: workers will seek higher wages in return for doing difficult, unpleasant or dangerous work, or for accepting a higher level of responsibility, or for higher qualifications or skills.

Business factors
1. Productivity.
2. Profitability of the business: the employer will seek to keep wages low in order to improve profitability and productivity.
3. Trade unions or other organisation of the employees.

Personal factors

These include merit and/or length of service. Workers will seek to be rewarded for long, good service.

Assessment of wages

Broadly speaking wages are usually paid on one of the following three general bases:

Time based

This is the traditional approach whereby an employee is paid for the time which he actually spends at his place of work. A pre-determined fixed rate per hour is paid. As far as the employer is concerned, the following advantages and disadvantages accrue. Weekly wages are simple to calculate and the total wages outflow is predictable. However, mere attendance does not necessarily mean productive work and because individual inefficiency may be hidden, supervision costs may be high. Advantages accruing to the employee are that wage computation is simple to check and that take-home pay is likely to be constant.

The disadvantages for the employee are that there is no recognition of ability in the monetary sense; a ceiling on earnings exists and there is the possibility of excessive supervision. Comparatively recent developments of the time – based principle include the payment of a basic high day rate and the adjustment of basic time rates by a merit rating. The latter makes some allowance for such characteristics as punctuality, loyalty, skill and efficiency.

Output based

This approach attempts to ensure that an employee earns his wages by his efforts rather than by his attendance. Schemes may be straight 'piece-rate' schemes where a flat rate per unit of output is paid, or a differential piece-rate scheme where more than one rate is paid depending upon which the employee qualifies for by virtue of his performance. The rate of differential piece-rate schemes will be set at such a level that the tendency of employees on straight piece-rate schemes to slow down their rate of production when an optimum level of earnings has been obtained, is reduced. Piece-rate schemes may become difficult to operate in cases where different employees work with very different levels of efficiency as less experienced employees' wages may fall below statutory minimum levels.

Combination schemes

Piece-rate schemes are often treated with suspicion by some trade unions. They dislike a system which relies on individual ability and effort. To some extent this prejudice has been overcome by the introduction of a guaranteed minimum wage which is overlayed by a piece-rate scheme. Such a system of payment ensures, in the event of an employee failing to achieve a particular level of output, that a mutually acceptable minimum wage will still be paid.

Additions to wages and salaries

A basic wage may be uplifted by such additional payments as:

- overtime payments, eg time and a quarter for time spent at work in excess of normal hours on usual working days;
- weekend working, eg time and a half for Saturdays and double time for Sundays;
- shift allowances – an addition for irregular or 'unsocial' hours;
- area differentials, eg London weighting/allowances;
- special payments, eg dirty money for dockers;
- productivity bonuses.

Collective bargaining for wages

Traditionally, wage rates for the majority of workers were settled through a process known as 'free collective bargaining'. This process was one in which wages and conditions of employment were decided by negotiation between employers and workers' organisations. Such agreements were wide ranging and the bias in favour of one party or the other often resulted from the respective negotiating position of each party. Trade unionisation often ensured that the negotiating position of the employees was strengthened, relative to that of the employers. Despite this, the basic principle underlying collective bargaining practices is one of voluntary acceptance between the parties involved. This principle carries the implication that there will be no outside interference in the negotiation procedures. However, economic circumstances often necessitate a measure of government control to be exercised over both incomes and prices.

The conclusion of most wage negotiations is a compromise between the respective views of each participant. Their arguments have traditionally been based on the following factors:

1. cost of living;
2. comparability with similar work in other industries or businesses;
3. prosperity of a firm or industry;
4. tradition;
5. levels of employment, influencing the balance of supply and demand for labour.

It is normally the aspiration of workers' organisations to achieve pay increases which at least equate with increases in the cost of living as indicated by the Retail Prices Index. It is also important that total earnings rather than basic wage rates be considered. In this way average earnings for average hours worked can be compared with movements in retail prices to show whether real wages – purchasing power – have risen or fallen.

Where work of a comparable type is carried out in different industries, there will be union pressure to keep wage rates comparable. While comparability is important to ensure uniformity of treatment of different groups of productive workers, it is vital when attempting to establish levels of pay for indirect or non-productive workers. The most widely known examples of comparability in practice are the Civil Service Pay Research Unit and the Armed

Forces Pay Review Board. These attempt to apply techniques of fair comparison with other organisations in the private sector, on the assumption that market forces in the private sector will determine the 'true' reward for a given type of work.

The relative position of the firm or industry is an important consideration for both sides when pay settlements are being negotiated. An upward trend will encourage unions to press for higher settlements, a downward trend will limit the funds available. Whatever the state of the firm or industry, it must not be forgotten that there are many claimants on a firm's resources, eg shareholders, capital equipment replacement programmes, working capital requirements and investment projects for the future. It may be advisable for management to take unions into their confidence regarding the financial position and future financial plans.

The tradition of high wages and additional benefits in an industry will be a significant force during the negotiation process. This is particularly relevant when one group of workers feels it is losing its position vis-à-vis other groups.

A high level of unemployment means that the supply of labour exceeds the demand, with the result that wages are likely to be reduced. The reverse will, of course, apply when unemployment is low.

The system of collective bargaining outlined above is reasonably effective as a method of negotiating minimum wage rates to be used as a basis for local agreements. Only a minority of workers earn only the basic minimum rate.

Hours of work

About a century years ago the standard working week was 60 hours or more. With the passage of time and the improvement in conditions of employment brought about by the activities of the trades unions and the growing social conscience of the nation as a whole, the normal working week is now one of 40 hours or less. Despite this reduction in normal hours of work, actual hours worked have not reduced due to the amount of overtime now recorded. Overtime has, in fact, become an established feature of the working life of many employees – particularly wage-earners.

Overtime is primarily worked by adult males. The availability of youths for overtime working is limited by their need to study to obtain advancement and their desire for leisure time. Many people are also limited in overtime working by their family responsibilities.

The amount of overtime working also varies by type of employment. Labourers tend to work longer hours than skilled men, presumably because the higher basic rates earned by the latter are more likely to be affected by the regressive labour curve. Time rate workers, skilled or not, tend to work more overtime than piece rate workers. Clerical workers generally work little overtime because very often they receive only a flat rate of payment with no provision for overtime earnings. In cases where clerical workers do work in excess of their conditioned hours, they are often given time off in lieu at a later date.

Traditionally, employers have opposed any attempts to reduce worked hours because it is in their interests to achieve the greatest utilisation possible of their resources such as plant and machinery. Shorter hours means less utilisation and therefore less output. Hence, unit costs increase – fixed costs spread over a smaller base. Where they cannot resist the pressures for shorter conditioned hours the next best alternative to achieve an optimum level of utilisation is to pay a premium to workers prepared to exceed their conditioned hours – overtime. While this is often acceptable to the employees, the trades unions would prefer the engagement of additional workers – perhaps on a shift basis. The additional workers would boost union membership and therefore union influence vis-à-vis the employer. At the present time the government would also wish to see a reduction in overtime hours worked in favour of the engagement of additional workers as this would ease the unemployment situation. However, from the employer's point of view, it is cheaper to pay an overtime premium than to engage additional employees unless such additional employees can be utilised, with existing employees, in a shift system. A three-shift system per 24 hour period for perhaps six or seven days a week will obviously produce the maximum utilisation of capital equipment and resources. However, once regular overtime is an established practice, it can only be eliminated if management are prepared to uplift employees' earnings to a comparable level through the payment of shift bonuses and similar devices. Also most employees need overtime to maintain their current standard of living.

Should a reduction in actual hours worked per week result from a reduction in conditioned hours, it should not be assumed that individuals will work fewer hours. Often, they will take a second job. A considerable proportion of workers in the United Kingdom have a secondary form of employment and millions of others require one and are prepared to work up to an extra twelve and a half hours per week.

Alternatives to a shorter working week in terms of hours worked include longer weekends, the same daily conditional hours worked per four-day period, and longer paid holidays. An extra week's paid holiday is equivalent to an increase in the hourly rate of pay of 2.7 per cent and is, from the point of cost to be preferred to a substantial reduction in weekly hours worked. This practice is commonplace on the Continent where workers generally have a greater entitlement to paid holidays per year.

The four-day week discussed above would be a popular innovation as far as the employee is concerned even when he would use the spare time to take another job. The increased freedom of choice enjoyed by the employee would probably be good for his morale, and this will provide benefits to his main employer in the form of increased motivation. In France, businesses have moved to a 35-hour week, resulting in greater profits and employment prospects in the leisure, entertainment and retail industries, all of which benefit from workers' increased free time.

Another variation of the traditional pattern of working within a 40 hour week is the concept of flexitime. The flexitime system, which is normally most appropriate to office workers, splits the working week into two parts:

1. There is a daily period, often referred to as 'core time', when all employees must be at their places of work. 'Core time' is stipulated by the employer – for instance, between the hours of 10 am and 4 pm.
2. The balance of the daily conditioned hours may be made up either before 10 am or after 4 pm or perhaps through a combination of both.

Control is obviously necessary to ensure that employees work their full working hours over a given period (normally a month). The administrative problems have largely been eliminated with new 'computerised clocks' which automatically record, for each employee, hours worked.

The advantages claimed for the flexitime approach to hours of work include:

- improvement in morale by allowing employees to arrange their days to fit their individual needs. Considerations include the availability of transport, family requirements – particularly for married women with families – and leisure activities;
- reduction in strains on individuals resulting in improved health and efficiency;
- reduction in absenteeism. Employees on fixed time employment frequently claim to be sick rather than risk getting into trouble for being late.

Productivity agreements

Productivity bargaining differs from normal collective bargaining in that some positive benefit, such as increased output per worker, is required in return for an increase in remuneration above the norm. It is important that the productivity increases result from the increased efforts of the workers and not merely from improvement or expansion of the plant used in the production processes. In this context the term 'increased efforts' often refers to the voluntary elimination of some restrictive practice. Alternatively, in a period of rapid technological change, productivity bargaining may be associated with a planned redundancy programme.

Considerations which arise during the negotiation and implementation of productivity agreements include:

- Wasteful work practices should be eliminated.
- Managers may tend to reward their favourites with work that attracts a high productivity payment.
- Necessary work that does not attract many opportunities for productivity payments is seen by workers as of limited value and little interest.
- Some agreements involve increased payments before the effects of increased productivity are a reality. This could cause difficulties for management in cash flow terms. On the other hand, if increased payments are withheld until a productivity threshold has been reached, problems may arise if management and workforce have conflicting views of the actual level of productivity attained at any point in time.
- Productivity bargaining is obviously unsatisfactory for workers in areas of employment where there is little scope for achieving productivity increases and for white collar workers where the measurement of productivity is very imprecise.

Back in the 1970s/early 1980s certain companies found that productivity agreements had increased production output but sales had remained relatively static, thus causing a high level of stock with consequent strain on financial resources. Also in the same period it is generally agreed that productivity agreements increased the level of unemployment. This demonstrates that productivity agreements need to be integrated with the corporate plan to increase sales as well as production.

Company pay policy

Company pay policy should be formulated with two main objectives. Firstly, it should seek to provide an adequate level of reward in order to facilitate the recruitment and retention of the optimum balance of employees. Secondly, it should encourage individuals to seek promotion within the company structure by ensuring that there is adequate reward for additional responsibility and improved skills. Important considerations in the attainment of these objectives include:

1. the availability of the requisite types of skill on the labour market;
2. the effect of higher rates of taxation which tend to level down differentials, thus removing any incentive for advancement;
3. the different terms of employment and bases for calculating remuneration of wage and salary earners. Salaries are normally subject to regular increments, while wage rates are varied by collective bargaining – subject to any government controls. The effect of this is that wage earners have tended to keep pace with increases in the cost of living rather more effectively than salaried staff.

National wage agreements do not necessarily solve the pay problems of individual firms. While such agreements might stipulate a minimum level of payment for given categories of workers, they do not lay down a maximum. The actual level of wages in excess of the minimum is a matter of company policy in the light of local conditions such as local availability of labour, wage levels of competing employers and the activities of local trade union representatives.

A sound company pay policy will treat the question of differentials with great caution. An increase to a small group of employees or even to a single employee as a reward for good performance will inevitably set up a chain reaction throughout the organisation because the established differentials will have been destroyed. All other groups of workers within the organisation will clamour for a restoration of the differentials, not through the withdrawal of the original increase, but through the payment of a similar increase across the board. The chain reaction is unlikely to be contained within the firm. The company's rates of pay will become higher than those of comparable firms, a situation which the unions are unlikely to accept for long. Thus, the initial small increase in some obscure company could lead to a pay demand on a national scale involving millions of pounds. This situation can only be avoided if all proposed increases are negotiated and agreed by all parties concerned, including all local union representatives before any payments or promises are made.

Company pay policy should therefore be formulated at the highest level in any organisation. In practice the individual responsible for the implementation of the policy is the personnel manager, but this does not absolve the other members of the management team from the responsibility of having a working knowledge of the policy, particularly with regard to their own departments.

Financial incentives

We have considered previously the three general bases for the assessment of wages. The consideration of financial incentives embraces the same general principles but in this section a more specific approach will be followed.

Incentives are designed to increase personal effort which should be quantifiable in terms of increased production, for direct workers. In practice incentives tend to be financial, but the theories of A H Maslow and F I Herzberg (discussed in Chapter 21) should not be forgotten or the anticipated increase in output will not be realised. When production can be increased through a good incentive scheme workers and management both benefit, in that improved efficiency in turn creates conditions favourable to further incentives.

Rate fixing is critical for any incentive scheme. Rates should give a return commensurate with the effort required to increase production to the stated level. They should not be reduced except in agreed circumstances, and the threshold for the payment of increased rates should be attainable by the average worker. On the other hand, management should be careful not to offer over-generous rates in case these become the 'norm'. Provision must be made for loss of output which results from circumstances beyond the control of the employee – for example raw material stock-out and machine breakdown situations.

Financial incentive schemes normally fall within one of the following categories.

1. Additions to basic earnings: these come in the form of bonuses, cost-of-living additions or profit-sharing schemes.
2. Piece rate and differential piece-rate schemes: the term 'piece rate' may be defined in the conventional context of units of output for direct workers or it may also be applied in situations where an individual's effort is quantifiable in indirect terms: for example a salesman's efforts reflected in the volume of sales which he achieves.
3. Lieu (place) bonuses: these are paid to indirect workers where individual effort is not quantifiable even in indirect terms.
4. Geared incentive schemes: these are applied in situations where the volume of work fluctuates. Earnings are stabilised in relation to average levels of output by a decreasing rate of incentive payment as output increases.
5. High day rates: workers are paid a high basic wage provided that they can maintain a specified level of output. The advantage of this system, which is now widely used in the car industry, is that both earnings and output levels tend to be consistent and the high degree of wastage normally associated with piece rate systems is avoided.

Incentive schemes may be based on individual or group performance. The main problem with group incentive schemes is that the additional complications inherent in such a scheme necessitate a time lag between the earning and the receipt of the incentive. Workers are therefore less able to identify the extra effort with the extra reward and the sense of urgency necessary to maintain the impetus is lost. In addition individual effort – and idleness – go unacknowledged.

Profit sharing and co-partnership

The aims of profit sharing and co-partnership schemes are to allow the workforce both a share in the profits and a voice in the management of the organisation.

In theory this involvement of the labour force in the formulation of its own destiny should encourage such qualities as loyalty, thrift and industriousness and help build up the reputation of the organisation as a good employer. This in turn should help to reduce the level of labour turnover and build up the level of skill within the organisation. The cycle is completed by a fall in unit cost due to improved efficiency and a larger profit for distribution to all parties. Expressed in this way, profit-sharing and co-partnership schemes are both a form of group incentive scheme. The main disadvantages therefore are similar:

1. The profit share-out is often delayed too long to fulfil its function as an incentive.
2. The efficient and the inefficient worker are equally rewarded.

Other disadvantages include:

3. Employers tend to benefit most from the workers' additional efforts.
4. Employees distrust profit statements largely because they do not understand them. They are particularly suspicious when profits are low.
5. Although members of the management team are required to share a profit, they must bear a loss themselves.
6. Profits are influenced by a variety of factors, many of which are beyond the control of both workforce and management – for example, the general economic climate.

Profit distributions may take the form of cash payments or the issue of shares to employees. Normally the latter method is adopted, or the advantage of worker involvement in the future of the company is lost. Indeed, it is for this very reason that there is often some form of restriction on the transferability of any shares issued in this way. Also there are tax advantages of not making the distribution in a cash form.

It is generally accepted that more highly paid executives are usually better motivated by a profit – sharing scheme which enables them to build up capital in the form of shares.

Co-partnership is a form of profit sharing where the share of the profits attributable to the worker is retained in the business. The retention may either be effected through the issue of a normal share, in which the situation is very similar to that described above, or a co-partnership committee of workers is formed which represents that portion of the capital of the organisation which has been attributed to the workforce. This committee has a voice in the management of the organisation.

The disadvantages of profit sharing also apply, to a greater or lesser extent, to both forms of co-partnerships. A further disadvantage is that, in the event of the failure of the firm, the worker loses both his savings and his job. Despite these disadvantages there have been some notable successes in excursions into both profit sharing and co-partnership. They are ICI plc and the John Lewis Partnership respectively. In the latter case the employees, who are all partners, are able to make a significant contribution to the running of the business in a variety of ways.

Pensions

Although the state system provides a basic pension, it is usually at a minimal level and so most employees could suffer a dramatic reduction in income on retirement and may need to claim additional social security benefits to survive. Most companies today have a company pension scheme which provides for a benefit during the years of retirement.

The scheme may be either contributory, in which the employee has a deduction from his salary which is usually matched or exceeded by the employer – for example an employee contributes 4 per cent of salary and the employer 6 per cent – or non-contributory, in which the total contributions are borne by the employer. It must be remembered that pension costs are high (a figure of 10 per cent of total salary bill is often used) and must be regarded as part of the salary 'package'. They are that part of earnings set aside (normally invested) to provide income in retirement.

Pension schemes may be classified as defined contribution or defined benefit schemes. In defined contribution schemes, the employer's and employee's contributions are invested in a pension fund, which may be managed by a fund manager outside the company and which owns shares and other investments in a range of companies. On retirement, the employee's share of the fund, including a share of the profits made by investing, is used to purchase an annuity from a financial institution.

In defined benefit schemes, the employee is guaranteed to receive a definite level of pension, calculated according to a formula (which may vary from scheme to scheme) based on final salary and years of service (eg years of service divided by sixty multiplied by average salary for the last three years).

Chapter Nineteen

Welfare, discipline and termination of employment

- Introduction

- Employee welfare

- Absence through sickness

- Discipline at work

- Redundancy

- Dismissals

- Redundancy counselling

- Resignation

- Retirement (including early retirement)

- Conclusion

Introduction

Labour is one of the four traditional 'factors of production' and as such is vital in the modern industrial society in which we live. The contribution which labour can make to a national economy is dependent on many factors, one of the most central of which is the relationship which exists between it and its employers. A good relationship and the co-operation between the parties which originates from it, stems from the planning and implementation of a positive personnel policy based on an understanding of the needs of the individual human beings who make up the labour force. Such needs embrace social, economic, physical and psychological considerations and it is these which, if it is to be successful, the personnel policy of an employing organisation should satisfy.

Within an employing organisation, it is the personnel manager who will have the responsibility for a continuous examination of the relationship with its employees and for ensuring that the needs of the workers are met. The execution of these responsibilities will require a thorough understanding of the topics discussed below and much more besides. His success is sometimes considered to be measurable by the effect of the adopted policies on the morale of the employees.

Employee welfare

It has been suggested by many industrial psychologists that concern on the part of the employer for the conditions and terms of service of the employee is almost as important as the payment of wages as far as the motivation of the individual is concerned. Certainly, above a subsistence level of income these factors play an increasingly important role. Historically, employers like Rowntree provided for the welfare of their staff because of their Quaker principles. Nowadays employee welfare is regarded as one of the social responsibilities of management irrespective of any benefit which might accrue to the employer through improved motivation.

An active welfare programme might include the provision of some of the following services, amenities and fringe benefits:

- subsidised canteen facilities;
- sports and social facilities;
- assistance with accommodation and relocation expenses if the employee has to move house because of work;
- sickness benefit and medical facilities;
- pensions and life insurance;
- travel allowances and expenses;
- training and education facilities;
- nursery schools, crèches and day care for infants, particularly important in encouraging mothers of infants to return to work.

Benefits arise in the following circumstances:

1. Welfare facilities minister to the needs of the worker and generate goodwill resulting in increased productivity.
2. A fit, healthy workforce is more productive than one which is bedevilled with absenteeism through sickness.
3. There is a reduction in labour turnover through greater job satisfaction and loyalty to the organisation.

The provision of sickness benefits is of such importance that it deserves separate consideration. If no payment of sick pay is made by a firm, there is a tendency for sick employees to return to work before they are fully recovered and to spread infection among their colleagues. Many firms have therefore found that a generous sick pay policy is advantageous and little, if any more, expensive in the long run than none at all. Care is required to ensure that any such scheme is not abused. This can be achieved through the maintenance of complete records and perhaps the employment of a welfare officer whose duties might include the visiting of sick employees to establish the validity of any claims.

Absence through sickness

The Office of Health Economics published a report entitled *Off Sick*, in which they claimed that the number of days lost through absenteeism in the United Kingdom exceeded the number of days lost through strike action by up to a hundred times. The report indicated that the main determinant of the rate of absenteeism was level of morale and motivation of the employees. There is a marked trend towards frequent and short absences for minor ailments which in themselves would probably give insufficient cause for absence, but when associated with boredom, stress or dissatisfaction at work give poorly motivated employees the excuse they need.

It is therefore suggested that the investigation of the reasons for absence is as important as the maintenance of sickness records. Persistent absence of staff in any particular department is often an indication of poor supervision or poor working conditions. Management will need to tackle these problems to improve the situation.

Discipline at work

The efficiency of an organisation depends upon many factors, but the two most closely associated with the activities of its employees are the willingness with which instructions issued by supervisors are carried out, and the acceptance of rules of conduct and standards of work.

For rules and instructions, both written and oral, to be obeyed willingly, they must be seen as reasonable and relevant. If they are not they will be actively disobeyed or ignored. Positive and intelligent leadership on the part of managers and supervisors has a vital part to play in this respect. Such leadership is only possible if managers and supervisors themselves are disciplined in their approach to their responsibilities. The type of discipline which will result from good leadership based on these principles is known as constructive self-discipline.

The rules of conduct and standards of work applicable within an organisation should be published and always be readily available to the employees and supervisors. The number of rules should be kept to the minimum consistent with efficiency, safety and good conduct, because a large number of rules will be more easily forgotten and therefore ignored. New employees in particular should have the rules fully explained and they should be drawn to the attention of all employees at regular intervals. Supervisors should also be given guidance in the interpretation and enforcement of the rules to ensure consistency. At all times the rules should be promptly and impartially enforced.

A further facet of discipline and the compliance with regulations is that of the 'range of toleration'. This refers to the degree of divergence from the stated regulations which the supervisor will accept without exercising his authority. The range of toleration will vary with the circumstances of the situation. For example, in a fireworks factory strict obedience of regulations concerning the control of smoking will be required for obvious reasons and the workers will accept them. On the other hand, the workers may not be so willing to obey a rule which prohibits eating at the place of work unless there is some good reason which is explained to them. Where no such reason exists, supervisors will not be inclined to enforce such a rule and will therefore, consciously or unconsciously, allow a greater 'range of toleration' in the exercise of their authority than in the former case.

Conflict often arises when the range of toleration is perceived differently by workers and supervisors. What workers consider reasonable in any given circumstances may be considered as unreasonable by the supervisor. It should also be recognised that conflict, when it arises, may take the form of a flagrant breach of the rules. An unreasonable no-smoking rule can be avoided by frequent visits to the toilet.

The 'range of toleration' evident in any particular workplace will depend on the overall attitude of management towards the employees and also, as previously indicated, by the particular requirements of the work being done. Some of the considerations which might be relevant are outlined below:

1. Production objectives: poor time-keeping may be tolerated as long as production objectives are met.
2. Labour shortages: a wider range of tolerance may well result when there is a shortage of a particular grade of labour. Management might fear that disciplinary action, even if justified, would cause the individual(s) punished to leave.
3. The desire for status and prestige by the managerial and supervisory grades may well result in an exercise of authority which tolerates no divergence from the rules.
4. The need to maintain order: non-observance of rules may be tolerated when only a few individuals are involved, but when larger numbers are involved, any relaxation of the rules might cause widespread disorderliness. The implications of this are that the smaller the work group, the greater the range of toleration to be expected, all other things being equal.
5. Natural or human needs: on one hand such considerations require strict enforcement of medical and safety rules, and on the other they lead to a relaxation of discipline, allowing such activities as smoking and chatting at the place of work within reasonable bounds.

Disciplinary committees involve worker participation. The principle involved is that rules which have been formulated as a result of joint consultation between the workers affected and management will have a better chance of being understood and accepted. This principle can be extended by involving the workers in the enforcement of the rules. Such involvement might include the election or appointment of workers to a joint appeals committee which is created to hear appeals against decisions taken on disciplinary matters. Similarly, the Robens Report entitled *Health and Safety at Work* suggested that accident prevention is best achieved by placing the responsibility for the enforcement of safety regulations in the hands of those workers who create the risks which must be safeguarded against. A safety committee should therefore include worker representation.

Despite these arguments, the number of joint committees in existence is probably less than might be expected because of a management prejudice that workers generally lack the ability and impartiality necessary to make disciplinary judgments and to award punishments. The criteria stipulated by Rowntree if workers are to make a real contribution to committee work include:

- coincidence of workers' and employers' interest;
- a knowledge of all relevant facts;
- the independence of mind and sense of responsibility to make individuals' judgments irrespective of the view of less talented workmates.

Redundancy

Under the Employment Rights Act 1996 an employee is redundant when:

- the employer has ceased, or intends to cease, to carry on business either for the purposes for which the employee was employed or in the place where the employee was employed; or
- the requirements of the business for employees to carry out particular work, or to carry out that particular work in the place where the employee was working, either no longer exist or are expected to diminish or cease.

The redundancy may be individual, but in recent years there have been 'mass redundancies' when a factory or unit is closed and all or many of the employees made redundant. There are legal provisions for redundancy payments and the statutory minima are reasonably simple. However, redundancy, particularly on a large scale or in an area of high unemployment, creates many human problems which are the concern of personnel management.

As well as dealing with the problems of the employees made redundant, personnel management will also be heavily involved in maintaining the morale of those employees kept on.

The following are some of the major problems in dealing with a mass redundancy:

1. Who should be made redundant first? The normal practice is 'last in, first out' applied to the varying categories of employees. This is the most equitable method and also limits the amount of redundancy payment due.
2. When should employees be advised?
3. How should employees be advised?
4. Are any jobs available elsewhere in the group or in the local area? If so, is there any training or disruption of home life necessary?
5. The calculation of the redundancy payment: there is a statutory *minimum* payment, but many organisations negotiate, often with trade unions, higher levels of payment.
6. How is the morale of the remaining employees, who will, almost inevitably, feel insecure, to be maintained?
7. The organisation of a systematic close-down, when appropriate: in the past there have often been worker 'sit-ins' which have prevented management access to the assets of the business, eg stock, plant and machinery, land and buildings, etc.
8. How will customers and suppliers be affected? This is a marketing and purchasing problem, not a personnel one.

Dismissals

These comprise two main categories, as follows:

'Lay-off' or 'suspension'

These are minor aspects of termination of employment involving temporary parting on the initiative of the employer but without prejudice to the employee. They may be brought about by:

1. lack of work; for example, building workers are often laid off in bad weather and then recalled when work once more becomes available;
2. suspension for a breach of the rules or regulations, usually for a short fixed period of time.

Discharge

It was considered until quite recent years that it was the sole right of management to hire and fire, and such a practice is obviously feasible so long as supply of labour exceeds the demand for it and is unorganised. However, this concept has little acceptance in industry today, and modern practice protects the employee against arbitrary discharge. Generally, the reasons for dismissing an employee are limited to:

1. breach of the terms of the employee's contract;
2. gross misconduct; even then dismissal comes usually after a preliminary warning, followed possibly by suspension.

Redundancy counselling

The legislative restrictions on the employer's right to dismiss do not cover the whole of the personnel manager's concern in this area. In particular they do not eliminate the role of the personnel officer as welfare worker in the old sense.

There remains a good deal which he can do to help a person who is redundant, even if all the public policy requirements have been met. This help focuses mainly on helping the individual by advice and by organising facilities which he or she might be incapable of mobilising on his or her own behalf, eg PAYE/social security advice, retraining or re-deployment.

Resignation

Whereas discharges are initiated by the employer, resignations come from the employees. It is most important here to have exit interviews to find the real reasons why people leave. These may well reflect on the efficiency of a firm and its management and lead to a review of its policies and practices on pay, training, supervision, promotion and other conditions of employment. Alternatively, they may arise from personal circumstances, eg pregnancy, house move.

This gives rise to other complex questions, however, centred on the problem of the lengths to which a firm should go in trying to retain the services of a person, for example, on whom much expense has been incurred in training. Should his salary be raised to match or better outside offers? If so, how will such an increase affect the salaries of others in similar jobs?

Retirement (including early retirement)

This may be in accordance with company policy or as a result of a decision by the individual on reaching a certain age (in which case he will need to give notice). In any event a full interview should be granted before a person retires. From this may be gleaned reasons for discontent which the individual would not normally complain of for possible fear of reprisal.

A number of companies now run seminars on retirement for employees in their last year(s) of work. This shows the problems and opportunities retirement brings.

A relatively recent occurrence is 'early retirement' when employees within say five to seven years of retirement are asked to retire early in return, normally, for a lump sum payment and maintenance of pension rights. Early retirement is often a more acceptable method of reducing the labour force than redundancy. There are obvious benefits, in early retirement, for both employer and employee.

Conclusion

Termination of employment is a complex matter involving statutory provision, company policy and, most important, human emotions. Dismissal and redundancy often cause great personal sorrow and distress and personnel management must do all it can to alleviate this. Action taken must be fair and equitable, prompt and decisive, but always with regard to human dignity.

Chapter Twenty

Individual, group and organisational behaviour

- Introduction

- The individual at work

- Attitude

- Organisation roles

- Status

- Social groups

- Organisation design

- Formal and informal organisations

Introduction

The management of the human resource is a vitally important aspect of business and a very important part of the syllabus. In Chapter 5 we examined the organisation of work and the people who have to carry out the work, from a structural point of view. In Chapters 15–19 we examined the tasks which have to be performed by the personnel function. In the next two chapters we examine the human resource from the human behaviour point of view.

The first section looks at the individual and the individual's place in business. The next section considers the importance of the group, and the final section expands this into a consideration of the organisation. Chapter 21 looks at the leadership and motivation of the human resource.

The individual at work

The study of the individual at work is the task of the industrial psychologist. It commences with selecting the most suitable job, which can be achieved in two ways:

Fitting the person to the job

This involves:

1. vocational guidance: scientifically assessing the individual in order to give guidance as to the field of work where he is likely to be most efficient and derive most satisfaction;
2. personnel selection: using such means as questionnaires, interviews, intelligence and aptitude tests as well as group methods, to select the best person for a particular job (see Chapter 16);
3. training: advising on methods, duration, teaching and learning practice, who should do the training and what should be the content of the training course. Scientifically devised training schemes can do much towards increasing the satisfaction of trainees, instructors and management, as well as reducing training costs. Training thus supplements the selection process (see Chapter 16).

Fitting the job to the person

For this the following must be considered:

1. Design and layout of equipment: a piece of machinery or layout of a plant should never be designed without reference to the people who must work there. Much can be done to design machinery and layout work space to fit in with the average worker's capabilities and thus reduce fatigue, boredom and time delays. (The design of equipment to fit the person is the science of ergonomics.)
2. Physical conditions of work: increasing efficiency in carrying out a job as well as improvements in lighting, heating, ventilation and reduction of noise should be a matter of continued examination.
3. Psychological conditions of work: accidents, absenteeism, rest periods, wages and bonus systems, types of supervision and consultation should all be examined in relation to the individual concerned, and the reasons for any major variances from normal should be identified and, if necessary, remedied.

This field is not, of course, exclusively the concern of the psychologist. He frequently works with other branches of science, engineers, doctors, time and motion engineers, designers and ergonomists. It is, however, here that the psychologist has a definite contribution to make to industrial life; the industrial psychologist is trying to help industry in the following ways:

1. To increase productivity by increasing the efficiency of people (as opposed to machines): this does not mean that he will only be looking for ways of getting people to work harder; productivity can be raised, for example, by better selection and/or training, eg in a shop employing 100 people, the average output is 100 units per hour, with the best producing 150 and the worst only 50 units per hour; if in future only those people are selected who could produce over 100 then productivity would rise proportionately without extra effort.
2. To increase the satisfaction derived from one's work: dissatisfaction, once it starts, tends to spread.

3. To improve relationships between people at work: it is a basic assumption that the better these relationships are the more will productivity and individual satisfaction be increased.

Attitude

An individual's will to work and performance at work will be largely influenced by his attitude to work in general, the job in particular, his colleagues, superiors and subordinates.

An attitude is a mental stance or set, a predisposition to form certain opinions. Attitudes give meaning to facts, minimising or neglecting those facts which do not agree with the attitude adopted. We tend to select from a mass of information facts that favour our attitudes and to ignore those that are unfavourable.

Attitudes have important implications for management. The attitudes which the workers have towards work, the firm and management can influence the relations between them and the management. Managers must understand what the attitudes of the workers are if they are to understand what motivates the workforce towards different courses of action.

The attitudes that the workers hold can do much to explain their behaviour in particular circumstances. For example, the management of a firm may introduce a scheme which will be beneficial to the workers. However, such a scheme may not be greeted with enthusiasm by the workers. The workforce may be suspicious of the motives of the management because they have the attitude that the management of the firm is not to be trusted. Similarly, many managers treat suggestions from employees with a great deal of suspicion because they hold an attitude that workers are basically lazy and therefore any suggestion that comes from them is designed to reduce the amount of work they have to do.

Open-mindedness on both sides can do much to alleviate the situation as can careful education to reform attitudes. It is possible to change attitudes and management and workers must make every effort to achieve attitudes of co-operation if the firm is to prosper.

Attitude surveys

Many firms are attempting to overcome the problem described above by conducting attitude surveys among their employees.

Attitude surveys are important tools of management because without a knowledge of exactly what motivates the workers, of how they feel about the work, the leadership in the firm, the working conditions and the pay, managers will be unable to construct feasible policies. Such knowledge is essential if managers are to understand their workers.

One of the main reasons for industrial disputes is a lack of understanding between managers and workers. This comes about because neither side knows what attitudes are held by the other. A knowledge of these attitudes would lead to an understanding of each other's point of view, thus promoting better industrial relations.

Organisation roles

All individuals play roles, both at work and in their private lives. Roles are defined by their title, by their position and by the expectations of other people. Thus, throughout life we variously play the roles of father, mother, husband, wife, child, student, subordinate, superior. In business we may be factory workers, office clerks, salesmen, foremen, supervisors, managers, directors – each of these roles consists partly of a range of tasks which the role-occupant has to carry out but also of a pattern of behaviour in carrying out the task, which is expected of the role-occupant by the people with whom he comes into contact. If this seems to be a difficult concept to grasp ask yourself what you expect a mother to do, or a salesman or a manager? Perhaps more significantly, ask yourself what sort of behaviour you would *not* expect of these roles.

Role is the fundamental organisation concept. There are parallels with the animal and insect world, where organised specialised behaviour has been noted (as with the queen and the drone among bees); it is the basis of all specialisation of function. The role describes the job, whether the function is to be financial director or setter operator. In simple informal situations people divide themselves into roles. In more formal complex situations the role becomes the job offered, its functions and limitations possibly outlined by written 'terms of reference'. More than this, the role becomes 'the formal behaviour expected of the actor (role occupant)'.

Behaviour in a role is dominated by the expectations of more than immediate superiors, and is further defined by formal organisational rules and informal relationships. It is also increasingly prescribed by people outside the organisation in the wider society. Demands for more participation are increasing the role of many shop floor jobs, just as demands for more social responsibility are changing the role of board level functions. The role then is defined by a set of expected behaviours on the part of superiors, subordinates, formal worker representatives such as shop stewards and other union officials, and colleagues. Additionally, the role is defined by the hierarchy of the formal organisation (ie the authority associated with the job-title), the control system of the organisation specifying what information the role occupant is entitled to receive, the organisational reward system (ie the payment system), and the status system (see 'Status', below) which reinforces the reward systems.

Further influences on the role are largely external to the formal role from the society and its culture, and the individual's *latent roles* – each person has various latent roles involving different expectations such as those of friends, parents, wives, children. Such expectations and the influence they exert are receiving more attention nowadays, sometimes in ways which many find disturbing as, for example, when a company interviews the wife of an applicant for a senior position.

In a bureaucracy, the formal role, ie, the official position, title and function, should be impersonal (see 'The bureacratic model', below), but this cannot be achieved since the individual has personal views, skills, abilities and needs. These can rarely be an exact fit to the formal and informal expectations which define a role.

Role problems

In practice, an individual's role will vary according to circumstances. Various problems may then arise:

1. Role conflict: this arises when the demands of different parts within the set are incompatible, as in the example just given.
2. Role overload: this happens when too many demands have primacy. This can often arise when a position has too many bosses or too many subordinates. Role overload can also be the case where role conflict becomes unbearable for the individual concerned.
3. Role ambiguity: this is the situation when one does not know what is expected, which may come from an inability to find out who gives the orders in a hierarchy, from an inconsistent boss or from role overload.
4. Role stress: role ambiguity, conflict or overload can lead to this. Stress is not necessarily bad; some element of it can secure good performances. This is termed *role pressure* in order to distinguish it from *role strain,* which is the situation when stress is harmful.

These problems are not necessarily mutually exclusive but can occur together.

Effect of role problems
If the role is a poor fit for the person's needs and abilities, then tension and conflict will occur, both in the individual and in the organisation. This can take the form of:

- rejecting the formal role;
- fighting to have the role changed;
- refusing to acknowledge some of the responsibilities of the role, or wilfully misunderstanding instructions;
- leaving the organisation;
- using impersonality and formality, eg working to rule, refusing to accept unwritten orders;
- procrastinating – delaying completion of some demands in the 'hope that the problem will go away';
- prevaricating – eg lying about tasks having been done in the hope that they will be forgotten or not discovered;
- 'scapegoating' – blaming someone else for sins of omission or commission.

Many organisational problems find their source in the incompatibility of people and their roles. For the individual the problems and inconsistencies can be very serious, for not only can they modify personality in time but they can also lead to ulcers, heart attacks and mental illness. Some formal roles, eg product manager, foreman, are especially vulnerable to problems like those above.

Role behaviour and adjustment

The options available are to accept the role; change the role; train the person.

Accepting
Acceptance of role need not always lead to the problems examined above. People have been known to:

1. set personal targets to beat;
2. develop pride in their skill;

3. compensate with hygiene factors (see below);
4. concentrate on the social aspects of the job;
5. seek alternative satisfaction outside the job.

Changing

Changing the role to fit the person depends upon other variables. One of the problems of mass production technology, for example, is the limited possibility of changing roles by job enrichment, except at prohibitive cost. The more specific the tasks to be carried out, the less the possibility of changing the role to suit the person.

Training

Training the person involves changing:

1. his attitude and values – by sensitivity training, T groups, internal communication techniques and the like; and
2. his skills and abilities – by on-the-job and outside training schemes.

Status

The idea of status reinforces the organisational role, since status denotes the rank or relative importance. A broader definition of status is the 'degree of popular prestige attaching to the holder of a position in the social system'. The status system supports the authority system and is an important component of hierarchical organisations. Status within organisations broadly reflects the status system within society. As in society, status is both conferred (title, position) and inferred (from behaviour, life style).

Derivation of status

Status derives from one or more of the following job-related factors:

1. The authority and power (see Chapter 21, 'Authority v power') which are attached to a position in a hierarchy.
2. Knowledge and education: this suits the theory of bureaucracy – knowledge is graded up to topmost position. Staff with higher education than line managers raise problems of status (problems of lateral relations). Craft jobs needing high levels of training and expertise have high status.
3. Differentials: high pay is valued for more than its obvious financial benefit, since higher pay accompanies higher rank. Many industrial disputes spring from arguments over pay differentials. Often the amounts of money in question seem trivial in terms of extra purchasing power. What is really at stake is money as a symbol of status, a differential which lets everyone know that one job is of higher status than another.
4. Exclusiveness: an organisational hierarchy forms a pyramid in which there are fewer positions available for promotion as one rises. At the top is but one job, that of chairman. Status tends to increase as the number of people holding the rank declines.

---

5. Reward system and symbols: apart from pay there are many other elements in a reward system, of which status is one. Those which are tangible become symbols of status, such as car parking spaces, a car itself, key to executive dining rooms, personal offices etc.

These status symbols often begin to be looked on as personal 'rights'. Such symbols are much more easily given than taken away. Practically anything, however trivial, can become a status symbol, and can be a major cause of industrial disputes.

6. 'Clean' versus 'dirty' jobs: white collar jobs are usually recognised as having higher status than blue collar jobs. (This applies even when they are less well paid.) Labouring jobs have lower status the dirtier they are (working in a sewage works tends to have less status than cleaning buses). Attempts are made to increase status by giving jobs fancy titles, like rodent operative for rat catcher.

7. Conditions of employment: it is common to find different conditions of employment within the same business. People are paid by the hour or by the week or by the month. Pension schemes differ for different grades of employee. Hours of work may differ as may reporting times (hourly paid personnel often have to be in an hour before other employees). These differences all become questions of status.

8. Location: from shop floor to executive suite, the actual physical location in which a person works confers status. Businesses often site head offices in locations with status.

9. Association with status: status can also be conferred by being associated with high status. For example, the secretary of the managing director has more status by association and access to knowledge, than other personal secretaries (and often junior management). Some businesses also confer status upon their employees by the public esteem in which the business is held.

10. Self-direction: the degree to which self-direction and self-control can be exercised may confer status. Close supervision of experienced, highly skilled workers is resented by them as lowering their status and undervaluing their skills.

Status also derives from factors which an individual brings to a position, such as class (as identified by society generally), charisma and personality, age (which has high status, particularly in some oriental cultures) and personal qualities such as height, looks etc.

Status may be inconsistent when some factors do not correlate with others, eg age and authority, and may be ambiguous when a person is unsure of his own status. In either case the individual involved experiences stress and difficulties and tensions arise in the organisation.

Importance of status

It is essential to recognise that status is important to everybody, because it is closely related to self-respect, and industrial disputes arise when there is no respect for the other person's self-respect. In negotiating between management and unions it is important that the 'winner' concedes a point to the 'loser', so that the 'loser' does not 'lose face' among his peers; the loss of 'face' can often be the cause of the next dispute because of the resentment left from the previous dispute.

It is also important to recognise those aspects of status which are essential and those which are inessential and potentially causes of resentment. Japanese-managed firms, for example, have achieved considerable improvements in industrial relations by scrapping the management dining-room and insisting on managers and workers eating the same food together, by insisting on managers starting work at the same time as the shop-floor workers etc.

Social groups

Having considered some of the issues facing the individual at work, such as the problem of fitting the right person to the right job, role problems and status, it is now necessary to recognise that nearly all business activity is performed by people working together in groups; indeed most of the problems facing the individual arise from his relationships with other people.

Over 2000 years ago Aristotle described man as a 'social animal' and thus summed up what appears to be a natural propensity for men to form themselves into social groups. We are all, with very few exceptions, 'social animals'. We are born into a social group – the family – and we maintain our membership of such groups throughout our lives. We are great 'joiners'; we join clubs and societies; we work within a group, and we form our own groups of friends around us. We are never isolated.

Thus, the social group is an important aspect of human behaviour and its importance cannot be stressed enough. As the group is so important to us it follows that it is also important to our work.

What is a group? A social group has been described by one eminent sociologist thus:

'A social group consists of a number of persons whose relationships are based upon a set of interrelated roles and statuses. They interact with one another in a more or less standardised fashion determined largely by the norms and values they accept. They are united or held together by a sense of common identity or similarity of interests which enables them to differentiate members from non members.' (Chinoy).

Social groups can normally be identified by three major characteristics:

1. a standardised pattern of behaviour between one member and another;
2. shared or similar beliefs or values;
3. the ability to differentiate between members and non-members.

A family group demonstrates all the characteristics of a social group. Other groups such as a firm or a club or a society may well manifest these characteristics in different ways:

Behaviour patterns
The interaction between members and their roles and statuses may well be formally created. Thus the managing director of a firm or the chairman of a society has his role formally created while the structure of the organisation will formally bestow upon the other members their various roles and statuses dependent upon their position within the structure.

Shared beliefs
In the case of a club or society, it is fairly obvious that the members will share common beliefs for it is usually for the furtherance of such beliefs that the group was formed. In the

case of the firm, the shared belief could well be that such organisation is the only way to further the economic aims of the members.

Differentiation of members and non-members

As we have already seen, it is possible for members to differentiate other members from non-members if they are known to each other. In other cases, some other form of differentiation may well be adopted, eg a style of dress or a manner of speaking.

There are many different forms of social group, varying from the family to a large commercial organisation. However, whatever form the group takes it will still display the above characteristics in one form or another.

There are many different kinds of groups but they can be classified into four major categories:

1. primary groups – with frequent face to face contact, eg family, work group;
2. secondary groups – less frequent contact and normally larger than primary groups, eg a company, a social club, a trade union;
3. membership groups – the group to which a member belongs;
4. reference groups – the group with which an individual compares himself in evaluating his status.

The Hawthorne experiments

Between 1924 and 1932 Elton Mayo (1880–1949) (a founder of the 'human relations' school of management theorists) and his colleagues carried out a detailed study of worker behaviour at the Hawthorne factory (near Chicago, USA) of the Western Electric Company. Production at the factory was thought to be low and Mayo was asked to advise management on the reasons therefore. Originally, the experiments concentrated on the physical aspects of the work, eg, illumination, but it was found that improvement in lighting did not improve output and, on some occasions, production improved when lighting was made worse. Mayo realised that the factory unit taken as a whole was too varied to be suitable for definite conclusions. He therefore carried out two major long-term experiments with a limited number of employees.

The first experiment was in the relay assembly test room where five female operatives were selected to work in a separate room and over the years 1927–1929 variations were made to working conditions and output measured under the varying conditions. It was found that output gradually rose even when conditions were worsened. The main reasons for this were found in interview to be that the operators felt united with a common purpose and also because management appeared to be interested in them. This led to the conclusion that group morale and a sense of participation could overcome poor working conditions.

The second experiment was in the bank wiring room where a group of male operators were studied, but other conditions remained as previously. There were 12 operators and two inspectors in the team who were observed during the six- month period of November 1931 to May 1932. From this experiment it was concluded that the men worked as a group to restrict output (even at a loss of earnings) to their unofficial level and reported a consistent (but false) output each week and also that there was an unofficial leader, not the supervisor. Any operator in the group who did not conform to the group pattern was regarded as an outsider and verbally abused by others.

The Hawthorne experiments thus showed that group behaviour could override working conditions or payment-by-results schemes. In one case (relay assembly) the group effects were beneficial and in the other case (bank wiring) adverse to management.

Morale

The Hawthorne experiments – and many other observations – demonstrated the close correlation between morale and performance.

Morale tends to be high when human beings feel that their personal needs and objectives are being satisfied by the environment in which they are working. It is revealed in a continuing state of mind and may be thought of as a group attitude which is a by-product of satisfying group relationships. Morale is affected by the comradeship of other people with a similar outlook who are engaged on the same job. To work with others and to be accepted by them gives a feeling of well-being and strength.

There are a number of ways in which high morale can be encouraged:

1. Active participation in the pursuit of a common goal must be promoted.
2. The members of groups should be compatible with each other.
3. Each group should be given every chance to be aware of and experience the fact that it is making progress.
4. The work should be shared equitably between the members of the group.
5. A free and tolerant atmosphere within the group should be cultivated while rules and penalties should be kept to a minimum.

High morale within a group will show itself in:

1. a sense of common purpose shared between the members of the group;
2. the belief that the task being undertaken by the group is worthwhile and the goal attainable;
3. a resistance to frustration among the members of the group;
4. co-operativeness and esprit de corps.

Low morale will be demonstrated by the converse of the above.

There can be no quantitative measurement of morale. If it is to be appraised at all, an attempt must be made to encourage the employees to give expression to their feelings and emotions. There is no way of measuring the correlation between productivity and morale, which further serves to make the quantification of morale difficult.

It must also be appreciated that morale is an element that pervades the whole firm. The structure of the firm, its organisation, its management, the nature of the supervision and leadership, the administration and procedures within the firm, and the attitudes of workers and management all go to creating high or low morale.

Worker participation

The logical extension of recognising the importance of the group and group morale is 'worker participation'.

Everyone should be aware of the bad effects of poor 'industrial relations'. Successive governments have attempted to produce a formula to bring together the two sides of industry ('manager and worker' or 'them' and 'us').

The concept of worker participation (of which 'Worker Director Schemes' are specific examples) is an attempt at solving this dilemma.

'Participation' is the right of a person to take some part in the decision-making processes of the organisation for which he or she works. As such it helps to satisfy the natural desire of human beings to exercise control over their own working lives.

Any successful 'worker participation' scheme can only help to achieve this objective and thus help resolve bad industrial relations situations. Job enrichment, job enlargement and the restructuring of responsibilities which are necessary in order to achieve participation should have beneficial effects on the morale and efficiency of the workforce. Also, it is argued that quite apart from increasing efficiency it is equitable that those who do the work should have a voice in the policy making process which dictates their working existence and livelihood.

The concept of 'worker participation' aims at much more than achieving a degree of worker involvement at board level. It also envisages closer participation at most other levels. Examples of such participation are direct personal involvement by workers in the setting of standards, rate fixing, quality control, the democratic organisation within groups (including group determination of roles and the division of group remuneration) and many other aspects of policy-making. Recent experience and investigations into results of enlightened worker participation schemes seem to confirm that the effects are favourable and often lead to overall improvements in working relationships. Such improvement can be quantified in terms of reduced labour turnover and absenteeism, better quality work, reduction of scrapped work in production and fewer closedowns caused by industrial unrest.

Genuine worker participation will only be possible if workers are truly involved in the affairs of the business, its objectives, plans policies and performance, and such involvement will only be possible if management accept a responsibility to divulge to their workforce a wide range of facts and figures about the business and its success (or failure). A large proportion of the workforce is denied all but the basic information, and management efforts to introduce changes and improved methods, which are often resisted by workers, could in many instances be facilitated by discussion with workers' representatives and the publication of relevant information. Businesses are increasingly becoming aware of the need to issue more information to their employees.

The concept of having worker participation on the board of directors represents radical alteration to the traditional working relationship existing between management and workers. There are many potential problems. One well known problem is that worker directors are elected to the board of directors to represent the workers' interests but, once there, increasingly start to identify with the management rather than the workers who elected them.

It is doubtful that legislation will create the correct environment for genuine worker participation. Participation is an attitude of mind which cannot be regulated by law, but must develop from an awareness of the mutual benefits available to both sides of industry. The government can use its influence, lay down laws, establish the correct conditions and even offer appropriate incentives, but it cannot make 'worker participation' successful without 'grassroots' support. Such success will come from the favourable attitudes of managers and workers who must use it and accept it.

Note: this topic is charged with political overtones and students should be careful, when discussing it, not to betray political bias or to make 'hostile' remarks about one side of the argument or the other.

Organisation design

The subject of organisation design has already been introduced in Chapter 5; students are advised to re-read that chapter before reading this section.

Chapter 5 concentrated on the structure of organisation. The first part of this chapter introduced the concept of individual roles and the last section stressed the importance of the group. Understanding all of the concepts – structure, roles and groups – is essential to the understanding of organisations.

The organisation is the basic arrangement of roles within which people will be allocated the tasks by which a firm's central purpose and objectives can be achieved. The role has specific tasks, a defined degree of authority, a clear relationship with other roles, and a position in a role structure; in addition, a certain kind of behaviour is expected of the person occupying the role. This kind of basic organisation based upon division of labour can be seen in any task-oriented concern, even a voluntary club in which the treasurer and the secretary fulfil different roles.

The organisation is also a social system. People relate to and become friendly with those with whom they work and share interests. They build up loyalties to their group and have their own cliques. Since the biggest shared interest is work and similar tasks, then the work group becomes a social unit. The interaction between the members of the group and between the groups themselves may not be according to the official channels of communication.

The organisation as defined by its roles and tasks is often known as the 'formal organisation' and the social interaction as the 'informal organisation'.

Managing the structure of the organisation in its technical and social aspects is a task for higher management through appropriate organisational design.

The process

The kind of organisation structure which a company will set up depends on many variables. The process of organising is iterative; it is something which managements must constantly pay attention to in order to avoid major organisational dysfunctions.

Clearly three factors will have the prime effect on the structure of the organisation:

1. the kind of business or businesses in which the organisation is engaged;
2. the values and priorities of the senior management;

3. the size of the organisation.

As any of these change over time, so will the organisational structure to reflect changes in the business's product/market strategy, its style of management or its size.

The bureaucratic model

The concept of bureaucracy was propounded by Max Weber, early in the last century, as the 'ideal' form of organisation. This form, if it were perfectly achieved, would lead to a permanent structure of offices (roles) which would be 'rational-legal' and transcend the people in the roles. The characteristics of this model are:

1. Division of labour: specialisation is by task and, hence, operative. Specialisation entails succeeding vertical and horizontal links.
2. Hierarchy: compatible with the notion of vertical division of labour is that of hierarchy, or authority structure, in which authority is increased in successive grades.
3. Impersonal roles: the concept of roles is closely allied to the idea of division of labour. The role is the function which one is appointed to undertake. The function is quite separate from the person undertaking it, and is thus impersonal.
4. Rules: bureaucracy has specific rules, both written and unwritten. In the course of time unwritten rules become written ones, and new rules are added, as in case law.
5. Expertise: specialisation demands expertise, therefore the higher a person's expertise, the higher his position in the hierarchy. Thus positions are based upon the technical and educational qualifications needed.

These characteristics form an élitist view of organisation in which ultimate power and authority reside at the top, and is diffused in accordance with grade. The model indeed is from Weber's analysis of authority in society.

In practice, the modern form of bureaucracy would exhibit further characteristics such as:

1. Centralisation: the bureaucratic tendency is implicit in the ideas of centralisation of authority.
2. Size: the bigger the organisation, the more authoritarian and centralised it becomes.
3. Controls: there are especially strong financial controls and budgets, and cost procedures.
4. Technology: the larger and more costly the modern technology involved the more the tendency to the features of bureaucracy. Thus mass or process production has the greatest tendency to bureaucratic characteristics.

A bureaucracy, through its rigid role structure and technical specialisation, is the medium by which scientific management is exercised. The principles of classical organisation theory such as 'span of control' or Fayol's precepts of 'unity of command' are based upon similar assumptions. As Weber noted, a bureaucracy is rational since its system of roles and impersonality legitimises a hierarchical authority while its rules legalise it.

Dysfunctions of bureaucracy
Some dysfunctions of bureaucracy can be examined under the same headings.

Division of labour. Over-specialisation of tasks, whether manual or clerical, leads to jobs becoming boring and repetitive, often needing little attention from the worker. This leads to what Durkheim called 'anomie' and Marx 'alienation', when the workers' boredom with, and antipathy for their tasks leads, perhaps not to revolution, but to strikes and bad industrial relations generally, plus poor quality products. It is often argued that the production technology of the car industry is responsible for most of its problems, hence attempts by companies such as Volvo to eliminate the non-stop production line. Lack of interchangeability of workers and hence an inability to respond to technological or market changes is a further problem.

Hierarchy. An authority structure becomes dysfunctional when it becomes so inflexible that change cannot take place. The idea that the boss knows best in every instance is as untenable as the notion that things should always be done in a certain way. Since organisations must adapt to changing environments, there is a need for flexible and more organic organisational forms.

Impersonal roles. In practice it is not possible for the role to be impersonal. People bring their own attitudes, needs, values, expectations and skills to the functional role and thus help to shape it. More importantly perhaps, a role is determined by other people's expectations, bosses, subordinates etc (see section on Organisational Roles) so that it can never be completely impersonal. The role must also be adapted to changing circumstances which means that the incumbent has to be allowed discretion and the less discretion he can exercise the slower the organisation can adapt. Also people see it as unfair that rewards attach to the role (rigid pay scales), while punishments attach to the person (tellings off, sackings). Promotion (which may not be possible) is then the main way to recognise merit or long service.

Red tape. Rules are what most people understand as 'bureaucratic red tape'. Every procedure must be codified, and each standard laid down, so that when a new challenge crops up, the organisation is unable to cope, since there is no room for discretion. The more rules are written, the more they become 'ends' in themselves, rather than means to ends. Formalism and ritualism then take over. The more the rules appear to reinforce a hierarchical authority structure, the greater the tendency to conflict and tension. The ultimate is reached when 'working to rule' is used as a form of industrial protest.

Expertise problems. Expertise can involve problems of staff and line conflicts, career blockages, discrimination against experience in favour of formal paper qualifications, discrimination against people outside the system by means of qualifications granted only within, and possibly control of the organisation by 'apparatchicks', or 'thinkers' rather than 'doers'.

Being hidebound. When lower and middle grades in the hierarchy begin to feel that the organisation is too hidebound, they begin to question the system and its legitimacy. This leads to problems of authority.

Bureaucracy has become a pejorative word, associated with delays in service, ludicrous errors which no one has the apparent authority to resolve, over-staffing and time-wasting, inefficiency, 'red tape' and general bumbledom.

Yet bureaucracy has become the most common pattern for large organisations. As organisations, private or public, grow bigger they tend to become more bureaucratic. Such large bureacratic organisations account for a growing share of national output, well over 50 per cent already. The features of bureaucracy are thus both common and important.

The practical model
As noted above with the work to rule, there is often a paradox involved in bureaucracy in the sense that only by disobedience of the rules or refusal to accept the authority structure, can the bureaucracy be kept functioning. Some dysfunctions can therefore be beneficial rather than harmful. Employees may solve problems without keeping records, or groups may institute their own unofficial norms. Formal channels of communication may be by-passed, or 'natural' informal leaders may emerge to take all except the titular authority from the official manager.

The bureaucratic kind of organisational form demands predictability rather than creativity, stability rather than change, consolidation rather than entrepreneurship. In situations where the environment is predictable and stable, and the product market changes slowly, it can be argued that bureaucracy is the 'ideal' form, becoming dysfunctional only under the pressure of changing circumstances. Bureaucracy exists because it is inherently logical, organisations need allocations of tasks and roles, managers need information to control what is going on and the authority to see that organisational objectives are achieved. At the same time, as Wilensky notes, 'In a complex system, hierarchy, specialisation and centralisation are blockages of intelligence'. In other words, the logic doesn't always work!

In practice, the totally machine-like bureaucracy is at one end of a continuum and as unlikely as its opposite, the fully rule-less, role-less free form organisation. Thus, such characteristics of bureaucracy are adopted as seem appropriate to environmental circumstances, the complexity of the business and the technology involved. Moreover, the characteristics must change to fit the evolving needs and attitudes of people as demands increase for more democracy and participation in the work place.

A further point to consider is that some parts of a business may be more open to change than others, or may in practice have different value systems in operation. It is therefore not unusual to have departments in a bureaucratic organisation which are more flexible, more democratic and more 'free form' than the whole (task force squads in the police for example). Even within a 'free form' high-technology business, not all divisions will be faced with the same amount of pressure for change, and those less exposed may exhibit more bureaucratic tendencies. Some writers argue that ever-increasing rates of change in the environment, combined with the 'knowledge explosion' and a 'communications revolution' from higher standards of education and modern information technology, will lead to a natural erosion of the bureaucratic form.

Formal and informal organisations

To attain an objective beyond the capacity of one individual, work has to be divided into many different tasks, capable of being done by one man or by a number together. This results in the horizontal and functional aspects of organisation where jobs are defined, differentiated and allocated to appropriate personnel, who, for a reward, are willing to co-operate to attain the objectives desired.

Simultaneously with the horizontal and functional organisation, a vertical or hierarchical line of co-ordinators and decision makers comes into being. From manager to superintendent to supervisor there is a downward flow of authority, delegation and communications. In a healthy organisation the flow of information upwards is constant and keeps management informed on progress made.

An organisation chart can indicate the formal position of each person in the organisation, horizontally and vertically, and the channels of interaction between them.

From the formal chart we get an idea of the levels of power and decision, of the task and job specialisations, of the formal linkage. Even in this formal structuring, however, errors can be made. You can have too many levels of command which may indicate unclear objectives, excessive bureaucratic timidity and inaccessibility, or over-centralisation.

Inevitably communication flow can become distorted and the organisation can become unwieldy. There can be too many people reporting to one individual. Again, there can be a situation where there may be a department concerned with the entire plant, but reporting to the production manager. Job titles may not be descriptive; functions may not be clearly designated: there may be a multiplicity of co-ordinators with no clear job responsibility.

Thus, the formal chart can never mirror what actually happens in the organisation for there can be many hidden factors which are not revealed in a simple chart. The likes and antagonisms of personnel in the same or different functions can affect communications. The stresses upon, and the inadequacies of, supervisors and managers can have an impact upon decisions. The informal influence of the shop steward, the rivalries and pressures of groups and individuals, the skills, competence and reputations of individual managers, create, underneath the formal structure, an informal organisation that dare not be overlooked by one who would manage effectively.

In the constitution of informal groups, physical location, similarity of jobs and interests, and special interests may contribute to their particular form. Sheer physical nearness and constant face-to-face relationships can establish a feeling of togetherness between individuals. People with similar jobs tend to come together and talk a special jargon of their own and have similar hopes, aspirations and outlooks. People with like interests, technical, artistic, musical and social, may be drawn together both inside and outside the workplace. Sometimes special issues, political, ideological and religious, can unite or divide people at work.

Informal groups and informal organisations, like all social groupings, often act as agents of social control. They can establish certain norms of behaviour which in turn demand conformity from group members. However, these standards may conflict with those set by the formal organisation, as found by Elton Mayo in the Hawthorne experiments (see above).

Even today there are a number of organisations where the output level is determined by the 'informal organisation'.

271

The ways in which the informal organisation can work against the aims of the formal organisation can manifest themselves in many different forms. Work methods may be affected; men in a working group may exchange repetitive jobs, one man may do two jobs while a colleague rests; the men can change the sequence of operations to reduce monotony or tension or as a short cut. All of these, however, can result in the standards of the formal organisation being undermined. This is particularly relevant on night shift work when supervision and control are often at a lower level.

What has been called the culture of a firm embraces its entire way of doing business, its manner and style of production, its particular objectives, its level of technical and personal sophistication, the customs of management, and the value placed upon different types of work in a manner far beyond the formal concept of the business. Culture is a wider term than organisational structure which describes the tasks, the positions of people and their formal roles. But roles are not people and as a result a man's formal role may differ greatly from his conception of that role and from the functions and activities associated with that role. This again widens the gap between the formal and informal structure of business.

To summarise, therefore, the informal organisation of a business represents the human aspect of the business. It is the consequence of placing people into the formal structure. The particular capabilities of the personnel, their likes and dislikes, their attitudes and prejudices, their social affiliations, create an undercurrent within the organisation which the wise manager must take account of if he is to manage effectively. The informal organisation can work quite effectively against the aims and goals of the formal organisation. A knowledge of this phenomenon will permit the manager to understand the reasons why his plans are not being achieved, or how best to use the informal organisation to his advantage.

Chapter Twenty One

Leadership and motivation

Introduction

How well the individual works, to what extent groups work together constructively or destructively, how flexible the organisation is in adapting to change – to a large extent all these things depend on the quality of leadership.

Evidently one of the roles of anybody in a managerial position is to lead. This may be seen merely as the exercise of authority and discipline. These concepts will be examined first in this chapter.

However, this is to take a very narrow view of leadership. More important are the skills of team management and the resolution of conflict. These concepts are examined next.

Above all, leadership depends on motivation. Understanding what motivates workers and using this knowledge in the design of organisation, in communicating with workpeople, in the design of reward systems is what leadership is essentially all about.

Finally, this chapter draws together some of the main theories of leadership, many of which conflict with each other but which have to be understood.

Authority

In a hierarchy, authority is assumed to reside in greater or lesser degree according to the level of the position. The higher the level, the greater the authority. By the same token, the higher the level the more the power.

It is necessary to draw a clear distinction between 'authority' and 'power'. *Authority* is given by the role and built into the structure of organisation. It is a right which brings with it responsibility and accountability. Thus, authority is legitimate, and has been called the 'right of the last word'. In fact, the extent of the right is built into the definition of the role.

By contrast, *power* need not be legitimate, since it is not the right but the ability. It might be defined as the 'ability to make things happen or to get one's own way'. Power exists with authority, when authority is exercised.

Bases of authority

The bases of authority include:

1. the terms of reference of the role;
2. position in the hierarchy;
3. control of, or access to, resources (eg factors of production, information);
4. ownership or proxy ownership, ie professional managers are 'authorised' by the owners, the shareholders (or the State in the case of nationalised industries);
5. charismatic leadership;
6. superior knowledge;
7. tradition;
8. devolved authority from superior;
9. factors concerned with subordinates, such as their:

   a) expectations, aspirations and needs;
   b) values;
   c) contracts of employment;
   d) conditioning from:

      i) childhood – acceptance of parental and other authoritarian discipline;
      ii) learning – the extent to which they are conditioned by the job.

In fact, without subordinate acceptance there can be no effective exercising of authority, for it is the subordinate who confers legitimacy on the superior, who must therefore meet his subordinate's aspirations, needs and values, through effective leadership so that his authority continues to be recognised.

Problems of authority

Forces affecting the manager include:

1. His own values, as shaped by society: in a less authoritarian society he is unlikely to see total authority as achievable or desirable.
2. The exercise of authority is limited by the costs and benefits to be granted, especially if resistance is involved.
3. The acceptance of authority incurs matching responsibility. Not all managers, rightly or wrongly, are willing to accept the obligations and accountability.

Forces affecting the subordinate include:

1. Some may be ideologically opposed to the general society within which the business operates.
2. Subordinates acquiesce to managerial authority for reasons of self-interest, which depend on their motivations.
3. People accept others' authority only up to a point or for some aspects and not others.
4. Authority may be acceptable simply because some aspects of the situation seem not to matter, or have never been tested.
5. Authority may be acceptable because subordinates are in too weak a position to challenge it.

Forces affecting the situation include:

1. Authority may not be accepted in situations of long-term or historical conflict.
2. Economic circumstances, especially in respect of employment prospects, may make acceptance of authority more or less likely (eg it will be less likely if there are many similar jobs being advertised).

Authority v power

Management's power relies, of course, on the same factors as those which confer authority. But more basically, power comes through the control over resources; money and jobs, and also information and knowledge. The use of power is coercive.

Authority and power can thus be seen as a continuum ranging from 100 per cent legitimate accepted authority to the 100 per cent illegitimate abuse of power. Managers use a mixture of authority and power to achieve organisational objectives, depending on their assessment of the requirements of the situation and of the appropriate leadership style. However, an over-use of power means that subordinates no longer legitimise managerial actions, and signals that the organisation is in a poor state of health.

Leadership and discipline

Some of the important leadership and disciplinary techniques applicable to large organisations are outlined below:

Maintaining the authority of the position

An executive is a leader by virtue of the position he occupies in the hierarchy, rather than because of any personal leadership qualities (though these may have helped him to achieve his present position). It is therefore important to maintain the *authority of the position* if the executive is to be an effective leader of his group. This forms a substantial area of behavioural research, ie role playing.

Impersonalising the authority relationship

If the subordinates' acceptance of decisions made by superiors becomes an obligation imposed by the organisation rather than a personal obligation to the superior, the maintenance of authority is facilitated. This also helps a superior when unpopular decisions have to be made and implemented, as the decision making becomes an organisational responsibility, and the organisation rather than the superior, is taken to be the 'culprit' by the subordinates.

Participation by subordinates

Leadership may be authoritarian (in which the leader takes all the decisions) or democratic (in which the leader invites participation from subordinates in the decision-making process).

However, specialisation and division of work tend to limit the scope of participative decision making in complex enterprises. Also if the subordinates' views are not acceptable to the organisation and have to be overruled by the superior, frustration may result.

Keeping subordinates informed

Undesirable behaviour by a subordinate may simply be due to lack of information about the behaviour patterns or goals of the organisation. A good leader ensures that his subordinates have knowledge of the norms of appropriate behaviour and the consequences of non-conformity.

Consistent interpretation and enforcement of rules

Superiors should be consistent in interpreting and enforcing the rules of the company. Erratic and inconsistent enforcement can create frustration, insecurity and distrust among subordinates.

Modifying unpopular decisions

Executives should not make decisions that will not be obeyed by subordinates. It may be better to modify a decision than be faced with an open challenge to authority.

Use of disciplinary measures

The effectiveness of disciplinary measures against subordinates depends on how highly they value their connection with the organisation.

Leniency

Some superiors are more lenient in enforcing decision and organisational policies than others. A lenient superior may countenance several minor infringements of rules by his subordinates and thereby create goodwill and a sense of personal loyalty which will help him carry his subordinates with him in achieving the major organisational objectives.

However, leniency must not be carried to the extreme of departing from the standards of the organisation.

Team management

We have seen how social groups have an important part to play in the modern business environment. If a manager is to carry out his tasks effectively, he must have the ability to manage the various work groups which he may come into contact with.

The basic skill involved in the effective management of social groups or work teams is that of leadership. Leadership is the process of obtaining willing co-operation from a group. Mary Parker Follett in her papers 'Leader and Expert' and 'Some Discrepancies in Leadership Theory and Practice', published in 1927 and 1931 respectively, went further in that she saw the power pertaining to the leader as being the result of the capacity of the group to accept a particular individual as a leader. Continued effectiveness of a work team therefore involves the manager in securing the interest, loyalty and participation of all the members of the team. A good leader, as Fayol contends, should both possess and infuse into those around him the courage to accept responsibility.

To maintain teamwork, therefore, means that the manager must lead by involvement. It is not sufficient for the leader to foist a problem upon the group, he must establish with them whether they have a problem. This requires of the manager a knowledge of the principles of group discussion as well as a knowledge of the forces in play within all social groups. He must be aware of how social groups can influence the behaviour of individual members and of how group decisions are reached.

An effective work team which is well managed can be expected to display the following characteristics:

1. It is cohesive; its members will subordinate individual interests to group objectives and there is a real esprit de corps within the group.
2. It has defined and accepted objectives.
3. Its application of policy shows a high degree of co-ordination of activities.
4. It shows adaptability in meeting changing circumstances.
5. It shows timeliness in its decision making and actions.
6. There is an intelligent use of communication channels.
7. The group will use meetings productively.
8. There is a permissive atmosphere about its discussion of issues and possible changes; it makes use of constructive criticism.

Conflict

In any human organisation, however well run, there will always be an amount of stress and unrest.

This has resulted in conflict becoming more and more important to the modern manager and in focussing attention upon the manager who is unable to manage such conflict.

The classical school of management theorists tended largely to ignore conflict depending upon the force of management power to solve any problems which may have arise in this area. However, in the 1920s Follett in her essay 'Constructive Conflict' suggested that rather than the managers aiming to remove conflict, usually by force, they should aim to manage such conflict in such a manner that it could be directed to the good of the undertaking.

Follett suggested that there were three methods of solving a situation which had resulted in conflict, usually between the men or the trade unions and management. These were by domination, compromise and integration. Of these, only integration can offer a permanent solution to the problem.

Domination

One can solve a conflict by domination; by sheer massive power one can destroy an opponent. This means that a strong management can bring down a weak union, or a strong union can destroy an enterprise. This often results in new grievances coming to the fore yet again.

Compromise

One can solve disputes by compromise, the most favoured and frequent form of solution. In compromise each side asks for what it wants and then trades for the final result. This is a temporary settlement, which does not search for the less obvious and real issues in contention. In addition, compromise usually concentrates on the short-term, ad hoc solutions and often leads to a repetition of the conflict after a brief period.

Integration

One can also solve conflicts by integration. This approach assumes that the conflict is seen as a many-faceted problem with the solution lying in the satisfaction of the essential needs of both sides of the conflict. For integration you require a common value system between the disputants to ensure that both sides know exactly what the other side is talking about. One of the most common reasons for conflict remaining unresolved is that far too often each side to the dispute is talking about different things. Thus, for instance, suppose ABCDE are the disputed elements. It can happen that management may well regard A and B of great importance, C of some importance and D and E of no significance at all. The men and their union on the other hand, might put most value on D and E and consider A, B and C insignificant. In solving a conflict by integration, the dispute would be broken down and analysed into its component parts, and the different weightings attached by each side to the items ascertained. The needs, desires and aspirations of both sides are brought together to be viewed and valued. From such an elevation, a revaluation of interests may result.

The obstacles to the integration process are that:

1. It requires intelligence, perceptiveness, discrimination and inventiveness on both sides.
2. Many managers have acquired the habit of domination which may be difficult to break.
3. Cultural prejudices may emphasise differences rather than common ground.
4. Many managers lack training in the art of co-operative thinking.

However, by careful training and development of managers, many of these obstacles can be overcome.

Conflict is not necessarily a bad thing. Although it can be very destructive, it can, however, serve to clear the air between operatives and management and to clarify long-standing points in disputes.

The effective manager cannot, and does not attempt to, eliminate all conflict. What the manager must do is to solve the problem by the process of integration and thus bring about a clarification of the goals and objectives of both sides. Constructive criticism within the consultations will mean that management can gain as much as the workers. Procedures, working practices and personnel policies can all be improved as a result of such consultation serving to improve managerial performance in the long run.

Motivation

Since 1880, when Frederick Winslow Taylor began his systematic study of management techniques, most research has been about motivation. Taylor made four basic assumptions about human behaviour at work:

1. Man is a rational animal concerned with maximising his economic gains.
2. People respond to economic situations as individuals.
3. Men, like machines, can be treated in a standardised fashion.
4. Work can be scientifically analysed, and it is the responsibility of managers to *instruct* the workers.

Taylor believed that all the workers wanted, beyond anything else, was high wages.

Taylor's theories were applied for many years in the form of incentive payment schemes (piece-work schemes etc) without any great change. However, in the late 1920s the work of Elton Mayo at the Hawthorne Works of the General Electric Company did much to disprove Taylor's theories and point the way to the modern theorists. The basis for most modern theories, though, rests upon the theories of motivation put forward by Abraham Maslow, an American psychologist (1908–1970).

Maslow's hierarchy of needs

Maslow suggested that a person is motivated to satisfy an ascending series of needs which fall into a hierarchy or pyramid of five broad strata. In ascending order these are:

1. physiological or basic needs: food, warmth, shelter, sex etc;
2. safety or security needs: freedom from danger;
3. social needs: the need to belong;
4. esteem needs: including self-esteem and the esteem of others (eg 'status symbols');
5. self-actualisation needs: the need to develop to one's fullest potential and realise all one is capable of.

Maslow puts forward the proposition that the needs are, in the simplest way, satisfied one after the other. Thus as one need is satisfied it ceases to be a motivator and the person will look to satisfy the next need in the hierarchy and so on. But, if while trying to satisfy a higher group of needs a more basic need emerges, the individual will turn his attention to it until it is satisfied.

From a 'motivation to work' standpoint, the employer who thinks that man lives by bread alone will be baffled if his adequate provision of loaves leaves his work people unhappy and unmotivated. As Maslow said, 'Man only lives by bread alone – where there is no bread.'

Three important points have to be remembered about Maslow's theory:

1. The hierarchy closely resembles the ordinary development of a person from birth to

maturity – the infant first needs food and warmth, safety and love and as it grows up gradually needs to develop a reasonable self-assurance (or self-esteem) and finally emerges as a self-motivating adult capable of and desiring achievement.

2. The disappearance of needs as they are satisfied and the emergence of others as motivators is an unconscious process – once one has got a job one will quickly forget, and even deny, how pleased one was, and automatically start looking for promotion, status, or recognition; if one does not get them one will feel just as unhappy as one did when one had no job at all.

3. As Maslow points out, the five steps in the hierarchy are not rigid. There is a certain degree of interaction between them. It is more a matter of decreasing percentages up the steps, because most members of society are both partially satisfied and partially unsatisfied in all their needs at the same time.

Maslow's thinking goes on to suggest that, since the need for the satisfaction of the basic needs in the hierarchy is as important as the satisfaction of the need for, for example vitamins, then the healthy man is the one who is motivated primarily by his self-actualised need – the need to develop to his fullest potential. If a man is thwarted in the substantial satisfaction of the lower needs then the higher needs cannot emerge. Thwarting of the satisfaction of a need is, however, something that the individual does not do himself – it is imposed on him from outside. Since management is the major force outside the individual at work, then the implications of this theory for management are far reaching.

The business organisation as a satisfier of needs

The business organisation has an important part to play in the satisfaction of needs. It contributes significantly to the satisfaction of the physical needs (eg food and clothing) through financial rewards, and to the security needs by means of long-term employment. The employee satisfies his needs for acceptance and belonging through associating with his work colleagues and through identifying with his work group.

However, it is the esteem and self-expression needs which are particularly relevant to the consideration of employee motivation. Esteem is satisfied through recognition and consideration of personal feelings. The self-expression needs involve the expression of the person's abilities and skills. They show themselves in the desire for some measure of responsibility on the job, and for jobs which are interesting and challenging.

Recent research in job enlargement indicates that when jobs are made more challenging by introducing more responsibility and variety, they not only increase the satisfaction of the job-holder but also lead to increased job performance.

Herzberg's 'motivation/hygiene' theory

One of the most important concepts of motivation at work to stem from Maslow's views is that put forward by Professor Frederick Herzberg (born 1923), another American psychologist, who developed the 'motivation/hygiene' theory.

The origins of this theory lie in research by Herzberg into what people think about their jobs – what made them happy or unhappy, satisfied or dissatisfied – by investigating events in the lives of a number of engineers and accountants. (These investigations have been carried out many times since by other researchers, with many kinds of people and in many countries, and there is a high degree of verification of the results.)

The research suggested that the factors that caused satisfaction at work (and genuine motivation) were of a different nature from, and had to be considered separately from, those that caused dissatisfaction. Looked at this way, the removal of a dissatisfier does not cause satisfaction, it merely causes no dissatisfaction. As a result, satisfaction and dissatisfaction are not opposites. In Herzberg's view the opposite of job satisfaction is no job satisfaction and the opposite of no job dissatisfaction is job dissatisfaction.

Factors that contribute to the avoidance of dissatisfaction, Herzberg labels hygiene (or maintenance) factors; those that contribute to satisfaction he labels as motivators.

Motivators improve performance; hygiene factors only serve to bring an individual's performance back to 'normal'.

A man's working situation – the actual job he does and the conditions surrounding and attached to it such as pay, supervision and so on – can be seen as a mix of motivators and hygiene factors. But great care has to be exercised not to confuse one with another. The job should be kept 'clean' by hygiene factors so that there is no dissatisfaction, but this in itself will not motivate the worker – and if he is not motivated he will not work without being pushed.

The research that Herzberg carried out established that it was possible to distinguish between, and classify, the hygiene and the motivating factors.

The hygiene, or maintenance, factors include:

1. security;
2. status;
3. working relationships;
4. salary;
5. working conditions;
6. supervision;
7. company policy and administration.

The actual motivators found in the research, the things that brought satisfaction , include:

1. psychological growth (Maslow's self-actualisation);
2. advancement;
3. responsibility;
4. the work itself;
5. recognition;
6. achievement.

In the motivation-hygiene theory, therefore, the needs of the individual are regarded as falling into two groups.

1. Animal needs: these are those needs relating to the animal needs of human beings such as satisfying hunger or avoiding pain, together with the learned drives associated with them, such as earning money.
2. Spiritual needs: this second group relates to those qualities which are uniquely human, such as the need for achievement and psychological growth (the upper end of the Maslow hierarchy).

Herzberg also pointed out that catering for both sets of factors will be beneficial to both employee and employer. Hygiene factors will maintain performance but the motivating factors are needed to bring about real improvement.

McGregor's X and Y theory

Douglas McGregor (1906–1964), an American management consultant, carried out studies on theories of management and employee motivation. He described various assumptions which managers make about the behaviour of employees. McGregor compared the traditional management philosophy of direction and control with the more modern approach of job satisfaction and the uplifting of the human spirit as a motivating force. He called the two propositions Theory X and Theory Y respectively.

Theory X ('traditional' view)

Theory X forms the traditional management philosophy of direction and control. The manager tells people what to do and resorts frequently to rewards and punishments to get things done. He works on the following assumptions:

1. The average human being has an inherent dislike of work and will avoid it if he can.
2. Because of this particular human characteristic, most people must be coerced, controlled, directed and threatened with punishment to get them to put forth adequate effort towards the achievement of organisational objectives.
3. The average human being prefers to be directed, wishes to avoid responsibility, has relatively little ambition and above all desires security.

Theory Y ('modern' view)

Theory Y, in contrast, is a new management philosophy based upon the findings of the social scientists and rests upon the following assumptions:

1. The expenditure of physical and mental effort in work is as natural as play or rest.
2. External controls and the threat of punishments are not the only means for bringing about effort towards organisational objectives. Man will exercise self-direction and self-control in the service of objectives to which he is committed.
3. Commitment to objectives is a function of the rewards associated with their achievement. The most significant of such rewards, eg the satisfaction of ego and self-fulfilment needs, can be the product of efforts directed towards organisational objectives.
4. The average human being learns, under proper conditions, not only to accept but to seek responsibilities.
5. The capacity to exercise a relatively high degree of imagination, ingenuity and creativity in the solution of organisation problems, is widely, not narrowly, distributed among the population.
6. Under the conditions of modern industrial life, the intellectual potentialities of the average human being are being only partially utilised and should be developed further.

This proposition represents two widely divergent views of man at work and, if they were adopted in either form, would result in opposite styles of management. However, in practice, management styles vary considerably. The various styles and theories of leadership are described below.

Leadership

Theories

Although many expositions of leadership have been proposed, as yet there is a lack of general acceptance of any one of them as being truly explanatory. Because the development of a theory of leadership is such a vital aspect of management, it is appropriate to examine some of the attempts.

1. The 'trait' theory is based on the proposition that all successful leaders possess common personality traits that have causative bearing on success.
2. The 'situation' theory is based on the proposition that the individual perceived to be best suited for leadership in a given situation will emerge from the group as a leader. Following this approach candidates for leadership might be placed in various informal situations calling for specific interaction and those who assumed positions of leadership in the informal group situation could be selected for formal leadership positions.
3. The 'eclectic' theory of leadership is synthetic; it is a combination of components of other theories. It brings explanatory phrases or information from other theories into one body of thought in an effort to explain leadership.

The eclectic theory is perhaps the most useful of the theories, since it draws information from several sources to explain leadership.

Characteristics and skills of a leader

Leadership can perhaps best be defined as:

> 'the will to dominate the proceedings in which one finds oneself, accompanied by a character which inspires confidence in followers, so that they are persuaded to do the acts required of them'.

or more simply as:

> 'the ability to persuade people to do things they would not do, or think, voluntarily'.

Some of the generally accepted characteristics of a leader are acceptance of responsibility, confidence, decisiveness, integrity and intelligence.

The required skills can therefore be established. Certain of these skills will be inherent in a person's character and personality, whereas others can be taught. The skills include:

1. organising ability;
2. acceptance by other people at all levels;
3. vitality/energy;
4. encouraging initiative;

5. delegation;
6. man-management;
7. tact;
8. self-discipline.

Likert's styles of leadership

Dr Rensis Likert (1903–1981), an American industrial psychologist, carried out research into the use of human assets ('human resources accounting'). Likert asserts that to achieve maximum profitability, good labour relations and high productivity, every organisation must make optimum use of their human assets. The form of organisation which will make the greatest use of the human capacity is one of highly effective work groups linked together in an overlapping pattern by other similarly effective groups.

Organisations at present have widely varying types of leadership styles and Likert has identified four main systems:

The exploitive-authoritative system
In this:

1. Decisions are imposed on subordinates.
2. Motivation is characterised by threats.
3. High levels of management have great responsibilities but lower levels have virtually none.
4. There is very little communication.
5. There is no joint teamwork.

The benevolent-authoritative system
In this:

1. Leadership is by a condescending form of master-servant trust.
2. Motivation is mainly by rewards.
3. Managerial personnel carry responsibility but lower levels do not.
4. There is little communication.
5. There is relatively little teamwork.

The consultative system
In this:

1. Leadership is by superiors who have substantial, but not complete, trust in their subordinates.
2. Motivation is by rewards and some involvement.
3. A high proportion of personnel, especially those at the higher levels, feel responsibility for achieving organisational goals.
4. There is some communication (both vertical and horizontal).
5. There is a moderate amount of teamwork.

The participative-group system
In this:

1. Leadership is by superiors who have complete confidence in their subordinates.
2. Motivation is by economic rewards based on goals which have been set in participation.
3. Personnel at all levels feels real responsibility for the organisational goals.
4. There is much communication.
5. There is a substantial amount of co-operative teamwork.

The fourth system is the one which Likert considers ideal for the profit-orientated and human-conscious organisation; he says that all organisations should adopt this system.

To convert an organisation, Likert considers that four main features of effective management must be put into practice. These are:

1. Motivation of work must be fostered by modern principles and techniques, and not by the old system of rewards and threats.
2. Employees must be seen as people who have their own needs, desires and values and their self-esteem must be maintained or enhanced.
3. An organisation of tightly knit and highly effective work groups must be built up which are committed to achieving the objectives of the organisation.
4. Mutual respect within the work groups must be fostered for the groups to be effective.

While Likert's industrial experience was considerable and his theory deeply researched, many observers argue that practical experience disproves his theory. These observers point out that management in the 21st century is often about quick action and rapid reaction.

The managerial grid (Blake/Mouton)

A more recent classification of leadership or managerial styles has been introduced by Dr Robert Blake of the University of Texas. Blake and Jane Mouton suggest the concept of the managerial grid which is reproduced below:

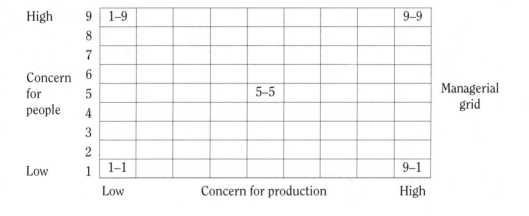

The grid is an attempt to evaluate managers and leaders on the assumptions that there are two areas of managerial concern, namely people (which is on the vertical axis of the grid) and production, or performance of tasks (which is on the horizontal axis of the grid), and that a proportion of the leader's time is devoted to each. It can be used in conjunction with psychological tests to assess strengths/weaknesses of managers.

Blake's grid provides a one to nine scale so that a manager can be given a rating for each area, nine being the highest rating in either case. Some of the possible ratings are as follows:

1. 1–1 management: this is impoverished management, with ineffective performance in production and lazy and indifferent workpeople.
2. 1–9 management: Blake describes this as 'country club' management. Production is incidental to lack of conflict and the preservation of good fellowship.
3. 5–5 management: this represents middle of the road management, with some drive generated for output but with nobody exerting themselves to their full capacity.
4. 9–1 management: this style of leadership, with a high rating for concern for production and a low rating for concern for people, is sometimes known as task management. In this situation men and women are looked upon as a commodity, much as machinery is. In such an environment, to challenge orders and procedures is interpreted as a lack of co-operation. Little attention is paid to the thoughts, attitudes and feelings of the workers.
5. 9–9 management: this is team management with high productivity flowing from the integration of task and human requirements.

Note: in every case the rating for concern for production is the first of the two ratings.

The three-dimensional grid (Reddin)

However, Blake's managerial grid has not been the only approach to the problem. An alternative has been Reddin's three-dimensional grid which extends Blake's original concept by the addition of a third factor, that of effectiveness. Reddin's grid is reproduced below:

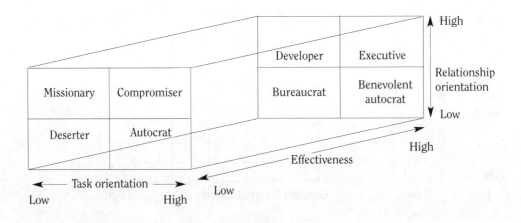

A central part in the three-dimensional theory of management or leadership styles is an eight-style typology of management behaviour resulting from the eight possible combinations of the three factors. These three factors are task orientation, relationship orientation and effectiveness.

Task orientation
This is the extent to which a manager directs his own and his subordinates' efforts towards goal attainment, characterised by planning, organising and control.

Relationship orientation
This depends on the extent to which a manager has personal job relationships; characterised by mutual trust, respect for his subordinates' ideas and consideration of their feelings.

Effectiveness
This is the extent to which a manager achieves the output requirements of his position. Four of the styles – missionary, autocrat, compromiser and deserter – are less effective, while the other four styles – developer, benevolent autocrat, executive and bureaucrat – are more effective.

Here is a capsule description of the eight styles as they are and how they could be perceived by others:

Executive. A manager who is using a high task orientation and a high relationship orientation in a situation where such behaviour is appropriate and who is therefore more effective: he is seen as a good motivator who sets high standards and is a good team manager.

Compromiser. A manager using high task and relationship orientations in a situation which requires high orientation in only one or neither and who is therefore less effective: he is seen as a poor decision maker and as one who allows various pressures in the situation to influence him too much. Seen as minimising immediate pressures rather than maximising long-term production.

Benevolent autocrat. A manager who is using a high task orientation and a low relationship orientation in a situation where such behaviour is appropriate and who is therefore more effective: he is seen as knowing what he wants, and knowing how to get it without causing resentment.

Autocrat. A manager who is using a high task orientation and a low relationship orientation in a situation where such behaviour is inappropriate and who is therefore less effective: he is seen as having no confidence in others, as unpleasant, and as being interested only in the immediate job.

Developer. A manager who is using a high relationships orientation and a low task orientation in a situation where such behaviour is appropriate and who is therefore more effective: he is seen as having implicit trust in people and as being primarily concerned with developing them as individuals.

Missionary. A manager who is using a high relationships orientation and a low task orientation in a situation where such behaviour is inappropriate and is therefore less effective: he is seen as being primarily interested in harmony.

Bureaucrat. A manager who is using a low task orientation and a low relationship orientation in a situation where such behaviour is appropriate and who is therefore more effective: he is seen as being primarily interested in rules and procedures for their own sake, and as wanting to maintain and control the situation by their use. Often seen as conscientious.

Deserter. A manager who is using a low task orientation and a low relationship orientation in a situation where such behaviour is inappropriate and is therefore less effective: he is seen as uninvolved and passive.

Conclusion

In the last two chapters we have covered a lot of what must, for many students, be completely new ground. It is not, however, difficult. If you think about yourselves, and your own behaviour, and relate this new knowledge to your own experience, you will find that it falls into place quite easily. The behaviour of individuals and particularly their pattern of behaviour in groups needs to be considered by management when making decisions.

Chapter Twenty Two

Financial planning

- Introduction

- Cost accounting

- Management accounting

- Generation of profit targets

- Capital expenditure

- Budgets and budgeting

- Budgetary control

Introduction

(Students are advised to reread Chapter 6 before starting this chapter.)

Financial planning is an essential ingredient in the corporate planning process. Every manager, whatever his functional interests, should be conversant with the mechanics and implications of the formulation, implementation and control of financial plans, at least as far as his own activities are concerned.

The most important aspects of the role of the financial planner are to:

1. ensure that financial plans make the optimum contribution to the corporate objectives and that:

    a) they are consistent and compatible with the corporate plan;
    b) the assumptions on which the projections are based are clearly stated, indicating the relevant elements of change and uncertainty anticipated in the future;
    c) the conflicting interests of stakeholders (ie share-holders and internal and external interest groups) are recognised;
    d) the financial consequences of adopting the proposals in terms of profits, costs, selling prices, turnover and resource deployment are analysed and made clear;

2. plan the corporate cash flow, so that the company is able to meet its planned commitments. If periods of financial strain are in prospect, the financial planner should

ensure that top management are aware, so that alternative courses of action can be considered, either:

a) to reduce the proposed activities to levels achievable with the existing financial resources; or

b) to raise the additional necessary finance;

3. analyse and evaluate any proposals which have financial implications, projecting the probable consequences of adopting suggested alternatives, indicating those which appear to offer the best prospects and presenting the analyses and recommendations in a format which can be understood by non-accountants.

Obviously, financial planning necessitates the specialist skills of cost and management accounting defined below.

Cost accounting

Costing is the ascertaining of the amount of expenditure incurred on a single item, or group of items or activity. The function of cost accounting is to collect data concerning factory costs and other operating costs. To gather this data the cost accountant needs: to understand the component of manufacturing cost, a knowledge of the production process, an efficient cost-gathering system, and the ability to determine the total cost for a given volume over a specified time period, and the cost per unit of production. All data used by the cost accountant originates from production or some other activity. When costing a job the cost accountant will need to know:

1. the time spent and the grade of labour used;
2. how much material was used and the cost of the material;
3. the overhead expenses incurred.

The cost accountant's responsibilities include the following:

1. the formulation, implementation, and operation of cost systems and procedures;
2. the determination of costs by product, unit of service, department, function, activities, responsibilities, time periods, geographical areas, and any other appropriate cost centre or cost unit;
3. comparisons for different time periods of actual costs with estimates or pre-determined standard costs;
4. the interpretation and presentation of costing information useful to management for decision making and control of the company's operations. Many of these reports are made on a regular basis, others are made on an ad hoc basis.

Management accounting

Definitions

'Management accounting is the application of accounting techniques to provide all levels of management with information to assist them in planning and controlling the activities of an organisation.'

The *Glossary of Management Techniques* produced by the Treasury defines management accounting as:

'... the application of accounting knowledge to the purpose of producing and of interpreting accounting and statistical information designed to assist management in its functions of promoting maximum efficiency and in formulating and co-ordinating future plans and subsequently in measuring their execution.'

The management accountant

The management accountant is concerned with decision accounting and control accounting. Decision accounting is concerned with the analysis of the returns, or profitability, of the various alternative allocations of resources. Most of these decisions occur at irregular intervals. Control accounting produces data at regular intervals in a standard form, so that actual performance can be compared with the pre-set standards formulated in the planning stage. The analysis would indicate any deviations, or variances from the planned performances. Summary information of this kind enables managers to take corrective action if and when necessary.

Generation of profit targets

There are many factors which directly influence the composition of profit targets. The most important of these are discussed below.

Shareholders' expectations

This factor requires the company to establish a minimum long-range profit target which would produce a yield which its shareholders might reasonably expect to earn during the period under review, taking into account:

1. the potential dividends and opportunities for capital appreciation;
2. the element of risk involved in the business – in low risk industries, the profit earned by member companies tends to be low, whereas it tends to be high in high risk industries; and
3. what shareholders might have earned elsewhere from a comparable risk investment.

As the vast majority of shareholders have no detailed knowledge of the current or potential problems which face the companies in which they invested, their yield expectations for the period under review are almost invariably unrealistically high. The degree to which their expectations will be taken into account depends on the power which they are able to bring to bear on their companies; usually, if they are disenchanted they simply sell their shareholdings.

Return on capital employed

The conventional calculation to measure the return on capital employed is:

$$\frac{\text{Profit} \times 100}{\text{Capital employed}} = \text{ROCE (\%)}$$

The calculation is simple, but the composition of the figures used in the calculation is open to many interpretations. It is rarely possible to calculate the ROCE on a year-by-year basis, because the cash flows arising from heavy capital expenditure usually take much longer than one year to materialise.

Capital employed is the total amount of long-term financial resources invested in the company by shareholders and others and therefore extends to:

- share capital;
- any retained profits reinvested in the business;
- long term loans from banks and debenture holders;
- principal amounts outstanding on hire purchase agreements and finance leases (the amount still left to be paid less the interest element);
- permanent bank overdrafts.

Because ROCE is intended to show the total return made for all the providers of finance, the profit figure used should be before interest expenditure, which represents the share of the return paid out to loan providers such as banks, debenture holders and hire purchase companies. The question of whether or not to take account of taxation is more difficult, because taxation is in one sense an unavoidable cost to the providers of finance but in another sense is not an actual business expense but merely an appropriation of profit to the government.

The capital employed figure may also be adjusted to exclude short term investments which are not necessary for the business's operations, as these represent spare cash which the company cannot presently use and has therefore invested or deposited in order to earn interest until it is needed. It is therefore actually unemployed capital. If these investments are excluded from capital employed, of course, the interest and dividends earned on them must be excluded from profit.

Capital employed should be calculated as an average of opening and closing capital employed for the period in question, in order to show what the average return on this capital was.

The more competitive the industry, the greater the pressure on its member companies to invest in new and improved plant and equipment, research and development, training and computerisation – none of which is likely to show any significant returns or benefits in its introductory year and perhaps not even in the following year. Furthermore, the uncertainty of demand and the associated revenue flows caused by changes in fashion, tastes, consumer behavioural patterns, technological advances, the irregularity of the business cycle and competitive pressures will be reflected in the wide margins of error which are usually allowed when generating profit targets.

The financial planner has to decide how to define both the value of the capital to be used as the computational base and the profit (or loss) assigned to each relevant profit period. Both 'capital employed' and 'profit' tend to be highly subjective terms because of the number of associated factors which have wide variations in interpretation. Most values shown in a typical balance sheet represent original costs and, as a consequence, bear little or no relation to their market value or to their value to the company as a going concern. Land and buildings bought in, say 1912, may not have been revalued, while plant and machinery may have been depreciated at artificially high or low rates. Similarly, stocks are conventionally valued at cost or market price (whichever is the lower) even when inflation or price increases have boosted their replacement costs. Patents, trade marks and goodwill are often shown at zero or nominal values only.

Thus, when using contemporary balance sheet figures as the basis for computing ROCE, caution must be exercised.

If the balance sheet figures are updated to reflect current conditions, the return, expressed as a percentage, will change, but the profit expressed in absolute terms will probably remain unaltered.

Potential earning capacity

In its most simplistic form, this approach requires the financial planner to derive his profit targets from the earning capacity of the corporate assets, assessed according to the present values of the cash flows which they are expected to generate.

Capital structure

The success of the corporate plan and the associated financial plan is directly dependent on the soundness of the capital structure of the company. The capital structure may help or hinder the efforts of the company to raise additional finance. It also directly influences the profit target, because of the fixed-interest component which has to be paid on debentures and preference shares, irrespective of the projected level of operational activity. If the company has a high interest debenture component, it may find it difficult to raise additional risk capital and find its expansionist ambitions restricted by lack of adequate capital. (See 'Gearing' in Chapter 6 above.)

The capital structure of a company can be broken down into long term and short term finance. This finance is required to pay for the company's assets. Obviously, fixed assets and stocks have to be paid for, but in fact the amounts owed by the company's debtors are also assets which have to be funded, as the company needs the cash from somewhere to survive in the period between goods or services being sold to its customers and the customers paying for them.

The company's assets may include:

- tangible fixed assets, such as land, buildings and machinery;
- intangible fixed assets, such as amounts expended on research and development on projects which are expected to earn money in the future;

- stocks;
- debtors;
- cash and bank deposits.

All of these assets have to be funded by shareholders' own funds or by liabilities. Sources of funding include:

- share capital;
- retained profits;
- long term loans;
- government grants;
- bank overdrafts;
- unpaid creditors, including suppliers and tax authorities;
- receipts in advance from customers.

Amounts owed to suppliers and tax authorities are a source of short term financing to the business, because the company is able to use the money which will eventually have to be paid in the period before payment actually falls due. In effect, with suppliers of goods and raw materials, the supplier continues to fund the stocks which have been delivered to the company up until the moment when the company pays for them. Receipts in advance are also a form of short-term financing.

Bank overdrafts may constitute long or short term financing, depending on whether or not they are expected to be called in by the bank in the near future (in published company accounts, however, overdrafts must be shown as current liabilities). The other sources mentioned above – share capital, retained profits, long term loans and government grants – are long term sources of finance (government grants are usually not treated as income on the date when they are received, as they are usually provided to fund large assets and long term projects and are therefore realised as income in the company's accounts over the period of time during which the asset is used or the project is in progress, with the unrealised part being shown on the company's balance sheet as a source of financing).

A company's total assets must be balanced by its total sources of finance. This is usually expressed by the equation

Assets – Liabilities = Capital

Capital here represents the owners' (shareholders' in the case of a company) interest in the business, including share capital, retained profits and any revaluation reserves created in the company's books to balance revaluations of assets. Liabilities are amounts of money owed by the company or the amount paid in advance by customers for goods and services not yet delivered.

A company will usually have a permanent level of current assets (stock, debtors and cash) and a permanent level of current liabilities (short-term creditors, receipts in advance and overdrafts repayable on demand). The level of current assets does not have to be the same as the level of current liabilities. For example, a supermarket may have very low levels of current assets because stocks will be held for short periods and customers will usually pay cash rather than receiving credit, while suppliers may extend credit for a substantial period, enabling the supermarket to spend the cash (eg on wages or new fixed assets) as it comes in. On the other hand, a furniture shop selling on hire purchase may have much higher levels of debtors than creditors, because suppliers may have to be paid within one or two months, while customers may have up to three years to pay. Because every asset has to be funded from somewhere, the furniture shop's current assets may need to be financed from long term loans, whereas the supermarket's short term creditors may be helping to finance investments in fixed assets.

The difference between current assets and current liabilities is called working capital (or net current assets) if the current assets exceed the current liabilities, in which case it represents an additional amount of permanent assets which has to be funded from long term sources. If there are more current liabilities than current assets, the difference is called net current liabilities and represents an additional amount which is available to support long term investment.

A company's capital structure may therefore look something like this:

Capital structure				
Assets			Sources of funding	
Current assets	Stock Debtors Cash	Working capital {	Current liabilities	Short term creditors Receipts in advance Short term overdrafts
Long term assets	Land and buildings Plant and machinery Research and development Intellectual property Strategic investments		Long term funds	Bank loans Long term overdrafts Hire purchase agreements Share capital Retained profits Government grants Revaluation reserves

It is axiomatic that the capital structure should be relevant to the operational activities and requirements of the company. Cash should be available as and when required, while the proportions of loan and risk capital should be such as to provide the (reasonable) shareholder with a satisfactory return on his investment. Flexibility in being able to change the composition of the capital structure may be a vital ingredient of success. Short-terms loans are generally easier to negotiate and at a lower rate, than medium and long-term loans. Short-term capital can provide for the expected and unexpected fluctuations in cash flow, whereas medium and long term finance will be required mostly on a permanent capital base or for projects lasting several years, such as an overseas expansion programme. The relationship between risk and loan capital will have a bearing on the size (and risk element) of the profit target.

Capital expenditure

Evaluation

The capital originally invested in a company, and supplemented by retained profits, will be reinvested in a multiplicity of assets such as land and buildings, plant and machinery and long-term new product development programmes, for the express purpose of generating future income and profits. Capital expenditure cannot be justified without the prospect of it making a contribution to income and profit.

A proposal to invest can be assessed in many ways, but the following two questions are basic to any evaluation:

1. What level of net cash flow (income less outgoings) will the investment create over its working life?
2. What net value (ie profit) is the investment expected to add to the company during its working life?

In the long term – which may be classed as the life of the asset or product – both concepts should provide identical results and conclusions, but in the short term there can be wide differences in interpretation and application, because when the asset is first acquired or the product developed the cash outflow is generally at its heaviest whereas cash inflow is either low or non-existent. The following investment appraisal techniques are discussed below:

1. pay back method;
2. average rate of return method;
3. discounted cash flow methods.

These techniques can be applied to new product development, for which see Chapter 8.

Pay back method
This is the simplest assessment indicator and is based on:

1. the number of years a project needs to recover its initial investment outlay; and
2. the annual contribution, which is calculated by deducting the annual operating costs from the annual revenue.

Example

Initial investment outlay		£40,000
Forecasted annual revenue		
10,000 units @ £3.00 per unit		£30,000
Forecasted annual expenditure		
Material	£5,000	
Labour	£17,000	
Direct overhead	£3,000	
		£25,000
Forecasted annual contribution		£5,000

Payback period $\dfrac{£40,000}{£5,000} =$ 8 years

The apparent advantages of the payback method are that it is simple to understand and calculate, it shows the initial investment required, and it allows an easy ranking of projects, based on the length of the relative payback periods. The disadvantages are that it ignores the return on capital employed (ie it does not measure profitability), and it gives the same value to the same level of receipts and expenditure, irrespective of their occurrence (that is, £1,000 received in the first year is rated no more highly than £1,000 received in the fourth year).

Accounting rate of return

This method is similar to the payback method, except that it takes depreciation and capital employed into account. The advantages claimed are that it is simple to calculate and understand, and it allows a better comparison of alternative projects, because it is related to the initial investment outlay; in addition, the total income over the expected life of the project is taken into account, and depreciation is taken into consideration.

The disadvantages are that it ignores changes in the levels of income and expenditure in different periods, as it is based on an anticipated average performance, and it disregards the fact that money received at a later date does not possess the same value in present day terms as money received earlier (ie £1,000 in the first year is accorded the same value as £1,000 received in the fourth year).

Example

In simple computational terms:		
Initial investment outlay		£40,000
Forecasted annual revenue		£30,000
Material	£ 5,000	
Labour	£17,000	
Direct overhead	£ 3,000	
Depreciation		
(10 years @ £4,000 pa)	£ 4,000	
		£29,000
Forecasted annual contribution		£ 1,000

Profitability $\dfrac{£1,000}{£20,000*}$ x 100 = 5% pa

*The £20,000 is the average capital employed over the expected life of the asset:

$$\frac{£40,000 + £0}{2} = £20,000$$

The investment in the asset is £40,000 when the asset is new but the asset, and therefore the investment in it, is worth nothing (£0) when it is scrapped ten years later. The average value of the capital employed in the asset is therefore midway between £40,000 and £0.

Discounted cash flow (DCF) methods

There are several variations of discounted cash flow, all based on the universally accepted assumption that money to be received (or expended) in the future has less value than now. The compound interest formula which enables us to calculate the present value of future receipts is as follows:

$$P = \frac{S}{(1 + r)^n}$$

where P= present value of S; S = amount to be received at the end of the nth period from now; r = rate of interest; n = number of time periods; and $(1 + r)^n$ = present value factor.

If a company can earn 10 per cent on its investments, it will be indifferent as to whether it receives £100 now, £110 in one year's time, or £121 in two years' time. Similarly, £100 to be received in two years' time is only worth £82.645 now, derived from the present value factor:

$$\frac{£100}{(1.10)^2} = £82.645$$

Cross check

Initial outlay	£82.645
10% interest, year 1	£8.264
Balance, year 1	£90.909
10% interest, year 2	£9.091
Balance, year 2	£100.000

Most investment or project calculations involve cash flows of different levels at different time periods, so the present value calculations are not quite so straightforward. Let us assume that the expected receipts for three years are £4,000, £6,000 and £2,000 and that the rate of interest remains at 10 per cent throughout, then the appropriate present value factor for years one, two and three will be 0.909, 0.826 and 0.751 respectively:

Year	Cash flow		Present value		Present value factor
1	£4,000	x	0.909	=	£3,636
2	£6,000	x	0.826	=	£4,956
3	£2,000	x	0.751	=	£1,502
	£12,000				£10,094

Net present value (NPV)

The net present value of evaluating and priority-rating capital investment proposals is now in fairly common usage. It uses DCF to sum the present values of the net cash flows anticipated during the asset life.

The NPV of an investment is the balance of the total present values of the related cash flows calculated using the minimum discount rate (which is the rate of return the company has decided its investment proposals must achieve before they can be considered viable).

Let us assume that a proposed investment promises receipts of £45,000, £75,000 and £42,000 at the end of the first, second and third years, and that after an initial capital outlay of £120,000, the related expenditures at the end of the first, second and third years are £5,000, £8,000 and £2,000 respectively, while the minimum discount rate is 10 per cent.

Year	Net cash flow		Present value factor		Present value equivalent
0	-£120,000	x	1.000	=	-£120,000
1	+ £40,000	x	0.9091	=	+ £36,364
2	+ £67,000	x	0.8264	=	+ £55,369
3	+ £40,000	x	0.7513	=	+ £30,052
			Net present value		£1,785

The £1,785 over the required minimum rate of 10 per cent may be considered to be the safety margin. When the business has to choose between several alternatives, the proposal offering the highest net present value is usually selected.

Note: students sometimes question why money to be received in the future has less value than now.

Imagine that you lent £1 to your best friend in return for an IOU. Because you have complete confidence in your friend the IOU would be worth £1, even if he didn't pay for several days.

But imagine that you lent £1 to an unknown, disreputable-looking beggar in return for an IOU. You might well say that the IOU was worth nothing!

In between, you might lend £1 to an acquaintance with a reputation for forgetfulness. If you assessed your chances of being repaid as 1 in 2 or 50:50 you are subconsciously 'valuing' the IOU as £0.50 – and that value might fall the longer you have to wait for repayment.

Similarly, in business all future payments are attended by risk, which will vary according to the reputation of the debtor and other relevant factors, including current interest rates. Interest rates also fluctuate according to the demand for money and the degree of risk.

If inflation is to be taken into account in such calculations (and in order to give a true perspective it ought to be), then a slight modification is necessary to calculate its effect. The present value *in real terms* of future monies is reduced by the effect of inflation in the same way that the present value of future monies is reduced by the value of interest foregone. Thus, if the inflation rate is calculated at 12 per cent per annum and the rate of interest 10 per cent per annum, then the present value of future monies is calculated as follows:

$$P = \frac{S}{(1 + r + F)^n}$$

where P = present value of future monies; S = amount to be received at the end of the nth period from now; r = rate of interest; and F = rate of inflation.

The revised discounted rate would be 22 per cent, so at this rate £100 to be received in four years' time would have a present value of:

$$\frac{£100}{(1.22)^4} = £100 \times 0.451$$

$$= £45.10$$

Capital investment projects

Capital investment proposals, including new product development proposals, should be analysed and evaluated systematically, so that top management can decide whether or not to proceed.

Although it is not essential for capital investment details to be incorporated on a standardised form, a routinised approach is advisable, otherwise important data may be excluded. The following standardised headings and questions are suggested as guidelines:

Preliminary survey

What is the project intended to achieve? The total cost of the proposed investment and a broad indication of the return expected, together with the proportion of total corporate assets that will be directed towards the proposal.

What impact will the project have on current and projected operational activities? How will the organisational structure be affected by it? How long will it take for it to be operationally effective?

Does the business possess the necessary expertise to exploit the opportunities which the project is expected to generate? What expertise might have to be brought in?

What risks, financial and otherwise, might be involved in adopting the project? How might they be reduced?

To what extent will the business have control of the associated costs of purchase, construction, implementation and operation? How fixed are the agreed costs?

Evaluative criteria

What are the overall objectives? To what extent are they consistent and compatible with the corporate plan? Other functional plans?

What criteria are to be applied to decide whether the project is acceptable? Profit? Profitability? Market Share? Expansion of product range? Welfare? Replacement of plant and equipment? Product quality? Customer service?

Cash flow

This will cover:

1. capital expenditure: site preparation, land and buildings, plant and equipment, installation and training.
2. operational expenditure: material, labour and services.
3. revenue: cost savings, sales and royalties and governmental grants.

Conclusions

Acceptance or rejection. Responsibility for decision, implementation, control and review. Who should be notified of decision?

Budgets and budgeting

A budget is:

> '... a financial and/or quantitative statement, prepared and approved prior to a defined period
> of time, of the policy to be pursued during that period for the purpose of attaining a given
> objective. It may include income, expenditure, and the employment of capital.' (CIMA.)

The overall control budget, or master budget, is the end product of detailed functional budgets which are integrated into the master budget. The number of functional budgets will vary from one company to another depending on size, products or service, methods of production, methods of marketing, and the competence and structure of the management.

The main functional budgets to be found are for manufacturing, marketing, administration, research and development, capital expenditure, and cash. In detail a budget is:

1. a projected plan of action, expressed in monetary or quantitative terms, aimed at securing available resources; and
2. a means of:

   a) directing and controlling specified activities towards defined objectives;
   b) generating operating standards to measure and evaluate actual performance;
   c) assigning responsibilities for action;

d) determining priorities; and

e) identifying significant variations from standards, so that effective remedial action can be instituted.

Budgeting has three primary objectives:

1. planning and forecasting, including the formulation of policies;
2. co-ordinating the activities of the company, so that they can be directed towards unified goals;
3. controlling the implementation and measurement of performance so that the forecasted goals can be achieved and any necessary remedial action instituted.

Budgetary control

Definition:

'... the establishment of budgets relating the responsibilities of executives to the requirements of a policy, and the continuous comparison of actual and budgeted results either to secure by individual action the objective of that policy or to provide a basis for its revision.'

Process

The budgetary control process:

1. encourages managers to consider how they can improve the efficiency of the functions and activities for which they are responsible;
2. makes them more aware of the impact that their decisions have on their colleagues and associated activities;
3. demands precision of thought and expression on the part of managers in order for them to quantify their plans in monetary and other terms.

The whole budgetary control process consists of a multiplicity of revenue and capital budgets based on functional activities plus a master budget which summarises all of them. The relationship of the revenue and capital budgets and the master budget is illustrated diagrammatically on the next page. The comprehensive nature of master budgets tends to cover longer periods and be projected further into the future than functional budgets.

If the budgeted levels of activity are achieved, then the monitoring and comparison of actual and planned expenses is straightforward, but where the level of activity is greater or less than planned, then the actual expenses cannot be compared directly with the budgeted expenses. Flexible budgeting may provide the answer. As expenditures can be categorised as fixed, variable and semi-variable, companies with fluctuating levels of activity can adapt their expenditure allocations over a wide range of activity levels, so that expenditure allocations change with each activity change.

Advantages

Budgetary control:

1. facilitates the optimum utilisation of corporate resources by compelling management to consider the substitutability of machines and manpower and the costs of idle resources.
2. prevents or reduces waste of corporate resources as it regulates expenditure for predetermined purposes and within the confines of the corporate income.
3. assigns responsibility to specific individuals and departments and, by monitoring actual performances, pinpoints the degree of under- and over-achievement.
4. focuses attention on the need to ensure that adequate finance is available at crucial times during the budget period.
5. reduces the dangers of undue optimism and pessimism by forecasters, because the resultant budget targets provide the yardstick by which the forecasts are judged.
6. compels management to adopt systematic and routinised reporting procedures which are intended to trigger off corrective measures.
7. emphasises the need for executive and departmental co-operation and co-ordination in order to avoid the dangers inherent in unbalanced performances.

Relationship of master and functional budgets

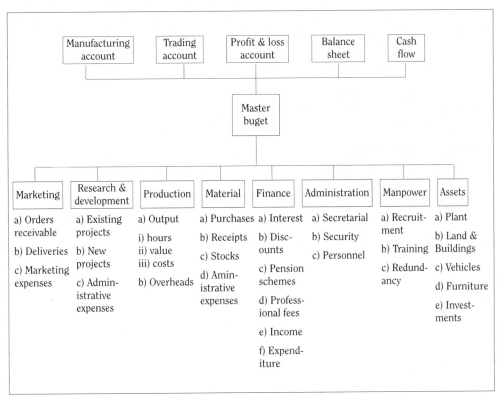

As seen in the discussion on sales forecasting in Chapter 9, logic requires that a tentative sales plan is prepared first in the functional budgeting process. The 'first shot' sales plan offers a working basis for the next planning stage by suggesting the sales volume and selling prices of the product lines it is proposed to market. Thus, the functional planners have to assess the practicality of the sales plan relative to the corporate facilities currently and potentially available. Production capacity, in its broadest sense, involves the availability of materials, labour, machinery, space and finance. If any of these factors is not available in sufficient volume to achieve the sales plan, then the latter will have to be scaled down or arrangements made to acquire the necessary additional facilities.

Financial implications of the sales plan/budget

The sales plan should be expressed in monetary terms to decide whether it can achieve the profit target, and if the available finance is adequate.

The financial cornerstones of a sales plan are income and expenditure. So far as income is concerned, the two elements are sales volume and selling price, whereas expenditure can be categorised under four main headings: manufacturing cost, distribution and selling cost, administrative expenses, and financing the business. Expenses should be divided between fixed and variable costs, so that the impact of under and over-capacity can be studied more closely. It is useful to remember that any revenue derived from the utilisation of an asset over and above its variable cost is a contribution towards covering the total fixed costs. The break-even point occurs at that operational level where:

Total variable costs + Fixed costs = Total revenue

(See 'Break-even pricing', Chapter 10.)

Once this point has been reached, additional revenue minus additional variable cost is profit. Suppose that:

Selling price is £10.00 per unit
Variable cost is £ 7.00 per unit
Total fixed cost is £60,000

then the break-even point can be calculated:

$$\text{Break even point} = \frac{£60,000}{£10.00 - £7.00} = 20,000 \text{ units}$$

Cross check.

Revenue	20,000 x £10.00	=	£200,000	
Variable cost	20,000 x £ 7.00	=	£140,000	
Contribution		=	£ 60,000	= Fixed cost

If 25,000 units are sold then the profit will be:

(extra) 5,000 x £3.00 = £15,000 (5,000 x contribution per unit)

If the business decides that it requires a £15,000 profit, then the sales level required to generate the £15,000 profit will be:

$$\frac{\text{Fixed cost} + \text{Profit}}{\text{Unit contribution}} = \frac{£60,000 + £15,000}{£3.00}$$

$$= \frac{£75,000}{£3.00} = 25,000 \text{ units}$$

(See 'Target pricing', Chapter 10.)

Usually the selling price will have to be reduced if a larger volume has to be sold, so the unit contribution will be lower at a projected higher sales volume, but the principle is exactly the same. Where the sales demand is elastic, then a severe drop in the selling price will be required to achieve the higher sales volume, which may be offset by a lower unit cost of production and distribution at the higher output level.

Financial planners should be able to show how the unit costs of production vary according to output levels, because the change in variable costs is rarely proportionate to output changes. Many variable costs increase in large steps rather than in direct ratio to output. Although variable costs cover production, direct labour, direct material (including bought out parts and components) and direct overheads (covering production, selling and distribution overheads) there is not a precise linear relationship with production levels. For example, additional machinery may be required for each additional 5,000 units produced and may be treated as a variable cost, even though the cost of the new machinery is the same whether it is needed to produce 5,000 units or just one unit which existing capacity could not cover.

Cash budget

The cash budget summarises the expected receipts and payments of a business within a given time span. Corporate liquidity and cash budgeting are often of greater importance in the short term than profit targeting, as it is quite possible for a company which is achieving a large profit to go bankrupt because of a lack of cash to pay its current expenses.

Chapter Twenty Three

Financial reporting

- Financial accounting

- Directors' report

- Accounting Standards Board

- Audit

- Accounting policies

Financial accounting

Financial accounting is concerned not only with the internal requirements of managers but also with external requirements of creditors, Registrar of Companies, Inspector of Taxes, shareholders and potential investors. Financial accounting is concerned with stewardship. It is the job of the financial accountant to record the revenue received for the sale of goods and/or services, and the expenditure incurred in such a way that the overall trading position can be ascertained at any given point in time. A good financial accounting system classifies, records and interprets, transactions and events of a financial nature. These facts and figures can be summarised and presented to management and outside parties. The forms of reporting financial information periodically are as follows:

1. The balance sheet, which covers current, fixed and other assets, and current and long-term liabilities.
2. The revenue accounts, which covers income and expenditure, and the manufacturing, trading, and profit and loss accounts.

Companies are governed by the Companies Acts 1985 and 1989 which require them, among other things, to publish their profit and loss account and balance sheet each year, by lodging a copy with the Registrar of Companies, who holds it available for public inspection. A copy is also sent, of course, to every shareholder and debenture holder.

Companies are not required to publish a fully detailed set of accounts. The Companies Acts lay down certain minimum disclosure requirements.

The detailed requirements of the Companies Acts 1985 and 1989 are complex as to disclosure of information in the accounts for small, private companies. They are more complex for public limited companies, and even more complex for listed companies, banks and insurance companies.

At this stage of your studies it will be sufficient to see one of the standard models for a profit and loss statement and a balance sheet, all as shown in the Companies Acts. An example is therefore shown in Appendix A, to be found at the end of the book. A profit and loss account shows what profit the company has made over a given period, and the balance sheet provides a 'snap-shot' of the company's financial position as at one particular day, normally the last day of the company's accounting period. The Companies Acts provide several different formats for these accounts, which broadly speaking are followed by most companies. The formats provide for some discretion on the part of the directors as to how exactly the accounts are laid out, but it is important that having established a favoured format the directors do not change it without good reason.

Small companies are not required to provide as much detail as larger ones, and public limited companies, listed companies and some private companies either are required or choose to produce additional accounts, such as a cash-flow statement, which indicates from what sources the company receives cash and on what that cash is spent. The Accounting Standards Board, which lays down financial reporting standards for companies and other organisations, has laid down detailed requirements for cash flow statements.

Directors' report

A directors' report will be attached to the company's final accounts. The contents of the directors' report is summarised as follows:

1. principal activities of the company and a review of the year's performance;
2. names of directors throughout the year;
3. the amount to be recommended by way of dividend;
4. the amount carried to reserves;
5. significant changes in fixed asset value and any marked difference between the book value and the market value of land and buildings;
6. directors' and their families' interests in shares and debentures of the company or of any other group company;
7. information about political or charitable donations if greater than £200 in value;
8. any insurance taken out for the benefit of the company's directors or auditors to indemnify them against any liability to the company;
9. particulars of any important events affecting the company or its subsidiaries or likely to affect them in the near future;
10. an indication of the activities of the company and its subsidiaries in the field of research and development;
11. details of any acquisitions of a company's own shares;
12. a statement narrating the policies the company operates for the employment of disabled persons;
13. the extent of compliance with Health and Safety at Work regulations.

Accounting Standards Board

Although the Companies Act 1985 contains some accounting rules, the details of accounting practice, in particular the items which may and may not be included in each of the figures on the balance sheet and in the profit and loss account, are laid down by the Accounting Standards Board, an independent body appointed by the Financial Reporting Council, whose members include of representatives from industry and the accounting and legal professions.

Audit

All companies, unless they are exempted on grounds of size, are required by the Companies Act 1985 to have their accounts audited by a registered auditor, who must be a member of an accountancy body geared to company financial reporting and permitted to act as an auditor under the rules of that body, a privilege only extended to members who have some years' experience in working for auditor firms.

The accountancy bodies which can grant registered auditor status in the UK are:

- Institute of Chartered Accountants in England and Wales (ICAEW)
- Institute of Chartered Accountants of Scotland (ICAS)
- Institute of Chartered Accountants in Ireland (ICAI)
- Association of Chartered Certified Accountants (ACCA) and its subsidiary the Association of Authorised Public Accountants (AAPA)

The purpose of an audit is to determine whether or not the company's financial statements are reasonably truthful. The audit will therefore involve an inspection of the company's accounting records and a comparison of those records with evidence such as invoices and payroll and personnel files to establish whether or not the accounting records are accurate. The auditor will then check that the financial statements themselves agree with the accounting records.

The auditor must write a report, for inclusion in the financial statements, stating whether or not in his or her opinion the financial statements give a true and fair view of the company's financial activities for the year and its financial position at the year end.

Accounting policies

In order to help to give a true and fair view, the company is required by the Accounting Standards Board to include a statement of its accounting policies, meaning the methods that the company used to arrive at the figures shown in the reports. Accounting policies include details such as the ways in which fixed assets are depreciated for accounting purposes, the periods of time over which different assets are depreciated, the methods for calculating stock values and whether or not the costs of any research and development activities have been included in the fixed assets on the balance sheet.

Chapter Twenty Four

Interpretation of accounts

- Introduction

- Parties interested in accounts

- Interpretation techniques

- Overtrading

- Internal comparisons

- External comparisons

Introduction

The interpretation of accounts is a vital accountancy function, concerned with the assessment of financial strength and commercial soundness of a business. In spite of the importance of interpretation, it is in an area which students tend to neglect; they do so at their peril, since the subject of interpretation provides the examiner with an excellent opportunity for posing searching questions.

Parties interested in accounts

The first point to establish before attempting a question of interpretation is to decide the probable viewpoint of the party for whom the interpretation is being carried out. The main parties interested and the information likely to be required by them are summarised as follows.

Management
Management will need to know if capital is being efficiently employed and that the return thereon, compared with competitors in the same line of business, is favourable.

Shareholders
Both ordinary and preference shareholders will be concerned with the safety of their dividends and thence the profitability of the business. The ordinary shareholder, unlike the preference

shareholder, may also have an interest in making a capital gain on his shares and to this end he may be content to forego large dividends so that the company can build up its reserves.

Creditors
A business's creditors will need to be satisfied that the company has the ability to pay its debts, as this will determine the amount of credit that they will allow the business.

Debenture holders
Debenture holders require regular payments of interest on their loans and they also need to be satisfied that any fixed or floating charge on the assets of the company, for the benefit of the debenture holders, is sufficient to ensure the repayment of the loan in the event of a winding up.

Interpretation techniques

The accountant has three main interpretation techniques at his disposal:

1. sources and application of funds statement.
2. straightforward appraisal;
3. ratio analysis;

Sources and application of funds statement

This shows all the sources of finance employed by the business (see chapter 6) and the way in which the money has been used. It analyses the information contained in the profit and loss account and the balance sheet.

Straightforward appraisal

Taking the profit and loss account and balance sheet in turn, straightforward appraisal will consist in part in examination of the following items.

Profit and loss account
Sales. Compare the figure for sales with previous years and also with budgeted figures if these are available. The probable causes of differences in the figure for sales are many and the following possibilities should be considered:

- price variations: have prices changed between the periods being compared?
- sales volume variations: has the sales volume (number of units sold) changed?
- sales mix variations: has a larger proportion of high or low priced goods been sold?

Gross profit. Any change in the percentage of gross profit to sales will be due to either sales variations or changes in the cost of sales. The causes of any change in the cost of sales must be in either the valuation of stocks or the cost of production of stocks or the prices paid for purchases.

Net profit. Expenses, under the main headings of administration, distribution and interest, should be compared both as a percentage of gross profit and in absolute terms with the previous years' figures and current budget estimates.

Balance sheet
Share capital. If there is any uncalled share capital (the company having issued partly paid shares), this will represent a reserve of capital which may be called up if necessary.

Loan capital. The repayment dates of debenture and long-term loans will have a profound effect on the company's cash flow unless a sinking fund has been set up for the specific purpose of redeeming debentures. Alternatively debenture holders may have the option of converting their debentures into ordinary shares, instead of cash repayment. In this situation it is more difficult to assess the amount of cash that the company will require to redeem its debentures.

Fixed assets.
Land and buildings. These may be freehold or leasehold; in the latter situation the imminence of the renewal of the lease is significant since the company may well be faced with an increased rental bill.

Plant and machinery. If these items are heavily depreciated then it is certain that they are old and possibly inefficient, and the company will face a heavy bill for plant and machinery replacement.

Working capital. The excess of current assets over current liabilities is known as working capital. The business should have adequate working capital to conduct its everyday operations and the amount of working capital required will vary according to the size of the business and type of trade which it is engaged upon. Too little working capital results in the business being in an overtrading situation; usually this occurs when the business is expanding and large stocks are required to increase sales which in turn leads to a vastly increased debtors figure. On the other hand, too much working capital means that the company's assets are not being utilised in the most profitable manner.

Intangible assets. Goodwill is an intangible asset recognised when the company purchases another company. It represents the excess of the price paid over the actual value of the purchased company's net assets, in other words the amount that the company pays to acquire the results of the past endeavours of the employees of the purchased company in building up the business. Other intangible assets such as research and development costs and costs of acquiring brands and trademarks may have no realisable value. In assessing the financial position from the balance sheet, consideration needs to be given to the future revenues that the company can realistically hope to generate as a result of possessing these assets.

Contracts for capital expenditure and contingent liabilities. In a limited company's published accounts, the notes attached thereto must disclose the company's capital expenditure commitments including any amounts not yet specifically contracted for. For obvious reasons any contingent liabilities such as lawsuits should be noted, as should the company's proposed action to deal with them.

Ratio analysis

A ratio is the relation that one item bears to another, thus large absolute figures may be reduced to readily assimilable information on which top management can act promptly. The total number of these relationships which it is possible to extract is very large but it is not necessary at this point in your studies to be able to produce an exhaustive list.

A word of caution: the examiner is looking for conclusions drawn from study of ratios which have been extracted from the accounts, in other words: the interpretation. If the ratio of A Ltd's current assets to current liabilities is 2 : 1 and the corresponding ratio of B Ltd is 1 : 1 the question that should be answered is: are the companies engaged in similar activities? If not, then the causes of the difference should be examined; perhaps B Ltd is in the retail trade while A Ltd is a manufacturer, and their working capital requirements will then be quite different.

If both companies are in the same field, the constituent items in the working capital block should be examined in order to ascertain the adequacy or otherwise of each company's working capital:

1. How many days' stocks are held by each company?
2. What is the repayment period allowed to debtors?
3. How many days credit are allowed by suppliers?
4. Has the company sufficient liquid funds to discharge immediate liabilities?

Ratios may serve many purposes but, in general terms, they assist management in its basic functions of forecasting, planning, co-ordination, control and communication. If they are used properly, they can improve efficiency and, therefore, profits. However, in inexperienced hands, they can mislead and result in the wrong conclusions being reached.

Single ratios are of limited value, primarily because overall trends are of more importance to management. In addition, a change in one ratio may be of significance only when examined in relation to other ratios. The most common specific uses of ratios include:

1. Past ratios indicate trends in costs, sales, profit etc, and are therefore very useful for forecasting likely events in the future.
2. Future plans can be 'targeted' by accounting ratios and so ratios become an integral part of the management control system.
3. Ideal ratios can be established and the relationships between primary ratios may be used to establish effective co-ordination.
4. The control of performance (eg sales quotas) as well as control of costs, may be materially assisted by the use of ratios.
5. Ratios can play an important part in communication both internally and externally for both management and shareholders.
6. Ratios may be used as measures of efficiency. This applies to a single company when making comparison between different periods and also to a group of companies when making comparisons between divisions.

Important financial ratios

Some of the more important ratios and percentages are demonstrated by reference to the following condensed set of final accounts.

XY LTD
BALANCE SHEET AS AT 31 DECEMBER 20XX
FIXED ASSETS

	Cost £	Dep'n £	WDV (written down value) £
Land	20,000	–	20,000
Buildings	144,000	40,000	104,000
Plant and equipment	36,000	12,000	24,000
	200,000	52,000	148,000
CURRENT ASSETS			
Stocks	72,000		
Debtors	100,000		
Bank	20,000		
		192,000	
Less:			
CURRENT LIABILITIES			
Trade creditors		(64,000)	
		128,000	
TOTAL ASSETS LESS CURRENT LIABILITIES			276,000
LOAN CAPITAL 10% DEBENTURES			(50,000)
NET ASSETS			226,000
FINANCED BY:			
SHARE CAPITAL			150,000
REVENUE RESERVES			76,000
TOTAL SHAREHOLDERS' FUNDS			226,000

TRADING AND PROFIT AND LOSS ACCOUNT FOR THE YEAR ENDED 31 DECEMBER 20XX

SALES	£400,000
Less: Cost of sales	£300,000
GROSS PROFIT	£100,000
Less: Expenses	£19,000
Less: Interest on debentures	£5,000
PROFIT BEFORE TAX	£76,000
Provision for taxation	£28,000
PROFIT AFTER TAX	£48,000

Notes:
1. Opening stock valued at £88,000.
2. Dividend per £1 share: 15p.
3. Stock market price per £1 share, £2.50.

Financial ratios. *The primary ratio* measures the return on capital employed.

$$\frac{\text{Profit after tax} + \text{Debenture interest}}{\text{Total assets } less \text{ current liabilities}} \times 100$$

$$\frac{(£48,000 + £5,000)}{£276,000} \times 100 = 19.2\%$$

The general definition of 'capital employed' is total assets (at market value) less current liabilities; many other definitions do exist but this is a good starting point. The return on capital employed (ROCE) is a good measurement of the efficiency of management.

The profit margin ratio measures the acceptability of selling prices and to some extent the efficiency of production.

$$\frac{\text{Profit after tax}}{\text{Sales}} \times 100$$

$$\frac{£48,000}{£400,000} \times 100 = 12.0\%$$

The capital turnover ratio measures the extent to which net assets employed generate sales. Note that it is expressed as a ratio and not as a percentage as in the previous examples.

$$\frac{\text{Sales}}{\text{Capital employed}}$$

$$\frac{£400,000}{£276,000} = 1.45 \text{ times (or each £1 of capital employed has generated sales of £1.45)}$$

Note:

Primary ratio = Capital turnover ratio x Profit margin before interest

19.2% $= 1.45 \times \dfrac{(£48,000 + £5,000)}{£400,000} = 1.45 \times 13.25\%$

The current ratio indicates the strength of the working capital and the degree of solvency of the business.

Current assets	:	Current liabilities
£192,000	:	£64,000
= 3	:	1

The liquid ratio, 'quick ratio' or 'acid test' provides a measure of the firm's ability to meet its current liabilities.

Liquid assets (current assets less stocks)   :   Current liabilities

£120,000 : £ 64,000

= 1.9 : 1

Operating ratios. *Stock turnover* indicates the efficiency of stock control. Excessive stocks must be avoided otherwise working capital will be tied up uneconomically.

$$\frac{\text{Cost of sales}}{\text{Average stock}} = \frac{£300,000 \times 2}{(£88,000 + £72,000)} = 3.75 \text{ times or every 97 days (approx)}$$

Average debt collection period will indicate the rate at which customers are paying for credit sales. It is therefore a measurement of the effectiveness of credit control.

$$\frac{\text{Debtors}}{\text{Average daily sales}} = \frac{£100,000 \times 365}{£400,000} = 91 \text{ days}$$

Creditors' turnover period is an indication of how quickly creditors are paid and the extent of short-term capital. A long creditors' turnover period may indicate that the company has problems in paying its suppliers or, alternatively, that it has no problems in paying its suppliers and therefore receives generous credit terms.

$$\frac{\text{Creditors}}{\text{Cost of sales or purchases (if known)}} \times 365 = \frac{£64,000}{(£300,000 + £72,000 - £88,000)} \times 365 = 82 \text{ days}$$

Earning ratios. *Dividend yield* is an indication of the rate of return on ordinary shares related to the market price.

$$\frac{\text{Dividend}}{\text{Market price per share}} \times 100 = \frac{£0.15}{£2.50} \times 100 = 6\%$$

Earnings yield is an indication to the ordinary shareholder of the yield if all available profits were distributed. 'Earnings' is the profit after tax attributable to the ordinary shareholders ie excluding any preference dividends etc.

$$\frac{\text{Earnings per ordinary share}}{\text{Market price per share}} \times 100 = \frac{48,000}{£2.50 \times 150,000} \times 100 = 12.8\%$$

Earnings per share is the profit attributable to ordinary shareholders divided by the number of ordinary shares in issue.

$$\frac{\text{Profit attributable to ordinary shareholders}}{\text{Ordinary shares in issue}} = \frac{£48,000}{150,000} = £0.32$$

The price/earnings ratio measures the number of years that it will take the earnings per share to equal the market price.

$$\frac{\text{Market price}}{\text{Earnings per share}} = \frac{£2.50}{£0.32} = 7.8 \text{ years}$$

The capital gearing ratio is an indicator of the relationship between the fixed interest capital (preference shares and debentures) and the ordinary share capital. A company with a greater amount of ordinary share (or equity) capital is said to be 'low geared', while a company where the fixed interest capital is the higher, is said to be 'high geared'. Gearing is neutral when ordinary and fixed interest capital is in a ratio of 1 : 1. It will be seen that XY has a capital structure that is 'low geared'.

(Preference shares if any) + Debentures = £ 50,000
Ordinary share capital = £150,000
Gearing ratio = 1 : 3

Overtrading

Overtrading is a problem which arises from increasing sales at too rapid a rate. The ultimate result is a serious shortage of cash which means that wages, creditors and corporation tax cannot be met.

A typical pattern of events may commence when the company takes on additional orders. This would then be followed by engaging additional workers or working overtime. At the same time, extra materials would be purchased on credit. If the production cycle is fairly long this means that, although extra cash has to be paid out more or less immediately, additional revenue may not be forthcoming for a considerable period. This assumes that the additional production will be sold without delay, but in some circumstances the process may take the form of a build up of stock. If this is the case, then the shortage of cash may necessitate an emergency sale at greatly reduced prices and this is likely to have adverse effects on profitability.

When analysing the situation shown on a balance sheet, it is very important to watch for signs of overtrading. Some of the most important of those signs are summarised below:

1. A business is taking a much longer time to pay off its creditors. This fact may not always be easy to determine. An increase in the total creditors or an increase of creditors in relation to debtors may be an indication. Similarly, a comparison of the period of credit being taken with the norm for the particular trade may also be a guide to solvency.
2. A stock increase has occurred without an increase in turnover; an even more positive sign is an increase in stock and a reduction in turnover.
3. There is a growth in the rate of borrowing so that the proportion of borrowing in relation to the assets owned by shareholders is excessive.
4. The total profit (gross and/or net) begins to diminish.
5. There is a sudden upward or downward swing in any figures, or the appearance of new items such as short-term loans.

It should be remembered, however, that a single ratio is of limited value, and, if possible, three or more successive years should be compared because only then will a trend be discernible.

Internal comparisons

Internal comparisons can be made between divisions and product groups, as well as between years. However, in many cases a comparison between divisions will be difficult to undertake with any degree of accuracy because of the problems involved in calculating the capital employed and the profit of each division, without arbitrary apportionments of corporate overheads.

External comparisons

The results of a company can be compared with those of its competitors, but this is often of limited value for the following reasons:

1. The accounts are prepared on a historic cost basis.
2. Different companies will have different classifications of revenue and cost.
3. Different companies will have different accounting policies and measure revenues and costs in different ways.
4. There are problems in identifying separate trading activities when the accounts have been consolidated.
5. Transfer prices are used between different companies in a group.

A more meaningful comparison can be carried out when a business participates in an interfirm comparison scheme.

Chapter Twenty Five

Management information and communications

- Management information

- Routine reports

- Non-routine reports

- Interpretation and selection

- What the accountant can provide

- Work study departments

- Management services department

- Marketing department

- Manpower information system

- Purchasing department

- Analysis and presentation of data

- Information technology

- Business communication

Management information

We have seen that one of the functions of the cost and management accountant is to provide data on which to base financial plans and other business decisions. But the accountant is not the only provider of information. We have seen that marketing research is an essential source of information, not only for marketing but for production, purchasing, accounting and personnel. We have seen that personnel use information about employees in order to avoid human relations problems arising and to devise better personnel policies. Purchasing use information about the supply and demand for raw materials in order to decide how much to purchase at a time and they maintain records about suppliers in order to know the most reliable sources. Production is dependent on information from sales in order to plan production schedules. Accountants themselves require information about interest rates and the actual costs of operations in order to produce financial and cost accounting information.

Remember that our basic business model, introduced in Chapter 1, saw each business function operating in its own 'market' and interacting with every other function. Remember also that our definition of a market assumes that buyers and sellers have knowledge (or information) about each other and you will realise that information is fundamental to the conduct of business.

The question arises: should we leave each department (or function) to gather its own information? In one way it would be sensible: they know what they want and how best to get it, but this argument is more than outweighed by the fact that much of the information gathered by one department is also needed by another and the duplication of effort if everybody was to collect their own would be costly and inefficient.

There is therefore a strong case for an integrated 'management information system' which would leave specialist departments to collect their own specialist information, which would then be automatically transmitted to other departments who needed it but would not be transmitted unless it was needed.

In designing such a system the following questions need to be asked:

1. Who needs the information?
2. What information is needed?
3. Why?
4. Where is the information to be obtained?
5. When is it needed?
6. How should it be gathered and disseminated?

Who needs the information?

These will be:

1. all managers who have to make decisions;
2. all managers, supervisors and foremen who have to inform or instruct subordinates;
3. all workpeople who need to be kept informed about matters affecting their own working conditions or personal circumstances;
4. external agencies who have a statutory right to information about the company's affairs;
5. other stakeholders who may have a 'right' to be kept informed about matters affecting their interests in the company.

What information is needed?

This depends on the answer to the question 'who?' The degree of detail and the style of presentation of the information will vary according to the intended recipient.

Management's requirements are many and varied depending on the nature of individual jobs. The higher a manager is up the organisation chart, the more general the information he requires and it will probably be void of complicated detail. Furthermore, it will usually only be required at monthly intervals. For example, the managing director is most likely to want a monthly profit and loss account and balance sheet (probably in a form suitable for his particular needs). And he will usually prefer to see cumulative comparisons between budgeted forecasts and actuals accompanied by an explanatory narrative, where appropriate. On the other hand, the shop foreman is likely to be concerned with daily reports on such items as labour efficiency or waste.

It follows from this that an initial decision is not only 'what?' but also 'what not?' – what information can be left out or simplified without distorting the facts. The answer to this is to ask 'why?'

Why the information is needed

Why the information is needed will give a clear indication to the degree of detail required.

Managers are often unable to specify their information requirements in precise terms and so the onus is usually placed on the provider of the information. The manager expects information to help him make decisions preferably without becoming too personally involved in the actual process of getting it. However, he will want the information in the right form, at the right time and not obscured by irrelevant information.

Where is the information to be obtained?

Obviously this depends on what is required. We have already seen the importance of monitoring the external environment for information which may affect our business. Other information will be generated within the business.

We have also seen the importance of using secondary information before collecting primary information.

When is it needed?

Out of date information is useless – in fact it is worse than useless because there is a danger that decisions may be based on information which no longer applies. The user and the provider of information will need to plan very carefully the timing of a report – an interim report may be necessary rather than waiting for the final report.

How should it be gathered and disseminated?

Once again this depends on the nature of the information, why it is needed and the identity of the recipient. In some cases a computer print-out of figures, meaningless to anybody but the recipient, may suffice, but in others there will have to be a carefully argued and fully illustrated report.

Coupled with the question of 'how?' is the subsidiary question 'how much?' How much can be afforded in the process of gathering and disseminating information?

The answer again lies in the answer to the question 'why?' If the information is essential then virtually any cost may be justified, but if it is only desirable then the marginal cost of gathering the information needs to be compared with the marginal gain from having the information. This is a very difficult question for which some sophisticated statistical techniques offer theoretical answers. In practice it may be easier for the manager to ask 'how much do we stand to lose if we don't have the information?'

Having taken this overview of the management information system let us now consider some of the detailed items of information in regular use by most companies.

Routine reports

A list of the routine reports which may be provided for a company's managers might include the following:

Daily

1. analysis of materials wastage (by causes);
2. labour efficiency statistics, measuring fluctuations in output per man-hour;
3. analysis of lost time (by causes);
4. orders received.

Weekly

1. analysis of overtime worked and the reason(s) for it;
2. jobs completed;
3. project control – critical path analysis, identifying any delays in the completion of work critical to the completion of any major projects.

Monthly

1. departmental operating statement;
2. labour variation analysis, showing differencies between budgeted and actually employed labour;
3. material variation analysis, showing differences between budgeted and actual material usage;
4. overhead variation analysis, showing differences between budgeted and actual expenses;
5. sales analysis, showing sales by type of product, customer etc;
6. capital expenditure project report, showing progress of major capital projects;
7. stock discrepancy, showing differences between stock records and actual stock;
8. sales variation analysis, showing differences between sales invoiced and delivered;
9. profit and loss account;

10. source and application of funds;
11. balance sheet;
12. accounting ratios analysis;
13. orders received, analysed by type of product/customer;
14. cash position, analysed by account;
15. overdue accounts, and how many days overdue.

Quarterly/bi-annually/annually

1. profit and loss account;
2. balance sheet;
3. source and application of funds;
4. departmental operating statements.

Non-routine reports

In addition to all the above there may be continuous monitoring and surveillance reports, and ad hoc reports, that is those on investigations into particular problems.

Interpretation and selection

It is not only necessary to present the information to management; it should normally include some indication of suggested action. The principle of management by exception emphasises that management needs to be informed only of those items which fall outside the previously determined tolerance limits. The manager does not need to know specifically when things are going according to plan, but he must be informed as soon as possible if there are significant differences between forecasts and actual performance. It is as important to bring management's attention to favourable variances as it is to highlight the unfavourable ones. In the case of either an adverse or favourable report the budget or standard may be suspect and require investigation and revision.

What the accountant can provide

The accountant's day-to-day work

The accountant is not the only person concerned with presenting and interpreting information for management, but in many small companies he is the one most personally involved. By the very nature of his work, the accountant has to deal with practically every aspect of the company's activities. His work starts with the recording of the receipts and disposition of funds for capital and revenue expenditure purposes. There is a legal requirement placed on the accountant whereby he must keep proper books of account that will satisfactorily explain the transactions in which the company is involved. This will necessitate keeping records of the purchasing of materials, the payment of wages and salaries and other types of expenditure. Similarly, details of sales made and amounts owing by customers must also be correctly recorded. At the end of the accounting period, management will wish to know whether the company has been operating at a profit or a loss and whether the company is financially stable and successful or not.

Emphasis on control

It is seldom sufficient to know the relative profitability of each of its products, processes, departments, services and other activities. The accent is very much on control. Over the years the management accountant has developed sophisticated control techniques including:

1. budgetary control;
2. standard costing;
3. marginal costing;
4. break even analysis;
5. differential costing;
6. project cost control using networks;
7. capital investment appraisal techniques using DCF;
8. operational research techniques:

    a) optimisation;
    b) statistical forecasting;
    c) financial models;

9. organisation and methods of office procedures;
10. computerised accounting; and
11. a complex of costing systems including:

    a) job costing;
    b) process costing; and
    c) operating costing.

Work study departments

However, it must not be supposed that the accountant is the only person who is able to present meaningful information for management. In many large efficient companies there are management services departments. This development arose from the formation of organisation and methods departments which themselves tended to be clerical offshoots of the work study departments. Work study is one of the earliest branches of the management control sciences. It comprises both method study and work measurement. Working conditions must be standardised before the best method is suggested and the measurement of the work content in standard hours will then follow. Work study is, therefore, a valuable aid to efficiency in the factory and it is also often used as a scientific basis for the installation of bonus incentive schemes.

Management services department

A typical management services department would carry out the following functions:

1. management accounting;
2. internal audit;
3. organisation and methods;
4. data processing facilities (computer hardware and software);
5. operational research.

Marketing department

The marketing department, either through formal market research or through sales reports and analysis of environmental and competitive change, will continuously monitor and report on factors affecting the company's product market. (For a detailed discussion of this, see Chapter 9.)

Manpower information system

The function of a manpower information system is to collect and process manpower data covering the acquisition, deployment and control of manpower resource, and to distribute it when and where required in the most efficient and cost-conscious manner. It is only comparatively recently that the main focus of manpower information systems has expanded from payroll applications and aspects to wider issues such as manpower resource planning. Traditionally, a manpower information system is based on individual records, showing:

1. personal details;
2. professional qualifications;
3. previous job and grade;
4. present job and grade;
5. training;
6. department;
7. performance;
8. promotion prospects.

Individual records may be aggregated to provide data necessary for calculating labour turnover figures by department, type of work, age of employee, length of employment etc.

Purchasing department

The purchasing department will monitor changes in the supply and demand schedules for essential raw materials, with a view to securing the best bargain by buying short or long, in bulk or in smaller quantities. Purchasing will also monitor performance by suppliers regarding quantity of material supplied; delivery dates, compared with promised delivery; prices, and quality of material supplied, so as to build up a 'vendor rating', indicating the suppliers from whom it is best to buy.

Analysis and presentation of data

A broad distinction between data and information is that data are raw facts which become information only when they are in a processed format suitable for control and decision-making purposes.

Data usually comes alive when trends and comparisons can be extracted. Extrapolative techniques can be applied to forecast or predict future performances. Interfirm comparisons in the same industry can be of inestimable value when they can be focused on absenteeism, labour turnover, recruitment, rates of pay or manpower costs, or on market shares, advertising expenditure etc.

The presentation format should be geared to the ability of the recipient to understand the content of the information (eg a non-accountant might easily be confused by undefined accounting jargon terms). It is often worthwhile to add explanatory notes to reports and schedules on major points of interest or explanations on significant variances.

The use of data

A considerable amount of attention has been given to the development of information systems with the increasing use of the computer. This recognises the fact that many items of input data may be useful for a number of different outputs. For example, stock control data is useful for accounting, purchasing, production and sales (eg stock availability). Similarly, payroll data is useful for accounting, labour cost control, labour turnover, pensions and production. Data should not, therefore, be gathered independently for special purposes, but rather the same basic input should be made available for multiple end uses. For instance, data may be a by-product of an operation, or series of procedures, designed for a specific purpose, such as details of the flow of raw materials or payroll calculations and should be made available for other purposes.

Some procedures are designed primarily to guide managers in making decisions (eg stock control procedures which are essential to accurate interim accounts and for providing information necessary for financial planning and purchasing decisions) and should therefore be used as a basis for future planning.

Principal information systems

The multiple uses of data and the demands for economy in the processing of data into information has resulted in the concept of a complete management information system being developed. Research has indicated that there are three major information systems in the typical company: financial, personnel, and logistics.

The basis of the financial system is the company's cash flow, while the personnel information system is concerned with the flow of information about people. The logistics system, on the other hand, applies only to those data which reflect the physical flow of goods through a company and through distribution channels to the final customer. There are other identifiable information systems concerned with marketing, research and development, strategic planning and employee remuneration.

The Data Protection Act 1998

Although access to data is extremely important for any form of decision making, it is necessary to strike a balance between the need for access to data and people's right to ensure that any records or information about themselves is accurate and available for inspection and, if necessary, correction. As so much information is now stored on computers or in paper form, it is inevitable that some of it will be inaccurate. There have been many cases of persons being wrongfully refused credit from banks merely because by chance they happen to have the same name, or to live at the same address, as someone who has not proved creditworthy.

The Data Protection Act enables any inaccuracies to be corrected. This remedy is open to employees working in a business, to students at a university, to customers of a bank and to most other individuals on whom records are being kept. Failure by the holders of the records to remedy any inaccuracies can lead to penalties – as well as being bad publicity. Organisations are also required to register with the Data Protection Registrar the uses to which data will be put and notify individuals of the use for which the data is required.

Information technology

The most dramatic happening in business in recent years has been the development of 'information technology'. Combining the technology of computing, with its ability to handle a mass of data very rapidly, with the technology of satellite and fibre optics and other electronic communication, with its ability to communicate across great distance instantly, it is now possible for much of the data used by business to be transmitted instantly and globally.

Major retailers now have a direct link from barcode readers at cash desks to stock control systems which are instantly updated. Products may be computer-designed in one place and the production line set in motion to produce the goods somewhere else. Vast sums of money may be electronically and instantly transferred from one country to another, with serious implications for foreign exchange. 'Teleshopping' permits customers to order goods via their television screens, without visiting the shops.

Business communication

Introduction

The importance of effective communication is implicit throughout the study of business:

- Market research enables the market to 'communicate' its needs and wants to the business.
- Advertising communicates promotional messages to customers.
- Salesmen negotiate through two-way communication.
- The personnel manager uses the interview as a form of two-way communication.
- Managers communicate instructions to subordinates.
- Subordinates communicate their attitudes to management through their behaviour.

Communication may be formal, officially concerned with matters relevant to the business, or informal, concerned with social or other matters not concerned or only indirectly concerned with the conduct of the business. It may be friendly or hostile, easy to understand or confusing, and may take many forms, oral, written or non-verbal. Above all, communication may be either effective or ineffective. It is effective when it achieves the objectives of the communicator, ineffective when it doesn't. It follows that the onus is on the communicator to ensure the effectiveness of his communication, not to blame the recipient for not understanding.

This is a vitally important point: ineffective communication may be worse than just ineffective; it may cause the opposite effect from that which was intended. Thus, bad advertising may lose customers; bad management/worker communication may cause industrial disputes; badly worded reports may lead to the wrong decision being taken.

Definition

Communicating is the transmission of ideas, emotions or attitudes from one person or persons to another person or persons. As far as possible this should be done with 100 per cent accuracy. It should be remembered that neither the transmitter nor the recipient need be a single person.

Some principles of communication are:

1. There must be lines of communication.
2. There must be persons at each end of the line capable of using the line.
3. There must be some means of ensuring the lines are used.
4. There must be sufficient inducement to use the lines.
5. The correct form of communication must be selected, ie oral, written, diagrammatic or pictorial.

The communication process

The elements of this are:

1. Intention/analysis: this is concerned with the What? Who? Why? and When? of communication.

2. Attention: communications should be designed to appeal to a variety of senses. Capture attention at the start by answering 'What's in it for the person receiving?' and 'What form of communication will best capture attention?'
3. Perception: it is essential to understand the receiver's perception – it is essential to help the receiver to see things as the sender does. Communication should be in terms which he is able to understand.
4. Retention: the mind tends to understand, accept and retain the simple rather than the complex; the logical rather than the confused; the known rather than the unknown; the concrete rather than the abstract. The mind prefers positive data.
5. Participation/feedback: this must be built in and encouraged by the sender at every stage. He must build in feedback, spoken or written words, actions, behaviour and must leave the receiver in no doubt who does what next. Feedback ensures that the receiver has received and understood the message.

The easiest thing to do when communications go wrong is to blame the receiver. The most difficult thing to do is to ask which of these principles were forgotten – or were not even appreciated.

Psychological interaction in two-way communication

Diagrammatic model of communication (see opposite)
Whatever the communication, it follows the same basic system.

The diagram is composed of the items and stages which make up any communication flow, from the origin, *information source* – the ideas, thoughts, orders, plans – *distortions* by selectors/filters (in human terms these will be the attitudes and perceptions of the sender). Next, those ideas become a *message* (order, plan, information) which must be *encoded* ie put into a suitable means of 'framing' the message (written or spoken words; signs, symbols or gestures etc) which can be *transmitted*, via the voice, muscles etc through suitable *channels* (post, telephone etc) again running the risk of *distractions* and interferences (undelivered mail, pneumatic drills etc). The *receiver* will pick up the transmission signals via the eye or ear and *decode* them to make sense of them. The receiver's *understanding* will be greatly influenced by his attitudes, perceptions, expectations. His 'interpretation' will determine the *destination*, ie what he thinks or perceives the *source is transmitting to* him.

If the flow stays on this one-way linear basis then the chances are there will be faulty communication producing subsequent behaviour. However, if the broken line linking the destination with the information source is *closed* then the flow becomes a *loop*, a continuous closed loop. In ordinary human terms, the receiver checks with the source to make sure that he has properly understood – ie he asks a *question* – he establishes a *two-way* communication system. Or by some reaction he 'communicates' *his* interpretation. In an *interview* where both parties are *face-to-face* these 'transmissions' can be picked up straight away. If by telephone or letter then the *feedback* is also established if both parties can question, ask for clarification and so on.

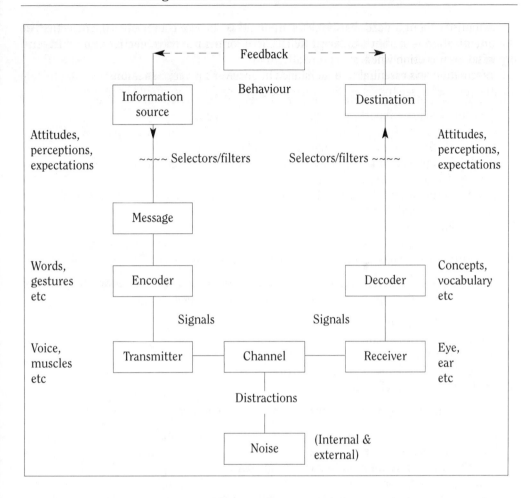

Problems of business communication

A reasonable argument can be put forward for the view that most of any organisation's problems stem from faulty communication.

Business communication models

All organisations have a variety of functions, structures and systems which must be controlled and co-ordinated. An organisation chart is a very simplified model of a firm; it shows the 'line' with its straight up and down, one step up and one step down *chain* of communication and command; the *network* of interdependence between departments within the firm. It may be extended to show communication links between each department and its external contacts (the micro-environment). An organisation cannot function without communication. Communications tie together the component parts of an organisation and impel people to action. In order for group and organisational activity to take place there must be communication among the participants.

In industry thoughts are shared for a purpose, this purpose is to further the objectives of the organisation – in short, to facilitate the achievement of the objectives for which the organisation was established.

Information and meanings are exchanged in business for various reasons:

1. to transmit orders and instructions so that they will be carried out effectively;
2. to ensure adequate reporting on how things are going;
3. to pass on information and advice from specialists to managers in charge of operations;
4. to appraise the performance of individual employees;
5. to advise employees on their progress so that their development and promotion can be furthered within the organisation;
6. to inform the owners (shareholders) of the organisation about its progress usually by balance sheets and profit and loss statements;
7. to train employees;
8. to inform middle and lower management of the decisions of top management;
9. to inform top management about the reactions of employees.

An employee's understanding of his job and its duties obviously depends on the quality of communication in the organisation. All employees want to know:

1. how to perform their jobs;
2. why they are doing them;
3. how well they are doing them;
4. why changes in the job are contemplated;
5. what the effect of such changes will be.

More sophisticated employees want to know much more:

1. how their jobs are related to the objectives of the organisation;
2. how secure their jobs are;
3. how they can secure the attention of management;
4. how they stand for promotion;
5. how their working groups are affected by job changes;
6. how they can participate in the thinking and decision making of their organisation.

The effectiveness of managers depends directly on the effectiveness of communication within the organisation, including their own effectiveness to communicate. They want:

1. their orders to be understood and to be implemented;
2. to know what top management is thinking;
3. information essential for planning and control;
4. to know how their employees are reacting.

An organisation is a complex of groups, all of which depend on communication:

1. There are many management groups, sometimes distinguished by levels of responsibility and authority, which have to communicate.
2. Departments have to communicate.
3. Working groups are held together by their internal communication.

4. Co-ordination of groups is based on communication.
5. The avoidance of tension between groups and the organisation requires continuing communication.

Forms of communication

By speaking
Face-to-face communication, by the spoken word, is a most important method. The supervisor/manager's main purpose is to arouse action. This calls for firm leadership, which implies readiness to meet people face to face. If he is cheerful and equable in his face-to-face contacts, he will tend to call forth a friendly response; if he is sarcastic and tight-lipped, he will arouse resentment.

By writing
Written communications play an increasingly important part in business administration – web pages, policy statements, rules reports, e-mails, memos, control documents, financial statements and standing procedures/orders are all well-known examples of documentation. There are handbooks or manuals, house magazines, notice boards and information racks.

The key steps in preparing the message are:

1. define the purpose of the message: for example, what change in knowledge or behaviour it is intended to bring about;
2. consider the recipients: their present knowledge and behaviour, their level of linguistic understanding and literacy, their culture etc;
3. plan the sequence of the message: arousing interest, capturing attention, giving information and encouraging feedback.

By listening
When listening to someone, the listener looks interested and shows that he is giving his undivided attention. This is both courteous and businesslike. A friendly, patient and attentive listener helps people to talk freely and is likely therefore to gain a true insight into their thoughts, moods and feelings.

Listening is an active process, requiring concentration, selection of core issues, commitment to memory and willingness to ask for clarification.

By reading
The effectiveness of a written communication depends as much on the receiver as on the communicator.

The reader tries to evaluate the communication, eg is this page consistent with the previous one, are the facts and opinions consistent with the facts that other people give and with what is known from experience.

By non-verbal behaviour
Attitudes, tones of voice, expressions, even silence itself, are occasionally acts of communication. There are also a sign language (gestures, facial expressions), an action

language (running) and an object language (clothes) as well as a word language. If non-verbal communication is intended, it must be as clear and precise as speech and writing. Always remember that fingers can often turn out to be pointing at far more objects or people than the pointer intended. Smiles, nods, winks, chin-scratching and arm folding are unlikely to convey any message to the audience and even less likely to convey the intended message.

Communication failure

Even a well-designed communication system can break down. The following is a brief summary of potential reasons for breakdown:

1. too little information (especially the holding back of 'bad news');
2. too much information (obscuring the essential message);
3. too soon, leaving time for the recipient to forget the message;
4. too late, after the recipient has already acted wrongly;
5. structural and network deficiencies, eg over-extended lines of communication, incomplete transmission of the message;
6. structure too large, too rigid, too centralised (requires better delegation, especially in decision making);
7. complexity of products or of processing, making it difficult for the recipient to understand or respond;
8. absence of key person/personnel to whom the message is primarily addressed;
9. by-passing of formal channels (although the informal channel is often a very efficient way of communicating);
10. language, terminology, concepts, jargon, which may be clear to the sender but not to the recipient or, worse still, may mean something totally different in the recipient's present or past environment (especially if the recipient has been recruited from another organisation that uses terminology in a slightly different way);
11. technical breakdowns.

Graphic communication

An important visual form of communication is graphic. The following have all appeared in relevant examinations and students should be familiar with the techniques.

Graphs show the relationship between one variable and another. Conventionally, the independent variable is plotted on the horizontal axis and the dependent variable on the vertical axis. Students should take care to use all the available space on the graph paper supplied and to ensure that the axes are clearly labelled and intervals accurately plotted.

In a *bar chart* data are represented by a series of bars or strips, the length of the bars being proportional to the quantity represented. *Percentage component bar charts* show how the percentage make up of data may vary from one situation to another.

Pie charts show the composition of data in the form of a circle in which each segment is proportional to the proportions of each component.

Chapter Twenty Six

Government, the community and business

- Introduction

- Government and business

- Government as legislator

- International trade and its impact on United Kingdom business

- Exchange rates

- The European Union and its impact on United Kingdom business

- Integrated nature of business

Introduction

Throughout our study frequent reference has been made to the economic, political and legal environment, and examples have been given to illustrate how these environments affect business decision-making. The first section of this chapter endeavours to highlight some of the ways in which the government, as manager of the national economy, affects business. The next section examines how the government, as legislator, has influenced the legal environment.

Government and business

Controlling the economy

These are the methods open to government: fiscal; monetary; direct intervention.

Fiscal policy
This is the direction of the economy through taxation and government expenditure. If taxation exceeds expenditure this is described as a 'budget surplus' and will have the effect of reducing national income by taking discretionary spending power out of circulation. Conversely, a 'budget deficit' is when government expenditure exceeds taxation, thus increasing national

income. In times of high unemployment, a budget 'deficit' will increase spending power, thus increasing the demand for goods and, therefore, labour. In times of high inflation a budget surplus will reduce the availability of money and thus reduce inflation, but in the process also the demand for goods and labour.

Monetary policy

The government controls the supply of money through the Bank of England. Since 1997, this function has been delegated to the Bank of England's Monetary Policy Committee. This removes the decision-making process from the hands of politicians, thereby reducing the danger of decisions to cut interest rates (making it easier to spend money on credit and reducing home-owners' mortgages) in order to gain short-term popularity at the risk of causing high inflation. If there is excess money in circulation this will have an inflationary effect; a classic definition of inflation is 'too much money chasing too few goods'.

The supply of money is controlled by interest rates, making money either more or less expensive to obtain. If borrowing is expensive, individuals and institutions are less likely to borrow and spend. There is therefore less money in circulation. The Bank of England influences interest rates by setting the rates at which it will lend to other banks. This in turn has a strong influence on the rates at which banks can afford to lend to their customers.

The Bank of England also controls the physical supply of bank notes. This is important, as Bank of England banknotes are legal tender and ultimately every transaction based on monetary exchange is an agreement to settle in banknotes or their equivalent. Debtors are legally entitled to settle their debts in legal tender and depositors can also withdraw money from their bank in Bank of England banknotes. If fact, every high street bank will always have a supply of these notes.

Alternative monetary policies can therefore be summarised:

Policy	Action	Effect
Dear money	Raise interest rates	Deflationary
Cheap money	Lower interest rates	Inflationary

Direct intervention

Alternatively, the government can intervene directly through legislation to control business activity.

Government objectives

What are a government's objectives? Possibilities are the control of unemployment and of inflation; a surplus balance of payments, that is, surplus in trade with the rest of the world; and economic growth. While all parties agree on these objectives there is obviously disagreement over priorities and policies. In the US and UK in the 1960s, unemployment was seen to be the most important issue, but by the mid-1970s lax monetary and fiscal policies and the increase in oil prices had led to high inflation in the UK, making it impossible for businesses with lengthy stock turnover periods, especially in manufacturing, to remain profitable without continually raising prices faster and faster, thereby increasing inflation and leaving the problem unsolved. Since 1973, both Labour and Conservative governments have therefore accorded higher priority to fighting inflation, initially by means of prices and incomes policies (which were largely unsuccessful because they were based on a denial of workers' and businesses' economic realities) and later by means of fiscal and monetary measures.

The problem for government is the virtual impossibility of pursuing all objectives simultaneously.

The problem for business is the difficulty of long-term planning when the cost of capital over the life-span of a project may fluctuate according to political priorities, when the demand for the company's products may be seriously affected by variation in the cost of money and when the availability and cost of labour is similarly affected.

Taxation

Direct taxes include:

- personal income tax (which determines the individual's discretionary spending power and therefore his behaviour either as a consumer or as a worker);
- corporation tax levied on companies' profits. This may be offset against capital investment;
- inheritance tax when assets are inherited;
- capital gains tax on the profits made from selling property and investments.

Indirect taxes include:

- customs and excise duty, levied at specific rates;
- VAT (value added tax) levied at either 8 per cent or 17.5 per cent on the selling price;
- stamp duty, on the sale of land, buildings, stocks and shares.

Indirect taxes often hit poorer people harder because they are taxed on expenditure and poorer people spend a higher proportion of their incomes.

From the business point of view the details of taxation can affect the proportion in which wealth is distributed and therefore the demand for different types of good from different segments of the market. Corporation tax influences financial planning, national insurance contributions add to variable production costs and capital gains tax has a direct impact on the workings of the Stock Market.

Inflation

Inflation is undesirable because of its effect on savings and the value of wages and on the costs of purchase and manufacture of stock to replace what has been sold. High inflation can turn nominal profits on the sale of old stock into real losses when stocks have to be replaced. This makes inflation especially damaging for manufacturers and retailers. Under fixed exchange rate mechanisms, inflation can also have a severe effect on exports, as other countries within the system may have central banks which are more successful at controlling inflation and, therefore, over time, a larger price differential will arise. At the same time, imports become relatively cheaper, resulting in higher imports and loss of domestic markets by home producers. This means that high inflation in one country within a fixed exchange rate system can result in a deterioration of that country's balance of payments and reduce its gross domestic product.

Conclusion

Students should keep up to date, by collecting government statistics on rates of taxation, interest rates, balance of payments and inflation and unemployment rates – so as to be able to illustrate answers to questions – and by reading political and economic articles in the quality newspapers. You should also 'think through' a variety of business and economics related problems, so as to reach an understanding of the interaction between these forces. For instance, if indirect taxes hit poorer people hardest what would you expect an increase in the tax on coffee to do to the demand for a popular brand and to the demand for an exclusive high quality brand? If interest rates are higher in the US than they are in the UK, what would you expect to happen to investment capital and therefore what effect would this have on long-term British productivity?

Posing such problems and 'thinking them through' will help you to understand the major economic forces facing business and will stand you in good stead when faced with unexpected examination questions.

Government as legislator

The legal environment

Legislation affects business in three main areas:

1. Companies Acts define a company's financial obligations and reporting requirements.
2. Consumer legislation, such as the Trade Descriptions Act, protects the consumer.
3. However, the most controversial and politically sensitive area of legislation is that concerning the employment of labour.

Government intervention

In 1998 the government implemented the National Minimum Wage Act, which set up the Low Pay Commission, whose function is to recommend a national minimum wage.

At the time industrialists expressed concern that a national minimum wage would make the UK uncompetitive but, despite some inevitable inital difficulties, the legislation has been reasonably satisfactorily implemented.

Equal pay

The Equal Pay Act 1970 and the Sex Discrimination Act 1975 (see below) aim to eliminate discrimination between men and women in employment on the grounds of sex. The Acts are complementary and should be read together.

The Equal Pay Act 1970 is concerned with remuneration and other terms and conditions of employment. Its most important provisions include the requirement for pay to be equal where it can be shown that a woman's work is the 'same or broadly similar' to the work of a man in the same employment or where a woman is employed in a job which has been given an equal value to men's jobs under a job evaluation scheme even though the nature or content of the job itself may be different.

The Sex Discrimination Act 1975 is much broader and according to the House of Commons Official Report Standing Committee 8 dated 1 May 1975, seeks 'a common strategy and philosophy, a parity of treatment approach and attitude'. It complements the earlier Act.

Sex Discrimination Act 1975

The Sex Discrimination Act also covers discrimination in the provision of education, housing, goods and services, discriminatory advertising and discrimination on grounds of marriage. Complaints of sex discrimination at work can be made to an employment tribunal.

The Equal Opportunities Commission has been established to help enforce the legislation and to promote equal opportunities between the sexes.

Definition of discrimination

Part 1 of the Act defines two kinds of conduct which constitute sex discrimination, *direct* discrimination which involves an actual or inferred intention to treat a person less favourably on the ground of his or her sex; and *indirect* discrimination involving practices which are discriminatory in their effect (whether or not this is intentional) and cannot be shown to be justifiable.

Employment

Part 2 of the Act applies to employment and related matters. It is unlawful under the Act for an employer to discriminate in the recruitment of new employees or in his treatment of existing employees (for example, in such matters as promotion, training, transfer and dismissal).

The Act permits employers and vocational training bodies to provide training on a single-sex basis for work in which comparatively few members of that sex have engaged and to encourage persons of that sex to take advantage of opportunities for such work, and there is a corresponding provision as regards single-sex training for posts in trade unions and employers' associations. Trade unions, employers' associations and professional bodies are also permitted to make special arrangements to ensure the representation of one sex on elected committees where that sex might not otherwise be adequately represented. The Act also makes provision for vocational training bodies to provide single-sex training for married women returning to work and others who have been out of the labour market for domestic or family reasons.

Certain jobs in social services may also be legally restricted to employees of one sex on the grounds that clients are of that sex.

Goods, facilities and services

Discrimination in the provision to the public, or a section of the public, of goods, facilities and services (including, for example loans, finance, mortgages and facilities for recreation and entertainment) and of housing accommodation is unlawful.

Equal Opportunities Commission

The Equal Opportunities Commission has the strategic role of working towards the elimination of discrimination and promoting equality of opportunity between men and women.

Race Relations Act 1976

The Race Relations Act is modelled on the Sex Discrimination Act 1975, and such concepts as direct and indirect discrimination are replicated in the Race Relations Act. It is unlawful to discriminate against a person on the grounds of his race in terms of employment, education, the provisions of goods and services, union membership or housing. In respect of employment there are a few exceptions for genuine occupational qualifications, as for example, waiters in an ethnic restaurant, but generally anyone who has been a victim of discrimination can complain to an industrial tribunal, and, if successful, can obtain compensation.

The Commission for Racial Equality was set up to work towards the elimination of racial discrimination, to promote equality of opportunity between different racial groups and to keep the Race Relations Act under review.

Safeguards against dismissal

Until 1971 the law did not require the employer to give any reason for dismissing the employee. Unless prevented by the employment contract, the employer was able to dismiss employees justifiably simply by giving due notice.

In 1965 the Redundancy Payments Act established the presumption that every dismissed employee would be regarded as having been dismissed by reason of redundancy and therefore be entitled to statutory redundancy money.

In 1971, the Industrial Relations Act established the concept of unfair dismissal, and placed the onus of proof on the employer.

The law relating to the right of the individual not to be unfairly dismissed may now be found in the Employment Rights Act 1996.

In particular, an employee who has 26 weeks continuous employment with an employer may now demand a written statement of the reasons for his dismissal and the employer is required to accede to the request within two weeks, on pain of having the tribunal award the employee a sum equivalent to two weeks pay if it finds the complaint justified.

This stipulation is designed to help the dismissed employee determine whether he has been fairly or unfairly dismissed, and whether he therefore has a complaint which could be put to the tribunal.

The European Union's directive on acquired rights of workers on transfers of undertakings also protects an employee in the event of redundancy following a takeover of his employer's business.

Health, safety, welfare and physical conditions at work

The legislation relating to health, safety and working conditions is very wide-ranging and complex. It is increasingly being influenced by European Union law; for example, Council Directive 89/391 sets out to improve workers' conditions.

The principal statute on this subject is the Health and Safety at Work Act 1974 (HSWA), which is a consolidating statute. Regulations and codes of practice made under HSWA are gradually replacing the provisions of the earlier Acts, such as the Factories Act 1961 and the Offices, Shops and Railways Premises Act 1963. Current regulations include Management of Health and Safety at Work; Personal Protection Equipment at Work; Provision and Use of Work Equipment; Workplace (Health, Safety and Welfare); Manual Handling of Loads; Health and Safety (Display Screen Equipment).

The aim of HSWA is to protect employees by means of obliging employers to maintain safe premises and promote safe conditions of work. If the employers fail to provide safe premises and working conditions, the employers can be prosecuted. Prosecution is, however, relatively rare as the inspectors under HSWA prefer to encourage employers to co-operate with the statutory requirements rather than punish them for their failure to adhere to them. The inspectors can issue improvement notices, which require that the premises or working conditions be improved within a certain time period, or they can issue prohibition orders, if the premises or conditions of work are seriously dangerous. If the employer fails to obey these notices or orders he can be prosecuted.

Another important concern of HSWA is to encourage greater awareness of the need to promote health and safety at work.

The enforcement of HSWA is delegated to the Health and Safety Executive, who appoint the inspectorate, but local authorities decide on the appropriate rules for their regions, and the Health and Safety Commission provides overall guidance on policy matters.

Obligations under the Health and Safety at Work Act 1974

Duties of employers. Under the Act it is the duty of employers:

1. to provide and maintain premises and systems of work that, so far as is reasonably possible, are safe and without risk to health;
2. to ensure, so far as is reasonably practicable, safe practices and absence of risks to health in connection with the use, handling, storage and transport of articles and substances;
3. to provide adequate training and instruction to ensure the health, safety and welfare of employees;
4. to provide written statements of the general policy for health and safety at work in respect of employees.

Employers are not necessarily obliged, but are encouraged, to set up safety committees and to consult with safety representatives from that committee.

Rights of employees. Employees are not to be dismissed or disciplined for refusing or failing to carry out dangerous acts or bringing matters concerning the health and safety of employees to their employers' attention.

Duties of controllers of premises. Even where premises may not necessarily contain employees, HSWA requires controllers of premises to have regard for the health and safety of those who are using the premises, eg students within a university or guests at a hotel.

Duties of manufacturers. Manufacturers are obliged to produce their articles so that they can be used without risk to the health or safety of the user.

Duties of employees. Employees are obliged to act sensibly with due regard for the health and safety of both themselves and their fellow employees.

Civil liability arising from the Health and Safety at Work Act 1974

The Health and Safety Commission is continually updating the health and safety regulations, consulting with safety experts about codes of practice and generally doing what it can to promote the highest standards of health and safety in the working environment. Although lapses from these standards by employers or controllers of premises may not always be a criminal matter, it is likely that any failure to adhere to industry norms of health and safety at work would on the face of it give rise to an inference that the employer or controller of premises had been negligent.

Trade unions

The Trade Union Amendment Act 1867 contained the following definition of a trade union, which is still recognised today:

> 'A trade union is any combination, whether temporary or permanent for regulating the relations between workmen and masters, or between workmen and workmen, or between masters and masters, or for imposing restrictive conditions on the conduct of any trade or business.'

It is important to realise that, in accordance with this definition, employers' associations are also classified as trade unions. Historically s4 of the Trade Union Act 1871 debarred the courts from enforcing any agreement between one trade union and another. The effect of this was that any agreement between an employers' association and a trade union was not enforceable at law. Such agreements were regarded as 'gentlemen's agreements' which were binding in honour only. Under s179 of the Trades Union and Labour Relations (Consolidation) Act 1992 this rule was maintained, but it is now possible for an agreement to be legally enforceable if the parties wish to make it so – which often they do not. The non-enforceable status of such agreements should be borne in mind when considering the functions and aims of the trade unions in this country.

The aims of the trade unions can be summarised as follows:

1. The process of efficient production should be achieved with the minimum human cost.

For example, changes in jobs or conditions of work should be made in order to avoid or minimise stress between management and workers;

2. Working conditions should be maintained or improved, particularly in the areas of:

   a) fair wages and guaranteed earnings;
   b) reasonable hours;
   c) paid holidays;
   d) security of employment;
   e) adequate procedures for dealing with grievances;
   f) opportunities for promotion.

3. They will press for the internal development and expansion of authority, membership and influence of the trade union organisation itself. The attainment of these objectives will ensure freedom from aggression by employers or competitive organisations and freedom from government interference in the collective bargaining process.

Trades Union and Labour Relations (Consolidation) Act 1992 and the Employment Act 1990

Traditionally the Labour Party has been sympathetic to trade unionism and the Conservative Party suspicious of it. During the Labour governments in the later 1970s much of the previous Conservative government's legislation on trade unions was repealed. In due course, when a Conservative government was re-elected, the Conservatives introduced legislation to prohibit some of the activities that in their view were unacceptable, such as picketing of suppliers and distributors, obligatory closed shops, wild-cat strikes and a perceived lack of democracy in unions' own management. With the return of a Labour government, various rights have been returned to trade unions and their members, but in general many of the reforms introduced by the Conservatives remain in place in the interests of accountability and social responsibility.

The main effects of the current legislation are detailed below.

1. Trade unions may now be liable in tort for unauthorised strike action or for secondary picketing.
2. They must be registered and produce accounts regularly.
3. They must hold proper meetings and vote by secret ballots.
4. Terms in any contract which require one party to the contract to recognise a closed shop or to recognise a union will be void, and employees cannot be dismissed either for belonging to a trade union or for not belonging to a trade union.
5. Individual members of a trade union lose their right to claim unfair dismissal if they participate in unauthorised strike action.
6. If a trade union wishes to organise a strike, it must give seven days' notice of the date and timing of the strike.

Employment tribunals

These tribunals have existed since 1964 and their jurisdiction now covers matters arising from a variety of employment type legislation. Their main concern is for appeals against unfair dismissals. Tribunals have the power to award compensation and to make orders determining the rights of individuals or organisations. Their procedures are informal and they are required to attempt conciliation between the parties to the dispute before hearing a case. There is a right of appeal to an Employment Appeal Tribunal, and ultimately on a point of law to the House of Lords.

The Advisory, Conciliation and Arbitration Service (ACAS)

The Advisory, Conciliation and Arbitration Service (ACAS) was set up in 1974 and is now governed by the Trades Union and Labour Relations (Consolidation) Act 1992. Its powers and duties include:

- offering conciliation and other assistance to help settle any trade dispute;
- providing conciliation officers to promote the settlement of complaints made to industrial tribunals;
- referring matters in dispute to arbitration or to the Central Arbitration Committee;
- offering advice to employers, employers' associations, workers and trade unions on industrial relations and employment policies and publishing general advice;
- inquiring into any question relating to industrial relations, generally, or in any particular industry or undertaking or part of an undertaking;
- issuing codes of practice containing practical guidance for promoting good industrial relations (including codes on specified matters).

Many organisations use the ACAS codes of practice. The codes are generally reckoned by both employers' representative bodies and trade unions as being reasonable and fair to all parties concerned.

Trade union recognition

Independent trade unions may refer recognition issues to ACAS, which may decide on the manner of establishing the views of the employees concerned. Conditions for the arrangements and for notification of the results of a ballot, if that method is used, are laid down; the ballot should be secret.

A trade union would be able to complain to ACAS that an employer was not complying with a recognition recommendation.

Disclosure of information

Employers will be required to disclose information necessary for collective bargaining purposes, and which it would be good industrial relations practice to disclose to representatives of recognised trade unions.

Complaints

A trade union may complain to the Central Arbitration Committee that an employer has failed to disclose information. The complaint may be referred for conciliation; if conciliation fails, the Central Arbitration Committee may consider the complaint and may make a declaration specifying the information which is relevant, the date on which the employer failed to disclose the information, and the date by which the information should be disclosed.

Employment Rights Act 1996

This Act consolidated much previous legislation and deals with the following matters:

Guarantee payments

An employee will be normally entitled to a guarantee payment from his employer if he is not provided with work on a normal working day because of, say, a power cut or floods. A guarantee payment will not be payable if the employer is unable to provide work because of a trade dispute involving other employees of the same employer or of an associated employer. An employee will not be entitled to guarantee pay if the employer has offered him suitable alternative work which he has refused.

Medical suspension

An employee will be normally entitled to be paid by his employer if he is suspended from work on medical grounds. The employee will not be entitled to pay if he refuses an offer of suitable alternative work.

Maternity

An employee who is dismissed because she is pregnant, or for any reason connected with pregnancy, will be treated as unfairly dismissed. If she is incapable of working or is prohibited from working by a statutory provision because of her pregnancy and her employer cannot offer her suitable alternative work, she may then be fairly dismissed, but she will retain her right to maternity pay and reinstatement if she is otherwise eligible.

An employee has a right to return to her job, or a similar job, for up to 29 weeks after the birth of her child.

An employee will be able to complain to an employment tribunal if her employer does not allow her to return to work. The complaint will be treated as a complaint of unfair dismissal. If she cannot be re-employed because she is redundant she will be entitled to compensation under the Redundancy Payments Act.

An employee is also entitled to take time for ante-natal care and to insist that her place of work be suitable for new or expectant mothers.

Trade union membership and activities

An employee will have the right not to have action taken against him by his employer which would prevent or deter him from becoming a member of an independent trade union or from taking part in its activities at any appropriate time. An employer must not compel an employee to be a member of a non-independent trade union. Provision is made to deal with the situation where there is a trade union membership agreement, or where an employee will not join a union because of religious belief.

Time off

An employer will have to allow officials of independent recognised trade unions reasonable time off work, with pay, to carry out duties concerned with industrial relations between the employer and the employees they represent. Trade union officials will also be entitled to time off for training to help them carry out these duties. Time off must be made available to employees performing public duties (such as being an elected member of a local council); to employees caring for dependants; and to young employees receiving training. Under further regulations effective from December 1999, fathers are entitled to parental leave.

Insolvency

If an employer is insolvent, certain debts due from him to his employees (including guarantee and medical suspension payments, payments for time off and remuneration under protective awards) are to be paid in priority to other debts.

Employees whose employment has terminated because of the employer's insolvency may obtain payment of the debts mentioned above, plus arrears of pay and holiday pay, and unfair dismissal compensation from the Redundancy Fund. Contributions to an occupational pension fund which were unpaid when the employer became insolvent may also be paid from the Redundancy Fund.

Remedies for unfair dismissal

In a case of unfair dismissal an employment tribunal will have to give priority to examining the practicability of reinstatement or re-engagement. If this would be practicable and the complainant wants reinstatement or re-engagement, the tribunal may make an order and may order the terms of reinstatement or re-engagement.

An award of compensation for unfair dismissal will consist of a basic award and a compensatory award. The basic award will be related to the period of service the employee had had with the employer.

The compensatory award will take account of any loss sustained by the employee as a result of his dismissal. The award may be reduced to take account of any contributory action by the employee.

Itemised pay statement

Employers must provide employees with itemised statements of pay which contain details of their gross earnings, net pay and fixed and variable deductions.

Procedures for handling redundancies

An employer who proposes to make employees redundant and who recognises an independent trade union for those employees will be required to consult the trade union as soon as possible.

The employer must disclose prescribed information about the redundancy and how it is to be effected, and will be required to consider and reply to any representations from the trade union concerned.

Notifications must be given a minimum number of days before the dismissals take effect, depending on the numbers involved (90 days for 100 or more dismissals, 60 days for ten or more). Where appropriate, a copy of the notice must go to the recognised trade union.

If an employee unreasonably refuses an offer from his employer of a new contract or a renewal of the old contract, he would lose his entitlement to remuneration under the award.

Industrial relations in practice

Industrial relations in the United Kingdom are primarily a voluntary system despite the volume of statute laws. Any study must take into account the current industrial climate and all students are strongly advised to follow, in the national and professional press, developments both in the law and in practice.

International trade and its impact on United Kingdom business

Background

The United Kingdom is a major trading nation. Many United Kingdom businesses are involved in producing goods and providing services for export to the rest of the world, while others are involved in importing goods and services from the rest of the world. This international trade also affects those United Kingdom businesses which are not themselves engaged in import or export. The health of all United Kingdom businesses is dependent either directly or indirectly on international trade, and the health of the United Kingdom economy is heavily dependent on the nation's trading links with the rest of the world.

The pattern of the United Kingdom's trade with the rest of the world changed during the 20th century and particularly since it became a member of the European Union. This shifting pattern of international trade affects all United Kingdom businesses either directly or indirectly and will continue to do so in the future.

Prior to the United Kingdom's entry into the then European Economic Community (now the European Community or European Union) in 1973, much of its trade was with the former colonies (the Commonwealth). This trade had grown out of the former British Empire, and consisted to a large extent of the United Kingdom exporting manufactured goods (largely low tech) to former colonies and importing raw materials and agricultural produce from them. Because of the historic links between the 'Mother Country' and the former colonies, the United Kingdom's trade with the Commonwealth countries was to some extent 'protected', at least until the end of the second world war. After that the United States of America, in particular, began to call for 'free trade' in order to open up formerly protected ex-colonial markets to United States businesses (see the discussion on GATT and the World Trade Organization below). As a result of this global move in the direction of less protected and more open markets, the United Kingdom's traditional trading patterns began to change.

Following the United Kingdom's membership of the European Union, a large and increasing part of its international trade is now with its European Union partners. It also trades extensively with the United States and other Advanced Industrial Economies. Only a fairly small percentage of its international trade is with Third World countries. It is possible that this situation may change in the future, particularly as a result of the change of the formerly communist countries of Eastern Europe towards market economies and the improvement of the People's Republic of China's relations with the capitalist world. The completion of the Internal Market of the European Union in 1992 has already had an impact on United Kingdom trading patterns, and will continue to do so. The implications of this internal market for United Kingdom businesses is enormous (see 'European Union', below).

Multinational companies

International trade is becoming increasingly globalised. The rise of multinational companies (alternatively called 'transnationals') which trade in several different countries, has major implications for United Kingdom businesses and jobs. Multinational companies are able to move the production of their goods between different countries and different parts of the world in order to obtain the lowest cost production. For complex manufactured goods (eg cars) they are able to source different components in different countries. They are able to take into account not only production costs, including labour costs, but also such factors as industrial climate (are there strong trade unions and/or many industrial disputes?). Multinational companies are said to be 'footloose', meaning that they may potentially pull production out of a country, or a region, and move to another country or region where costs are lower. This may have a serious (and sometimes) devastating effect on the economy of a small country, or on the economy of a particular region. Not only may many jobs be lost directly as a result of a pull-out by a multinational, but there will also be indirect jobs losses resulting from the impact on other local businesses.

Labour costs

The ability of multinational companies to move production to lower-cost countries is potentially very serious for United Kingdom businesses and jobs. Although labour costs in the United Kingdom are low in comparison with some European Union countries, in world terms it is a high labour cost country. It is not able to compete with labour costs either in Third World countries or in the Pacific Rim countries (the so-called 'Asian Tigers' and 'Asian Dragons', the recently industrialised countries such as Korea).

Labour costs consist of two elements: direct wage costs (wages and salaries), and the so-called 'social costs of labour' (things such as redundancy and unfair dismissal provision, pensions and health and safety standards). The labour costs of the European Union are very high in world terms, and this is having a serious effect on the businesses of the Union. In Third World countries and in recently industrialised countries not only are the direct costs of labour lower than in the European Union, but the social costs are also much lower (for example, there are much lower health and safety standards, and there is little or no redundancy provision).

Competition

What is to be done? Clearly, the member countries of the European Union, including the United Kingdom, need to concentrate on those areas of economic activity where they currently still have a comparative advantage over the Third World and Pacific Rim countries. These areas are primarily those of the knowledge based industries, utilising Europe's comparative advantage in education. The United Kingdom also needs to ensure that its per worker productivity continues to rise, and becomes more competitive with that of the other advanced industrial countries.

The global economy

In the global market place, maintaining international competitiveness is vital to the survival of businesses and countries. Even those businesses which are not directly engaged in international trade are dependent for survival on the health of the economy in which they operate. Those businesses engaged in exporting are also very dependent on the health of the global economy, and in particular on that of the economies to which they export.

The economies of the world are now inextricably interlinked, and hence interdependent. International trade since the Second World War has undergone exponential growth. We are all now part of the global economy, and dependent for our livelihoods on the health of the world economy as a whole. It is now possible to talk in terms of a 'global growth' or 'global recession' which affects us all to a greater or lesser degree. The United Kingdom has always been a very open economy, which means that it is heavily engaged in international trade, both imports and exports, and this makes it particularly vulnerable to events in the global economy.

Balance of Payments

Just as two businesses which trade with each other keep a set of accounts which lists all transactions, so do countries. Each country has a 'Balance of Payments', which is ₍ simply a set of accounts which shows its global trading position vis-à-vis the rest of the world.

United Kingdom

The United Kingdom Balance of Payments accounts are published regularly by the government, and it is possible for anyone to go along to any large library and inspect them. They show the United Kingdom's international trade in all goods and services, broken down into 'visibles' (which means goods: items which 'you can drop on your foot' (Lord Robbins)), and 'invisibles' (which means services: items which you cannot drop on your foot).

The Balance of Payments accounts are also divided into a current account and a capital account. The current account deals with the import and export of goods and services, while the capital account deals with transactions in external assets and liabilities. The capital account includes items such as the building or acquisition of a production plant in a foreign country by a United Kingdom business (this will initially cause an outflow of funds from the United Kingdom to pay for it, but will ultimately lead to a stream of profits flowing into the United Kingdom), and the building or acquisition of a production plant in the United Kingdom by a foreign business (which will initially cause an inflow of funds to the United Kingdom, but ultimately will cause an outflow of profits from the United Kingdom). It also includes short-term monetary flows between the world's financial centres (eg the City of London, New York, Tokyo), and transactions in the gold and foreign currency reserves held by the Bank of England (normally as a result of the Bank buying or selling sterling, as discussed in 'Exchange Rates', below).

There are often references in the media to a 'Balance of Payments Deficit' or a 'trade deficit'. This means that for the period in question (usually a month, a quarter, or a year) the United Kingdom has received less income from its exports to the rest of the world than it paid for imports. In other words, it has either had to borrow to finance the deficit, or had to dip into reserves. While this may not be a serious matter for an individual month, it *will* be serious if it continues at too high a level. All imports must be paid for eventually, from current or future revenues.

It is not only *how much* the United Kingdom sells and buys internationally that is important. What we buy and sell, and their relative prices also matter (or may matter for the future) . If, for example, the relative prices of the exported goods change compared with the prices of the imported goods, then this will affect the so-called 'terms of trade'. If exports produce less while imports cost more, then it is said that the 'terms of trade have worsened'. This is potentially serious.

Oil

The United Kingdom Balance of Payments has benefited since 1979 from North Sea oil, which has contributed significant revenue. This oil 'bonanza', however, is now contributing less, and will continue to decline. The Balances of Payments of most of the major advanced industrial countries were seriously affected during the 1970s and beyond by several major increases in the price of oil, imposed by the Organisation of Petroleum Exporting Countries (OPEC), which formed a cartel of some of the major oil exporting countries (mostly the Middle Eastern states). The non-oil producing advanced industrial economies are very vulnerable to increases in the price of oil, and as a result these affect the health of the global economy.

General Agreement on Tariffs and Trade (GATT) and the World Trade Organization

Bretton Woods

The General Agreement on Tariffs and Trade was set up in 1947 at the post-war Bretton Woods conference which involved the United States, the United Kingdom and more than 40 other countries. The purpose of the conference was to set up systems designed to ensure economic stability, and not only GATT but also the International Monetary Fund (IMF) (see below) and the post-war exchange rate system known as the 'Bretton Woods' system (see 'Exchange Rates' below) were created.

On 1 January 1995, the GATT was replaced by the World Trade Organization (WTO), based in Geneva.

Purpose

The purpose of the WTO is to regulate the international trading system, to attempt to reduce the degree of protectionism, and to promote free trade in goods and services. The United States was very keen to promote free trade, in order to open up the then protected colonial markets to its businesses. Since the European economies had virtually collapsed as a result of the second world war, the United States held the purse strings and hence was able to mould GATT (and the other post-war institutions) to its wishes.

Most of the major economies of the world are members of the WTO, which means that they agree to abide by its decisions and policies. Throughout the GATT's history, various 'rounds' of agreements took place, with the aim of both extending free trade to further areas of goods and services and further reducing protectionist measures. The last GATT 'round' was the Uruguay one, which was concerned with agricultural produce and services. Protection of agricultural produce has been the source of major rows between the United States and the European Union.

Free trade

What is 'free trade'? Why is it alleged to be so beneficial? If it is so beneficial, why do all of the world economies take protectionist measures of one sort or another?

Free trade means that goods and services should be freely traded between countries without any let or hindrance, with no additional costs or conditions being imposed on their importers or exporters or eventual consumers. It is alleged to be beneficial not only to individual countries but also to the global economy. The economic theory of comparative advantage, first formulated by David Ricardo, demonstrates that if each country specialises in producing those goods and services which it can produce more cheaply than other countries, and countries then trade these goods between each other at agreed rates of exchange, total world production will be higher than it would otherwise have been, and each individual country will benefit. For example, if the United Kingdom specialises in knowledge-based activities (in which its relatively highly educated and trained workforce creates an advantage) then it can trade these goods and services with countries which have specialised in agricultural production (because they have better climates than the United Kingdom), and in theory both should be better off as a result of the trade, and total world production should be higher than it would otherwise have been.

Envisage a world economy which involves only two countries trading with each other (a simplification for illustration purposes only) and producing only two goods (again, a simplification). It may be that country A can produce both types of goods cheaper than can country B (in other words country A has what economists call an 'absolute advantage' in production). It will still be worthwhile for country A to specialise in producing the goods in which its advantage over country B is relatively greater. Country B will then concentrate on producing the other goods so that both countries and the global economy as a whole will benefit. Both countries will have a higher standard of living (higher income) than they would otherwise have had, and total world production will be greater.

This is the economic theory of comparative advantage which underpins the idea of the alleged benefits of free trade. One problem is that, in the current real world global economy, those countries which can offer only agricultural produce or raw materials (mostly the Third World countries) are at a major power disadvantage vis-à-vis the advanced industrial economies which can offer the more complex advanced goods and services. As a result the terms of exchange between these two categories of goods are not freely agreed, as per the theory, but enforced on the poorer countries (see 'Third World debt' below). Hence free trade is not necessarily beneficial to Third World countries, as it tends to benefit the strong economies and be detrimental to the weaker ones.

Protectionism

Advanced industrial countries (including those which are signatories to GATT) also employ protectionist measures from time to time. The reason for this is that governments feel the need to protect their industries and particularly their jobs from competition from other countries. Increasing globalisation of industries has resulted in many job losses in advanced industrial countries, with resultant demands for government to 'do something to protect "our" jobs', to prevent them from moving to Third World and/or newly industrialising countries. Faced with a recession, governments have tended in the past to raise protectionist barriers against the goods and services of other countries. This is what happened during the 'slump' of the 1930s, and it unfortunately results (and resulted then) in other countries retaliating, and barriers going up all round. This is undesirable, and it is one of the primary aims of GATT to avoid this situation.

There are various forms of protectionist barrier, some of which are more obvious than others. In some cases it may be difficult to distinguish whether a particular measure is employed with the aim of reducing imports or for a different reason. For instance health and safety standards may sometimes be used to ban specific goods from one particular country. Is this purely for the protection of the population, or in order to keep out the exporting country's goods? For example, Germany has in the past attempted to prevent imports of British beer, on the grounds that it contains additives. Other forms of protectionism may include time-wasting formalities and unnecessary paperwork (which adds to costs), or understaffing of customs posts which deal with particular types of imports (the French have done this in the past, with the result of slowing down imports of certain Japanese goods).

Protectionist barriers are normally divided into 'tariff' barriers and 'non-tariff'.

Tariffs involve imposing a charge on top of the cost of any particular good (for example, cars from Japan would have an extra import charge added to their cost, making them more expensive to consumers, and so discouraging people from buying them). Import quotas are a non-tariff barrier and mean that only a certain number of a particular good or of a good from a particular country are allowed in per year (for instance, in the past there has been a limit on the number of Japanese cars allowed to be sold in Britain per year).

The GATT agreement and subsequently the WTO recognised certain situations when protectionist barriers should be permitted. One of these is the so-called 'infant industry' situation: governments may argue that a new industry (or one which is new for them) should be protected initially from global competition, until it has established itself and is able to compete. Another permitted exemption is a situation which may have major employment implications (for example, an industry should be protected because its loss would cause massive job losses). An illustration of this is the textile industry, which in the European Union is protected from the competition the textile industries of Third World Countries by the Multi-Fibre agreement.

A further exemption permitted by the WTO is the protection of strategic industries (eg defence industries). The imposition of tariff barriers against particular goods from a particular country may also be permitted where 'dumping' can be proved. 'Dumping' means that a country sells its goods in another country for a price lower than it would ask in its own country, a price by which indigenous producers are unfairly disadvantaged. Dumping is quite difficult to prove, and allegations of it are quite frequent and generate acrimonious arguments between countries.

The International Monetary Fund (IMF)

The International Monetary Fund was set up in 1947 at the Bretton Woods conference, with the remit of ensuring international economic stability by lending money to those member countries which were suffering temporary Balance of Payments problems. Member countries contribute funds in accordance with an agreement – a quota system in relation to their importance in the global economy – and may draw upon the fund as necessary, according to an agreed set of rules.

Although originally envisaged as dealing with temporary imbalances, the IMF has increasingly come to be involved with attempts at solving longer-term structural imbalances in many Third World countries (see 'Third World debt', below). The IMF has a team of experts who will examine the economy of a country which is experiencing problems, for example with regard to debt repayment, or restructuring currently being experienced by the transitional economies of Eastern Europe), and produce a package of measures (a 'restructuring ' package). The loan needed is normally advanced when the country agrees to carry out the restructuring prescribed, and successive tranches (allocations of money) are normally dependent upon achievement. For example, Third World countries are normally recommended to concentrate production on goods for export, and an austerity package is usually suggested to reduce inflation and external debt.

Third World debt

During the 1980s, Third World countries were encouraged to borrow heavily at what were then very low interest rates (too much money was then looking for projects) in order to build 'modern' economies, with modern infrastructures, modern industries etc. Interest rates subsequently rose sharply; many countries were unable to repay and found themselves in serious financial difficulties. The Western banks and financial institutions which initially loaned them the money have pressed hard for repayment, but have been obliged to reschedule much debt and to write off some of it. Some countries (eg Mexico) have reneged on the debt, as the repayments imposed are too heavy a burden. Some Third World countries which were advised by the IMF to concentrate on export industries (in order to reduce debt) found themselves selling their commodities on a falling commodities market (ie prices lower than anticipated). This has meant that some Third World countries have been spending up to one half of their income on debt servicing. This is a very heavy burden, and no solution to the problem appears to be likely in the near future. The IMF-imposed restructuring programmes have in some cases caused serious social unrest (eg in Jamaica) because of their impact on jobs and living standards in some very poor countries.

Exchange rates

An exchange rate is the price of one country's currency in terms of another country's currency. In order for international trade to take place, it has to be possible for businesses to be able to buy and sell in other currencies. If a business in the United Kingdom sells goods or services to Germany, then it will want to be paid not in Euros but in pounds sterling. The German business will therefore need to be able to buy pounds sterling in exchange for its Euros in order to pay for the goods. Similarly, if a United Kingdom business wishes to buy goods or services from Japan, then it will need to buy yen in exchange for its pounds sterling.

The price of different currencies is quoted daily in the media: the rate of the yen against the pound sterling, the rate of the pound sterling against the dollar etc. A whole global system of shifting exchange rates of currencies against each other exists, and is crucial for international trade.

There are many factors which influence the price of different currencies; one of the major ones is the supply of and demand for each currency, which is in turn dependent on the amount of imports and exports of each country, and on the health of each economy. This factor is also influenced by things like differing inflation rates between countries, the perceived ability of each government to manage its economy, the overall budget deficit, etc.

In eras of 'floating' exchange rates (see 'Floating exchange rates', below) a major factor may also be currency speculation. This is theoretically based on the overall health of each economy (speculators preferring to hold 'strong' currencies rather than 'weak' currencies), but there are times when the amount of speculation against a currency may bear little resemblance to economic factors. An example of this was 'Black Wednesday' in September 1992, when sterling was driven out of the Exchange Rate Mechanism (see 'Exchange Rate Mechanism', below). Currency speculation has been fuelled not only by the removal of exchange controls (the United Kingdom removed controls in 1979) but also by the new technological era of computer-driven buying and selling of currencies, which may result in automatic selling of a currency which has fallen below a critical level and is therefore perceived to be on a downward trend.

The post-war Bretton Woods conference (see 'Bretton Woods', above) set up a system of exchange rates which was effectively fixed (technically an 'adjustable peg') system. This enabled international trade to take place within a certain exchange environment. Businesses and governments knew not only what the exchange rates between any pair of the world's main currencies was at any time, but also what it would be in six months' or a year's time (there were very infrequent adjustments to the exchange rates within the system). This certainty is crucial for businesses involved in importing and exporting. Uncertainty as to what the exchange rates will be in the future is very bad for businesses, and discourages international trade.

Floating exchange rates

The Bretton Woods system of exchange rates broke down in the mid 1970s, and was followed by the era of 'floating' exchange rates. This means that most of the world's major currencies are allowed to find their own rate against each other, based on the factors discussed earlier. The price of each currency is theoretically fixed by the global market place, and responds to changes in the factors which affect each country's economic health. In practice, governments have frequently been reluctant to allow their currencies to float freely and find their own rate. This is partly due to the uncertainty for business which freely floating currencies cause. It is also because the exchange rate has a serious impact on the price of exports, which affects the amount of exports which can be sold. A low exchange rate makes a country's exports cheaper than those of other countries (and hence helps to sell more); a high exchange rate makes goods and services more expensive compared with those of other countries (and hence makes exporting more difficult). Nevertheless, governments have sometimes wished to maintain a high exchange rate because it means that the cost of imports, which are often crucial to economic survival, is reduced. Maintaining a high exchange range can also give a short-term illusion of financial health until economic reality causes the currency to crash. A high exchange rate has sometimes been used as a disciplining device, to keep wages and costs down; the United Kingdom government attempted to do this with the high entry price to the ERM (see 'Exchange Rate Mechanism', below).

In order to achieve the exchange rate which it or the government wants, the central bank of a country (in the United Kingdom the Bank of England, in the United States the Federal Reserve Bank) will 'intervene ' in the currency market by buying or selling its own or other currencies. This will drive the currency in the desired direction; for example, if the United Kingdom government wishes to stop the price of the pound sterling falling, then the Bank of England will buy up pounds to force the price up; if it however, wishes the price of sterling to fall, then it will sell pounds, driving down the price. Other central banks do the same with their currencies. This is known as a 'dirty' float. In recent years, several central banks have sometimes acted together to achieve an objective which the various governments view as desirable. Instances of this include: several major central banks acted in support of the dollar by buying up dollars to force the price up; the very highly priced yen was the cause of concerted action by several central banks; on the occasion of the massive speculation against the French franc in 1992, the German Bundesbank and the French central bank bought up large amounts of francs in an attempt to support it.

European Monetary System (EMS)

The European Union has its own internal exchange rate system, the European Monetary System, covering the Euro zone and other EU countries. The EMS has in the past operated an Exchange Rate Mechanism (ERM), requiring governments and central banks to intervene to limit fluctuations in the comparative value of members' currencies. The Maastricht Treaty (1992) effectively requires membership of an Exchange Rate Mechanism for a period of time before any country is allowed to adopt the Euro.

The United Kingdom's pound sterling entered the ERM in 1990 at a rate against the German Deutschmark and other European currencies which was widely perceived to be too high (ie sterling was overpriced), and this had a serious impact businesses on United Kingdom and jobs. Following intense speculation against sterling in September 1992, the United Kingdom currency was forced out of the ERM. The impact which the ERM and monetary union have had on United Kingdom businesses is discussed below.

European single currency

In January 1999, under the terms of the Maastricht Treaty, eleven European Union countries (France, Germany, Italy, Spain, The Netherlands, Belgium, Luxembourg, the Republic of Ireland, Austria, Finland and Portugal – joined by Greece in 2001) abolished their separate currencies and adopted a single currency, the Euro (with Euro-denominated banknotes and coins replacing the old national currency banknotes and coins in 2002). This entailed the establishment of the European Central Bank (ECB) in Frankfurt to control the money supply and set interest rates with the statutory aim of controlling inflation. The United Kingdom, Sweden and Denmark chose to remain outside the Euro zone at the initial stage.

The advantages of a single currency include the following:

- Governments and industry lose the ability to disguise declining competitiveness and falling real incomes through inflation and currency devaluation as all income has to be earned and all payments made in a hard currency over the supply of which the government has no control.

- Transfers of money between countries are made easier because there is no need to negotiate exchange rates and calculate the equivalent values in one currency of amounts in another. Banks and money brokers are also deprived of one method of charging for transactions because of the removal of the opportunity to charge commissions or to buy and sell currencies at a profit.
- The value of prices to be charged for overseas contracts become more predictable.
- Prices of capital goods and other large items for which a fully international market is practicable are more easily compared.

The disadvantages include the following:

- Money supply and inflation rates in one country are affected by fiscal decisions of overseas governments. Although this can to a certain extent be controlled by stability pacts limiting budget deficits and government debt levels, the European Commission may find these difficult to enforce in times of financial crisis or if a large number of countries decide to break the pact at the same time.
- A single monetary policy set for a larger area is always likely to be inappropriate for some parts of that area. Some areas may be suffering from high inflation and therefore need the restraint of higher interest rates, while other areas are suffering from declining production and need cheaper money to facilitate industrial investment.
- An international central bank established by treaty and only subject to limited control by ministers and commissioners acting on purely delegated powers is more remote from democratic control than a national bank for which an elected parliament can pass legislation.
- The temptation for governments to undermine the central bank's authority by negative briefings to the press is increased by the fact that the appointment of the bank's board was not the sole responsibility of any one government and therefore there is less implied self-criticism by the group responsible for attacking the bank's policy. This may be especially true if a government favourite has been disappointed in the appointment process.

The European Union and its impact on United Kingdom business

Treaty of Rome

The European Union (then called the European Economic Community (EEC)) was formed in 1957, initially with six member states (France, Germany, Italy, The Netherlands, Belgium and Luxembourg). Fundamentally, the aim of the EEC was to ensure that the European economies became so interlinked that war between them would be impossible. The precursor of the EEC was the European Coal and Steel Community, which concentrated deliberately on those goods (coal and steel) without which modern warfare would not be possible.

The founding treaty was called the Treaty of Rome, and it is still this treaty which with its articles forms the bedrock of European legislation/ regulations. The Treaty embodies the aims of the EEC: to establish a 'common market' within the member countries by reducing restrictions on the free movement of goods, services, capital and workers, by setting up an economic trading block with a Common Customs Tariff and a Common Commercial Policy.

The budget for the European Union comes from the member states. The majority of the budget of the European Union is currently spent on the Common Agricultural Policy (see below), which absorbs a disproportionate amount in relation to its importance to the European economies. This is due to historical and political factors.

The United Kingdom joined the EEC in 1973 and has since then been subject to European Union regulations. These include such areas as competition policy (monopolies and mergers; unfair competition), health and safety, pollution control, equal opportunities policy, etc. The European Union now has a major impact on all United Kingdom business, which must comply with the appropriate European Union regulations and directives.

The Common Agricultural Policy

The Common Agricultural Policy of the European Union has historically absorbed a major part of the budget of the European Union, which is not in proportion to the relative importance of agriculture in the European economies. The aim of the CAP has been to secure food supplies for the European Union population, and to protect European Union agriculture from world competition. The European Union is in world terms a very high-cost agricultural producer. This means that if European Union agriculture is not protected it will largely not survive, as European Union prices are higher than world prices for most agricultural produce. The CAP therefore imposes an External Tariff, a charge on foreign imports into the European Union, which makes them more expensive and hence less desirable for consumers. The CAP has also supported European Union farmers by setting 'intervention' prices: for each agricultural good, the European Union sets a price below which it will not allow the good to fall; if the prevailing market prices fall to this point (eg because there is a surplus), then the European Union will buy up enough of the good to maintain the price. This system, which effectively guarantees the producer a fixed price no matter how much is produced, has led to much over-production and the infamous European Union 'butter mountains' and 'wine lakes'. The European Union has in recent years begun to address this inefficient system, by imposing quotas on the production of some goods (eg milk quotas), and by encouraging non-production via 'set-aside' schemes which pay farmers for not producing. The CAP has been a source of problems over the years, but it is difficult to change radically in the direction of greater efficiency and lower prices for consumers since it is a very sensitive political issue in some countries.

Single European Market

On 1 January 1993 the European Union Internal Market (1992) was inaugurated. All goods and services may now pass freely around and among member states without internal customs duties, customs posts, border controls, the filling in of customs forms or other forms of restriction. The internal market has had and will continue to have a major impact on United

Kingdom businesses. Some European industries have restructured as a result of the new internal market (that is, there have been mergers between firms in different European Union countries in the same line of business) and more will do so. This poses both opportunities and threats for United Kingdom businesses: they can now trade freely within the countries of their European neighbours, on a par with indigenous firms (although they still have currency problems, known as 'transaction costs'). But other member states' businesses can also have free access to the United Kingdom's markets, so United Kingdom businesses need to compete vigorously.

In 1994, the European Union also negotiated a European Economic Area Agreement with four other European countries, Norway, Switzerland, Iceland and Liechtenstein, thereby extending the single market in goods, services, labour and capital futher.

The United Kingdom is disadvantaged by geography, by the costs of getting on and off an island, but the opening of the Channel Tunnel now provides easier access to and from mainland European markets. It remains to be seen whether United Kingdom businesses and the United Kingdom economy as a whole will benefit or lose out as result of the completion of the internal market. One important factor is the language barrier: United Kingdom businesses need to train workers to be able to do business in the languages of their customers.

A further issue in relation to the single market is the level of indirect taxation. UK duties on alcohol and tobacco in particular are higher than in many other countries, including France, which has led to many consumers crossing the Channel for the specific purpose of buying the same goods cheaper in French towns than in British ones. There has also been the difficulty of preventing retailers and smugglers buying goods at low duty rates in France to resell illegally in the UK, thereby evading UK indirect taxes.

The United Kingdom has benefited from being a relatively low wage country within the European Union – for example, Japanese multinationals have been keen to locate plants within the United Kingdom in order to get inside the European Union external trade barriers. But the United Kingdom may also suffer in that some production may be switched to the even lower cost southern states of the European Union (Greece, Spain and Portugal). Some areas of the United Kingdom are disadvantaged by being a long distance from the European Union mainland markets. These northern areas of the United Kingdom may risk becoming declining regions. The European Union in its drive towards full economic and monetary union has increased its so-called 'structural funds' in order to attempt to redress the balance somewhat and avoid some areas of the European Union turning into declining regions by funding projects in such areas through its Regional Development Fund. Also, in the aftermath of Maastricht, a 'Cohesion Fund' was set up in order to help the four poorest member states (Greece, Portugal, Spain and Ireland) achieve the convergence criteria of the treaty (see below).

Maastricht Treaty

The Treaty of Maastricht (signed at Maastricht in 1992) called for movement towards full economic and monetary union by 1997. It was recognised that, in order to achieve full economic and monetary union, it would be necessary for all the member states involved to harmonise their economic performance to some extent. A number of 'convergence criteria', which each country involved would need to achieve prior to full economic and monetary union were established. These criteria covered government deficits; inflation; exchange rate stability within the ERM, and stability of long-term interest rates. All of these were to be within defined boundaries close to those of the best performing member states. The main body of the Maastricht Treaty (which also amends the Treaty of Rome) was signed by the governments of all the then member states.

In addition, the social chapter of the Maastricht Treaty called for harmonisation of European social legislation – labour regulations, redundancy provisions, provision for part-time workers, etc. The purpose was to provide a level playing field throughout the European Union, and to ensure workers' and citizens' rights. The United Kingdom government believed (and to some extent still does) that this would make United Kingdom businesses uncompetitive and so lead to job losses. The Major government initially insisted on an opt-out from the social chapter but the opt-out was renounced by the Blair government in 1997.

The future of the European Union?

What does the future hold for the European Union? In the relatively near future the widening of the union to include several Eastern European countries, such as Poland. Membership for Turkey, which has been an Associate Member for some time, is also a possibility.

As well as widening, it is possible that the Union may also 'deepen' (ie become even more integrated). This is at present a problematic area, as United Kingdom governments have tended to resist political integration.

The further development of the European Union as a massive trading block in the world economy has advantages for both European Union citizens and businesses. The European Union currently wields enormous power in the global economy, and will continue to do so. This does, however, cause disadvantages for Third World countries, and for those small economies not part of trading blocks. Increasingly, the global economy seems to be heading in the direction of an oligopoly situation, where there are a small number of very large and powerful trading blocks and a large number of small powerless economies.

Integrated nature of business

This last section does not attempt to introduce any new material; its aim is to remind you of the issues previously discussed, particularly the more controversial ones. Controversial issues may arise in some form or other as the subject of an essay question in the examination, so it is well to have thought through some of the arguments first.

The thing to remember is that there is no 'right' answer to questions of this sort. The nearest thing to a 'right' answer is one that represents both (or all) sides of the argument; this means that you must keep an open mind, recognise all the different arguments, be aware of your own prejudices and avoid letting them colour your argument and, finally, if you wish to express an opinion make sure that you show it is an opinion rather than a statement of fact.

The following are possible controversial issues, arranged approximately in the order 'macro-environment', 'interface between business and its environment', 'internal issues'. Use this textbook, other readings and practical material collected from newspapers and journal articles throughout your course of study, to illustrate your arguments on both sides of the issue.

As appropriate, think about the issues posed from the point of view of:

1. the government;
2. the major political parties;
3. society at large, men, women, pressure groups;
4. current legislation;
5. shareholders;
6. directors;
7. managers, general and functional;
8. workers, supervisory, skilled and unskilled, clerical and manual;
9. manufacturing industry;
10. service industries;
11. customers;
12. suppliers;
13. trade unions;
14. financiers;
15. the environment;
16. international relations;
17. maintaining good public relations.

Recognise that the above roles are often duplicated – how does the effect of such role conflict affect the issue?

Macro-environment

1. What are the advantages and disadvantages of the mixed economy?
2. What is the best way of achieving effective ownership of big industries: through nationalisation or privatisation?
3. Should regulated industries pursue a profit or a welfare objective?
4. Identify changes taking place in society. Are they threats or opportunities?
5. Is innovation the same as progress?
6. What is the role of small businesses?
7. Do the workings of free enterprise ensure the best allocation of material resources?
8. If the marketing concept makes business customer-oriented, how do you explain consumerism?

Interface between 'business and its environment'

1. What are the arguments for and against government intervention in private business?
2. Does business change society or does society change business?
3. Are businesses forced to innovate?

4. Is conflict between society, owners, managers and workers inevitable? Is it desirable? How is it resolved?
5. Does business growth benefit society?
6. Should the state protect small businesses?
7. Should the state or private business be responsible for pollution control?
8. To whom is a manager ultimately responsible?
9. Should there be any limits to the 'duty of care'?

Internal issues

1. How do 'change' and 'innovation' affect the internal organisation of a business?
2. Should businesses pursue growth?
3. What are the advantages and disadvantages of (i) being big and (ii) being small?
4. How can small businesses protect themselves?
5. Which is the most important business function?
6. Are leaders born or made?
7. Can responsibility, authority and accountability be separated?
8. What are the costs and benefits of information technology?

Other issues

Other issues will arise during your course of study, some general, some specific. Make a careful note of them and analyse them within the framework outlined above. This will help you to realise the integrated nature of all business decisions.

Appendix A

Profit and loss account (format 1 from Schedule 4 of the Companies Act 1985)

1. Turnover
2. Cost of sales
3. Gross profit or loss
4. Distribution costs
5. Administrative expenses
6. Other operating income
7. Income from shares in group undertakings
8. Income from participating interests
9. Income from other fixed asset investments
10. Other interest receivable and similar income
11. Amount written off investments
12. Interest payable and similar charges
13. Tax on profit or loss on ordinary activities
14. Profit or loss on ordinary activities after taxation
15. Extraordinary income
16. Extraordinary charges
17. Extraordinary profit or loss
18. Tax on extraordinary profit or loss
19. Other taxes not shown under the above items
20. Profit or loss for the financial year

Balance sheet (format 1 from Schedule 4 of the Companies Act 1985)

A) Called up share capital not paid
B) Fixed assets

    I) Intangible assets

        1) Development costs
        2) Concessions, patents, licences, trade marks and similar rights and assets
        3) Goodwill
        4) Payments on account

II) Tangible assets

    1) Land and buildings
    2) Plant and machinery
    3) Fixtures, fittings, tools and equipment
    4) Payments on account and assets in course of construction

III) Investments

    1) Shares in group undertakings
    2) Loans to group undertakings
    3) Participating interests
    4) Loans to undertakings in which the company has a participating interest
    5) Other investments other than loans
    6) Other loans
    7) Own shares

C) Current assets

  I) Stocks

    1) Raw materials and consumables
    2) Work in progress
    3) Finished goods and goods for resale
    4) Payments on account

  II) Debtors

    1) Trade debtors
    2) Amounts owed by group undertakings
    3) Amounts owed by undertakings in which the company has a participating interest
    4) Other debtors
    5) Called up share capital not paid
    6) Prepayments and accrued income

  III) Investments

    1) Shares in group undertakings
    2) Own shares
    3) Other investments

  IV) Cash at bank and in hand

D) Prepayments and accrued income
E) Creditors: amounts falling due within one year

    1) Debenture loans
    2) Bank loans and overdrafts
    3) Payments received on account
    4) Trade creditors
    5) Bills of exchange payable

   6) Amounts owed to group undertakings
   7) Amounts owed to undertakings in which the company has a participating interest
   8) Other creditors including taxation and social security
   9) Accruals and deferred income

F) Net current assets (liabilities)
G) Total assets less current liabilities
H) Creditors: amounts falling due after more than one year

   1) Debenture loans
   2) Bank loans and overdrafts
   3) Payments received on account
   4) Trade creditors
   5) Bills of exchange payable
   6) Amounts owed to group undertakings
   7) Amounts owed to undertakings in which the company has a participating interest
   8) Other creditors including taxation and social security
   9) Accruals and deferred income

I) Provisions for liabilities and charges

   1) Pensions and similar obligations
   2) Taxation, including deferred taxation
   3) Other provisions

J) Accruals and deferred income
K) Capital and reserves

   I)   Called up share capital
   II) Share premium account
   III) Revaluation reserve
   IV) Other reserves

      1) Capital redemption reserve
      2) Reserve for own shares
      3) Reserves provided for by the articles of association
      4) Other reserves

   V) Profit and loss account

Appendix B

Some examinations consist of a compulsory structured question based on a case study. Case studies are descriptions of business situations, usually based on 'real life', although the amount of detail which they contain is necessarily reduced. They have two functions in your course, learning and examining. From studying cases you can learn the integrated nature of business, develop skills of analysis, recognise priorities and learn how to present a report, with your analysis and recommendation. The examiner will be looking for evidence that you have learned, and can apply, these lessons.

Cases vary from one to another but there are certain general rules which you should apply when analysing them.

1. Read the case through before you start to make any notes. This is to ensure that you have a good 'overview' of all the issues.
2. The case will almost certainly contain a problem or problems for you to solve. So remember how a doctor proceeds:

   a) Identify any 'symptoms' of the problem.
   b) Identify or suggest possible causes.
   c) Look for evidence of likely causes and select the most likely – 'diagnosis'.
   d) 'Prescribe' appropriate action to remedy the cause. This will be the 'recommendation' section of your report.
   e) Set revised performance targets and suggest ways of monitoring the company's performance to ensure that the problem has been solved.

3. If the case contains dates or times, carefully analyse the order of events to determine possible cause and effect.
4. If the case contains any organisational structure, carefully analyse this to determine the hierarchy, span of control and chain of command.
5. If the case contains any quantitative information such as accounting data, market shares, labour turnover etc analyse these very carefully and see how they may relate one to another.
6. If the case contains 'personalities', try to imagine how these people would behave in reality.
7. Above all, remember that the case is meant to simulate reality and make sure that your recommendations are sensible, within the context of the case described.

Index